FROM EMPIRE TO ANARCHY

METTE SKAK

From Empire to Anarchy

Postcommunist Foreign Policy and International Relations

HURST & COMPANY, LONDON

First published in the United Kingdom by
C. Hurst & Co. (Publishers) Ltd.,
38 King Street, London WC2E 8JZ
© Mette Skak, 1996
Printed in India

ISBNs
1-85065-248-1 (cloth)
1-85065-242-2 (paper)

PREFACE

The origins of the present work can be traced back to a research project, launched in 1987, on the changing Soviet-East European relationship. Within a few years, however, the wall came tumbling down and so did the Soviet Union. The sea-change of 1989-91 required a radically new concept – one that reflected the Springtime of Nations and foreign policies. Just as domestic revolutions brought a new agenda of transition studies, so the collapse of the Soviet international order brought postcommunist foreign policy studies to the fore. The new agenda is more demanding, but definitely also more exciting. As a political scientist trained in the humanities, I have come to look upon foreign policy as a field where international relations have the flavour of cultural interface. Not that I am romantic about nationalism, but there is a charm to the study of individual foreign policies which systemic analysis is unable to convey. The fact of self-determination not only legitimizes this kind of closer inquiry but necessitates it. How do the newly free states manage? What are the contents of their foreign policies? Why? These are the questions which occupy this volume.

Naturally, there is no way that a single person or monograph can cover the nearly thirty sovereign state-units which may be considered postcommunist when the emerging post-Yugoslav states are included. My approach is to provide the reader with a comprehensive functional introduction in principle covering all state-units and then to continue in the format of case-studies. The book is conceived as a text for university students, but I also hope to attract other readers with an interest in contemporary international relations as well as colleagues – post-sovietologists and other social scientists. I have included a historical section describing the Soviet imperial system in order to provide the non-area specialist with a frame of reference. Moreover my analytical approach builds on the antecedents to postcommunism. Yet it should be possible to read the chapters independently from one another.

It is my primary ambition to contribute to cumulative research. Except for a few conceptualizations and some less known findings, this is not a venture in theoretical innovation or empirical sensations, but an effort of synthesis. Throughout I draw on sources of insight from the vast pool of social science and sovietology in addition to empirical documentation. The result is a book rich in references with some academic jargon. However, I strongly believe in the political relevance of my topic. In order to communicate this, my own stance will occasionally be indicated – in the spirit of the Swedish economist Gunnar Myrdal, who recommended social scientists to be explicit about their own value premises and approaches.

References indicate a collective undertaking through the many authors on whom I rely. Even where there are no references, chances are that one or several of the many academics, diplomats and government officials whom I have met and interviewed in Bratislava, Brussels, Budapest, Moscow, Prague, Sofia, Vilnius, Warsaw and other European capitals influenced my writing. I am indebted to my Aarhus students and colleagues and to the Danish Committee on Security and Disarmament, SNU, which more than once sponsored my travels and provided me with sources. The same applies to several embassies in Copenhagen. I am also grateful for the moral support and technical and practical assistance of my husband, Peter – not to mention his patience. Needless to say, I carry the sole responsibility for any errors there may be.

Aarhus, March 1995   METTE SKAK

CONTENTS

MAPS

ACRONYMS AND ABBREVIATIONS

AFD	Alliance of Free Democrats (Hungary)
BALTBAT	Baltic peacekeeping battalion
BAM	Baikalo-Amurski Magistral (an extension to the Trans-Siberian Railway)
CAP	Common Agricultural Policy (within the EC/EU)
CBSS	Council of Baltic Sea States (March 1992–)
CEFTA	Central European Free Trade Agreement (the Visegrad countries)
CEI	Central European Initiative (formerly the Pentagonal/Hexagonal)
CFE	Conventional Forces in Europe (disarmament agreement)
CIS	Commonwealth of Independent States (December 1991–)
CMEA	Council of Mutual Economic Aid, or Comecon
Cominform	Communist Information Bureau (1947–56)
Comintern	Communist International (Third International, 1919–43 except for OMI)
CPSU	Communist Party of the Soviet Union
CSBM	Confidence and Security-Building Measure
CSCE	Conference on Security and Cooperation in Europe
EBRD	European Bank for Reconstruction and Development
EC	European Community (until 1 November 1993)
EFTA	European Free Trade Association (formulated 1960)
EU	European Union (since 1 November 1993)
GATT	General Agreement on Tariffs and Trade
GDR	German Democratic Republic (1949–90)
GNP	gross national product
GOSPLAN	Gosudarstvennoe Planovoe Buro (the Soviet planning agency)
GPU	Gosudarstvennoe Politicheskoe Upravlenie (Soviet secret police, 1920s)

G-7	Group of Seven industrialized countries
GSP	General System of Preferences
Gulag	Glavnoe Upravlenie Lagerei (the system of Soviet labour camps)
HDF	Hungarian Democratic Forum
HSP	Hungarian Socialist Party (formerly the HSWP: the Communist Party)
ICBM	Intercontinental ballistic missiles
IMF	International Monetary Fund
INF	Intermediate nuclear forces
KGB	Komitet Gosudarstvennyi Bezopasnosti (State Security Agency: the Soviet secret police from the 1950s till 1992)
LDLP	Lithuanian Democratic Labour Party (formerly the Communist Party)
MFA	Ministry of Foreign Affairs
MFN	most favoured nation (a general principle of trade preference)
MGB	Ministerstvo Gosudarstvennoi Bezopasnosti (Soviet Ministry of the Interior in the early 1950s, following the renaming of 'People's Commissariats' as ministries)
MGIMO	Moskovskii Gosudarstvennyi Institut Mezhdunarodnych Otnoshenii (the State Institute of International Relations of Moscow: the Soviet Diplomatic Academy)
MP	Member of Parliament
MTS	Mashinno-Traktornye Stantsii (machine-tractor stations: sovietization agencies during collectivization)
MVD	Ministerstvo Vnutrennykh Del (the Soviet Ministry of the Interior in the post-Stalin era)
NACC	North Atlantic Cooperation Council (inaugurated in December 1991)
NATO	North Atlantic Treaty Organization (1949–)
NEP	Novaia Ekonomicheskaia Politika (liberal Soviet economic policies of the 1920s)
NGO	non-governmental organization
NKVD	Narodny Kommissariat Vnutrennykh Del (People's Commissariat for Internal Affairs, *de facto* the Soviet secret police of the 1930s and 1940s)

OECD	Organization of Economic Cooperation and Development (formerly the OEEC: the agency implementing the Marshall Aid Programme)
OMI	Otdel Mezhdunarodnoi Informatsii (The Office of International Information, the secret successor to Comintern)
OMON	Otriady Militsii Osobogo Naznachenia (Soviet Ministry of Interior forces)
OSCE	Organization for Security and Cooperation in Europe (since December 1994, formerly the CSCE)
PCC	Political Consultative Committee (of the Warsaw Pact)
PfP	Partnership for Peace (a framework for cooperation launched by NATO, aimed at post-communist states)
PHARE	Pologne-Hongrie: Aide à la réconstruction économique (Phare = 'lighthouse' in French). An EU programme for economic and technical assistance originally targeted at Poland and Hungary, subsequently extended to all East Central European, Balkan and Baltic countries.
RSFSR	Rossiiskaia Sotsialisticheskaia Federativnaia Sovetskaia Respublika (Soviet Russia)
Samizdat	'sam-izdatelstvo', a pun in Russian = 'Do-it-yourself' Publishers Ltd.
SMERSH	'Smert nad Shpionam' = 'Death to Spies' (NKVD counter-intelligence batallions during the Second World War)
SOP	standard operating procedure
START	Strategic Arms Reduction Talks
TACIS	Technical Assistance to the Commonwealth of Independent States (and EU aid programme launched in 1992. Mongolia is included in TACIS)
TEMPUS	The EU academic exchange programme covering post-communist states
UN	United Nations
UPA	Ukrainian Insurgent Army (of the 1940s and early '50s)
USSR	Union of Soviet Socialist Republics (1922-91)
WEU	West European Union (an organization for security cooperation, 1955–)
WWF	World Wide Fund for Nature

1

INTRODUCTION

When Mikhail Gorbachev still resided in the Kremlin, a Soviet joke attributed to him the following statement: 'When I came to power, Soviet society was on the verge of a deep abyss. Now we have taken a bold step forward.' Indeed, the tide of change sweeping across the USSR, Central Europe and the Balkans has brought huge problems. Attempts at reform led to uncontrollable imperial collapse. The Warsaw Pact, the Council for Mutual Economic Assistance (CMEA), the Communist Party of the Soviet Union (CPSU), the Soviet Union itself – all were dismantled in the course of just three years, from 1989 to 1991. At the time of the *annus mirabilis* of 1989 it looked as if a peaceful transition from communism to democracy was taking place. The mood was optimistic, bordering on euphoric. Now pessimism prevails. The postcommunist world has become one of crisis, jingoism and conflict. The West is as cautious as ever.

It is easy to be too pessimistic when assessing the prospects for a successful transition from communism. Yet it is necessary to confront the dangerous international dynamics created by postcommunist nationalism. What is at stake is nothing less than peace, security and stability. This was realized as far back as the 1950s by Walter Kolarz, who chose to conclude his pioneering study of the Soviet colonial system with the following warning:

> The emergence of a multitude of small national states in Eastern Europe, in the Caucasus and Central Asia, in the territory of what today is the U.S.S.R., would increase the anarchy in the world and would not even benefit the nationalities concerned. (1952, p. 316)

In other words, the study of postcommunism must abandon the preoccupation with the domestic dynamics of transition[1] and turn

[1] For examples of 'domestic' transition studies see Przeworski, 1991; Bozóki *et al.*, 1992.

to foreign and security policy. More than ever, the essential research agenda concerns linkages between the internal and external aspects of society, linkages between the internal and external dimensions of systematic change. Sovietology[2] will continue to work as the frame of reference for this kind of venture, but given the fact of transition it is a field which must develop into 'post-Sovietology' in a marriage with other fields of social science, such as foreign policy analysis, security and Third World studies as well as the general study of international affairs. Linkages with the past represent another important agenda. The Soviet imperial order represented its own sub-system of international relations. In order to understand the complexity of transition it is necessary to examine the logic and drama behind the establishment of this order as well as the mechanisms behind its daily working. The very collapse of the Soviet Union still merits discussion.

This volume seeks to explore the basic features of postcommunist foreign policy and international relations. It begins with a fairly extensive conceptual and empirical introduction to the field as a general framework for analysis. There follows an examination of the foreign policy of individual countries and of the aspects of conflict and cooperation in postcommunist international relations. As already suggested, my approach highlights the imperial past of the newly free postcommunist countries. More specifically, the 'concentric circles of empire' are seen as a key factor behind the differing foreign policies and achievements of postcommunist states. The case studies are therefore preceded by an account of the rise and fall of the Soviet empire and its general features, including the foreign policy system. The countries then singled out for case studies are Russia, Lithuania and Hungary – representing the unique case of the imperial centre and countries of the internal and the external empire, respectively. The subsequent chapter on postcommunist international relations deals with three cases of conflict, regional cooperation and finally the post-Cold War East–West relationship.

Foreign policy is commonly understood as comprising decisions and actions involving relations between one state and other states or organizations – foreign policy as output, as it were (Frankel, 1963, p.1). The comparative study of foreign policy, however, has to look

---

[2] 'Sovietology' refers to the study of the communist Soviet and Eastern European polities, which used to be a somewhat self-contained 'area study'. See Fleron and Hoffmann (1993).

at the inputs determining such policy and examine decision-making within it (Clarke and White, 1989; Hermann *et al.*, 1987). In view of the frequent lack of substance in the foreign policies of the individual postcommunist countries and the drama of the domestic transition from communism, it is tempting to dismiss the study of foreign policy as irrelevant and superfluous. However, these objections clearly miss the point. For better or worse, foreign policy represents a vital medium for the pursuit of interests and for modifying external constraints. This is particularly so in an age of marked interdependence when the immunity and problem-solving capacity of the state is being eroded. While highlighting the 'cascading nature of interactions' that characterize politics in the multi-centric world of today, James N. Rosenau insists on the relevance of foreign policy as a 'conspicuous component' in international relations however turbulent they may be (1990, pp. 298, 402). Moreover, foreign policy is a key medium through which newly independent states can manifest themselves internationally as autonomous entities. In addition, the transition from communism enforces a foreign policy agenda of its own, a point to which I shall return (cf. Schroeder, 1992).

On 'anarchy' and 'empire'

In studying postcommunist international relations, it is my point of departure that the collapse of the Soviet international order, or 'empire', created a state of anarchy because of the emergence of sovereign states. This is no original observation, but an axiom among students of international relations (Wolfers, 1962, p. 67). What characterizes the international system of sovereign states, in contrast to national systems, is the lack of a sovereign, the lack of a supranational authority – for instance, a world government. This means that armed conflict and war are built into the structure of international relations as a mechanism for conflict-resolution. The birth of new independent states only adds to this logic.

An equally important observation within today's research on international relations, however, is that anarchy may be modified. Some actors display restraint in the pursuit of their interests. Moreover, there are instances of voluntary political and economic integration – in Europe and the Americas. The pursuit of interdependence is a motivating force in the foreign policy of some states, e.g.

Germany (named '*Einbindung*'). Accordingly, the pattern of conflict is superseded by one of cooperation – at least among the consolidated states of the 'old world'. Therefore, it may be more accurate to describe the pattern of interaction as one of 'mature anarchy' (Buzan, 1983, pp. 93–101; Bull, 1977).

As for the newly free postcommunist states, the absolutely essential question, then, concerns whether they will be able to establish a mature anarchy among themselves or they will resort to classical, unrestrained power politics. Rather than sweeping generalizations, this is a question which warrants careful empirical investigation. Because of its obvious policy relevance, it also needs to be addressed in terms of policy deliberations.

Nowadays it has become a matter of political correctness to describe the Soviet communist system as an 'empire'. Even in Moscow, the former imperial 'centre', it is commonplace to use the term. Evidently, it is the disintegration of the Soviet empire which forces scholars into this radical reinterpretation (cf. Mayall, 1992, p. 23). Similarly, the concept of totalitarianism, once branded unscientific and normative, is being rehabilitated as another key to understanding how the Soviet system worked (Odom, 1992). But whereas totalitarianism (if taken literally)[3] suggests a purely national analytical perspective, the concept of empire carries more apt connotations of an international system of dominance. Together, the twin terms of 'empire' and 'totalitarianism' serve to illuminate the depth and breadth of dominance within the Soviet international order.

The term 'empire' presupposes the existence of a centre of power, in this case the CPSU leadership. It implies the pursuit of a distinct imperial policy, in this particular case the policy of *sovietization*. The American Sovietologist David J. Dallin defined the Soviet empire as 'a large conglomeration of various nationalities forcibly held together by a great power' (1951, p. 1). Apparently, it was Dallin who pioneered the perception of varying perimeters of the Soviet empire, an approach reiterated by contemporary Sovietologists (Bialer, 1984). Accordingly, the 'internal Soviet empire' refers to the now defunct Soviet Union with its fifteen constituent union republics. The 'external empire' describes the small Warsaw Pact

---

[3] Friedrich and Brzezinski (1965, p. 21) define a totalitarian state as having the following six characteristics: an elaborate ideology, a single-party rule based on a one-man dictatorship, a secret police, a media monopoly, party control over armed forces and a centrally planned economy.

states and Mongolia. The 'fringe of empire' refers to former Yugoslavia as a country that liberated itself from Soviet control and as such represents a peculiar case of transition from communism. Albania falls into the same category.[4]

Decolonization and its outcomes: quasi-states?

Using empire as an analytical approach means looking upon the collapse of Soviet communism as the breakdown of an imperial order and, more specifically, as a process of decolonization during which the independence of peoples formerly under soviet rule was recognized. This interpretation has received official approval in the *Oxford Companion to Politics of the World* (1993). Here one finds the upheaval throughout the Soviet-East European region during 1989–91 under the entry of 'decolonization'. It was the explicit Soviet dismissal of the notorious Brezhnev doctrine of 'limited sovereignty' in the autumn of 1989 which marked the decolonization of the Soviet external empire (Skak, 1992a). Soviet Foreign Ministry spokesman Gennadi Gerasimov announced the replacement doctrine, dubbed the 'Sinatra doctrine', according to which the countries of Eastern Europe could now do it 'their way'.

To be sure, the degree of voluntary and controlled decolonization on the part of the Soviet leadership can be questioned as far as the internal Soviet empire is concerned. On the other hand, it was a fairly peaceful process reminiscent of the later Czech-Slovak 'velvet divorce', in stark contrast to the Yugoslav process of decolonization (Schmid, 1993). What happened was that Boris Yeltsin, acting on behalf of Russia, the core colonial subject within the Soviet territorial system, urged other republics 'to take all the sovereignty they

[4] The annual *Eastern Europe and the Commonwealth of Independent States*, launched by Europa Publishers in London will probably come to be the leading reference source on geographic, political, economic, social, historical and institutional data on the individual political units of the former Soviet empire. In addition there is Bogdan Szajkowski's *Encyclopedia of Conflicts, Disputes and Flashpoints in Eastern Europe, Russia and the Successor States* (1993). Unfortunately, Radio Free Europe/Radio Liberty's weekly *RFE/RL Research Reports* and *News Briefs* have been cancelled in their present format. These have been among the best sources for current coverage of political developments in the region. A successor-periodical called *Transition* published by the Open Media Research Institute in Prague began in 1995. The institute also brings out daily reports on developments in East-Central Europe and the former Soviet Union, the *OMRI Daily Digest.*

wanted' and formally acknowledged their independence in various bilateral treaties. This pulled the carpet from under the foot-dragging policy of Gorbachev. The August putsch of 1991 irreversibly sealed the fate of the Soviet empire; it was followed by the formal dissolution of the Soviet Union at the Minsk and Alma-Ata summits of December 1991. The whole process was facilitated by Russia's eagerness to take on Soviet legal commitments in exchange for the assets of the USSR, such as its permanent seat in the UN Security Council. Russia thus succeeded in establishing itself as the successor state of the Soviet Union. The red Soviet flag above the Kremlin wall was replaced by the Russian tricolour on 25 December 1991.

In legal terms, the decolonization of the Soviet internal empire followed the principle of African decolonization *uti juris possidetis* (the territory 'as you now possess'). It refers to the principle of territorial decolonization and sovereignty, in contrast to ethnic decolonization and sovereignty (Mayall, 1992, pp. 22-5; Chipman, 1993, pp. 149 ff.). Although most of the newly free post-Soviet republics are ethnically heterogenous, the EC's Badinter Commission decided on a policy of recognition according to which internal administrative borders were to become international borders. Doing anything else would have opened a Pandora's box of territorial issues and thus undermined a peaceful process of dissolution during which many representatives of non-titular nations in individual republics (such as the Russians in the Baltic republics) actually voted for independence.

The other side of the coin in applying the principle of *uti possidetis*, however, is the territorial disputes and subsequent lack of external and internal stability haunting most postcommunist states. The arbitrariness surrounding decolonization is only heightened by the arbitrariness of the preceding period of colonization. A few examples will suffice. Following the Second World War, the Ruthenian region of eastern Czechoslovakia became part of the Ukrainian Soviet republic, while Moldovans were separated from their fellow Romanians. Before that the Soviet Union absorbed the formally independent state of Tuva (bordering Mongolia). The immense proportions of the problem of territorial stability throughout the postcommunist world are indicated by the more than 274 trouble spots, disputes and ethno-territorial conflicts identified by one scholar in the former Soviet Union and Eastern Europe (Szajkowski, 1993a).

Decolonization is not necessarily a finite process, but can be likened to the peeling of an onion or opening a Russian *matrioshka* doll. It is an open question whether decolonization will continue, for example in the case of Russia, which is not a unitary state but a federation consisting of almost ninety administrative units. The Polish-British analyst Bogdan Szajkowski deems this a likely outcome in contrast to his Russian colleague, Sergei Saizew (Szajkowski, 1993b; Saizew, 1992). In support of the latter, less alarmist position one could cite the inflation accompanying secession, which means that latecomers risk gaining very little international attention, maybe even losing whatever attention they enjoyed. This, however, does not invalidate the basic point in this argument, namely that postcommunist foreign policy studies must prepare for the eventual dissolution or disappearance of some of the units of analysis – for instance Moldova, which Romania considers to be Romanian land. Territorial issues are legion among and within postcommunist states, implying that problems of security are just as much problems of internal stability as external hostility. Therefore the analysis of security cannot operate solely at the level of foreign policy, but must take the domestic context into account (Dick, Dunn and Lough, 1993).

The problem of the viability of the postcommunist state is a feature which the present work shares with studies of Third World foreign and security policy (Azar and Moon, 1988). This raises the question of whether postcommunist foreign policy-making units are actually 'quasi-states' like many Third World states, notably those of black Africa (Jackson, 1990). Because of the concentric circles of empire (to be examined in greater detail later), the concept of quasi-states would seem to have particular relevance for the newly free states of the internal empire.

A quasi-state is one that enjoys sovereignty only in the most formal sense of the word, in other words, a state whose autonomy and viability are highly debatable. Robert Jackson uses the expression 'negative sovereignty' to define quasi-states, namely states whose 'sovereignty' rests exclusively on the protection from foreign intervention embedded in international law (*ibid.*, pp. 5, 26 ff.). Quasi-states received their sovereignty through the act of decolonization, a kind of world historical affirmative action building on Western norms of equality and self-determination (*ibid.*, pp. 16–21). But the former colonial subjects were ill prepared for independence and hence display the following features even today:

[governments] deficient in political will, institutional authority, and organized power to protect human rights or provide socio-economic welfare. The concrete benefits which have historically justified the undeniable burdens of sovereign statehood are often limited to fairly narrow elites and not yet extended to the citizenry at large whose lives may be scarcely improved by independence or even adversely affected by it. These states are primarily juridical. They are still far from complete, so to speak, and empirical , statehood in large measure still remains to be built. (*ibid.*, p. 21)

As a result, the diplomacy of aid looms large in the foreign policy of quasi-states *vis-à-vis* the well-established states of the northern hemisphere. This again has to do with the fact that compensation for weakness and underdevelopment has become an international norm (*ibid.*, p. 24). By contrast, the sovereignty of states such as those of Western Europe, East Asia, and in some cases Latin America, need not be bolstered as they enjoy what Jackson calls 'positive sovereignty'. This is defined as 'the sociological, economic, technological, psychological, and similar wherewithal to declare, implement, and enforce public policy both domestically and internationally' (*ibid.*, p. 29).

The distinction between states and quasi-states is basically the same as that between weak and strong states, according to which small states need not be weak states, nor are great powers by definition strong states (cf. the case of Denmark as opposed to the Soviet Union; Buzan, 1983, pp. 65ff.). In practice, however, we are talking about a continuum of weakness and strength and not opposite poles. Therefore, the question of whether one or other of the newly free postcommunist states is a quasi-state or a state has to be settled by empirical inquiry.

To return to the distinction between the internal and the external empire, the point about the latter is the peculiar quasi-statehood this region enjoyed because of the mechanism of the Brezhnev doctrine and the extreme constraints on foreign policy it entailed. Today, the external empire is definitely moving from quasi- to full statehood, whereas this is less obviously the case for the newly free states of the internal empire. Yet circumstances vary, and analysts are generally optimistic on behalf of the Baltic states as some of the most viable states of the now defunct Soviet Union (Schroeder 1992; Armstrong, 1992). Given the immense destructive potential of Russia if it were to act to protect its external sovereignty and vast mineral resources, the Russian Federation hardly qualifies as a quasi-state. On the other hand, Russia faces a unique challenge in state-building, a challenge rooted in the country's imperial past as the core in a continuous expansion into contiguous regions. This creates enormous problems of self-demarcation and identity. On top of this, Russia has grown into a highly fragmented and regionalized political and economic system since 1990 or so.

Some of the obvious candidates for quasi-statehood in the former Soviet Union, namely the five republics of Central Asia, did in fact anticipate their meagre economic prospects as independent subjects. Their leaders stand out as most inadvertent founding fathers, to quote the analysis of one American area specialist. Rumour has it that support for Uzbekistan's independence bill was so lukewarm that President Islam Karimov had to make a formal motion to ensure that its passage was marked with applause (Olcott, 1992). Decolonization was definitely not what Central Asians wanted. Conversely, the leaders and peoples of the three Baltic states were pushing for independence in a way which left virtually no other alternative. Moldova also deserves mention for its energetic bid for nation-building in defiance of Romanian territorial claims.

As for the role of the international environment in the consolidation of the postcommunist states, mention could be made of the Nordic neighbours of the Baltic states, who do perceive a security stake in the latter's continued autonomy. Nevertheless, the process of state- and nation-building is and remains a domestic process which can only be brought about by the combined wills, efforts and responsibilities of governments and populations, to quote Robert Jackson once again (1990, p. 21). In other words, the burden of proof when it comes to manifesting their statehood rests with the governments and peoples of the postcommunist states themselves. The point in this perception is the opportunity for action inherent in the situation facing newly free states, irrespective of their size and other features (Papadakis and Starr, 1987).

By now it should be clear why I have chosen to paraphrase Rupert Emerson's classic (1960) study of Afro-Asian nationalism before independence, *From Empire to Nation*, in the title of the present work. I believe the comparison with Afro-Asian decolonization and Third World politics helps to illuminate the foreign policy situation in the postcommunist world. This, of course, does not mean that there are no differences, or that they are just differences in degree. Insofar as the terms 'empire' and 'anarchy' carry negative connotations, this is also not totally unintended. When studying postcommunism – as well as communism – it is imperative to maintain a critical attitude. The exciting thing is that the present sea-change in the eastern half of Europe offers immense opportunity for constructive criticism, making policy deliberations more relevant than ever before.

Postcommunism: the praetorian scenario

The point in using concepts and insights from studies of Afro-Asian and Latin American states is the coupling with sovietology and political science in general. As for the sovietological input, it is time to reflect on the concept of postcommunism so central for this study. As can be seen from Zbigniew K. Brzezinski's use of the term in his prophetic work on the birth and death of communism, the point about the term 'postcommunism' is the open-ended nature of the transition which it implies (1989). Except for the termination of one-party rule, postcommunism defies definition in a stricter and more positive sense. Hence it is premature to use the term 'the new democracies'. Authoritarian trends – or intermezzos? – are resurfacing in some postcommunist states (for example Romania, Turkmenistan). Some might develop their own type of society, because of the peculiarities of their political history and culture, an outcome which cannot be entirely excluded in Russia. On the other hand, a full restoration of communism can be discounted because of the changes already made and the immense coercion this therefore would require.

The ambiguity of postcommunism is reproduced at the level of foreign policy and further tends to repeat itself at the level of international relations in the shape of 'anarchy'. I shall return to this linkage between the domestic drama of transition and the field of foreign policy shortly. But in order to portray a likely scenario whereby democracy is paralysed under postcommunism, it is necessary first to make an excursion into the phenomenon of praetorianism. Originally coined by Samuel B. Huntington (1968) in his classic work on political order in changing societies, this concept has since gained widespread acceptance in Third World studies, including foreign policy studies (Korany, 1983; 1984). The syndrome of praetorianism characterizes many societies undergoing the transition from tradition to modernity. It can be seen as both cause and effect of their weakness as states. It was the American Sovietologist Jack

Snyder who pioneered the application of praetorianism to the study of postcommunist societies (1990-1).

Praetorianism is a syndrome of immature modernity. It refers to the pervasive politicization of all sorts of social forces and institutions which one typically finds during social upheaval. Its modernity stems from the spread of knowledge and information, both of which form the basis of political mobilization (Korany, 1983). In the narrow sense, praetorianism refers to the intervention of the military in politics, perhaps the most dangerous form of praetorianism because of the weaponry at its disposal (Huntington, 1968). Yet, Huntington insists that praetorianism in the shape of military intervention in politics is but one manifestation of a general phenomenon. He uses the term 'praetorian society' to define a society where there is

absence of effective political institutions capable of mediating, refining, and moderating group political action. In a praetorian system social forces confront each other nakedly; no political institutions, no corps of professional political leaders are recognized or accepted as the legitimate intermediaries to moderate group conflict. Equally important, no agreement exists among the groups as to the legitimate and authoritative methods for resolving conflicts. In an institutionalized polity most political actors agree on the procedures to be used for the resolution of political disputes, that is, for the allocation of office and the determination of policy.... This is true of both Western constitutional democracies and communist dictatorships. In a praetorian society, however...each group employs means which reflect its peculiar nature and capabilities. The wealthy bribe; students riot; workers strike; mobs demonstrate; and the military coup. In the absence of accepted procedures, all these forms of direct action are found on the political scene. (*ibid.*, p. 196)

Praetorianism does work as a mechanism for participation, but it is not a lasting system because of the chaos it produces. The mass praetorianism of the Weimar Republic was replaced by Nazi totalitarianism, and it is no coincidence that Huntington's sequence of praetorianism ends in a military coup. Similar outcomes cannot be excluded in the generally fragile postcommunist states. Institutional weakness in the shape of weak party systems, including the lack of parties truly committed to the advancement of the interests of the ordinary citizenry, is the key to understanding the praetorian scenario of political decay. Thus praetorianism does not presuppose dictatorship or authoritarianism; on the contrary, it thrives on a parliamentary structure if this is weakly consolidated and easy to manipulate. Praetorianism turns politics into a scramble for the protection of narrow interests, a scramble for control over the state, a scramble for politicizing for the sake of politicizing. Praetorianism is a model of decision-making in which parochial group interests paralyse governments to the detriment of ordinary citizens and their mundane interests. Sadly, this appears to be a fairly accurate description of political dynamics in Russia and much of former Yugoslavia, even when allowing for the possible lack of Bonapartist instinct in the Russian Army as a result of the political control exercised by the CPSU in the Soviet era (Tiller and Schröder, 1993; Gow, 1993).

Praetorian dynamics are indeed making themselves felt in Russian foreign policy-making (Skak, 1993a; cf. Crow, 1993a). The Russian language actually has its own word for praetorian-like turmoil: *Smuta*, literally 'confusion'/'lack of transparency' – an expression referring to the *Smutnoe Vremia* or 'Time of Troubles' from 1598 to 1613, a traumatic period in the history of Russia when multiple heirs-apparent to the Tsar made their bid for power and there were simultaneous Cossack insurrections and foreign interventions. Russian political analysts are more than willing to invoke *Smuta* in their interpretation of contemporary Russian politics. Cossack armies are also an element in postcommunist Russia's praetorian syndrome because of their autonomous role in conflicts, in which they tend to identify themselves with Russian chauvinism; this in turn makes populist Moscow-based politicians identify with them.[5]

Cossack military, economic and political activity, notably in places like the secessionist Dniestr Republic in Moldova, further points in the direction of 'warlordism', another concept used to describe dismal political development in quasi-states and the like

[5] Historically, Cossacks (not to be confused with Kazakhs – an ethnic category) were runaway serfs who settled on the borders of Russia where their former lords were unable to catch them and bring them back. The Tsarist government decided to legalize Cossack communities as their settlements and armies came to be seen as useful instruments for the protection of Russian state interests. Cossackhood was mostly repressed under the Soviet regime, but resurfaced during Gorbachev's *glasnost*. See also Gehrmann (1992) and Skinner (1994). Admittedly, it is difficult to assess the overall significance of Cossack activity, as little in the way of systematic research is being undertaken. Most analysts, however, are uncomfortable about their role in conflicts and their cooperation with Russian Army personnel.

(Kolstø *et al.*, 1993; Umbach, 1993). Originally used as a term for the seizure of power by local military leaders during the civil war in China before 1949, warlordism now characterizes political relations in Somalia, Afghanistan and other weak Third World states. As rightly observed by Robert Jackson, unrest in quasi-states is by no means confined to governments, but extends to their opponents as well (1900, p. 193). Warlordism is thus an apt term to apply to most military-political activity in former Yugoslavia, and to the nationalistic insurrection led by Colonel Dzhokhar Dudaev in Chechnia in the Caucasian part of the Russian Federation. The Dniestr Republic and Tadzhikistan are other regions of postcommunist warlordism. But there is no strong likelihood that warlordism will be the outcome of the postcommunist political struggle everywhere. However, it could spread to Russia proper via administrative regionalism, mafias and disgruntled army personnel and from there to other regions. Similarly, post-Yugoslav warlordism threatens security – in the Balkans and in Hungary.

As for possible alternatives to praetorianism, Jack Snyder offers two, namely *civic democracy* and *corporatism*. The distinction between these altogether three types of postcommunist pluralist politics stems from the institutional setting. Whereas praetorianism implies the lack of basic rules of game among political actors and institutions, civic democracy builds upon a stable structure of parties which compete for the favour of the average voter and therefore avoid extreme ideological positions (Snyder, 1990-1). In other words, this is a system of piecemeal social engineering, to use Karl Popper's famous phrase (1966, vol. 2, p. 222). The Czech political scene points in this direction, as does the Hungarian scene with its surprisingly stable party system.

However, the possibility of a more corporatist outcome cannot be excluded in these two countries, nor in other countries of Central Europe, because of the legacy of the pragmatic-corporatist style of the Austro-Hungarian empire which dominates Austria to this very day in the shape of the *Sozialpartnershaft*. Corporatist decision-making is characterized by direct bargaining between government and corporate interests – at the expense of parties and parliamentary structures (dubbed 'Harpsund democracy' in Sweden). In other words, this is another type of piecemeal social engineering, although one which may not allow necessary adaptations and alienate the public. Be that as it may, corporatism has played a conspicuous role in small states as a safeguard against adverse influences from the international economy (Väyrynen, 1989). Insofar as the so-called third way is synonymous with corporatist crisis-management during transition, it could thus help to consolidate democracy in postcommunist countries. However, the actual ideologies and political practices of third way protagonists are alarmingly demagogic, a point to which I shall return.

Following Seymour Martin Lipset (cf. Lipset 1964), who pioneered the perception of modern democracy as corporatist, one could argue that the criterion for the return to normalcy and to Europe for the newly free postcommunist states would be corporatism. Several Sovietologists came to look upon communism as its own peculiar type of corporatism, 'controlled corporatism' (Nørgaard, 1985). According to this point of view, corporatism represents a source of continuity, perhaps even legitimacy, appealing to less resourceful societal strata during the transition from communism. Corporatist foreign policy decision-making could boost governments externally and internally when negotiating their countries' future relationship with, say, the European Union. The pervasive corporatism and lobbyism characterizing this system of international cooperation only reinforce this argument. Most societies, however, feature a mixture of civic democracy and corporatism in the field of foreign policy (Denmark, for example). Therefore, the mixed scenario is probably the most likely for political recovery under postcommunism as an alternative to praetorian decay and dictatorship.

But there is a fourth possibility, namely '*consociational democracy*', which must be mentioned because of the ethnically heterogenous postcommunist world. Consociationalism refers to the principle of institutionalized power-sharing among segments in a society – be they ethnic, religious or regional (Lijphart, 1977). It involves the proportional allocation of political or other prestigious offices within the state, such as ministries and positions on public boards, and may include fixed quotas for access to the media (notably television and radio). Consociationalism may thus be conducive to integration in deeply divided societies and work as a tool for overcoming cleavages, yet it can also institutionalize these very cleavages. Consociationalism presupposes élite consent on behalf of the differing segments in society and can therefore be characterized as corporatist federalism. Cases in point are Switzerland and Belgium, but even the European Union displays consociational features, as did the

Soviet Union and Yugoslavia. The consociational principle would appear to have relevance for many postcommunist small states facing ethnic conflict, such as Estonia and Latvia, where it could help defuse tension in relation to Russia. Consociationalism need not be permanent, but can be a temporary device for ethnic conflict-management. Whether consociational or not, any kind of domestic security policy aimed at fostering tolerance and peaceful conflict cultures would have positive repercussions for foreign policy and European security.

2

ISSUES AND TRENDS IN POST-COMMUNIST FOREIGN POLICY

It was Kwame Nkrumah, the founding father of Ghana, who coined the famous motto: 'Seek ye first political kingdom and everything else shall be added unto you.' His bitter experience as head of state later drove him into writing treatises on neo-colonialism. Simon Bolivar, the liberator of Latin America, was always less sanguine about the blessings of independence:

> It is a terrible truth that it costs more strength to maintain freedom than to endure the weight of tyranny. Many nations, past and present, have borne that yoke; few made use of the happy moments of freedom and have preferred to relapse with all speed into their errors. (quoted in Emerson, 1960, p. 272)

Indeed, the argument so far is that independence is not the terminal point in a struggle for 'national liberation', but rather the beginning. Gaining independence thus represents its own kind of shock therapy that breeds nostalgia for the past. The superficiality of sovereignty via decolonization calls for prudence in all spheres of policy. Because of the newness of most postcommunist states, this requirement amounts to squaring the circle. Worse still, sovereignty places responsibility on the governments of the newly free states. This cannot be any different because of the opportunity for autonomy and participation associated with sovereignty, however unequally distributed it may be. By contrast, imperial and colonial systems offer the comfort of having someone to blame.

Evidence of the naivety surrounding the goal of independence and ignorance about what lies beyond in terms of organizational tasks and external demands is legion even when one turns to the Baltic states. Their interwar history of independent statehood might have inspired organizational initiatives, but the Baltic societies did not prepare for independence and could not because of international

16

isolation (Vares, 1993, p. 5). As a result, independence was experienced as a rude awakening in Estonia, Latvia, Lithuania and elsewhere. The wave of frustration and disillusionment was even greater in Ukraine, whose economy has been nose-diving. Opinion polls reveal that only 40 per cent of Ukrainian citizens were still in favour of independence by 1994, in stark contrast to the outcome of the December 1991 referendum (*The European*, 18-24 March 1994).[1] The Ukrainians expected to fare better than Russians because of Ukraine's abundant agricultural and mineral resources, but now they compare their opportunities in life with those of allegedly poor Mexicans, displayed in TV soap operas, who buy themselves coffee, which Ukrainians cannot. Only the leaders of Central Asia seem to have anticipated the unpleasantries that political kingdom would add unto them.

Russian post-independence or post-imperial blues are widespread. The post-imperial syndrome in Russia springs from the feeling of involuntary geographical isolation from the West, disruption of trade, and anxieties over the fate of the suddenly created Russian diaspora of about 25 million people – probably the biggest diaspora in the world even when compared to the Chinese diaspora. Gaining true sovereignty has also been a sobering experience for the countries of the external Soviet empire, in spite of previous self-government and the organizational apparatus at their disposal. The notable exception which proves the rule is the former GDR, which is subject to the shock therapy of having lost independence.

Nevertheless, the vision of independence and nationalism has an important role to play in mobilizing political energy. Determination and skill are certainly needed in order to overcome the misery inherited from communism. As illustrated by developments in South Korea since the Korean War, nationalistic determination can be a constructive tool for recovery and consolidation that is of obvious significance for foreign policy.

The present chapter is intended to give an overview of the foreign policy agenda and intricacies facing postcommunist states and to discuss how they manage their independence in comparison with other decolonized states. First the intricacies of transition from communism are explored, followed by an examination of foreign

---

[1] By December 1994, support for Ukrainian independence had climbed to 64 per cent as the result of improvements in overall political and economic stability (*OMRI Daily Digest*, no. 20, part III, 27 Jan. 1995).

policy building, including the problem of stabilizers. Next, the organizational challenge of founding a foreign ministry and international diplomacy is addressed. Then I look at the different functional aspects, such as problems and policies of security, as well as the development and welfare dimensions of postcommunist foreign policy. This is followed by a consideration of foreign policy decision-making in view of the highly ambiguous nature of 'foreign policy' in the context of transition and nation- and state-building. The final part of this appetizer to the later case studies of postcommunist foreign policy reflects on overall trends and linkages between domestic structural features and foreign policy outcomes.

Intricacies of transition

To summarize this reasoning, the proposition is that transition from communism in the Eurasian region is a special type of transition, namely imperial transition. There is general agreement that this differs from other movements away from authoritarianism because of its unique complexity. On the one hand, there is the political transition from communist authoritarianism to postcommunism and democracy; on the other, there is the economic transition from a centrally planned to a market economy. There is thus a double challenge in managing transition, in contrast to the situation in formerly fascist Southern Europe and in the decolonized Third World states where the economies had long been part of the international 'capitalist' division of labour.

The fact that the economic strategy of communism was basically one of autarky and minimal foreign economic exchange means that transition in the context of communism requires a fundamental foreign policy reform in terms of world market participation and openness (Segal *et al.*, 1992; cf. Holzman 1974). In spite of this, deliberations on the switch from the anachronistic foreign economic policy of communism to one of world market adaptation and integration are remarkably absent in many contributions on the economic transition (Przeworski, 1991).

The internal pressures for a policy of participation and reintegration stem from the economic crisis and the environmental disaster inherited from communism, as well as the institutional deficiencies of the newly free states. This creates a desperate demand for infusions of capital, technology and know-how from abroad. The work of

Geoffrey Pridham and his colleagues on the role of the European Community (now the European Union or EU) in the transitions of Eastern Europe, can be cited as evidence that cooperation with the outside world, and its active support, is a vital ingredient in the success of transitions (Pridham *et al.*, 1994).

The external pressures for a strategy of openness and participation stem from the need to cultivate the goodwill of private investors and international financial institutions such as the IMF. The political and economic conditionalities in the Europe Agreements of Association with the European Union are intended as a further stimulus for reform. Similar conditionalities are found in CSCE and NATO declarations, as well as in the membership provisions of the Council of Europe.

However, these last external pressures for a foreign policy of reintegration are controversial from the point of view of state sovereignty and may thus create tension at the domestic level. In itself the simultaneous introduction of representative democracy, freedom of the press and a market economy marks a tremendous political challenge. Economic restructuring inevitably results in economic deprivation and unemployment, which puts the government implementing reform in an extremely difficult situation. Inherent in this is a strong incentive either to return to authoritarian rule in order to paralyse criticism and avoid elections or conversely, to abandon reform and adopt a policy of muddling through.

Although never labelled as such, the populist notion of the third way does in fact work as a strategy for muddling through. It provides a platform for uniting left-wing and right-wing forces on the basis of a shared hostility towards reform, interdependence and internationalization. The appeal of this political constellation in a context of decolonization results from the skilful manipulation of nationalism by third-way protagonists. The very concept looks like a carbon copy of the 'third force' idea coined by Juan Perón during his presidency in Argentina, cf. his slogan *ni yanqui, ni marxista – peronista* ('neither Yankee nor Marxist, but Peronist').

Contrary to what might have been expected, the notion of the third way has proved to be something quite different from respectable welfare state aspirations and visions of a Germany-like 'social market economy'. The dangerous nature of the concept is revealed by the fact that it is often embraced by anti-urban, anti-cosmopolitan, if not anti-Semitic,[2] forces in society (Lendvai, 1990). At the level of foreign policy and international relations third-way populism threatens easy escalation to chauvinism and aggressive revisionism – as seen in Serbia and Croatia. The alliance between 'reds' (including Stalinists) and 'browns' (including outright fascists or Nazis), as often seen in Russia, is another reminder of possible extensions of the third way in the direction of domestic and international repression and warfare. In other words, the third way represents a tool for ideological manipulation in the hands of praetorian forces. The drama of transition tempts praetorian solutions consisting of 'aggressive populism, hyper-nationalism, militarism and economic demagoguery', to quote the analysis of Jan Zielonka (1992, p. 5).

As already pointed out, there are disincentives surrounding the third way. Slovakia's quiet recourse to a more conventional strategy of reform questions the whole premise that there is a tenable alternative to so-called shock therapy (Fischer, 1993).[3] Failure to introduce reform runs the risk of perpetuating the profound economic and ecological crisis inherited from communism, as illustrated by the Ukrainian slide into economic disaster. Conversely, a

[2] Anti-Semitism represents a peculiar, but curiously neglected problem in terms of brain-drain in studies of the economic transition from communism. Perhaps more than any other culture, Jewishness involves middle-class characteristics such as entrepreneurial spirit, civic culture and intellectual talent. For this reason, surges of anti-Semitism are certain to backfire upon the entire transition.

Interestingly, anti-Semitism appears to constitute less of a problem in today's Russia than in East-Central Europe. Russian ethnic intolerance is increasingly channelled in other directions, notably towards the Caucasian and Muslim nationalities of the former USSR because of the violent nature of many of their conflicts (Juchneva, 1993). This may help to stem the Jewish exodus to Israel, which would otherwise contribute to the economic malaise of Russia.

[3] The gradualist approach of the 'third way' economists, for instance those working within the framework dubbed 'Agenda 92' after the 16 March 1992 Bologna conference 'Agenda 92 for Socio-Economic Reconstruction in Central and Eastern Europe', seems to work primarily as a platform for criticism of shock therapy. If implemented, the gradualist policy of continuing subsidies to unprofitable state enterprises for the sake of avoiding unemployment could easily create a vicious circle of hyper-inflation, flight of capital and increasing foreign debt. As far as 'shock therapy' is concerned, it is in fact a fairly gradualist course when it comes to privatization and similar measures which take some time. The real issue is whether or not to transform the economy. I am grateful to my students Gitte Bjørg Andersen, Lars Thuesen, Jesper Rasmussen and Helle Willumsen for drawing my attention to Agenda 92.

determined strategy of reform probably represents the only way to build up a tax base for the necessary social security and the creation of an entrepreneurial class with vested interests in democracy and foreign policy moderation. It is a precondition for attracting foreign investment. Or, to quote the British dependency theorist Aidan Foster-Carter's aphorism, there is only one thing worse than being exploited, namely not being exploited.

The overall point about the intricacies of transition and reform in the context of postcommunism is that they do not limit themselves to the domestic sphere. The new political élites are also facing a 'Catch-22' situation at the level of foreign policy. In order to win external support for the transition and to normalize relations with the outside world, they have to launch a foreign policy revolution. But this revolution of participation and reintegration into the world order tends to clash with another foreign policy revolution, namely nationalistic mobilization for the purpose of gaining independence and sovereignty. The fact that the individual postcommunist country is not alone in this, but is surrounded by other newly free postcommunist states facing the same challenge, results in strong competition for international attention and national success.

In other words, the formation of foreign policy confronts postcommunist élites with stark dilemmas. Until recently, most Sovietologists and political scientists treated national mobilization as something of a sideshow in relation to the politics of transition. However, 'nationalism' – the ideological belief that each nation should live in a state of its own – has gradually conquered the political agenda in the countries undergoing transition from totalitarian repression, because of its connotations of struggle against foreign interference and dominance. Nationalism, ethnicity and religious cleavages can no longer be ignored (Brzezinski, 1989/90). If anything, the danger now lies in overemphasizing these dimensions. Be that as it may, the bottom line is that decolonization adds the politics of nation- and state-building to the agenda of reform in the countries undergoing transition from communism.

Foreign policy-building and the problem of stabilizers

New states often adopt a policy of 'nation-state-building', a concept that refers to the attempt of building state identity on the basis of (one single) ethnicity. At issue is the initiation of political development within a state. State-building entails the creation of modern citizenship, communal unity and state cohesion. Irrespective of the cultural history of the particular nation or state, it is very much an exercise in inventing tradition and identity, to cite the postmodern approach to nationalism. Drawing on the collective myths and history uniting people living in a given territory, building a nation-state is a process of ideological coalition-building which invites exaggeration, distortion, if not outright falsification, of history. Moreover, it is an exercise in self-demarcation which tends to undermine tolerance, confidence and security in relation to the surrounding world. Because of its bias towards exclusive and intolerant nationalism, nation-state-building in the context of multi-ethnic states tends to jeopardize internal security. Instead of reducing state vulnerability it may thus perpetuate it, as the history of Georgia since independence has shown.

State-building draws on contemporary institutions such as the army and defence, sport and culture, the launching of national airlines,[4] foreign ministries[5] and, indeed foreign policy. As the latter has to be invented too, one can speak of 'primary foreign policy formation' in roughly the same sense as when Marx wrote about primary capital accumulation. Needless to say, the territorial volatility and institutional weakness of the newly free state only add to the difficulty in this. In order to illuminate the problem of foreign policy-building, I should like to introduce the concept of 'stabilizers' invented by the Swedish political scientist Kjell Goldmann (1988) in his seminal work on change and stability in foreign policy.

Stabilizers are defined as any kind of phenomena tending to inhibit change even when there is a pressure for change (*ibid.*, p. xv). Goldmann identifies four basic types. First, there are 'international stabilizers', such as the norm of non-intervention or the Brezhnev doctrine which prevented Eastern Europe from leaving the Warsaw Pact. Secondly, due to the inertia of belief systems, one can speak of 'cognitive stabilizers', especially in the case of consistent,

---

[4] Thus the three Baltic states decided to establish national aviation companies in defiance of the economies of scale inherent in the model used by Denmark, Norway and Sweden (the SAS airline).

[5] As established by Maurice East (1973) in his examination of the workings of the Uganda Ministry of Foreign Affairs, the foreign ministries of new states often have a marginal role in foreign policy-decision making and act primarily as symbols of independence.

central and untestable beliefs such as enemy images. Thirdly, stabilizers may be 'political' in the sense that once a policy has gained legitimacy, reflecting a broad consensus, it will be difficult to challenge. It follows that institutionalization, support and salience work as determinants of political stabilizers. Finally, there are 'administrative stabilizers', that is inertia brought about by standard operating procedures within the bureaucracy, or the inertia of, say, policies of muddling through. Most people look with contempt upon inertia as a source of conservatism and an impediment to change, imagination and adaptability. But in this way inertia is conducive to stability or maybe even peace. Thus the point about stabilizers is that they contribute to the predictability of foreign policy.

As can be seen from this, the reasoning behind Goldmann's concept of stabilizers neatly summarizes the argument advanced by so-called institutionalists or regime analysts (Young, 1986; Wallander, 1992). It is a school of thought which challenges the 'realist' power approach to understanding political behaviour, including foreign policy. The institutionalists argue that the logic of power can be modified by institutions and regimes defined as persistent, and connected rules or norms whether formal or informal. As in the case of the concept of stabilizers, institutions and regimes need not be physical organizations. Mostly they are immaterial behavioural constraints – norms. Although regime-theorists and especially neo-liberal institutionalists tend to lean towards an optimistic outlook as they emphasize the possibility of moderation and cooperation, neither institutions nor stabilizers are by definition positive. As the example of the Brezhnev doctrine illustrates, stabilizers may negatively affect the lives of millions of people and threaten peace. The routinization of the Arab-Israeli conflict is another case of a problematic stabilizer. In other words, there is a complex nexus between peace and war and foreign policy change and stability. Here it is worth quoting Goldmann himself: 'In order to improve relations between long-standing adversaries it is necessary to destabilize their mutual policies of enmity. Once this has been achieved, the task is to stabilize their emerging policies of amity.' (1988, p. xv)

The overarching problem concerning foreign policy-building in new states is the inherent lack of 'stabilizers'. New states start from scratch; they have no experience or diplomatic tradition on which to rely, making their foreign policies highly volatile. As foreign policy actors, new states are thus similar to revolutionary states (cf.

Walt, 1992). The newly free postcommunist states cannot turn to the foreign policy legacy of the Soviet empire, because this cannot work as a source of legitimacy for them. This is very unfortunate, because under Gorbachev Soviet foreign policy did become a most respectable policy of *détente* and participation dubbed 'new political thinking'.

Building upon a recognition of the condition of interdependence, new political thinking grew into a Kantian vision of international democratization and security, a vision of evident relevance for postcommunist states because of the nature of their transition. Yet the rhetoric of new political thinking has disappeared. The tragic fate of this stabilizer is particularly pronounced in the case of Russian foreign policy. Being the successor state to the Soviet Union, Russia should be in a position to legitimize its foreign policy by drawing on relevant tenets from the Soviet era. But the Russian foreign policy discourse has come to look like an onslaught on new political thinking. In the assessment of the American Sovietologist Jeff Checkel (1994), this is not so very paradoxical given the low degree of institutionalization of Soviet new political thinking. Following Goldmann's terminology, the doctrine was never converted into a genuine political stabilizer but merely served as a cognitive stabilizer for liberal segments at the top of the Soviet system. These brief remarks are by way of introduction to the fascinating, albeit quite disillusioning, subject of Russian foreign policy, to which I shall return later.

The irony about the open challenge of new political thinking is that it is most clearly felt in Russia. Other postcommunist states are either simply indifferent to it, or they continue the rhetoric of interdependence and participation. This does not mean, however, that there is no problem of stabilizers for them. There certainly is a lack of administrative stabilizers such as routine and familiarity with the field (more on this later). The general problem of stabilizers also reveals itself in the way virtually all postcommunist states resort to 'national interest'. The emphasis on this concept as an overarching cognitive and political stabilizer is illustrated by the words of former Polish Prime Minister Tadeusz Mazowiecki on the national interest as 'the supreme criterion of our policy' (*Summary of World Broadcasts*, 26 November 1990). Similar statements can be found everywhere in official documents and speeches. Given the role of foreign policy in state- and nation-building, the emphasis on national interest should come as no surprise. The concept has a self-evident appeal for nationalists as a tool for legitimacy.

For this reason it is necessary to recapitulate the devastating criticism against the concept which has been made by political scientists. It is a concept which permeates the classic realist thinking of scholars such as Hans J. Morgenthau, who simply defines national interest 'in terms of power' and further characterizes it as the 'rational essence' of foreign policy (1967, pp. 5 ff.). But as James N. Rosenau, points out the concept of power is as elusive and ambiguous as the concept of national interest itself (1971, p. 244). The concept of power and the entire reasoning on the national interest tend to become tautological, as when Morgenthau assures us that the criterion of power will enable nations to follow 'but one guiding star, one standard for thought, one rule for action: *the national interest*' (1951, p. 242). It is necessary to ask in whose 'national interest' Russia is acting, for example, when it claims to act for the benefit of the national interest – is this only the interest of Russians, to the detriment of other peoples living in Russia (such as the many millions of Muslims)? As demonstrated by the British scholar Roy E. Jones, the concept of national interest is simply empirically empty in that it can denote anything which is held to be desirable in particular circumstances (1979, pp. 35-43).

Not only does the concept of national interest lack analytical rigour, but there is an important philosophical criticism to raise against it. The notion of 'national interest' as an infallible guide for action suggests a dangerously 'historicist' vision of foreign policy. In continuation of Karl Popper's (1966) vehement criticism of the historicist belief in the 'laws of history', 'the destiny of Russia', 'the sacred mission of Russia', 'the eternal fate of Serbia' and the like in his defence of the open society, foreign policy cannot and should not be anything but piecemeal social engineering. Historicist thinking is notoriously popular among intellectuals throughout the post-communist world – a legacy of communist mysticism and tribalism, to use the parlance of Popper, yet one which in the case of Russia has its roots in German historicism. Lev Tolstoi's novel *War and Peace*, for example, provides a historicist interpretation of the 'Patriotic War' of 1812 against Napoleon's France, in addition to extensive deliberations on the philosophy of history (Tolstoi, 1963). The geopolitical approach to foreign policy inspiring Russian politicians and politicians throughout the postcommunist world continues this historicist tradition. Halford Mackinder and his quite mysticist theory of the 'Eurasian Heartland' figured directly in the deliberations of Igor Malashenko when he was employed as a scholar in the International Department of the CPSU (Malashenko, 1990; Pozdnyakov, 1993).

A policy that insists on the principle of 'national interest' in neglect of interdependence and internationalization easily slides into parochial myopia and habitual thinking (Chipman, 1993). As a nation- and state-building device in an environment of competing nation-building processes, the reckless pursuit of national interest threatens to ignite inter-state conflict. The exclusiveness it suggests may spark intra-state conflict as well. The attraction of 'national interest' as a device for legitimacy for postcommunist élites, however, will not disappear simply through wishful thinking; neither will the realist 'power' mode of foreign policy behaviour it entails. This deplorable fact, combined with the general lack of stabilizers, erodes the relevance of the institutional approach when studying postcommunist foreign policy and resulting international relations. Incidentally, this is also the conclusion reached by one of the ardent institutionalists, Celeste Wallander, who opens up the possibility of 'a less important and more problematic role' for institutions in post-Soviet security policies (1992, p. 60; cf. Dannreuther, 1993). Stephen Burant (1993) offers a model in his application of the balance-of-power interpretation to Poland's policy towards its eastern neighbours. But his admission that there are motives beyond the logic of power and history in Poland's policy indicates that the best strategy for analysis may be one that seeks to test not only the realist hypothesis of the logic of power, but also the institutional hypothesis of alternative logics. In the analysis to follow there will be further elaboration of the institutional as well as the realist theme in postcommunist foreign policy.

The organizational dimension: making a foreign ministry

Whenever a colonial power retreats it leaves behind an administrative void. The chaos which followed the abrupt Belgian withdrawal from the Congo (Zaïre) in 1960 was one extreme case. All of a sudden, the Congolese had to fill over 4,000 vacated administrative posts from a recruitment pool of barely thirty university graduates. All over Africa totally inexperienced people had to fill such vacancies, or governments were forced to ask former colonial administrators to help keep things running. It took decades to Africanize the bureaucracy and to this very day Africa is haunted by inefficiency, corruption and nepotism among its civil servants.

On the surface, the situation in the postcommunist world seems much less desperate. Data in the ex-Soviet and CMEA statistical yearbooks show that the independent states of the former Soviet empire together have a pool of some 30 million people with higher education. Each Warsaw Pact member, union republic of the USSR and Mongolia had an intelligentsia numbering hundreds of thousands or even millions of individuals at the dawn of independence. However impressive, these figures should not obscure the very real of problems of over-specialization and irrelevance of education, or the problem of mental attitudes – work ethic, initiative and responsibility. Despite the high formal level of education, in contrast to many Third World states, most postcommunist countries do face major problems in organizing and staffing their ministries.

Foreign policy as a political practice involves the conduct of diplomacy, that is the conduct of international relations through negotiation, the essence of which is the accommodation of conflicting interests (Stoessinger, 1969, pp. 219 ff.). While the topic for diplomatic action may be the eruption of conflict, diplomacy in itself implies peaceful conflict-resolution. As such, diplomacy is a trade of atmost importance for newly free states aspiring to peace and security who find themselves in a competitive, conflict-rich environment. But the professional requirements of diplomacy can become a major barrier to the success of foreign policy, especially for the non-Russian states of the former internal empire, who have really had to start from scratch.

As already pointed out, the problem is not a general lack of education, let alone illiteracy, but inadequate professional training. Often postcommunist foreign ministers and diplomats hold degrees in international law, which is not in itself an irrelevant subject but is not enough to cope with the political, economic and technological realities of the contemporary world. Some are economists or historians and some have no relevant training at all. Virtually none have a training in political science. Many do not know foreign languages, nor do they know about the international organizations their country seeks to join. Only a few have experience of working or studying abroad. Most are ignorant about the working of market economies. The result is a rather messy and arbitrary foreign policy management in which foreign ministers have been seen distributing the mail or disregarding fundamental security precautions. In the analysis of the Estonian scholar Peeter Vares:

> [The Balts] had to create the security policies of their countries, but no local Balt had ever been involved in security studies. The only thing that the Balts did not lack was enthusiasm, but it could not substitute for their ignorance...numerous enthusiastic amateurs rushed to fill the outwardly attractive vacancies in the foreign services. (1993, pp. 5–6)

The vacancies mentioned refer to the fact that Soviet union republics did have 'foreign ministries' as the result of a constitutional amendment of 1944 (Aspaturian, 1960). But these ministries were purely fictional, as suggested by the deafening silence on their existence in the literature on Soviet foreign policy. A telling point is that only Kyrgyzstan chose to keep in office the 'foreign minister' left over from the Soviet era – Roza A. Otunbaeva, appointed in 1986.

The special case of Ukraine deserves mention because of its independent seat in the United Nations along with Belarus. For Ukraine this has come to serve as a platform for the country's emerging independent foreign policy and has provided a group of trained diplomats (Melnyczyk, 1991). Nikolai Kovalski, an international affairs expert at the Russian Institute of Europe who studied with many of today's post-Soviet diplomats, insists that one should not underestimate the skills of Central Asians, some of whom served as Soviet ambassadors to Mexico and other Third World countries (personal interview).

Kovalski's qualifications do not invalidate the point about the difficulty of organizing a postcommunist diplomatic service. The option of recruiting foreign policy personnel among emigré populations in the United States, Canada and elsewhere cannot solve the problem. In the assessment of Peeter Vares, their better formal qualifications are often offset by their lack of in-depth knowledge of the country whose interests they are going to serve. This points towards another big problem in staff recruitment, namely that of political reliability. This is a problem which is shared by the countries of the external empire and Russia despite the large pool of trained diplomats at their disposal (Crow, 1992a; McGregor, 1992; Reisch, 1992). Both Soviet and external empire diplomats were recruited on the basis of the notorious *nomenklatura* lists which ensured their political loyalty (see below, pp. 92, 107-8). Because of the privileges and fringe benefits accompanying the *nomenklatura* positions, they did attract talented people. Even external empire diplomats received training at the Soviet Foreign Ministry's Diplomatic Academy or the Moscow State Institute of International Relations (MGIMO); a practice that had to end, leaving new diplomats without any systematic training. The old practice of ensuring that 'experts' were also 'reds' meant that the new postcommunist states found themselves with many 'non-reds' who happened to be non-experts as well. The problem of amateurishness is therefore not limited to the internal empire (McGregor, 1992; Skak, 1991a). It was partly for the sake of maintaining continuity among public servants that post-communist Czechoslovakia re-adopted security clearances, dubbed *lustrace* ('screening'), with other countries following suit.

Countries of the Third World display a similar, if not higher, degree of arbitrariness in the organization of their diplomacy (Clapham, 1977). Sinecure diplomats fill many embassies, whether out of personal greed or because their governments lack operational programmes and vision with respect to their foreign ministries (Calvert, 1986; p. 83; East, 1973). Sinecurism is not unknown among diplomats in the postcommunist countries, but the low salaries offered to civil servants tend to discourage this and actually worsen the problem of cadre recruitment as people defect to private firms. There have been some instances of diplomatic relations being established for reasons of prestige and nation-building. Thus Latvia tried – partly out of ignorance – to maintain relations with both the People's Republic of China and Taiwan, thereby prompting the People's Republic to break off relations. Mostly, however, embassies are established where they are deemed necessary, for example in Washington, Brussels, Bonn and other capitals that are of importance if a country is to link itself with the sinews of international cooperation.

Most Third World countries represent poor role models for postcommunist states in the field of diplomacy. However, several analysts single out the Brazilian Ministry of Foreign Affairs, the *Itamaraty*, as by far the most professional and efficient foreign service in Latin America and – by extension – in the Third World in general (Calvert, 1986, p. 86; Kaufman, 1977, p. 153). The key to its success lies in the tradition of expertise – strict selection processes and extensive training – and continuity, built up by the Baron of Rio Branco, who served as Foreign Minister from 1902 till 1912. The

Chilean Ministry of Foreign Affairs also draws attention as one of the more successful on the Latin American continent, which, incidentally, is the least Third Worldish and most 'European' of the Third World continents. The Argentinian Ministry of Foreign Affairs has a less flattering record, due to its association with the fatal miscalculation in the conflict over the Malvinas/Falkland Islands in 1982. Naturally, there is always the option of drawing on the know-how of Western diplomatic services and sending future public servants on exchange programmes such as TEMPUS for language and political science training. Cooperation with western diplomats, officers and parliamentarians within the framework of NATO, for instance begins to resemble a senior-level exchange programme.

The very act of international cooperation represents an exercise in 'learning by doing'. Accordingly, one should not over-dramatize the difficulties ahead, provided that some sort of consolidation and return to normalcy take place. Yet this proviso brings into focus the policy recommendation of Peter Calvert: 'The advanced countries must...try to see the problems of the new states in their own terms, remembering that their political weaknesses also limit their capacity to explain their interests adequately' (1986, p. 171). Calvert further reminds us that war is not a remote possibility for new states, an observation that may serve as a prelude to the following section on conflict and security.

Problems and policies of security: reintegration I

Following the tradition of Hans J. Morgenthau and Barry Buzan, security may be defined as the ability of states to maintain their independent identity and functional integrity, a definition that includes other aspects of security and security policy than security in a purely military sense. This does not render protection from attack and absence of threats irrelevant as markers of 'security'. The tremendous significance of decolonization at the level of security policy lies in the decentralization or 're-nationalization' of security policy following the removal of colonial 'overlay'.[6] The replacement

[6] 'Overlay' refers to situations when an external power gains control over local conflict and security dynamics through direct colonization, imposition of Cold War dynamics or the like (Buzan, 1983). Overlay may intensify conflicts, but mostly it has a pacifying influence. The role of Marshal Tito in post-1945 Yugoslavia could be described as 'charismatic overlay'.

of *Pax Sovietica* by new sovereign states forces the latter to formulate their own security policy. As argued earlier, newly free postcommunist states tend towards a policy of nation-state-building inspired by the concept of national interest. This leads to a search for national security policies (Grizold, 1993; 'Military Policy Doctrine of the Republic of Bulgaria', 1992). Inspired by the National Security Council of the United States, Russia has launched a 'Security Council', Poland a 'National Security Bureau' and Bulgaria a 'National Security Council', with Belarus and other countries following suit. However, looking for national security – and 'national interest' – under conditions of international interdependence and globalization means looking for a mirage.

What is more, the concept of national security obscures the anarchy and the security dilemma facing new states born in a common process of decolonization. When groups or individuals strive to attain national-territorial security from attack, they 'are driven to acquire more and more power to escape the impact of the power of others', to quote John Herz's wording in his seminal article (1950) on the security dilemma. This breeds insecurity in the countries surrounding the state that is arming itself, which in turn motivates a stepping up of preparations and, ultimately, 'a vicious circle of security and power accumulation is on' (*ibid.*). Defensiveness and offensiveness, respectively, are therefore in the eye of the beholder. What one state considers legitimate and necessary defensive measures tend to be seen as offensive by others, in the sense that they threaten the *status quo* to the former's advantage (Wheeler and Booth, 1992; Buzan, 1983).

The security dilemma was what faced the newly free states of Latin America on their decolonization from Spain in the nineteenth century. It brought several inter-state wars to the continent: Paraguay against Argentina (1865-70); Chile against Bolivia and Peru (1879-84); and later El Salvador against Honduras (1969: the so-called Soccer War). India and Pakistan were subject to a baptism of fire on gaining independence. As for specific postcommunist security dilemmas, one could cite Ukraine's unwillingness to give up its nuclear weaponry: a hostile action in the eyes of Russia and a most controversial one from the point of view of nuclear non-proliferation, but nevertheless a necessary defensive measure from a Ukrainian point of view (Alexandrova, 1993a). Ukraine's decision to build up an army of 400,000-450,000 men shook governments in Central Europe until it was realized that this was being done as a deterrent in relation to Russia (Skak, 1992b).

Security dilemmas do not presuppose symmetry in relations between states. Russia's reaction to policy initiatives in the Baltic countries demonstrates that small and weak states may be perceived as threatening by great powers because of their very pursuit of security, notably in connection with imperial great power complexes as is the case here. In other words, the whole complex of cognitive and cultural disparities, that is disparities in perception and self-perception as well as more trivial (organizational) sources of misinformation and misperception, work as aggravating factors in the perception of threats and formulation of counter-measures.

The concept of security dilemmas is part and parcel of realism, including its neo-realist offspring (Waltz, 1979; Morgenthau, 1967). But is the security dilemma that inescapable? Here the optimists turn towards the type of regime as a crucial modifying factor. Immanuel Kant's treatise on 'perpetual peace' has sparked off a considerable body of research arguing that democratic countries are more pacifist than others. More specifically, democratic countries do not wage war against one another, but they do occasionally wage wars against non-democratic countries. Declining non-democratic countries in particular may be tempted into preventive war (Schweller, 1992). In this connection it is worth remembering that the transition from communism represents a process of democratization and hence bears the promise of peace. Opinion polls and voting behaviour at times reveal surprisingly sane political views held by the citizenry, as illustrated by the Russian referendum of 25 April 1993. Transition from communism is not just ethnic mobilization, or an economic revolution from above, but a pluralistic tide involving the creation of institutions of civil society – parties, independent organizations and so on. The traumatic experience of communist repression and one-party rule should prevent authoritarian forces from gaining legitimacy again.

Conversely, the initial element of democratization in Afro-Asian decolonization was crippled by the widespread perception of democracy as alien, as something imposed by the colonial powers in a deliberate preparation for neo-colonialism. This perception paved the way for military dictatorship and more or less authoritarian one-party rule (Emerson, 1960, pp. 282 ff.). Still, the embryonic postcommunist democratic structures and the fact that only one, the

Czech lands, out of almost thirty sovereign postcommunist states has a tradition of democracy worth mentioning serve as a cautionary note.

This qualification of the significance of postcommunist democracy leads to a reiteration that basically all are new states and often lack security policy stabilizers. Postcommunist states still need to be 'socialized' into the system, to use Kenneth Waltz's apt term (1979, pp. 127-8). As pointed out earlier, this makes these countries almost revolutionary, tending to wage wars against one another because the turmoil surrounding new states alters the balance of power, heightens the danger of misperception and tempts exaggerated assessments of how easy it is to win (Walt, 1992, pp. 322-3). In this Stephen Walt reasons not on the basis of worst-case analysis, but merely from the legitimate security concerns of sovereign states in a self-help, anarchic system (*ibid.*, pp. 360 ff.). There have already been several instances of inter-state war between postcommunist states; for example, between Armenia and Azerbaijan over Nagorno-Karabakh. Anthony D. Smith therefore emphasizes the instrumental nature of conflict and war in processes of nation-building, citing the decisive role of the war with Napoleon in 1812 in Russian nation-building, and of the Second World War in Soviet nation-building (dubbed 'the Great Patriotic War' in Soviet historiography). According to Smith, it is the army as an ambiguous institution in nation-building that is the culprit:

> With the growth in military professionalism, followed by mass military participation, the military's self-image and its stereotypes of the enemy assume disproportionate importance. In so far as the ideology of the military is necessarily ethnocentric or nationalistic, in view of their security function, the negative reference is reinforced on both sides [of the new state's border] and becomes generally aggressive and stereotyped.... In such circumstances, we should not be surprised by the many 'wars of liberation' and 'people's wars', from China to Angola and Cuba, which only serve to reinforce ethnic solidarity and 'nation-building'. (1981, pp. 377, 392)

Barry Posen offers even more sombre deliberations on the security dilemma at the grass-roots level under conditions of decolonization and deep societal transformation; deliberations which deserve to be quoted at some length:

> In areas such as the former Soviet Union and Yugoslavia,

'sovereigns' have disappeared. They leave in their wake a host of groups – ethnic, religious, cultural – of greater or lesser cohesion. These groups must pay attention to the first thing that states have historically addressed – the problem of security...there will be competition for the key to security – power...the process of imperial collapse produces conditions that make offensive and defensive capabilities indistinguishable and make the offence superior to the defence. In addition, uneven progress in the formation of state structures will create windows of opportunity and vulnerability. Across the board, these strategic problems show that very little nationalist rabble-rousing on nationalistic combat-iveness is required to generate very dangerous situations...the 'groupness' of the ethnic, religious, cultural and linguistic collec-tivities that emerge from collapsed empires gives each of them an inherent offensive military power...the drive for security in one group can be so great that it produces near-genocidal behaviour towards neighbouring groups.... The vulnerability of civilians make it possible for small bands of fanatics to initiate conflict.... The presence or absence of small gangs of fanatics is thus itself a key determinant of the ability of groups to avoid war as central political authority erodes. (1993, pp. 28-33)

The last paragraph concerns the phenomenon of warlordism which creates a drastically lowered threshold for the eruption of small, brutal and highly destabilizing wars. According to Posen, the wars in Yugoslavia erupted because the parties identified the re-emerging identities of the others as offensive threats.

Posen is not alone in observing that the security dilemma arises not only among states, but also among ethnic groups and other collectives as the previous overlay disappears. Bogdan Szajkowski argues that mobilization along ethnic kinship lines is not just manipulated from above in a deliberate process of nation-building, but from below as well because 'the retreat into ethnic socio-political boundaries and values offers safety at turbulent times' (1993, p. 173). Individuals may thus find greater security by resorting to ethnic collectivism instead of communist collectivism as a remedy for their security dilemma. The Western individualistic orientation may be by-passed as not attractive at all. Sadly, it is precisely collectivism which is easy to manipulate in the direction of violence. Failure to address all these immensely counter-productive effects of nationalistic myopia – for example in the relationship between

Hungarians and Romanians, or Russians against Estonians and Latvians – could prove fatal. The increased number of refugees is but one example of the pressure upon the entire postcommunist region during this era of 'the peace dividend'.

What about cultural orientations and their significance? It is increasingly being argued that the peaceful behaviour of democracies towards other democracies may be less a product of procedures than of democratic political cultures, notably participant cultures (Ember *et al.*, 1992). Although it is dangerous to make sweeping generalizations on the distribution of pacifist and violent cultures across countries, there are obvious differences between the acquiescent adaptation of the Czechs, symbolized by the anti-hero ('Good Soldier') Svejk, and the brutal macho-cultures of the Balkans and the Caucasus. The 'singing revolutions' of the Baltic peoples stand out as accomplishments in non-violent political struggle. But when roles are reversed under conditions of sovereignty, it is tempting to seek revenge and humiliate former 'master peoples'. Cultural change in the direction of participant cultures is not impossible, but it takes time and requires the same interplay of destabilizers and stabilizers as within political change in general (cf. Hahn, 1991; Goldmann, 1988). Hence the cultural factor is another cause for pessimism on the ability of postcommunist states to avoid war between themselves. The experience of Western Europe suggests that the cultivation of cultures and nationalisms of compromise and peaceful conflict-settlement necessitates the travails of war. If that is so, it is to be hoped that the fair share of war which the postcommunist region has experienced in the course of history will suffice.

Some might object that the breakthrough in the field of nuclear and conventional disarmament evidenced by the INF, CFE, START I and START II treaties must somehow alleviate the security dilemma facing the newly free postcommunist states. Many governments happily settle for much smaller national armies and, so far, the Baltic states have built up only mini-armies. Russia's plans for restructuring the armed forces inherited from the Soviet Union are bedevilled by acute financial problems, low morale and problems in housing the forces withdrawn from other postcommunist countries. The autumn draft of 1992 left the Russian Army short of almost a million men, meaning there were 630,000 officers against only 540,000 conscripts (*Nezavisimaia Gazeta* [hereafter cited as *NeGa*], 2 July 1993). Evidently, disarmament measures and resource problems significantly lower realistic force levels. But, as indicated in the earlier discussion on warlordism, the formation of national armies is not the entire story of the security problem. The real sore spot is the lack of control over men and firepower that characterizes some postcommunist military establishments. This brings the discussion back to the overarching problem of weak institutions and weak states, resulting from the combined turbulence of transition and decolonization. The fact that security problems of postcommunist states are just as much problems of internal security and stability makes it more appropriate to speak of societal security (Dick *et al.*, 1993; Zielonka, 1992; Wæver *et al.*, 1993; Nørgaard, 1993). Consolidation and normalization represent vital security concerns for postcommunist governments.

All this reasoning on the security problems facing postcommunist governments as well as individuals would seem to point towards one single, utterly pessimistic conclusion. Fortunately, the actual record of postcommunist security policies gives reason for optimism. In spite of the rhetoric of national security policy, many governments pursue astonishingly healthy security policies involving various sorts of mutual confidence and security-building measures (CSBMs). A case in point is the eastern policy of Poland, which is fuelled by a genuine wish for reconciliation with Lithuanians, Ukrainians and Byelorussians to overcome the conflict-ridden legacy of the past and at the same time is inspired by balance-of-power considerations in relation to Russia (especially concerning Polish-Ukrainian relations; Burant, 1993). Another example of reasonable foreign and domestic security policies is provided by Bulgaria, which used to practise 'ethnic cleansing' towards its Turkish minority under the communist regime of Todor Zhivkov but which now seems to be a factor of stability in the Balkans, including in regard to Macedonia (otherwise considered 'lost' Bulgarian land; Karasimeonov and Skak, 1994).

The successful efforts of the leaders of Uzbekistan and Kyrgyzstan in defusing the conflict in the ethnically mixed city of Osh on the Kyrgyz side of their common border also deserve mention as a case of Central Asian conflict-management. Romanian-Hungarian tension notwithstanding, the two countries were the first to sign a so-called Open Skies Agreement in May 1991. The Hungarian side has spoken with warmth about this military agreement (*Népszabadság*, 30 December 1990). After their liberation from Soviet tutelage,

Poland, Hungary and Czechoslovakia swiftly organized a network of bilateral military cooperation treaties. Recently, the three Baltic states launched a joint peacekeeping battalion of 650 men, dubbed BALTBAT, to be trained for UN operations (*RFE/RL News Briefs*, 22-6 November 1993). Estonian, Latvian and Lithuanian cooperation includes monthly meetings at the level of foreign affairs' ministers. However limited their scope, all these East-East CSBMs are vital elements in European security today because they serve to de-nationalize security policy and conflict-management. They definitely need further encouragement and attention as a core principle of conditionality in the East-West economic relationship, together with an emphasis on human rights (cf. Walt, 1992).

As stated at the outset, the concentric circles of empire are a key factor shaping postcommunist security policy. Putting relations with the former hegemon on a new footing characterized by reciprocity is one foreign policy task confronting the newly free states of the internal and external Soviet empire. In practice, this amounts to restoring and renovating links with Russia. Here one senses the defining difference between the internal and external empire: the degree of sovereignty and foreign policy experience. The small member countries of the now dismantled Warsaw Pact have had markedly fewer difficulties in arriving at a new relationship with Russia, building on mutual respect, than, say, Estonia and Latvia, not to mention Moldova (Reisch, 1993a; Haramiev-Drezov, 1993; de Weydenthal, 1993). In a typical outcry, the Estonian Minister without Portfolio responsible for relations with Russia, Juri Luik, had to remind Russia and the world that 'little Estonia isn't stepping on Russia's toes' (*International Herald Tribune*, 24 August 1993). Without doubt, the Balts' lack of diplomatic experience hampers pragmatism, but this has to be weighed against Russian unwillingness to let the recognition of Baltic sovereignty translate into foreign policy (Kionka, 1992). Likewise, Moldova has been victimized in the Russian praetorian maelstrom of 'overbidding' on issues of foreign policy in the 'near abroad' (the internal empire). At one time, the then parliamentary Speaker Ruslan Khasbulatov made the Russian parliament's position on the inviolability of Moldova's borders conditional upon Moldova's membership of the Commonwealth of Independent States (CIS) (*RFE/RL Research Report*, 8 May 1992, p. 59).

It is against the background of this hardline Russian policy and a perceived threat to independence from Russia that the initial Baltic,

Ukrainian and Belarusian policies of neutrality have to be viewed. Belarusian neutrality as pursued by the now-expelled parliamentary chairman Stanislau Shushkevich was intended as a safeguard against CIS systems of 'collective security', building upon Russian dominance (Mihailisko, 1993). Similarly, Ukraine's neutrality as fixed in its 1990 declaration of independence quickly ceased to be seen as a goal in itself. It was above all a non-provocative measure of security aimed at consoling Moscow (Alexandrova, 1993a). Since then Ukraine has joined the NATO framework of Partnership for Peace (PfP), as have the Baltic states and nearly all residual CIS countries. Lithuania has formally announced its intention to become a full NATO member, as Albania did before this. Neutrality is simply becoming irrelevant in the eyes of postcommunist governmental élites – even more so, if one turns to the former small Warsaw Pact members, such as Hungary, which also for a brief period leaned towards neutrality (Reisch, 1993b; cf. Vaclav Havel in *International Herald Tribune*, 20 October 1993). This pursuit of membership is not limited to NATO, but extends to the Council of Europe, the EU and WEU, as emphasized by Hungarian Minister of Foreign Affairs Geza Jeszenszky (*ibid.*, 22 October 1992). However, insofar as it marks the emerging approach to managing relations with the former imperial centre and the security dilemma in general, the NATO component of postcommunist foreign policy attracts particular attention. Some Western analysts have difficulty in accepting this search for military alignment, deeming it off the mark given the many non-military security challenges facing postcommunist countries. But this objection does not address the problem of the re-nationalization of security policies, for which the only remedy is transparency through international military and security policy commitments. Seen in this perspective, it is encouraging to observe that the determined pursuit of membership of all European organizational structures has come to be shared by the Slovak and Romanian governments (Melescanu, 1993; *Den Slovakiske regerings programerklæring*, 1994).

This strategy of participation is what distinguishes the foreign policy of postcommunist countries from that of Third World countries, who began by pursuing the policy of non-alignment in relation to the Soviet-American conflict of the Cold War and later switched to a policy reminiscent of class war against all the industrialized countries of the 'North' (Rothstein, 1976). By contrast, postcommunist countries have not even bothered to contact the Non-Aligned Movement, which happens to be caught in its own post-Cold War crisis of identity. The only exception is Uzbekistan, which joined it in 1992 (*NeGa*, 4 September 1992). In order to explain these starkly differing patterns of participation and rejection of participation in the East and the South, it may be useful to introduce the concepts of 'entrapment' and 'abandonment' as employed not only within the analysis of alliance formation, but in economic integration too (Snyder, 1984; Kelstrup, 1991).[7] Thus states as sovereigns face a dilemma of cooperation in their relations with the surrounding world, be this military, political or economic cooperation. The stakes involved are security, identity, welfare or any combination of the three.[8] If a state opts for cooperation with the surrounding world it runs the risk of becoming 'entrapped' in the problems and conflicts surrounding the cooperative framework in question. It was this perception of entrapment (in this case neo-colonial entrapment) that inspired foreign and security policy of the Third World. Perceptions of entrapment also influence the policy of non-Russian countries towards Russia. Thus the Lithuanian parliament has adopted a Constitutional Act banning the country from joining any economic union relating to the former Soviet Union. Conversely, if a state opts for a policy of non-participation and non-alignment it runs the risk of being left alone with its problems, of being 'abandoned' by the world. The postcommunist policies of participation build on this perception of abandonment, which incidentally links logically to the perception of interdependence as a basic condition in international affairs. Third World foreign policies too increasingly follow the pattern of participation in acknowledgement of the very real problem of abandonment, not least in the case of black Africa. As stated before, there seems to be only one thing worse than being exploited, and that is not to be exploited.

Both perceptions have to be viewed in a historical perspective. The Third World view of entrapment is rooted in the experience

[7] The twin concepts of entrapment and abandonment have been used to analyse both Danish policy towards NATO and the ambiguities of Danish EU policies (Petersen, 1993; Kelstrup, 1991).

[8] The game of international cooperation may be analysed from the angle of the multilateral framework in question, but for the time being only the angle of the individual participant matters.

of forced Europeanization and modernization, whereas most non-Russian countries of the now defunct Soviet empire look upon their sovietization – to be elaborated upon later – as a forced de-Europeanization and de-modernization. In its European 'near abroad' the Soviet Union was never a role model, in contrast to the pattern in the Latin American-United States relationship, where people would shout 'Yankee go home' and secretly add 'but take me with you' (Rupnik, 1988). In fact, sovietization combined the worst of both possible worlds in that isolation from the West was accompanied by subjugation to the Kremlin power structure. The rhetoric of today's postcommunist élites speaks volumes about the historical, yet still vivid trauma of abandonment, e.g. 'those of us in the Cold War's "forgotten" part of Europe' (Melescanu, 1993, p. 12) and 'in 1956 the Western world showed us they would abandon Hungary' (*International Herald Tribune*, 3 February 1994). Elsewhere I have analysed the powerful cultural drive that lay behind the postcommunist approach of abandonment under the heading of Europeanization (Skak, 1991b). It is not a conception that excludes Russia, although the Russian approach to Europe was always more ambivalent (Skak, 1993b). Russia's fears of itself being abandoned can thus partly explain its opposition to an enlargement of NATO.

Indeed, the policy of participation on the basis of membership has developed into a security policy concept of its own, which could be termed a 'policy of reintegration'. In much the same vein, the German Sovietologist Heinz Timmermann (1992) speaks of Central European and Russian strategies of *An-und Einbindung* (*Anbindung* means 'joining', '*Einbindung*' means 'webbing', 'binding into' or the like). The reason why I have settled for using the term 'reintegration' rather than just 'integration' is the postcommunist perception of 'returning to Europe' after a traumatic hibernation as subjects in an alien Soviet empire. A further consideration is that the postcommunist issue of joining Europe should not be confused with the topic of integration among the present EU members. Legitimitized by Gorbachev's pursuit of a common European home, reintegration used to be a policy centred on the All-European CSCE process, but then disillusionment grew because of the CSCE's lack of clout. Subsequently, it developed into a policy that insists on full-scale integration into Europe, with full membership of NATO, WEU, EU and the Council of Europe as the ultimate goal.

A further argument why the postcommunist policy of reintegration must be seen as a security policy strategy centres on the reunification of Germany. This is still causing concern in the Czech Republic, Poland and Hungary, whose élites employ the same reasoning of *Einbindung* with respect to Germany as the Germans do themselves when arguing for the necessity of the country's integration into the EU and as Bonn's allies do concerning NATO – whose alleged role it is 'to keep the Germans down' (in addition to keeping 'the Americans in and the Russians out' in Lord Ismay's famous phrase; Skak, 1993c). One aphorism of Czech President Vaclav Havel (1990) illustrates the parallel reasoning of Central Europeans: 'The process of European integration should not stop at the reunification of Germany; it should go on. Only then will Europe be a safe place for Germany. Only then will Germany be a safe place for Europe.' The same logic of *Einbindung* ought to apply to perceptions of Russia, which many postcommunist countries perceive as threatening (Wettig, 1993). However, except for the all-encompassing CSCE (now OSCE) and NACC cooperation, this line of thought rarely inspires non-Russian postcommunist élites vigorously to pursue the reintegration of Russia *vis-à-vis* the West, let alone to engage themselves heavily in international cooperation with Russia (e.g. the CIS). This is quite understandable given the double complex of entrapment and abandonment created by sovietization, which remains a living memory. What is more, reintegration cannot but be a self-help race for success in which the West will be inclined towards rewarding commitment to reform and superior performance. Against this background it is interesting to note that some postcommunist countries which look upon themselves as 'buffers' – e.g. buffers in relation to Russia – have tried to formulate a concept that links their policy of reintegration and their policy of balancing relations with the former imperial core and other less stable neighbours – the concept of 'bridge'. A case in point is Poland's Eastern policy. The notion of bridging further seems to inspire Slovak, Hungarian and Romanian policies towards Ukraine, and Baltic policies towards Russia, as well as the Russian vision of Russia as the bridge or geopolitical 'balancer' between Europe and Asia (Pozdnyakov, 1993). In other words, postcommunist states often seek to place themselves as 'strategic' Europeanization and 'reintegration-patrons' for other postcommunist states located further off the centre of Europe, a concept to which we shall return. Thus, the Polish offer in relation to Lithuania, Ukraine, Russia and

Belarus is 'a positive response to their aspirations to be part of Europe' in exchange for 'their compliance with European and other standards, which are the only alternative to the extremely dangerous vacuum of rules that obtained after the failure of the [Soviet] Union' (Kostrzewa-Zorbas, 1992, p. 149).

Unfortunately, the strategy of posing oneself as a necessary bridge has become victim of substantial inflation – there are too many 'bridges'. Peeter Vares makes the sobering observation of Balts displaying susceptibility towards the West and indifference towards the East, as a contemporary comment on the Estonian-American scholar Rein Taagepera's vision of the Baltic countries as a gateway to Europe (Vares, 1993, p. 20). Nevertheless, bridge-thinking continues to influence Baltic foreign policy establishments (Friis Hansen and Jørgensen, 1993; *Frankfurter Allgemeine Zeitung*, 28 October, 1993). It is thus an approach which should be saluted as another attempt at seeking to overcome the security dilemma without jeopardizing reintegration; in other words, an effort towards reconciling entrapment and abandonment, this time in a bid to achieve the best of both worlds.

The terminology of reintegration is not meant to suggest that conventional theories of integration do not apply to postcommunist processes of reintegration. As argued by the British Sovietologist Richard Sakwa (1991), it is possible to identify a 'functionalist imperative', not to say a federalist imperative (the logic of abandonment), as well as more subtle neo-functionalist dynamics if one undertakes an in-depth analysis of the process of reintegration of individual countries. The culturally determined urge towards integration with Europe points towards not only logics of *Gesellschaft* ('society', i.e. contract-based relationships or procedural logic), as within conventional theories of cooperation and integration, but also towards logics of *Gemeinschaft* ('community', i.e. the emotional forces of identification and feelings of belonging). The twin concepts of *Gesellschaft* and *Gemeinschaft* are taken from the classic German sociologist Ferdinand Tönnies. Karl Deutsch's (1957) thoughts on 'security communities' reiterate the interplay between the two.

Where postcommunist policies of reintegration clearly differ from West European integration is in the concomitant domestic process of transition. This adds an entirely new, dramatic twist to the topic of integration. As I have exposed in greater detail elsewhere, postcommunist thinking on reintegration is preoccupied with the domestic feedback from integration (Skak, 1993c). At issue is the *Einbindung* into European international structures, commitments and norms as a vital, if not decisive factor in the success of the transition towards democracy and market economy. This breeds a search for membership commitment from organizations like the EU and NATO, a search for commitments as 'bastions', to use the parlance of adaptation theory (Mouritzen, 1988). Bastion-building is a typical political instrument for actors who feel vulnerable in one sense or another, including states who feel vulnerable on the domestic front.[9] In the postcommunist process of reintegration, membership commitments from international organizations work as bastions in the sense that they help to stem the tide of frustrations over the speed and scope of domestic recovery. They provide the light at the end of the tunnel. The approach of bastion-building has found its most explicit expression in contributions from Hungarian and Polish analysts. It amounts to a theory of democratization and a theory of internal security too. To quote the Hungarian political scientist Attila Agh:

> The point is that it is above all out of political necessity that we need the EC [EU].... The political future of the country is still open and a positive political coercion is...necessary for us.... Europe is a protection against proponents of parochialism.... Evidently, the democratic transition can only be finished if political and economic consolidation take place inside the EC. (*Népszabadság*, 15 February 1992)

As can be inferred from this, what disqualifies neutrality from the point of view of reintegration is the fact that it does not offer international *Einbindung;* it represents no bastion from which to fight aggressive populists, jingoists and praetorians. This is not to deny the value or the necessity of visionary non–military national security policies seeking to address the internal dimension of security, as is

---

[9] This emphasis on domestic determinants behind adaptive foreign policy behaviour falls into line with the founding fathers of this tradition, although empirical studies of adaptation tend to be biased towards external pressures for adaptation. See Rosenau (1970) and Petersen (1977). Rosenau's intellectual path towards adaptation as his conceptualization of foreign policy led him through the concept of *linkage*, chosen because it highlighted the role of foreign policy as an intermediary between intra- and extra-societal pressures (Rosenau, 1969). This position has since worked as a *raison d'être* for foreign policy analysis as a sub-field within comparative political science.

also made clear in the policy deliberations in connection with the quasi-state. The point is that postcommunist reintegration differs from integration in Western Europe because of this dimension of 'internal integration'. The task is one of overcoming the communist legacy of abandonment or isolation by providing for what might be termed 'primary integration' as one particular task within postcommunist foreign policy formation.

With due allowance for the substantial variations across countries, the overall conclusion remains that postcommunist security policies are conceptually far more sophisticated than one might expect, considering that they are launched by *de facto* brand new states. The élites of the new postcommunist states do not only follow national security policies focused on the pursuit of what Arnold Wolfers calls possession goals, i.e. those relating to the territory and the state in a narrow sense. In many respects they seem to acknowledge the virtue of pursuing what Wolfers calls 'milieu goals', i.e. those relating to the overall structure and development in the international environment (Wolfers, 1962, pp. 73-4). In this way they demonstrate their recognition of the fact that not least small states have a vital interest in the creation of strong institutions or stabilizers to provide for the *Einbindung* of great powers.[10]

Problems and policies of development: reintegration II

In order to continue along the lines of the argument of the preceding section, the initial discussion here concerns the policies of development. The functional division of foreign policy into policies of security and development – 'warfare' versus 'welfare' – is a quite conventional and handy analytical distinction. The concept of reintegration, however, encompasses both dimensions in appreciation of the broad, non-military conception of security. Thus postcommunist policies towards NATO are not devoid of economic welfare

[10] The concept of milieu goals has an equivalent in Ole Karup Pedersen's concept of 'normative interests' (1970, pp. 66-7 and *passim*). The foreign policy writings of Czech President Vaclav Havel are permeated by this kind of reasoning, e.g. the lesson he draws from the Munich deal of 1938 which sealed the fate of Czechoslovakia (*International Herald Tribune*, 20 October 1993). The legacy of Thomas G. Masaryk (1972) and his thinking on European integration appears to have inspired Havel as well.

aspects insofar as some of the cooperation with NATO relates to conversion of military production. Likewise, the policy of seeking EU membership does have undertones of military security policy because of the organic relationship between the EU and WEU and hence NATO. Figure 2.1 below recapitulates the logic of reintegration as it relates to consolidation of the domestic regime change in the shape of a vital feedback relation:

Fig. 2.1. REINTEGRATION—ELITE PERCEPTIONS IN THE POST-COMMUNIST WORLD

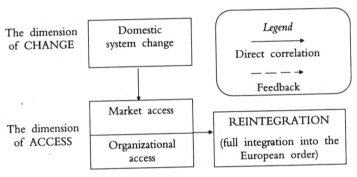

The same broad approach to reintegration, albeit focusing on what is in it from a Western point of view, reappears in a statement by François Heisbourg, the former director of the International Institute of Strategic Studies in London: 'If reform fails because of a lack of financial support, or through a lack of openness to Central European exports to Western Europe, or because of excessive reticence towards membership of the EC system, then we will all pay in security terms' (*International Herald Tribune*, 30 May 1991). Nevertheless, the question of market access is most directly related to economic recovery. Coined as a theory of democratization, the reasoning behind Figure 2.1 seems to be that only improved access to Western markets can sustain the fledgling entrepreneurial middle classes throughout the postcommunist region. Entrepreneurs and middle classes, in turn, represent the crucial social guarantee of the change towards market economy and democracy, because they tend to have a more vital stake in this change than any other social segment in society. This perception of the strategic role of middle classes in processes of democratization is fundamental in research on the topic (cf. Schöpflin, 1991a). Postcommunist privatization often turns out to be *nomenklatura* or mafia privatization, which gives the entire transformation an image of conspiracy that could have fatal consequences at the level of popular support. All the more reason, then, to seek to build up a class of real self-made entrepreneurs.

As for the necessity of external support in the shape of market access, there are two things to take into account. First, the break with the generally autarkic economic system of communism entails a break with a policy of import-substitution and a shift towards a strategy of foreign economic openness and export-led growth (Segal *et al.*, 1992; Holzmann, 1974). The very transition towards a market economy thus requires elbow-room in the field of exports. The collapse of the CMEA and the Soviet Union as regional trade systems only reinforces this point. Secondly, due to the low level of purchase power domestically, entrepreneurs cannot survive on the basis of domestic earnings. They will need additional sources of capital-formation and investment. Moreover, access to foreign markets helps to attract much needed foreign investment for modernizing the production apparatus. As already indicated in Heisbourg's statement, market access is one of the most powerful forms of 'aid' which the West could offer, as spelled out by many economists (Senior Nello, 1991, p. 183). It has proven rather difficult for postcommunist countries to gain market access, especially in the field of so-called sensitive goods (agricultural products, textiles, coal and steel), although the extension of GSPs,[11] Europe Agreements of Association (to countries of the external empire), free-trade agreements (the Baltic states) and partnership agreements (CIS countries: Ukraine and Russia at the time of writing) have helped a good deal.

In terms of economic development, the virtue of organizational access is not just a question of guaranteed access to the internal market of the EU, although this definitely plays a decisive role (Skak, 1993c). Gaining a firm commitment from the EU on full membership for postcommunist Europe is required to fix domestic systemic change with the specific motive of securing the necessary influx of capital and technology inflows (Palankai, 1990, p. 16). It is a question of unlocking the following chicken-and-egg situation: 'Foreign capital is distrustful towards us and refers to the lack of stability. But

---

[11] GSP refers to the 'Generalized System of Preferences', a system of tariff concessions which was extended to countries of the external empire in 1990 as a first step towards free trade that was of perhaps even greater significance than the Europe Agreements of Association in terms of market access.

the creation of stability is impossible without the help of this capital' (*Népszabadság*, 24 February 1990). In accordance with this, former Polish Prime Minister Jan Krzysztof Bielecki insists that 'the signal has to be made explicit *vis-à- vis* foreign investors that the EC really wants to include Poland. It is not a question of entry now or tomorrow' (Skak, 1993c). In other words, EU membership commitment is a question of bastion-building in more than one sense.

It has proven just as difficult to gain a firm membership commitment from the EU as it has to gain market access. Therefore many postcommunist countries resort to Germany as their crucial Europeanization and 'reintegration patron' (cf. *Frankfurter Allgemeine Zeitung*, 28 October 1993). They look upon the country as an influential advocate *vis-à-vis* other EU states, and so they want to conclude bilateral treaties explicitly stating Germany's commitment to bringing them closer to Europe and the EU, often treaties with explicit reference to the future goal of membership on behalf of the postcommunist signatory (Timmermann, 1992, p. 19). Past traumas and present worries over Germany notwithstanding, former Polish Prime Minister Bielecki is convinced that 'our path to Europe lies in Germany'. Germany has concluded such treaties with Poland, Czechoslovakia (before its break-up – still unchanged), Hungary, Romania, Bulgaria and Romania. Virtually all postcommunist countries, however, place relations with Germany high on their foreign policy agenda – be it Russia, Belarus, Kazakhstan or even faraway Mongolia.[12] Considering Germany's geostrategic location and its record of pursuing an accommodating policy towards the East – *Ostpolitik* – combined with its economic aid potentials, this pattern should not surprise. Together with Denmark, Germany has consistently pleaded for the eastward opening of the EU, and German Defence Minister Volker Rühe is more inclined towards extending NATO membership eastward than are his NATO colleagues. The other Nordic countries have come to work as additional reintegration patrons for the Baltic countries. Conversely, treaty-based reintegration patronage by e.g. France is seen as being of little practical utility (Garztecki, 1994).

---

[12] Mongolia's foreign relations include those with the EU, with which the country has signed a cooperation agreement; see Agence Europe, 16 June 1992. Mongolia has become eligible for technical assistance from the TACIS programme covering the CIS region. Japan is an equally important reintegration patron for Mongolia, which fears absorption by China.

The pressure for reintegration among postcommunist countries dominates foreign economic policy, but this does not make the issue uncontroversial on the domestic scene. As argued by the Lithuanian scholar Kornelija Jurgaitiené, there is a conflict between the romantic, if not anachronistic nationalism guiding the struggle for independence and the compelling task of modernizing and updating economic and political structures. In Jurgaitiené's assessment, 'Lithuanians are very much interested in the world opening to them, but they seem somewhat more reluctant to open themselves up to the world. They still see their state as their fortress, where they retrieve [*sic*] to rest after exhaustive experiences abroad' (1993, pp. 36-7). It is the perception of entrapment which also makes itself felt when it comes to the overarching issue of reintegration. As pointed out earlier, there is dilemma between what is demanded in terms of economic and political transition and what is demanded in terms of national liberation, where independence and sovereignty work as primary political bastions. As a dilemma of political development, this raises the question whether Europeanization entails cultural homogenization. As developments within EC/EU integration have shown (notably the rejection of the Maastricht Treaty in the first Danish referendum on the issue on 2 June 1992), culture and national identity are high politics even among the present EU member-countries. The trend is now towards less absolute demands of harmonization in continuation of the principle of subsidiarity, which should offer a solution for postcommunist countries.

Thus the chairman of the Hungarian Academy of Sciences, Domokos Kosáry, called on his country to work together with the small states of Western Europe – Belgium, Sweden, Portugal, Greece and Holland – 'who are going to face the same problems as us in relation to mechanisms of integration' (*Népszabadság*, 6 June, 1992). Inspired by Thatcherite laissez-faire the Czech Premier Vaclav Klaus airs frankly unenthusiastic views about the European Union, preferring it to devote itself to economic integration and free trade. Before the French referendum on the Maastricht Treaty, he was quoted as saying: 'Maastricht, which was an artificial and in my opinion unnecessary attempt to accelerate West European integration, is causing many problems.... The Czech government has resolved to refrain from intervention and there is no need to reinstate it through the EC' (*CTK-Business News*, 8 September 1992). Perhaps the most significant and explicitly nationalist opposition to European integration is found in Poland, however; an opposition that includes a radical Self-Defence Farmers' Union demanding protectionism (Sabbat-Swidlicka, 1992). Poland's Europe Agreement with the EC/EU did survive the procedure of ratification in the *Sejm* (parliament), but the remarks of one of the prominent sceptics, then Vice-Premier Henryk Goryszewski, struck a typical note: 'The small peoples of Europe who are going to be the first to lose their national identity will never permit this.... Poland will never become part of Maastricht-Europe.... The Europe of the Twelve will ultimately be a Europe of the German nation' (*Frankfurter Allgemeine Zeitung*, 3 September (1992).

As indicated in the section on security policy, considerations of neighbouring postcommunist states and of reintegration place postcommunist countries in another dilemma which is really a 'reintegration dilemma'. On the one hand, if they pursue a policy of involving themselves closely in economic cooperation with fellow-postcommunist countries, they run a risk of being trapped in their crisis and problems of transition and, what is more, they run the 'abandonment' risk of disconnecting themselves from integration and cooperation at the European level. These considerations legitimize a policy that neglects the immediate environment. On the other hand, the security dilemma, the need to uphold certain supply lines (for instance, of energy from Russia), and the wish for a strengthened regional identity based on mutual trade and cooperation prohibit an exclusive focus on the 'far abroad' of the West. Moreover, integration into the EU demands that postcommunist aspirants to membership harmonize and dismantle their trade barriers. Generally speaking, this dilemma is being resolved at the expense of East-East relations, for reasons highlighted by Bulgarian President Zheliu Zhelev:

> We do not reject this idea [i.e. Black Sea cooperation], we are ready to participate, but we fear that it might put a brake on our move towards modernity; we count on Europe because Europe will pull us towards progress. It [i.e. Black Sea cooperation] could mean the creation of a new CMEA, a new grouping of less developed countries. (*Le Monde*, 6 December 1991)

If anything, excessive Western interest in engaging postcommunist countries in close economic cooperation with themselves has backfired. This is illustrated by the crisis surrounding Visegrad cooperation (among Hungary, Poland, the Czech and Slovak Republics), a regional concept which according to Czech Premier Vaclav Klaus is simply a Western invention. Numerous practical difficulties and lack of enthusiasm therefore surround the Visegrad free-trade zone announced on 21 December 1992. Nevertheless, the Visegrad free-trade agreement – dubbed CEFTA – does represent a tangible result. The Visegrad formula has served to enhance the bargaining clout of these Central European countries at the international level (Vachudova, 1993). A Baltic free-trade agreement was initialled in Tallinn on 13 September 1993, and 'a common economic space' created between Kazakhstan, Uzbekistan and Kyrgyzstan, reportedly strengthening mutual trade and direct ties between firms (*RFE/RL News Briefs*, 14-18 February and 14-18 March 1994).

In terms of integration, the economic difficulties at the level of East-East relations all go back to the need for *dis*integration of the previous economic structure which – autarky notwithstanding – was an international edifice of integration along planned economic principles. The Soviet Union was a unitary economic system of immense proportions, with an added international superstructure in the shape of the CMEA. The planned economies' monopolist structure of production goes a long way to explain the economic chaos accompanying transition from planning to market economy. The endemic bottle-necks led to paralysis once the routine implementation of the plan was broken – suppliers of raw materials and sub-contractors let their partners down in the prisoners' dilemma of economic cooperation that followed (Kossikowa, 1993). A second factor that made it worse was the ubiquitous lack of hard currency, which placed a high premium on defection – abandonment of the others – by exporting to the West. A further aggravating point in this was the perception in the internal as well as the external empire that one's own republic or state was net contributor to the welfare of others, in defiance of the notorious difficulties of measuring such transfers (Orlowski, 1993).

The well-known result of this is the sharp decline in trade and production all over the former Soviet empire since 1989 (Slay, 1993). Rates of decline are higher than during the worst years of the Great Depression in the United States earlier this century, when

GNP declined by a maximum of some 10 per cent, compared to an East European average fall of 14.1 per cent and a Soviet average decline of 17 per cent, both as of 1991; in the case of the CIS the situation was worse in 1992 (Whitlock, 1994). The drop in regional trade is equally shocking; among the CIS countries, in constant rouble terms the level in late 1992 was half that of late 1990, while in the residual CMEA area between 1989 and 1991 there was an overall decline of 43 per cent (Whitlock, 1994; Slay, 1993). These figures illustrate the stark economic dependency brought about by an economically totalitarian Soviet order. Yet not all of these data reflect absolute economic losses, because of the extreme economic distortions of the planned economic systems: vast military industrial complexes, environmental destruction, combined with neglect of consumer industries and agriculture. The available macroeconomic data further tend to obscure trends towards recovery as the postcommunist statistical bureaux still fail to register activities in the private sector that is expanding all over the region. The picture is no longer uniformly depressing, especially not if we look at the Visegrad countries of Central Europe. Here there are instances of growth and trade reorientation – *inter alia* due to CEFTA (Slay, 1993). During 1992, 72 per cent of Poland's exports, 65 per cent of Hungary's and 66 per cent of Slovenia's exports went to the OECD region, primarily the EU market. Among the former Soviet republics only the Baltic republics are in a position to follow suit, but in theory this could change as the CIS states enter into bilateral economic partnership treaties with the EU.

Nevertheless, the general state of economic crisis and misdevelopment which the postcommunist countries share forces them to enter into the 'diplomacy of aid' as part of their reintegration policy. Compared to most less-developed countries of the Third World, postcommunist countries are much more resourceful and enjoy the further advantage of geographic and cultural proximity to the West, making it easier for them to argue their case in security terms. The Visegrad countries and Slovenia are already leaving the phase when they were clients in development and are now seen as attractive targets for investment and redeployment of production. Due to the immensity of Russia's proportions – be it in terms of area, mineral resources, economic destruction or neglect of agriculture and infrastructure – no amount of foreign aid will suffice in this case. Nevertheless, Russia does receive foreign economic and technical assistance, as do virtually all other non-Russian CIS countries, from the multilateral TACIS programme established by the EC. Similarly, the PHARE programme of the OECD G-24 grouping has been expanded to cover East-Central Europe, the Balkans and the three Baltic states (H. Kramer, 1993).

Criticism of these programmes as well as of the bilateral programmes of individual countries in Western Europe is frequent – for instance, complaints about lack of coordination between various donor frameworks, including the European Bank for Reconstruction and Development, or EBRD (Karaganov *et al.*, 1993). The role of private Western consultant firms carrying out feasibility studies in preparation for projects has become another contentious issue.[13] A recurrent theme is the call for a new Marshall Plan or at the minimum a 'long-term coordinated strategy for assistance' (*Beyond Assistance*, 1992; Karaganov *et al.*, 1993). Both *Beyond Assistance* and the report of Karaganov *et al.* are of special interest, as the former presents itself as 'the benchmark for future evaluation of Western assistance to postcommunist countries' and the latter as 'the first attempt to study Western aid to Russia at some length' – a Russian attempt that thus represents the receiver's end. These and other contributions are notoriously vague, however, when it comes to specifying the desired long-term strategy. In this they are quite revealing of the despair, the rising expectations and illusions surrounding programmes of economic assistance provided by the West.

As pointed out by Jurgaitiené (1993, p. 35) with respect to Lithuanians, it is a major problem that people in the postcommunist world have come to equate democracy with welfare, perceiving an automatic link between the two. Obviously, democracy in itself will not deliver welfare, because democracy is no guarantee of 'good politics' – optimal, socially just solutions to problems. This is the conclusion to draw from the position advanced by Joseph Schumpeter and the Danish analyst Alf Ross (Schumpeter 1950, Ross 1967). They propose looking upon democracy solely as a procedure for the orderly change of government, as a mechanism for correcting mistakes and for piecemeal social engineering (to reiterate Karl Popper). This leaves political responsibility with the citizenry and

---

[13] This problem caused one Western official to call for 'subsidiarity', i.e. by-passing both Eastern state bureaucracies and Western consultant firms by proceeding directly to local end-users for the sake of solely addressing their priorities (*Agence Europe*, 18 February 1994).

rightly so, as it is the citizens who carry the day-to-day burden of managing and implementing the transition from communism. This is what is implied, for instance, when the Russian economists behind the Karaganov report stress the absolutely decisive role of the Russian people in bringing about a successful transition.

It is the imperative of reintegration which forms the overall argument in this exposition of the development dimension of postcommunist foreign policy. This, however, points towards a most fundamental and unpleasant question for the newly free postcommunist states. Will their development efforts succeed? Are they economically viable at all? Here we should draw on the economic Sovietologist Gertrude Schroeder, who rejects the traditional geopolitical approach which expresses state viability in terms of national material resource endowment. In this, traditionalists neglect contemporary realities at the level of international economic exchange which often compensate for lack of national mineral resources and the like. Schroeder defines economic viability simply as the capability to exist and develop as a separate state in a world of highly economically interdependent states (1992, p. 549). The key point is the ability of a territory's population to perform within the larger global economy, rather than self-sufficiency. Like Robert Jackson, Schroeder highlights actor-based features such as a population bent on maintaining sovereignty at a cost and the pursuit of policies that are conducive to long-term economic growth and development. She continues:

> Probably the most crucial political requirement is a strong and stable government with an energetic leadership at the helm. This is essential for formulating and implementing the potentially unpopular economic policies that are conducive to long-run progress.... A supportive, or at least benign, foreign environment will greatly ease the adjustment process for new states – a factor that is especially important with regard to relations with neighbouring countries and with the former hegemon.... An ethnically homogenous population and a tradition of tolerance for the rights of minorities will lessen the danger of political instability and the sapping of the nation's energies by ethnic strife. (*ibid.*, p. 551)

Among the economic determinants of state viability, Schroeder includes an economy functioning adequately when independence occurs, a requirement which is only partially fulfilled in the case of postcommunist transition towards independence because of the simultaneous break from the planned economy brought about by stagnation and crisis. She stresses the role of trade with states other than the former hegemon or colonial core, a criterion which obviously excludes the states of the internal empire which did not have any independent trade links with the outside world. Particularly important is 'the ability to save and invest, raise the quality of the labor force through education and training, remove impediments to the effective allocation of resources (price controls, monopolies etc.) and promote foreign trade and investment' (*ibid.*, p. 552). The ability to produce goods and services that can be sold in competitive world markets is also crucial for small trade-dependent states. Schroeder rightly stresses level of education and qualifications as vital assets in managing the new tasks that independence brings. Countries with a developed infrastructure and geographic proximity to potential markets and reintegration-patrons are better off than others, but perhaps the most basic requirement is a fair level of industrialization, as seen in the European parts of the former Soviet empire.

The immediate foreign policy task is thus to establish a diplomatic presence not only in foreign countries, but in such international organizations as the IMF, GATT and the World Bank. Issues of debt[14] and distribution of assets have to be settled with the former colonial core, as well as the question of bases and presence of foreign troops. New arrangements for trade, communication and the passage of goods have to be made, and an entirely new legal framework providing for extensive economic exchange with the surrounding world – e.g. foreign direct investments – must be established, together with other measures of liberalization. In the event that the new state opts for a currency of its own, it needs a reliable central bank which does not engage in reckless printing of money and also needs to balance the exchange rate so that imports will not become too expensive, while on the other hand it will not hamper export competitiveness. Schroeder mentions the possibility of creating a payments union or clearing arrangements among postcommunist countries, but only as a temporary measure. The overriding long-

---

[14] In continuation of the line of participation, the states of the former external empire and Russia as successor of the Soviet Union uphold the principle of *pacta sunt servanda*, according to which international commitments are to be fulfilled, including the servicing of debt to the West. By contrast, the Bolshevik regime declared the debt of the former Tsarist regime null and void in early 1918.

term consideration must be world-market participation and rein-tegration. On the basis of these deliberations, Schroeder concludes that loss of independence is an unlikely outcome in most cases. Once established, states have shown surprisingly strong staying power. Dangers do certainly remain, in the field of ethnic fragmentation, lack of maturity among political opponents, lack of responsiveness on the part of governments, or military destruction – e.g. through interventions by outside parties.

The ambiguity of foreign policy and decision-making

Throughout the two preceding sections, postcommunist practices of foreign policy have been taken more or less at face value. It is time now to reflect more critically on the category of foreign policy and ask whether foreign policy can always be taken for foreign policy in the operational sense of measures targeted against the external environment. As the reader may have guessed, this is not always the case. It is certainly not the case when the object of scrutiny is new states in the midst of nation- and state-building and a simultaneous transition from one politico-economic system to another. In this context, the instrumental role of foreign policy in buttressing governmental and state legitimacy becomes particularly pronounced. For better or for worse, foreign policy has the capacity to bolster the patriotic legitimacy of individual politicians as well as parties and governments. For the latter, foreign policy actions help to create societal cohesion among the citizenry at large.

The domestic instrumentality of foreign policy may be quite harmless. At any rate, more often than not foreign policy fulfils functions of legitimization in the domestic scene in addition to its external purposes. Such could be argued of Iceland's pioneering diplomatic recognition of Lithuania and French President Mitterrand's visit to Sarajevo under siege in the summer of 1992. It is when foreign policy is solely or mostly pursued with domestic considera-tions in mind that the domestic functionality becomes dangerous. The danger arises when external considerations are brushed aside in the reckless pursuit of popularity at home. This may mobilize a plethora of not necessarily trivial conflicts in relation to external actors. The problem is that relations with the external world inspire patent solutions framed in simplistic we/they terms of obvious attraction for ruthless politicians.

A further problem is the use of foreign policy as compensation for necessary domestic measures. The resort to foreign policy in avoidance of the highly demanding and not very glorious field of economic policy and its implementation is particularly tempting in the context of the tortuous transition from communism, when necessary measures are highly unpopular, if not politically suicidal. Foreign policy as diversion often takes the shape of scapegoating or nonsensical conspiracy theories, such as the Serbian theory of the Great German cabal (cf. Dunn, 1992).[15]

In short, foreign policy may degenerate into what biologists term 'displacement activities'. No one captures foreign policy as displacement activities better than the Polish journalist Ryszard Kapuscinski, whose book *The Soccer War* contains a telling analysis of the case of Ben Bella who compensated for domestic failures by pursuing a self-aggrandizing foreign policy. With his energy, ambition and charm, he espoused the cause of Southern African independence and resistance fighters, hosted major Afro-Asian conferences and festivals in Algeria and so on, thus raising Algeria to a leading position in the Third World. But all this was at ruinous cost to his own country (1991, pp. 118-19).

Among postcommunist foreign policies, Russian foreign policy appears to be clearly blown out of proportion – the country's claim to greatpowerhood notwithstanding – as a result of such policy's immense attraction for all sorts of populists and opportunists inside and outside the parliament. Ukraine offers yet another example of excessive nation-building through foreign policy at the expense of reform (van Ham, 1994). The description above of Ben Bella's manic foreign policy activities illustrates the fact that foreign policy may grow into its own kind of absurd theatre. Peter Calvert carries this theatrical perception of foreign policy through in a chapter aptly called 'The Illusion of Foreign Policy':

> Much of the action with which we are familiar in the foreign policy field is relatively little concerned with real actions and real outcomes. It can best be understood in terms of a fourth model, that I am going to term the dramatic actor model.
>
> The dramatic actor model sees policy-making above all in

---

[15] As argued by Karl Popper (1966), the problem about conspiracy theories is not that conspiracies never happen, but that they so rarely succeed. Thinking in terms of conspiracies is a recipe for losing one's sense of proportion.

terms of a public performance. Once again the basic unit of analysis is the individual. The purpose of the individual is to present the best possible performance of the role to which society has assigned him. He finds, as he assumes this role, that there is already in existence a *stage*, namely the country concerned and its neighbours, the United Nations and its regional organizations and NGOs; a *script*, namely the historic documents of the past and the speeches of his predecessors; a *cast*, namely his political supporters and opponents; and *props* such as guns, ships and tanks, which may be made use of in the course of drama which is to follow. Nevertheless, the purpose of the drama is to be representational. Decisions are not primarily made for what they actually achieve, but rather for how they are seen contributing to the action and hence to the standing of the actors involved. (Calvert, 1986, p. 12)

This emphasis on the ambiguity of 'foreign policy' in the context of new states pulls the carpet from under conventional perceptions of foreign policy decision-making. This reasoning challenges the whole perception of rationality behind foreign policy behaviour – foreign policy rationality defined as external purposiveness. More specifically, it challenges the traditional realist model of decision-making dubbed the 'rational actor'. This model postulates the individual politician as the core decision-making unit. His (or her) calculus of costs and benefits among the various paths to follow is what brings about foreign policy decisions. The abstraction inherent in the model of the rational actor has provoked analysts inclined towards the view that decision-making is a collective process, such as the American political scientist Graham Allison.

Allison's alternative models of foreign policy decision-making, namely organizational process and governmental or bureaucratic politics, have grown into equally conventional wisdom for political scientists. The model takes organizations and their internal institutional dynamics, not to say inertia, as the point of departure. It borrows from Herbert Simon's notion of 'satisficing' behaviour – as opposed to utility maximizing behaviour in an absolute sense – within organizations (cf. Simon, 1947; Allison, 1971, pp. 71 ff.).[16]

---

[16] In coining the concept of 'satisficing' decision-making, Herbert Simon wanted to stress the limits to rational decision-making because of the impossibility of operating on the basis of full information in consideration of all possible goals and means, i.e. including all possible alternatives and their consequences.

To take one aspect, the way ministries produce and select information influences the options available in the eyes of their superiors.
As a result, the decisions arrived at may be sub-optimal in relation
to foreign policy interests and goals at the level of the state. Kjell
Goldmann's (1988) concept of administrative stabilizers, invoked
earlier, highlighting standard operating procedures and how they
shape foreign policy outcomes, provides a parallel to Allison's
organizational model. Both authors can be cited as evidence that the
routines of foreign ministries play no trivial role in foreign policy-
making. Neither do the political dynamics between ministers and
the bureaucracies they represent, the point of departure for the
model of governmental or bureaucratic politics. This model focuses
on foreign policy decision-making as a political game of bargaining
and compromise among actors pursuing their own ends. Foreign
policy outcomes depend not on the rational justification, but on the
relative power and skill of the bargainers.

Within the study of Third World foreign policy, consensus
prevails on the irrelevance of the latter two models of collective
decision-making in recognition of the highly personalized foreign
policy-making in this region of mostly weak, unconsolidated states
(Calvert, 1986; East, 1973, 1977).[17] To be fair, Allison never claimed
validity for his models beyond the industrial countries of the 'First'
World. Even more so than in the latter case, foreign policy-making
in the Third World is reserved for a small decision-making élite with
the president or premier at the apex. This was the pattern in India
under Nehru and in many other new states, including some in
Europe. Robert Rothstein (1976) lists Masaryk and Benes in interwar Czechoslovakia, Titulescu in Romania, Lange in Norway,
Spaak in Belgium, Luns in the Netherlands as cases of foreign policy
actors working on the basis of little or no interference from other
actors. Similarly, Jan Obrman (1990) has described postcommunist
Czechoslovakia's foreign policy decision-making structure as consisting of Vaclav Havel, his thirty year-old adviser Alexandr Vondra

---

[17] Not that Allison's model has not met with severe criticism when applied to the
study of foreign policy in the consolidated states of the 'First' World. One scholar
sees Allison's bureaucratic politics as 'an Unruly Baronial view of the world which
may unfortunately prove to be more useful analogical to England in the 1140s than
it is to any capital in the world other than Washington DC' (quoted in Clarke and
White, 1989, p. 120). Similarly, Lawrence Freedman finds this model extremely
culture-bound (1976, p. 436).

and the then Minister of Foreign Affairs, Jiri Dienstbier. This élitist pattern is clearly not limited to the Czechs, who do after all have a record of parliamentary democracy, but would apply to most other postcommunist countries as well.

Does this bring us back to square one, the model of the rational actor? The answer is both yes and no. On the one hand, the reconstruction of costs and benefits inherent in this traditional model is not a bad way to proceed. This method may, in fact, shed more light on foreign policy initiatives in postcommunist countries than the application of fashionable new frameworks such as epistemic communities.[18] The latter approach fails to address the isolation of most postcommunist decision-makers when they were still subjects of the Soviet empire, and the nationalization of their foreign and security policy as heads of independent states. On the other hand, the exclusive focus on foreign policy rationality within the rational actor model is a major shortcoming. The model disqualifies itself by its disregard of the domestic functionality of foreign policy and hence the ambiguity of such policy in terms of external and internal purposiveness. It is for this reason that Calvert (1986, pp. 7-17) introduces his dramatic actor as a fourth model. The dramatic actor thus serves as a framework for analysing foreign policy pursued for the purposes of bolstering personal legitimacy, nation-building, diversion from mundane issues of reform or the like.

So far so good. But is foreign policy-making in new states never a collective process in some sense or another? Is it at all valid to posit decision-making as the outcome of political calculus solely at the level of the individual? Of course not. This is where praetorianism comes into the picture as a conceptual umbrella for the highly idiosyncratic collective decision-making dynamics typical of institutionally weak political systems. Earlier I characterized praetorianism by its lack of consensus on the basic rules of the political game and disorder typical of societies undergoing systemic change. This offers windows of opportunity for ruthless actors. Praetorianism is thus 'dramatic actor' – i.e. foreign policy not for foreign policy's own sake – at the level of groups and individuals engaged in a reckless

---

[18] An epistemic community is defined as a group of specialists from different fields – or countries – who often meet and come to share one another's perceptions and assessments, a concept often invoked to explain the rise of new political thinking in the Soviet Union (Checkel, 1993). Learning – or group-think for that matter – is a closely related concept (see Breslauer and Tetlock, 1991).

struggle for power and influence (cf. Clapham, 1977, p. 169). In principle, Allison's focus on the government machine covers parliamentary inputs and lobbies (1971, p. 5). But in the turbulence of transition from communism, such inputs are better analysed under the heading of 'praetorianism'. Put in organizational terms, the praetorian model of decision-making works in roughly the same manner as the anarchic so-called garbage-can model of collective choice (Cohen *et al.*, 1972). It is a model where (praetorian) solutions – e.g. chauvinist solutions – look for problems, not the other way round. The point is the ruthless manipulation of agendas by powerful élites, resulting in arbitrary foreign policy decisions. The above discussion thus arrives at five ideal types of foreign policy decision-making within a four-dimensional frame, as illustrated in Fig. 2.2. These models may serve as an interpretative framework for the analysis of individual decisions within postcommunist foreign policy. Ideally speaking, all five should be subjected to empirical testing. The chances are that the two mainstream political science models of organizational process and bureaucratic politics originating in Allison's seminal work on the Cuban missile crisis will prove to have limited explanatory power.

Fig. 2.2. MODELS OF FOREIGN POLICY DECISION-MAKING

	Conventional models	Models covering new states
Individual as core decision-making unit	RATIONAL ACTOR	DRAMATIC ACTOR
Group as core decision-making unit	ORGANIZATIONAL PROCESS AND GOVERNMENTAL/ BUREAUCRATIC POLITICS	PRAETORIANISM

Still, the point is not to argue the virtue of the latter alternative conceptualizations of decision-making as such. What is important is to realize that the analysis of foreign policy in unconsolidated states must confront the disorderly nature of these polities. The application of state-of-the-art political science approaches such as new institutionalism has to be coupled with an awareness of possible domestic power struggles and foreign policy's resultant vulnerability. Notably in the case of former imperial centres like Russia, it is necessary to transfer the realist paradigm to the domestic scene to deal with the politics of *kto-kogo* ('who wins over whom'). This is the approach of the American political scientist Jack L. Snyder, who discovers a pattern of log-rolling among élites bent on expansion as the key dynamic of empire-building (1991, pp. 19 ff.). Neither the classic realists like Hans J. Morgenthau nor their 'Kremlinological' offspring within classic sovietology – e.g. the American historian Adam Ulam – did ever neglect societal dynamics to the extent claimed by textbooks arguing that they hereby 'blackbox' the state (e.g. Ulam, 1974). All the more absurd, then, to 'blackbox' the state in contemporary analyses in neglect of internal political dynamics.

Overall trends: the legacy of empire as pre-theory

The preceding analysis has established certain patterns worthy of recapitulation and further elaboration. Whether in the functional or in the legal sense or both, all postcommunist states are new states, implying that their foreign policy is circumscribed by a lack of stabilizers. As a determinant of foreign policy behaviour, this points towards unpredictability as a basic condition. The arbitrariness of the postcommunist territorial units reproducing internal as well as external disputes only reinforces this. The context of systemic transformation creating additional problems of state security represents another formidable domestic factor of vulnerability. This latter point is the key nomothetic determinant uniting postcommunist cases of foreign policy. The domestic transition in turn breeds the policy of reintegration – the pursuit of organizational and market access to the Euro-Atlantic order – most explicitly so among European postcommunist countries. The decolonization inherent in the transition from Soviet communism adds a further dimension of national liberation to the picture. The individual postcommunist state is not alone in this, but surrounded by equally new postcommunist states facing the same challenge of transition and nation-building. This brings forward another key foreign policy determinant working at the international level, namely the condition of anarchy and the security dilemma.

The quest for reintegration and the simultaneous management of relations to the fellow-victims of communist mis-development gives rise to a dualist pattern of foreign policy. On the one hand, there are relations with the Euro-Atlantic 'far abroad', governed by the perception of abandonment creating a push for participation. On the other, there are relations with the postcommunist 'near abroad' characterized by the fear of entrapment, a fear driven by the traumatic experience of the Soviet era 'partnership for crisis', as it were. For reasons of self-protection, relations between postcommunist states tend to have a touch of Cold War or, at best indifference.[19] The Russian sociologist and democratic veteran Dmitri Furman distinguishes between Russia's policy towards the West dressed in 'dinner jacket' and the policy towards the 'near abroad' in which Russia 'dons the flak jacket and rolls up the sleeves' (Teague, 1994). Indeed, the swiftness with which most postcommunist countries have embraced past enemies and hegemons of today, such as Germany, certainly marks a stark contrast to the foot-dragging towards former comrades in arms.

Nevertheless, this chapter's empirical introduction to postcommunist foreign policy can be taken as evidence that pessimism must not be carried too far when it comes to prospects for peace and stability. When all is said and done – in terms of lack of stabilizers, territorial and ethnic disputes, intricacies of transition, praetorianism and warlordism, infantile disorders of organizing diplomatic services, the security dilemma, pitfalls of entrapment and abandonment, the ambiguity of foreign policy threatening foreign policy 'overstretch' – what remains is an anti-climax in terms of bad news: there are several instances of prudence and pragmatism even at the level of East-East relations. The point of pursuing milieu goals and normative interests has not been wasted on postcommunist élites. The overall performance is not that bad. Postcommunist foreign policies are less idiosyncratic than those often seen in the Third World and they actually display trends towards continuity and consensus. The notable exception is the case of Russia, which stands out as a victim of factional strife and discontinuity, a topic to which I return shortly.

Not just in the new Czech Republic, but also in Slovakia a new consensus on the expediency of a consistent policy of reintegration is discernible, combined with improved relations with Hungary. In Poland and Lithuania leftist governments have taken over from rightist governments with little substantial effect on foreign policy (Kostecki, 1994). As observed by the *Frankfurter Allgemeine Zeitung* (28 October 1993), the Lithuanian opposition headed by the other-

---

[19] The dualist pattern is not unfamiliar in Third World foreign policies, as seen in the difficulties surrounding South-South cooperation, pan-Arabism and similar concepts.

wise uncompromising Vytautas Landsbergis cooperates closely with the government of Algirdas Brazauskas in a common effort to join NATO and the EU. In other words, the input from parliamentarians and foreign policy committees created after the collapse of communism emerges as a less disturbing factor within foreign policy than might be expected. If anything, the Hungarian parliamentary opposition worked as a factor of moderation when Hungary's first postcommunist government was in power (1990-4).[20] Accordingly, the élitist structure of postcommunist foreign policy decision-making may be less controversial than it appears at first sight. By inference, Robert L. Rothstein's point about the underlying consensus with respect to foreign policy goals and options being behind personalized foreign policy in the case of interwar Czechoslovakia and small West European states would seem to apply to the small European postcommunist states too.

Insofar as these trends towards continuity, consensus and moderation are significant, they call for further explanation. Cultural factors and differing levels of economic development will be treated as *ceteris paribus* factors although, of course, they are decisive in explaining the variations between Third World and postcommunist foreign policies. By mentioning the criterion of size, one possibility has already been indicated. Non-Russian postcommunist states are mostly small states and perceive themselves as such, in contrast to Russia, which is a mega-size power nourishing great power role-perceptions among its decision-making élites.[21] The postcommunist small-state pattern might be explained as evidence of the validity of newer, more optimistic 'small is beautiful' theories (Rosenau, 1981, pp. 113 ff.; Papadakis and Starr, 1987; Väyrynen, 1989). Following these contributions, the constraints confronting small states internationally

---

[20] *Frankfurter Allgemeine Zeitung*, 6 June 1991, reports the contacts between Eastern and Western parliamentarians. It is premature to term this 'epistemic communities', but nevertheless these contacts help to stabilize moderate postcommunist foreign policies.

[21] The concept of the small state is hotly disputed, as it is impossible to establish scientific criteria as to when a state is small or not. Size is relative, not an absolute criterion. In spite of this, decision-makers acting on behalf of states seem to identify with behavioural roles following the size criterion: small powers' conduct of foreign policy is often cautious and reactive, in contrast to that of great powers, whose foreign policies are also of broader scope. Superpowers in particular may be activist bordering on manic in their foreign policy behaviour for the sake of cultivating their image as superpowers (Jönsson, 1984).

should not be exaggerated, because of the diminishing role of power and security in the military sense under conditions of complex interdependence. Interdependence as a basic condition for both small and great powers creates windows of opportunity for the former in the shape of their greater efficiency and better organizational coordination. Small states simply have more manageable international agendas, whereas great powers may suffer from foreign policy overstretch. This could be cited as a reason why Iceland more or less defeated Great Britain in the Cod War of 1976. Cod represented about the only priority item on Iceland's foreign policy agenda.

Factors of efficiency are certainly not irrelevant in explaining the ease with which some small postcommunist states have formulated foreign policies and their overall performance. Once again we arrive at Schroeder's and Jackson's criteria for state viability, such as quality of leadership, domestic cohesion and determination; variables where small states need not be at a disadvantage. International factors of opportunity, such as the collapse of the Cold War and the Europeanization and multilateralization of security policies, provide the small European postcommunist states with greater room for manoeuvre. In this perspective, the boldness of the Baltic states *vis-à-vis* Russia, as maintained by Pertti Joenniemi (1993), is no anomaly but merely a reflection of the options available to small states: referring to norms of non-interferences, working towards participation and reintegration in order to avoid abandonment. At any rate, crying wolf served to mobilize Germany and others as brokers for the Baltic states in a diplomacy of mediation towards Russia, illustrating the small-state option of turning to influential third parties enjoying the confidence of the small state. The assertiveness of the Czech Republic following the dissolution of the Czechoslovak federation and the impressive performance of independent Slovenia also seem to underline that small may be smarter.

However, it is necessary to consider the traditional pessimistic power approach to explaining patterns of continuity, consensus and efficiency in small-state behaviour as well. The Danish political scientist Erling Bjøl (1971) offers four types of international systems surrounding small states, producing vastly different levels of stress and influence: hegemonial systems, confrontation systems, integration systems and security communities. In spite of the collapse of the Cold War, the non-Russian postcommunist small states still feel that they live in a hegemonic sub-system. For them Russia continues to loom large as a potential neo-imperial threat which decolonization cannot remove, for obvious geographic reasons. This Russian factor breeds caution, or pilot-fish behaviour towards the perceived shark, to use Bjøl's expression. Following this interpretation, the consensus on foreign policy is a consensus on the need not to rock the boat, while discreetly pursuing the course of reintegration all the more devotedly. This improves the international standing of the countries in question, which in turn furthers the domestic legitimacy of their foreign policy. The Czech and Slovenian self-confidence could be taken as a reflection of the fact that they have been removed geographically from their respective hegemonic threats – Russia and Serbia – through the establishment of the Slovak and Croatian buffer-states.

At any rate, balances and imbalances of power and the resulting perception of threat from hegemons at the core or fringe of the ex-Soviet empire must be taken into consideration as salient determinants of postcommunist foreign policy. It would be self-defeating for analysts to insist on the basic irrelevance of realist approaches to studying postcommunist foreign policy. This brings the analysis back to the legacy of empire and the structure of empire, more specifically to the Russian centre. Russia has recurrently been placed in brackets as an extreme, if not outright deviant case of postcommunist foreign policy. Among other things, Russia was singled out as suffering from 'too much foreign policy' because of foreign policy's role as diversion from reform. The case of the Russian great power as opposed to the residual, mostly small postcommunist states thus merits comment at this juncture. Since independence, the isolationist views of the supposedly influential Aleksandr Solzhenitsyn stressing the burden of empire have been swept away in a process turning communist internationalists and democrats alike into ardent nationalists urging a new assertive foreign policy. Russian parliamentarians, seconded *inter alia* by former Vice-President Aleksandr Rutskoi, turned into an opposition whose interference and direct attacks on the Foreign Ministry 'on all manner of issues went far beyond acceptable levels of intra-governmental squabbling' (Crow, 1993b, p. 1).

The parliament's obsession with foreign policy is not just a reflection of Russia's size and power. For lack of a Russian nation-state identity, the instinct of empire has the potential of serving as a political stabilizer. The combined effects of the domestic travails of reform and Russia's role as legal successor to the two preceding empires on Russian soil reinforce this logic. The instinct of empire becomes a lever for the many politicians preferring to mobilize on foreign policy in the domestic struggle for power. A case in point is the way the newly free neighbouring postcommunist states are being turned into a sphere of exclusive Russian influence. This perception has been launched officially along the lines of the US Monroe doctrine for the Americas by allegedly modern-minded political scientists such as Evgeni Ambartsumov and Andranik Migranian (*Izvestia*, 7 August 1992; *NeGa*, 12 and 18 January 1994). They are members of the Russian Presidential Council,[22] together with the equally influential Sergei Karaganov. The latter is another hardliner whose 'Strategy for Russia' – in its first and second versions – nevertheless reveals a more balanced view of Moscow's options, as if realizing the danger of slipping into a new burden of imperial overstretch through military overcommitment forever preventing Russia from catching up (*NeGa*, 19 August 1992, 27 May 1994; cf. Kennedy, 1988).

Western assessments of this development are divided into two groups, the optimists and the pessimists. The British analyst Neil Malcolm (1994) counts among the former when insisting that what we are witnessing is nothing but an exercise in consensus- building. He looks upon the domestic infight characterizing Russian foreign policy in its first years as a natural reaction to Russian Minister of Foreign Affairs Andrei Kozyrev's and President Yeltsin's preoccupation with their country's reintegration into the Euro-Atlantic order. What the pessimists – among which the present author counts herself – view as potential neo-imperialism is depicted by Malcolm as the outcome of 'the laws of political gravity' ultimately imposing a consensus around centrist positions. The pessimists on their part point, first, to the state of flux in Russian foreign policy decision-making as a result of vaguely defined organizational frameworks and divisions of authority as a factor inviting interference in a bid for power. Secondly, they advance the argument of the highly arbitrary nature of Russian coalition-building, due *inter alia* to the weak party

---

[22] Ambartsumov was appointed Ambassador to Mexico in 1994 and left the Presidential Council.

structure. This labile environment is a haven for rabble-rousers in the game of *kto-kogo* (Crow, 1993a; Skak, 1993a).

The situation is reminiscent of the death of Stalin, which unleashed a struggle for power in the CPSU Politburo. This time the catalyst is the implosion of the Soviet Union, its state and party structures. The point is the praetorian twist it adds to the present Russian power struggle. According to this perception there is no inherent stability in the Russian foreign policy neo-imperial consensus emerging since 1993. Potential neo-imperialism could grow into actual aggressiveness if deemed necessary in the domestic jockeying for position. Malcolm himself actually admits to the fragility of the prevailing centrist, semi-hawkish consensus. Its policy implication of intimidation bordering on subjugation of the 'near abroad' is by no means trivial, but may have tragic consequences for Russia itself as illustrated by its bloody and utterly misguided military intervention in Chechnia in late 1994. In this Russia repeated the archetypical imperial scenario of a voluntarist drift into expansionism without consideration for actual capabilities, as powerfully exposed by Jack Snyder (1991). It is this outcome that seems to worry Karaganov in his later 'Strategy for Russia', because of its implication of overstretch and international isolation (*NeGa*, 27 May 1994).

In other words, the Russian foreign policy establishment – be it *de jure* or *de facto* – has not entirely ceased to regard the country as the core in an imperial system. True enough, Russian moderates prefer to speak of the relationship between Russia and its 'near abroad' as a process of integration. The political vision, however, continues to have a Soviet ring, as when Yeltsin spoke of Russia's 'vocation to be the first among equals' in his opening address to the Federation Council of Russia (*Summary of World Broadcasts*, 12 January 1994). The very terminology of 'near abroad' is of post-Soviet Russian origin (*blizhnee zarubezh'e*). It is notoriously devoid of clarity in terms of its geopolitical reach. The countries of the CIS, which now include all three Transcaucasian states, undisputedly fall into the category, whereas confusion prevails when it comes to Estonia, Latvia and Lithuania – a confusion occasionally affecting even the former external empire. Migranian's contribution on the 'near abroad' places the Baltic states squarely in this category, whereas officials of the Russian Ministry of Foreign Affairs show discomfort when caught in such Freudian slips (personal interview; *NeGa*, 18 January 1994). In view of Migranian's position as presidential adviser, his deliberations qualify as a most significant attempt at reconquest at the verbal level. He displays 'concern' over the possibility that the Baltic states in their capacity as 'Russia's geopolitical sphere of interest' would become eligible for NATO security guarantees in the event of membership. He further warns against creating a *cordon sanitaire* around Russia in the shape of a Baltic Sea –Black Sea community. By presenting Russia as having the right and might to veto the foreign policies of the now sovereign states of the former internal empire, Migranian displays a perception of imperial suzerainty.

The concentric structure of the Soviet empire implies a variable legacy. This is confirmed in the more sporadic and subtler Russian attempts to define the countries of the former external empire as 'near abroad' in the neo-imperial sense. However, Russia does reveal a continued imperial complex towards these countries, as when it seeks to veto the extension of NATO membership to them. Russia is adamant on keeping Poland out of NATO whereas the Bulgarians, Slovaks and even Hungarians have been given a verbal green light to join it – as if deliberately playing old imperial subjects off against each other. (*RFE/RL News Briefs*, 22-6 November 1993; Reuter, 1 April 1994). In other words, it may be insufficient to speak of a dualist Russian foreign policy consisting of the respective policies towards the near and far Western abroad. 'Trilateralism' may be a more adequate conception of this pattern of Russian foreign policy growing out of the concentric circles of empire.

Is this trilateral pattern peculiar to Russia? Varying degrees of intensity and enthusiasm may be found in the foreign policy behaviour of the non-Russian countries of the external and internal empires. Poland, for example, pursues a policy towards Belarus that differs somewhat from its policy towards the Czech Republic because of the latter's attraction as a partner in reintegration. In other words, this is not a question of a Polish concentric approach of respect/disrespect for sovereignty but of varying geographic relevance reinforced by institutional handicaps. Russia's tendency to disregard its neighbouring states' sovereignty – notably those of the former internal empire – reflects a unique imperial complex. In addition, Moscow pursues a policy of reintegration towards the Western 'far abroad' that is more contradictory and ambiguous than is seen in other postcommunist states.

To conclude, one way or another the concentric circles constituting the Soviet empire do shape postcommunist interrelationships. When seeking to normalize relations with Russia – the ex-imperial core – postcommunist states face varying complexities, depending on their own position in the old Soviet empire. This position equipped the countries of the external empire with superior institutional resources compared to the countries of the internal empire, with the notable exception of Russia, the Soviet successor state. While these resources cannot be considered fully intact, because of the context of systemic breakdown and transition, the fact remains that the external empire did have an autonomous governmental apparatus prior to independence and Russia immediately received one. This marks an important difference from the non-Russian internal empire states, which were virtually born as quasi-states and share their institutional handicaps. The internal empire's route to 'positive' sovereignty may lead to the emergence of former party bosses as heads of state, as has been seen in Azerbaijan (Heidar Aliev), Georgia (Eduard Shevardnadze) and Lithuania (Algirdas Brazauskas). No one matches the organizational experience and power political savvy of these gentlemen.

This thesis of concentric circles of empire may be considered a 'pre-theory' of postcommunist foreign policy – a general hypothesis for distinguishing the performance and geographical structure of foreign policy among postcommunist countries. The concept of pre-theory was invented by James N. Rosenau to signify an early step towards explanation, the concept referring to a general frame of orientation (1971, p. 107, n. 40). Among his super-variables are the size and power factor discussed above, and the level of development which should perhaps be considered a constant rather than a variable in this context insofar as postcommunist countries have been subject to the same kind of mis-development. Much the same could be said about Rosenau's third variable, degree of openness. By definition, postcommunist countries find themselves in the same process of transition from closedness to openness. There are differing levels of development and reform in the postcommunist world, but they are differences in degree rather than in kind. In other words, Rosenau's universally applicable framework is far too general to be of much help here. It has to be complemented with 'middle-range' pre-theory, i.e. a pre-theory that addresses the specific regional or sub-systemic context, here that of postcommunist countries. To recapitulate the pre-theory of the concentric circles of the Soviet empire, my hypothesis sounds as follows: there is a variable legacy of empire that gives rise to varying foreign policy orientations and performances.

Against this nomothetic framework it might be objected that it blatantly misses the cultural variable and residual dimensions of history and geopolitics. The rise of nationalism has given new preeminence to the cultural factor, as for instance when Samuel Huntington (1993) argues that the clash of civilizations will provide the future theory of conflict – and foreign policy, presumably. In view of Huntington's trail-blazing conceptualization of the disorderly politics in changing societies under the heading of praetorianism, it is ironic that he suddenly takes 'civilization' at face value instead of addressing myths and manipulations of the civilizational variable. Generalizations of civilizations bound to cut-throat antagonism are always awfully reductionist and plain awful as policy prescriptions: they tend to produce self-fulfilling prophecies. This is not to say that culture or history and geopolitics do not matter, but in order to avoid reductionism it is better to place them outside the nomothetic framework and address them as the idiographic variables they are. Still, all three factors may express themselves at the nomothetic level in terms of degree of development and reform-commitment. Thus there is a certain reverse logic of empire among the newly free postcommunist countries in their performance in the field of reintegration.

A more interesting approach to falsifying the pre-theory of concentric imperial circles is found in the possession of nuclear arms as a determinant of postcommunist foreign policy. Rosenau abstains from singling out this factor, as if subsuming it under the size and power criterion. But given the unique status of nuclear weaponry as revealed in the international efforts of upholding a regime of non-proliferation, this is an impermissible reduction. Whereas the pre-theory of the concentric circles of empire hypothesizes roughly the same kind of Russian approach to the former internal empire – leaving some room for variation between CIS and non-CIS members – the pre-theory of possession/non-possession of nuclear weapons would argue another pattern. According to this theory Russia should concentrate its 'near abroad' activity on its nuclear neighbours Ukraine, Belarus and Kazakhstan and its far abroad activities on the United States rather than, say, on non-nuclear Germany. Certainly, the deployment of strategic nuclear weaponry on the territory of the three former internal empire states has served to draw the special attention of Moscow, but whether this has left the countries better off *vis-à-vis* Russia from the point of view of power relations is debatable.

It goes without saying that nuclear arms are a complicating factor in postcommunist international relations. However, the major flaw in the nuclear pre-theory is its inability to distinguish between political relationships. The significance of the strategic nuclear factor follows a starkly descending pattern, with Ukraine undisputedly at the apex, Kazakhstan in the middle occasionally signalling an intention not to give up nuclear armaments, and Belarus representing a trivial case from Moscow's point of view. There are many reasons for the Ukrainian-Russian nuclear dispute, and analysts willingly admit that the crux of the matter is the political and historical intricacies of this particular bilateral relationship in relation to which the nuclear issue is a sideshow (Morrison, 1993; van Ham, 1994). Ukraine does not possess operational control and the warheads continue to be targeted at the United States, not at Russia or *tous azimuts*. Notwithstanding this, Ukraine uses its nuclear weapons to bolster its position in the face of Russian muscle-flexing and a nose-diving Ukrainian economy. Migranian's remark that he considers Ukraine's nuclear weapons 'less important' are refuted by Russia's international campaign against Ukraine's refusal to give them up, a campaign that climaxed in the Russo-American-Ukrainian summit in Moscow in January 1994. There can be little doubt that Ukraine's nuclear option represents a key irritant for Russia, but hardly a threat. The significance of this factor derives primarily from its sabotage of Russia's strategy of projecting itself as the only true great power in the region – a topic to which I return later. Russo-Ukrainian relations constitute a special case, but for reasons of political history rather than military technology.

Insofar as nearly all the countries of the former internal empire have tactical nuclear weapons deployed on their territory as an expression of their position as internal empire countries, we are, in fact, back to the pre-theory of empire. The nuclear factor thus obscures more than it explains. Where the analysis arrives, then, is at a pre-theory of empire that does not claim explanatory power for all empirical occurrences, or even all patterns of general significance; nevertheless, it is a pre-theory that posits a relevant structural context for examining individual cases of postcommunist foreign policy, while escaping cultural stereotypes. Research must leave room for data going against the grain of this approach, such as varying dynamics within the two circles of empire. Yet the design of analysis has to display a basic commitment to the perception of concentric circles.

The design of the rest of the analysis

An indispensable way to demonstrate the validity of this geometry of empire is through historical analysis. Chapter 3 thus seeks to establish the concentric structure of empire by exposing the varying degrees of repression and direct rule employed by the imperial centre and the resulting different peripheral responses, ranging from guerrilla wars to acquiescence. It addresses the concentric circles at the level of foreign policy as a determinant of today's varying foreign policy patterns. Before that, however, it is necessary to reflect on the nature of the Soviet empire in a comparative light. Was it *sui generis* – *sui generis* also in the sense of marking a break with Tsarist past? What were the sinews of empire – the instruments for the establishment and exercise of control? Did they differ in a way corresponding to this author's distinction between the internal and external empire? Another topic for examination is the daily working of the Soviet empire, which ought to tell us something about its ultimate collapse: what went wrong? Which theories and explanations apply? Finally, what is the overall significance of the collapse of empire in the light of some years of postcommunism – was this a paradigmatic change or just a hiatus in a new process of integration with imperial undertones? The analysis of these highly complex and important issues of yesterday has to be brief, just to provide some background for appreciating contemporary complexities within the postcommunist world. As always, references to sources for further analysis are generous.

The diachronic section is followed by four chapters devoted to synchronous analysis, beginning with the case studies of postcommunist foreign policy. The method chosen is the comparative principle of selecting the apparently most dissimilar cases within the Soviet imperial frame (in itself a system of similar postcommunist cases; cf. Faurby, 1976). The reason for picking Russia – the former imperial centre and in that respect the single most dissimilar case available – as an object of inquiry is self-evident and needs no further comment. The motive of selecting Lithuania as an example of the internal empire case is rooted in the fact that this is one of the Western republics of the former Soviet Union with a Western cultural identity; moreover, it is a country with few problems in relation to Russia, due *inter alia* to the small Russian minority in the country. Lithuania thus ought to have every opportunity in its foreign policy and a corresponding record of success. It is not that Lithuania's performance has been bad, but it has had to struggle with numerous problems, including some of a very trivial nature stemming from fifty years of isolation and a resultant lack of international experience. In this respect the case of Lithuania illuminates the line of division between countries of the internal and external empire.

Hungary belongs to the category of the former external empire. The analysis of its foreign policy seeks to demonstrate the options available to countries of the external empire; options which admittedly were in no way symmetrically distributed, with Hungary in the group of countries having a broad room for manoeuvre. In fact, the ultimate test of the hypothesis of the concentric circles of empire would be a comparison of the foreign policy of Lithuania with that of Mongolia, the task being to demonstrate that the latter fares better than the former by virtue of its superior institutional legacy as part of the external empire. Clearly, this would be to stretch the hypothesis too far. Mongolia happens to have an extraordinarily weak legacy of nationally controlled state structures due to its unofficial position as the sixteenth Soviet republic (Hammond, 1975, pp. 107–44).

The organizing principle behind the case studies is to introduce the country in question in brief idiographic terms, to give an outline of resources and the present situation at the level of foreign policy. Then follows a longer section describing foreign policy, aiming to depict the basic orientation and portray developments since independence. This description is basically divided into two regional topics; namely policy towards neighbouring postcommunist countries and policy towards the advanced countries of the West under the rubric of 'policy of reintegration'. The analysis of Russia, however, is subdivided into ex-internal and ex-external empire policies. As argued above, Russian foreign policy displays instability and idiosyncratic inclinations whereas Lithuania has matured in the field of foreign policy in its pursuit of a balancing policy that seeks to avoid 'Finlandization'. Hungarian foreign policy has drawn strength from domestic consensus and will not be changed radically despite a change of government in 1994. Yet the social democratic-liberal government of Gyula Horn has a more pragmatic approach to relations with postcommunist neighbours than its nationalist predecessor had, and may prove more cautious on the issue of reintegration. The general hypothesis offered concerning Lithuanian and Hungarian foreign policy is one of relative foreign policy stability, and the inverse hypothesis of lack of stability concerning Russia.

Descriptive analysis invites explanation. The approach is to apply the two competing theoretical frameworks of interpretation, namely new or liberal institutionalism and then the realist thesis of balance-of-power logic. As should be clear by now, realism is best understood not as an approach that focuses exclusively on issues of military security, or as one pre-programmed into the neglect of domestic issues (including domestic balance-of-power issues), but merely as an approach that focuses on the logic of power, claiming this to be the essence of politics. What characterizes the opposite approach of liberal institutionalism is the claim that there is a logic beyond that of power, such as the logic of norms, regime maintenance and international cooperation (Wallander, 1992). The third and final step is to apply realism to the domestic scene through an analysis of competing institutions, factions and individuals. In all these respects, the peculiar case of Russia is subject to closer scrutiny than the other two. The peculiar logic of power politics in a context of systemic transition that includes foreign policy is exposed through the analysis of one particular event in Russian foreign policy decision-making, namely Yeltsin's cancellation of his visit to Japan in September 1992. Similar cases of decisions are examined for Lithuania and Hungary, the procedure being to apply the five frameworks of decision-making studies displayed in figure 2.2 above. All three chapters contain intermediate conclusions reflecting on the trends and overall viability of the foreign policy course chosen.

The analysis of postcommunist international relations in Chapter 7 is briefer and more condensed than the individual foreign policy studies. This disposition reflects the contention that the challenge of European security needs to be addressed on the state level of analysis allowing for closer examination of domestic dynamics. The expediency of addressing intra-state phenomena such as the growth of hypernationalism is admitted to even by John M. Mearsheimer (1990), otherwise known as a diehard neo-realist insisting on the primacy of structures over actors and national systems. The study of postcommunist conflict reflects on the lessons learned from the eruption of violent conflict in connection with the dissolution of the Yugoslav federation and the absence of violence when the Czechoslovak federation was dissolved. The aim is to formulate hypotheses about conditions for the eruption of violent conflict and see how they apply to the Russo-Ukrainian situation, as one of the most dangerous potential conflicts in the region of the former Soviet empire.

The topic of postcommunist regionalism has been chosen in order to investigate general determinants and patterns of interest in the multilateral interaction among postcommunist states and includes such themes as Visegrad cooperation, the Central European Initiative (CEI), Baltic Sea cooperation, Black Sea cooperation and the CIS. While the overall significance and viability of postcommunist regionalism should not be exaggerated, the overall conclusion remains that this phenomenon represents a significant, endogenous attempt at alleviating the structure of international anarchy facing the newly free postcommunist countries. As such it deserves far more encouragement from the outside world.

This brings the analysis to the final topic of East–West relations. While there is reason to criticize the foot-dragging response to the pressure for reintegration from the postcommunist countries, the analysis must confront the dilemma of reintegration facing the Western world in its relationship with the postcommunist world. As a dilemma between entrapment and abandonment this is no trivial affair but an issue that reaches into the complex trade-off between integration in depth and in breadth. Specific initiatives such as the EU's Pact on Stability in Europe and NATO's PfP concept are assessed. The final chapter reflects on overall trends of development within the postcommunist world in terms of anarchy and policy implications for the international community.

3

SHADOWS OF THE PAST: THE SOVIET EMPIRE

As observed earlier, it has become a matter of political correctness to look upon the former Soviet Union as an empire (Kiva, 1992). But what kind of empire? As the comparative scholarship on imperialism shows, the Soviet imperial system represents a peculiar kind of imperialism (Geyer, 1986; Mommsen and Osterhammel, 1986). Not that there are no similarities with other empires or continuities with the Tsarist Russian predecessor. Evidently there are. Yet what really characterizes Soviet imperialism is the unique institutions invented throughout its practice, including among other things the CPSU and Soviet Marxist ideology. It is therefore best considered *sui generis*. It was an empire that also stands out in terms of size. Due to the vastness of the Soviet Eurasian territory, it stretched about five times as far as the classical Roman empire. The fact that this was a contemporary and yet European empire with markedly colonial features makes it all the more anachronistic. Insofar as the subjugation of non-Russian peoples under the political control of the CPSU leadership was clearly involuntary and forced, this qualifies as a case of colonialism (Kolarz, 1952 pp. v. ff.).

It was thus no case of 'saltwater colonialism', to cite the incorrect criterion of colonialism launched by the United Nations. Like Tsarist Russian imperialism before it, Soviet imperialism was a matter of expansion into contiguous areas, not overseas territories. This expansionist logic bred another peculiarity, namely the concentric circles structuring the empire – the division into a distinct inner circle consisting of the Union of Soviet Socialist Republics proper and another equally distinct external ring consisting of the small Warsaw Pact members and Mongolia. Comparativists group the latter into so-called 'informal empires', that is empires where the centre refrains from direct political rule, preferring to exercise control in more subtle ways (Geyer, 1986, p. 61; David Dallin,

1951, p. 3). Viewed as a case of colonialism, the external empire thus qualifies as external colonialism. Conversely, several analysts use the term 'internal colonialism' when referring to centre–periphery relations within the internal empire, a concept to be explained further (Gouldner, 1977).

Before going deeper into the analysis of the Soviet variety of imperialism, it is necessary to pause and discuss the concept in general. As noted by the German historian Wolfgang J. Mommsen, one of the few to have studied imperialism for strictly analytical purposes, the utterly polemic, unscientific and inconsistent use of the term would seem to preclude just that (Mommsen and Osterhammel, 1986, p. ix). On the other hand, historians – not to mention political scientists – cannot just opt out of contemporary debates on the grounds that they are not to their liking. Controversial phenomena have to be analysed and discussed by scientists because they are controversial. The first point to make concerns the kind of motives giving rise to the phenomenon of imperialism in international affairs. Contrary to what is held by Marxism, imperialism at the level of the state is rarely determined solely by economic deliberations of profit, exploitation or more respectable types of economic expansion (Mommsen, 1977; Morgenthau, 1967, s. 41 ff.). Power and security represent far more relevant clues to what imperialism is about. This is tacitly acknowledged by one of the influential left-wing scholars, the Norwegian sociologist Johan Galtung, who deserves credit for his rejection of the economic reductionism of Marxism in his work on imperialism (1971). The essentially political nature of imperialism becomes all the more evident if we turn to the case of Soviet imperialism as openly acknowledged by Michael Barratt Brown, another exponent of the leftist approach to imperialism (1974, pp. 285–304). Today there seems to be broad consensus that it is interests in terms of power and security that provide the key to understanding the Soviet case.

Sovietization of the Russian centre

However, as argued by the British scholar Charles Reynolds, the power-security conception of the logic behind imperialism will not carry us any further unless it is applied at the level of the actor. In Reynolds' view, the outward manifestations of imperialism are more or less irrelevant tools for distinguishing whether or not something qualifies as 'imperialism'. Or, to be more precise, what really counts is the imperialist solution to problems of security, lack of power, economic profitability or whatever that may be reconstructed at the level of individuals. To take the example of Hitler, it is the connection between his reasoning – his perception of the operational environment – and his decisions and actions which is deemed 'crucial' by Reynolds (1981, p. 247). This seems to be an indispensable way of exposing the phenomenon of imperialism. In continuation of this, it is Stalin's embrace of imperial and colonial solutions to problems confronting the Bolshevik state that forms the decisive criterion for Soviet imperialism. Reynolds' own phraseology is quite instructive: e.g. 'Stalin insisted that the Soviet Union had a right...to maintain a sphere of influence in the border states...he did not deviate an inch over Poland' (*ibid.*, pp. 39-40).

Some might object to this personalized or hermeneutic approach to studying the complex phenomenon of imperialism. To be sure, in a highly pluralist context with deep divisions among leaders, imperialism may be the arbitrary outcome of domestic infighting between powerful segments in society, to use the parlance of Jack L. Snyder (1991). However, in view of the utterly totalitarian nature of the Soviet power structure under Stalin's reign this is a case where the personalized approach is indispensable (*ibid.*, p. 18). From this vantage point, Stalinism offers itself as a structural extension of the analysis. Stalinism is exactly what the American analyst Alvin W. Gouldner picks as the essence of Soviet colonialism. Taking E.H. Carr and other historians of the Bolshevik seizure and consolidation of power as points of reference, Gouldner depicts Stalinism as 'the avoidable outcome of unplanned, yet cumulative responses to the "chaos" of the post-revolutionary era' (1977, p. 9). Although it would have required a substantial redirection of policies and maybe events, forced collectivization need not have happened. It was not pre-programmed into history from the day the *Aurora* fired its guns. It took a Stalin to implement the policies and institutional practices of Stalinism. Stalinism, in turn, marked a Russo-centric interpretation of Lenin's organizational obsessions (Robert A. Jones, 1990, p. 85). Following in the footsteps of Gouldner, we may further define Stalinist imperialism as the reign of terror and expansion for the sake of state consolidations – 'socialism in one country', to quote Stalin's own nationalist slogan (cf. Geyer, 1986).

Stalin's willingness to resort to practices of coercion on an international scale is not refuted by the fact that he did display caution and restraint when necessary. One striking example of his imperial instinct is the absorption of the Baltic states as negotiated with Hitler and documented in the Secret Additional Protocol of the Molotov-Ribbentrop agreement of 1939, another his willingness to negotiate the degree of Soviet control over the Balkans in percentage terms with Churchill in 1944.[1] The most direct verbal testimony is provided by Stalin himself in a conversation with Milovan Djilas when the latter was Yugoslav emissary in Moscow during the Second World War: 'This war is not as in the past; whoever occupies a territory also imposes on it his own social system as far as his army has power to do so. It cannot be otherwise' (Djilas, 1962, p. 90). These words – made all the more emphatic by Stalin's final remark – in turn expose the logic of sovietization as a key operational principle. What characterized Soviet imperialism was the forced imposition of 'Soviet power' and Soviet institutions on foreign territories, albeit with substantial variations in the degree of homogenization and integration between the internal and external empire. It was no coincidence that Lenin chose the slogan '*all* power to the Soviets' for the revolutionary *coup d'état* of 1917. Lenin's role as the intellectual mastermind behind the policy of sovietization was also no trifle, but has to be mentioned on a par with Stalin's. It was Lenin who launched the élitist theory of one-party rule and coined the utterly centralist principle of 'democratic centralism' so as to ensure, first, the party's hegemony over the soviets (literally 'councils') and, secondly, iron discipline within the party. What is more, already Lenin insisted that 'the interests of Socialism are of higher value than the right of nations to self-determination' (quoted in Robert A. Jones, 1990, p. 41). As for Stalin's junior position as primarily the executor of policy while Lenin was alive, his instinct for power ensured him a place in history, as documented by subsequent events (Ulam, 1973; Deutscher, 1967).

The quest for control – political control by the party, economic control by the state – summarizes the teleology behind sovietization. *Monolitnost*, for example, was a catchword that always carried positive

---

[1] In its final version, the percentage agreement gave the Soviet Union '90 per cent influence' in Romania, '80 per cent influence' in Bulgaria, '50 per cent influence' in Yugoslavia, '10 per cent influence' in Greece and, perhaps most controversially, '80 per cent influence' in Hungary (Gati, 1986, pp. 28-33). By contrast, Soviet preeminence in Poland was non-negotiable.

connotations of unity and resolve in action. But control and power for what purpose? On this account the German scholar Dietrich Geyer mentions the twin motives of regime security and restoration of Russia's greatpowerhood. As for security motives, the Bolshevik regime did face foreign intervention, albeit not of a very determined kind. Geyer may have a point when he argues that the subsequent drive for industrialization gave the Soviet leadership an accomplishment to protect (1986, p. 53). Yet it is impossible not to notice the ultimately tautological nature of the Soviet power-security logic as revealed in the almost immediate and never-ending militarization of the Soviet economy and society. Ever since the early Bolshevik era of 'war communism', Soviet society was plagued not by having a military industrial complex, but by being one (Nove, 1982, p. 390). A more fruitful approach to imposing rationality upon the Soviet obsession with security and power is to invoke the historical legacy of both security problems and authoritarian-imperialistic solutions, and the resultant political culture of empire.

The history of Russian security policy is the history of how a defensively motivated urge towards state consolidation in the face of foreign invasions by Mongols and Western peoples gradually evolved into a more offensively motivated policy of state expansion (Riasanovsky, 1969). Ironically enough, it was these successful expansions which produced the slide towards a more fundamentalist approach to security, leading to repression and Russification in the western parts of the empire. The small state of Muscovy became a great power capable of demonstrating imperial resolve and quest for status, as when Tsar Peter the Great took the official title of 'emperor' in 1721. The Bolshevik regime was characterized by a similar development away from defensiveness towards imperial ambition. From an early stage, Stalin sought to legitimize Soviet rule by invoking the greatness of Russia and its past imperial rulers. The fact that Russian and Soviet imperialism was non-racial, multi-ethnic in its vision, made it possible for a Georgian like Stalin to identify with Russian imperial state interests in his approach to managing Soviet affairs and interests. Stalin's strategy entailed revision of the history of Russian colonial conquest into something far more rosy and progressive, as documented by Solomon M. Schwarz (1952). It is important to note that this resort to Russian nationalism – culminating in the years around the Second World War – was not unpopular with the Russian public, among whom it helped to repair

Stalin's image of being just a tyrant. This conversion of Soviet Marxism into an ideology and political practice of empire can further be traced back to the merger of Great Russian nationalism at the élite level and Bolshevism in the shape of national Bolshevism in the 1920s. Several prominent bourgeois nationalists united under the Russian name of *smenavekhovshchinists* ('Change of Landmarks') defected to the Bolsheviks, whom they saw as the only political force capable of restoring Russia (Agursky, 1987, pp. 203-66).

Nationalism and patriotism in the Soviet Union was thus very much Russian in substance and only 'Soviet' in form. More than any other nation, the Russians played the role of colonial settlers in the periphery of the Soviet internal empire in much the same way as during Tsarist colonization of contiguous areas. Between 1926 and 1939 alone, the numbers of Russians settled outside Russia (i.e. the RSFSR of 1939) grew from 5.1 to 9.3 million corresponding to a net outmigration of over 4 million. Of these 1.7 million went to Kazakhstan, where another 1.3 million had moved between 1864 and 1913 (Simon, 1986, p. 137). This pattern repeated itself in the Baltic states when they were reconquered in 1944. Between 1945 and 1953 – the peak years of immigration – some 400,000 Russian immigrants arrived, most of whom settled in the less rural republics of Soviet Estonia and Latvia (Misiunas and Taagepera, 1993, p. 112). Official propaganda and the work of the Central Resettlement Board established in 1939 did much to stimulate the Russian *wanderlust*, but, as during Tsarism, the motive was often one of seeking relief from repression, for instance in the hope that the collective farm statute would be less strictly applied than it was in the overcrowded provinces of central Russia (Kolarz, 1952). Arguably, this gave the imperial Stalinist policy the same kind of popular mandate as postulated by S. Frederick Starr concerning Tsarst Russan imperialism, turning it into a kind of Russian people's imperialism, to cite Walter Kolarz (1952, p. 3). Among more than 100 nationalities only the Russians were considered worthy of being prefixed 'great' – '*Velikii russkii narod* '.

However, to conclude from this that the position of Russians as a people within the Soviet Union resembled that of the German *Herrenvolk* within the Nazi empire would be a gross mistake. The lack of privilege accompanying the position of Russians as 'elder brothers' within the Soviet empire inspired the French Sovietologist Alain Besançon to renounce all talk of empire (1986, p. 10). The

Russians may have enjoyed advantages in terms of better opportunities for upward mobility – including better chances for moving to positions at the Kremlin pinnacle of power – but even more than the non-Russians, Russians had to display loyalty towards the party and the Soviet Union and ignore their cultural roots. The Russian political scientist Alexei Kiva tells a typical story about a man he knew who was summoned to the party committee to be transferred to one of the union republics. In terms of briefing, he was merely told that the personnel situation was bad, that he had to justify the party's confidence and that he further had to take the (unspecified) international situation into account, the party chairman adding: 'In short, you get the point!' Poor Comrade Petrov grasped neither head nor tail, but had to go and uproot his family. It ended in divorce and the drowning of his sorrows in vodka. To conclude in Kiva's own words, this man's life simply went to the dogs (1992, p. 21).

Kiva rightly insists that Stalin's repression and famine brought about by collectivization hit the Russian nation no less hard than it did other nations. Arguably, it was Russia that bore the brunt of the destruction of civil society and culture, leading to the following, highly dialectical outcome: full-scale sovietization of Russian society and the Russification of Soviet culture (Tucker, 1977, pp. 101-2). In order words, it is difficult to distinguish means and ends in the Soviet regime's use of the Russian nation, history and culture as a point of reference in its imperial policy. In fact, due to the Russian nation's numerical dominance within the Soviet Union there was no other alternative than to use Russians as the core centripetal force. The contradictory nature of Russian hegemony in the internal empire when analysed from the perspective of the Russian rank and file does not invalidate the conclusion that the Soviet state was essentially a Russian state whose macro-political pillar was Russian ethnic hegemony (Motyl, 1990, p. 84; cf. Motyl, 1988, pp. 36-52; Aspaturian, 1971, pp. 429-51).

And so the Soviet empire repeated and reinforced the 'autocracy, orthodoxy, and nationality' of Tsarist Russia, to cite Count Uvarov's doctrine of empire of 1832. While the similarities between the Tsarist and Soviet empires must not be carried too far, because of the evident dissimilarities in circumstances and political history, it is worth recalling S. Frederick Starr's interpretation of the logic of empire as a clue to understanding Soviet imperialism:

Whatever their actual cost to the metropolis, the non-Russian territories could certify Russia's status as a great power. Far from being an irrational factor, as Joseph Schumpeter suggested, imperialism – in Russia at least – endowed the state with an identity, a name, a place in the consort of nations, and a raison d'être that it would otherwise have lacked. (1978, p. 30)

Naturally, it is the contemporary implications that turn Starr's interpretation of the Russian political ethos into something controversial and disturbing. It is not that nothing has changed in contemporary Russian political culture; this is just to state the odds against change.

Sovietization of the internal empire

As for the names and locations of the more than hundred non-Russian nations and nationalities constituting the Soviet internal empire, the reader is requested to consult the special literature (e.g. Szajkowski, 1993a). The point of departure here is the Bolshevik leadership's decision to reconquer the erstwhile Russian empire. Admittedly, it is difficult to pinpoint this decision in terms of who, when and how. The 'decision' grew out of the ideologically-based belief in the 'progressiveness' of imposing the Soviet order on non-Russians and the Bolshevik élite's socialization into the political culture of empire. The catalyst for this imperial resolve was the establishment of incipient states along the rim of Russia proper in the wake of the collapse of the February Revolution (Pipes, 1964, pp. 50 ff.).[2] At first, the Bolsheviks could do nothing to prevent these secessions, but they were not inclined to tolerate them, as was demonstrated in the issuing of a 'Declaration of the Rights of the Toiling People',

---

[2] For an interesting political-science analysis of the rise and fall of secessionist states in the wake of the collapsing Russian empire, see Motyl 1990, pp. 103-18. Among these states wree Ukraine, Bessarabia (which adjoined Romania and is roughly today's Moldova), Georgia, Armenia, Azerbaijan, Belorussia, the Crimea, Bashkiria, the Volga-Tatar region, the Kazakh-Kirgiz steppe, Finland, Poland, Estonia, Lithuania and Latvia. Only the latter five survived as autonomous entities and then only for a limited period in the case of the Baltic states. While escaping Soviet annexation, Poland became subject to sovietization as part of the external Soviet empire. Finland was most successful in its bid for sovereignty, without doubt as a result of its fierce military resistance to the Soviet Union during the winter war of 1939-40. Yet Finland was subject to 'Finlandization', i.e. self-censorship in foreign policy.

ceding the right of self-determination only to 'toiling and exploited people' and not to nationalities as a whole (Jones, 1990, *loc. cit*). This was partly because they believed in the superiority of their own programme of emancipation. As a result of this clash of interest and due to foreign intervention, the Union of Soviet Socialist Republics was virtually born in a war, a war over sovietization. Officially, this lasted from 1918 to 1920, but fighting continued in some of the peripheral regions to the south till the late 1920s or even 1930s. As the principal combatants were not the non-Russian nationalities and the Bolshevik regime, but the latter ('the Reds') against its domestic opposition ('the Whites'), with the non-Russians caught in the middle, the war came to be known in Soviet historiography as the civil war. Yet it was also an international war in the literal sense of being a struggle among nations, a war waged between the centre and the periphery of the recently collapsed empire. As noted in one study of Soviet migration, the large influx of Russian and other settlers from the late 1920s onwards would not have been possible without the large-scale extermination of indigenous populations in the course of the 'civil war' (Titma and Tuma, 1992). The Kazakhs, for instance, were subject to genocide by both Reds and Whites. The Whites' unrestrained Russian nationalism contributed to tipping the scales in the Reds' favour, bringing about their ultimate victory. The Reds themselves were very skilful in issuing manipulative promises of national self-determination and federalism. Thus before 1922 the Republics enjoyed the right to maintain diplomatic relations, which was used by countries, like Azerbaijan (Pipes, 1964, p. 254). In 1922 the Treaty of Union established the USSR as a federal state, but this cannot obscure the fact of stepped-up centralization and oppression.

The terribly devastating civil war could be taken as a sign that the parties anticipated the horrors to follow. For a while, however, there was a temporary retreat reminiscent of the resort to liberal economic policies dubbed the NEP. The new policy towards the periphery came to be known as *korenizatsia* ('indigenization'). It entailed tolerance towards the many non-Russian nationalities and their culture, the aim being to create national élites who could be entrusted with the implementation of sovietization targets – i.e. cadres who were both 'Reds' and 'experts' (Liber, 1991; G. Simon, 1986, pp. 34–40). *Korenizatsia* did help to restore some of the prestige lost in the war. It was a battle against illiteracy, and for the emancipation of women, the formation of indigenous élites and restoration of culture. For this reason, *korenizatsia* was also instrumental in strengthening feelings of ethnicity and national pride (Suny, 1989, p. 505). In this way it served to sharpen the ensuing confrontation over the functional dimensions of sovietization: collectivization and industrialization as further dimensions to the initial nationalization of industry.

In Walter Kolarz's interpretation, what happened was a necessary shift in colonial strategy away from the predominantly agricultural colonialism of Tsarist Russia, which had to some extent outlived itself, towards a more modern colonial policy focused on industrialization (1952, p. 13). The Five Year Plans beginning in 1928 thus embodied the new colonial programme. As data cited above show, perhaps even more actively than during the time of the tsars, the Soviet centre mobilized Russians and other Slavs to settle in the new industrial regions and urban centres. The Russians had a double part to play in the industrialization drive, providing a skilled labour force and a political spearhead in this campaign of in-depth sovietization. Stalin's thesis of Russian supremacy and 'white man's burden' therefore had the following Soviet Marxist twist to it:

> We are told that one should not offend the nationalities. This is entirely correct, I agree. ... But to create from this [ideal] a new theory, that it is necessary to place the Russian proletariat in a position of inferiority in regard to the once oppressed nations, is an absurdity. ... the political basis of the proletarian dictatorship is in the first place and above all in the central, industrial regions, and not in the borderlands, which represent peasant countries. (quoted in Pipes, 1964, pp. 290-1).

These remarks, given as an answer to criticism raised against Soviet nationality policy at the Twelfth Party Congress in 1923, are instructive for the light they shed upon sovietization as a virtual onslaught upon the village.

It is therefore worthwhile to consider Alvin W. Gouldner's (1977) approach to internal colonialism as applied to the case of Soviet imperialism and colonialism in the internal empire. Gouldner addresses the topic solely in terms of the gap between urban and rural regions, thus ignoring specific ethnic dimensions in the internal Soviet centre-periphery conflict.[3] Contrary to other cases

---

[3] Internal colonialism refers to processes of unequal exchange *within* a state.

of allegedly internal colonialism, it is possible to identify truly exploitative and discriminatory features in Soviet agricultural policy. Among other things, Gouldner points to Preobrazhenski's institutionalization of internal colonialism through his system of prices that were deliberately rigged to the disadvantage of agricultural products. Preobrazhenski's idea was to provide a surplus for industrial investment ('primitive socialist accumulation'), and so by 1923 the prices of industrial products were about three times higher, relative to agricultural prices, than they had been in 1913, the peak year of the Russian economy (Nove, 1982, p. 93). Not surprisingly, the peasants reacted to this by withholding products. This in turn inspired the Bolsheviks to a genocidal solution, the horrors of which matched the Nazi *Endlösung*: forced collectivization.

In December 1929 Stalin decreed the 'liquidation of kulaks as a class', signalling the forcing of some 125 million peasants throughout the Soviet Union off their lands and onto collective farms (including the forced settlement of nomads; see G. Simon, 1986, pp. 121-9). As observed by Gouldner and repeated by Solzhenitsyn, this amounted to the reintroduction of serfdom. Collective peasants were denied the internal passes required since 1932 for travel inside the USSR. Collectivization thus marked the definitive ghettoization of the country's productive backbone. As a rural measure of nationalization, collectivization gave the state unrestricted access to the agricultural surplus and total political control over the peasants – the only civil society left. Preobrazhenski's 'price scissors' cut even sharper against peasants, who sometimes received 8 roubles for goods which cost the consumer 300 roubles. Those who survived collectivization faced a miserable slave-like life with even poorer infrastructure than was available to urban people. As for those who did not survive, estimates vary concerning the extent of this genocidal and class–cidal measure. We are talking about a death toll of several millions of people – peasants who starved to death because of the regime's

---

Gouldner's use of the terms linked to the original conception of internal colonialism as the exploitation of peasants by urban classes, an approach which was pioneered *inter alia* by Russian populists of the late nineteenth century and continued by Bolshevik economists like Evgeni Preobrazhenski. The British Marxist Michael Hechter (1975) sought to combine the point about economically disadvantaged regions with observations on cultural distinctiveness, thus turning the concept into a new theory of ethnic centre-periphery conflict. See also his article on internal colonialism in the *Oxford Companion to Politics of the World* (1993).

reprisals, peasants shot on the spot by secret police agents, and peasants with children sent to concentration camps (the notorious 'Gulag' archipelago. One source of Soviet origin puts the number of premature deaths for the years 1926-35 as high as 8.5 million, a conservative estimate insofar as Stalin himself casually admitted to 10 million 'liquidations' (Maksudov as quoted in Mace, 1984, p. 38). In the Ukraine alone, some 7.5 million people are estimated to have died in the terrible famine of 1932-3 (*ibid.*, p. 39). From a qualitative point of view it was, however, the Kazakh nomad civilization which was hit hardest, with a negative population growth rate between the 1926 and 1939 censuses of almost 22 per cent (G. Simon, 1986, p. 117). The British historian Hugh Seton-Watson mentions a figure of 1 million peasants in the north Caucasus having starved to death (1960, p. 158). These figures testify to the horrifying consequences of Stalin's 'class struggle' – a war against rural strata. As rightly observed by Gouldner, the absurdity in all this has less to do with a psychology of panic fostered by the Bolshevik siege mentality than with the sociology of internal colonialism which meant that any measure could be inflicted upon peasants and peasant nations with impunity (1977, p. 27).

As if this was not enough, another wave of terror followed, targeted at supposedly disloyal party members. According to Olga Shatunovskaia, a Stalin camp inmate herself and later a member of the CPSU Control Commission under Khrushchev, she had access to a KGB report – later removed from the Soviet archives – which documents the arrest of 19 million people between 1935 and 1941, 7 million of whom were shot and many more of whom died prematurely (Tolz, 1992). Later official revelations by the Russian Ministry of Security (formerly the KGB) admit to 7 million death sentences in the decade from 1935 to 1945, figures matching Robert Conquest's estimate of between 8 and 12 million inmates in 1937–38 at the height of the terror (*ibid.*). The catalyst for this additional slaughter was the murder of Leningrad Party boss Sergei Kirov, a murder which provided a magnificent pretext for terror. As in the case of collectivization, the subsequent wave of assassinations and senseless repression had undertones of ethnic extermination, among other reasons in order to reverse any hopes raised by the enlightened practices of *korenizatsia* (dubbed *Ukrainizatsia* in the Ukraine). In the periphery, the purges took the guise of a struggle against 'bourgeois nationalism', a struggle directed against the new ethnic élites as personified by Sultan-Galiev, Abdurakhim Khodzhibaev and Mikola Skrypnyk. It is revealing that the 'crime' of Fajzulla Khodzhaev, First Secretary of the communist party of Uzbekistan since 1925 appears to have been his fierce opposition to cotton monoculture. He was shot in 1938 after one of the notorious Moscow show trials (G. Simon, 1986, pp. 188-9). In Tadzhikistan alone, the number of party members fell from 14,300 in January 1933 to only 4,800 two years later (*ibid.*, p. 105). During the Second World War, the genocidal nature of the purges became even more alarming, for example when Stalin decided to dissolve the four autonomous republics of the Chechens and Ingush, the Volga Germans, the Volga Tatars, the Crimean Tatars and the Kalmyks (Kolarz, 1952, pp. 67-87). In the case of the ethnic Germans (who had settled by the Volga centuries ago) and some other peoples – including the Baltic peoples following the 1940 annexation – Stalin distrusted their political loyalty after the Soviet Union was drawn into the war with Nazi Germany. In other cases, such as those of the Tatars and the Caucasian peoples, the reason for the purges appears to have been their stubborn resistance to sovietization (G. Simon, 1986, pp. 225-33). Stalin's pre-war purges against his own officer corps adds yet another dimension to Stalinism as pathology; less well-known, perhaps, is the Soviet way of waging the Second World War. Military detachments of the NKVD, the so-called SMERSH (an acronym for 'death to spies'), stood behind Red Army units with their sub-machine guns, making it safer for the soldiers to advance than to retreat.

Reaction to sovietization in the internal empire. The stubborn resistance to sovietization marks another distinctive feature of developments within the internal empire. As should be clear by now, the Russians themselves would seem to have had plenty of motives for rising in armed struggle against sovietization. However, except for those who fought on the White side of the civil war – e.g. Cossacks, Siberians and Far Easterners – they did not. Following the innovative American-Ukrainian Sovietologist Alexander Motyl, whose argument is cast in terms of the cost-benefit analysis of rational choice, this acquiescent behaviour on the part of Russians and later non-Russians resulted from the evolving balance of power between the Soviet Russian state and potential insurgents (1988, pp. 1-19; 1990, pp. 30-45). Within a short period of time, the Bolshevik state grew into a formidable apparatus of coercion and control, dramatically changing the odds associated with resistance in favour of acquiescence (Motyl, 1988, pp. 107 ff). As mentioned earlier, the Reds were able to suppress the incipient states along Russia's rim, except for the Baltic states, which enjoyed the backing of Germany (Motyl, 1990, pp. 112-13). Later Stalin succeeded in annexing the Baltic States too.

This, however, should not obscure the fact that the non-Russians did originally rebel, as did some Russians initially. The story of sovietization in the internal empire is also the story of fierce guerrilla struggles against Bolshevik rule, fought for a host of political and cultural reasons as well as motives of simple survival, whether as individuals or as peoples. Examples are the Basmachi revolt in Central Asia in 1918 which flared up again in the early 1930s; the Dagestani *jihad* of 1920-1 in northern Caucasus; the guerrilla war of the Ukrainian Insurgent Army (UPA) from the early 1930s and again twenty years on; the struggle of the Lithuanian, Latvian and Estonian anti-Soviet partisans known as the 'forest brethren', which began in the 1940s and lasted in places till the early 1950s (Motyl, 1990, pp. 119-31; see also Pipes, 1964, pp. 256-60). At their peak, the Basmachis numbered 18,000, the Dagestanis 10,000 and the UPA as many as 90,000. The Baltic guerrillas were fewer: there were between 30,000 and 40,000 Lithuanian and from 10,000 to 15,000 Latvian and Estonian forest brethren, but as percentages of the populations concerned this matched the peak strength of the Vietcong in South Vietnam (Misiunas and Taagepera, 1993, p. 83). The Lithuanian guerrillas were able to inflict upon the Soviet side casualties numbering between 10,000 and 80,000, while they themselves lost from 20,000 to 50,000 fighters (*ibid.* p. 278). But the forces and the coercive power available to the Soviet side were vastly superior. Therefore the Lithuanians, like the other freedom fighters, were destined to lose from the beginning. Even under these circumstances, it still makes sense to analyse the phenomenon of armed resistance in terms of rational choice. For, as noted by Misiunas and Taagepera with regard to the Balts:

> ...by 1945 war and both occupations had engendered a feeling that one might die soon anyway. Life as a fugitive had become familiar to many, and scattered arms had become plentiful. However, the prime direct reason for resistance was the Soviet terror during the 1940-1 occupation and its reintroduction after reoccupation. ...Anyone who complained of some aspect of Soviet

bureaucracy or could not adjust to its demands (such as farm grain deliveries) [was a target]. The sloppy randomness of the MVD and MGB repression units...made almost everyone a potential target, the more so since the Soviets considered all who had survived the German occupation to be Nazi collaborators of some sorts. People went to the forests. ...when they could no longer tolerate the insecurity of civilian life. (1994, p. 84)

The sinews of the internal empire. Several of the sinews of empire[4] at hand in the Soviet case have already been mentioned in passing: the Red Army, the secret police and the Ministry of the Interior under their various acronyms, the CPSU, the doctrine of sovietization as an ideological tool for policy-implementation, the Russian nation, *korenizatsia* as a temporary policy measure, promises of national self-determination, federalism and even a legally enshrined right to secession as tactical instruments to win the confidence of the suppressed. Indeed, the problem is the numerous 'sinews' to consider when giving a full account of the institutional weaponry of the Soviet system. The sinews or institutional pillars of the Soviet internal imperial system were both formal (legal) and informal, macro- and microlevel. Space does not permit more than a summary of this point about the multi-dimensionality of the Soviet internal imperial system made by way of Fig. 3.1. Commentary is reserved for the more peculiar or less well-known of the Soviet sinews of empire.

To some extent, the list in Fig. 3.1. indicates the hierarchy among these 'sinews'. For instance, the Red Army was crucial at the operational level in reconquering the multinational Russian empire, but it was the party and the interpenetration of party and state apparatus which were the key institutions (cf. Pipes, 1964, pp. 242 ff.). The primacy of party rule was enshrined in the principle of dual subordination, making local administrative units responsible not only to higher bodies, but also to the soviet and via that to the party organization at the corresponding level of hierarchy. It is difficult to overestimate the significance of the Soviet bureaucracy, which in

[4] The 'sinews of empire' is a phrase often found in empirical analyses referring to the railways built in Africa to make European colonial rule and output more efficient. Tsarist Russia, too, had its infrastructural sinews of empire in the shape of the Trans-Siberian Railway. Similar projects in the Soviet era are the White Sea Canal (built by camp inmates and inaugurated in 1933) and the BAM Railway of the Brezhnev era.

turn confirms Shmuel N. Eisenstadt's theory of empires as a peculiar type of bureaucratic systems (1963; 1992). Stalin himself was nicknamed 'Mr index-card' and he clearly qualifies not just as a key macro-level actor, but as an institutional factor in his own right. As for the secret police and Ministry of Interior, these were bureaucracies in their own right with vast powers of interference and enforcement. Recent revelations document the KGB's role in Lithuania through its First Chief Directorate in the republic, for instance though infiltration of emigré groups abroad (Misiunas, 1994).

Fig. 3.1. SINEWS OF EMPIRE A: INSTITUTIONAL DEVICES FOR THE INTEGRATION OF THE INTERNAL SOVIET EMPIRE

Macro-level institutions. The CPSU; the doctrine of sovietization; Stalin (including the personality cult); the *nomenklatura* principle of interpenetration of party and state bureaucracy; the secret policy and ministry of interior; the Red Army; the Gulag system of forced labour camps; Russian hegemony including Russians as republican viceroys; Comintern (the Communist International of 1919-43)

Micro-level actors of implementation. Russian or other Slavic immigrants acting as colonizers; indigenous collaborators; the machine-tractor stations (MTS), etc.

Practices of implementation. Persuasion; terror; retreat

Economic institutions. Economic planning/resource allocation by GOSPLAN; autarky; the primacy of heavy industry and the military-industrial sector; the price scissors of primitive socialist accumulation

Military institutions. Service in the Red Army/Soviet Army

Administrative mechanisms. Russian as state language; imposition (or the annulment) of borders; Soviet law; internal passports (indicating ethnic affiliation)

Ideological doctrines/principles of repression. Marxism-Leninism; dictatorship of the proletariat, the leading role of the party; soviet power, *monolitnost, partiinost*, 'liquidation of kulaks as a class'; the concept of 'people's enemies'; 'socialism in one country'; atheism; the concept of the 'Soviet people'; the doctrines of *sblizhenie/slianie* ('coming together' 'flowing together', i.e., assimilation); the Stalin doctrine of limited right to secession, etc.

Principles of tolerance. Multinationality, *korenizatsia,* education for all; establishment of republican foreign ministries; legalization of republican armies.

Another interesting feature of the Soviet imperial system was the practice of appointing Russians as second party secretaries in the union republics, a practice only slightly modified after the death of Stalin (Miller, 1977). This is comparable to the system of viceroys in the British empire (the best-known example is probably Lord

Mountbatten, Viceroy of India prior to independence in 1947). Tsarist Russia also relied on 'viceroys' (governors-general) in the Caucasus, Poland and Lithuania – people who enjoyed greater powers and better access to the Tsar than ordinary provincial governors (Seton-Watson, 1952; p. 16). The Russian second secretary was in charge of organization and cadres; that is, in charge of the *nomenklatura* in the particular union republic, giving him the right to veto appointments (Miller, 1977).

The *nomenklatura* principle, in turn, represents a decisive sinew of empire and hence has to be discussed separately. The word refers to a system for the recruitment of politically reliable persons – trusted party members – to positions of importance within state and society, such as enterprise managers, leaders of institutions and public servants (e.g. diplomats), in other words a mechanism securing the recruitment of truly red experts. Introduced in the 1919 party rules urging party members to form cells within every organization to 'increase party influence in every direction and supervise the work', the *nomenklatura* system refers to a more narrow circle of people than the CPSU proper – some 3 million were involved (Harasymiw, 1969). There were *nomenklatura* lists of candidates and lists of *nomenklatura* positions at every level of the party hierarchy, including the CPSU Central Committee and Politburo. Appointment to the more inferior and numerous positions was the prerogative of party groupings in the union republics down to the level of district party committees, whereas the Kremlin head organization reserved for itself the right to appoint top leaders, including party secretaries of the union republics. Thus the last Soviet *nomenklatura* list was approved on 7 August 1991, naming 7,000 top government, state, military and KGB officials (Yasmann, 1993). The privileges associated with *nomenklatura* positions is what made this stratum the real ruling class within the Soviet imperial system. To conclude with a point made by Motyl, the way the *nomenklatura* system and the CPSU worked throughout the Soviet internal empire made them tools for the rule of Russians. Russians together with their Ukrainian and Belarusian *secunda inter pares* dominated the top echelons of power, including the army and diplomacy.

Another macro-level institution buttressing the Soviet imperial state and international system was the Comintern. Many analysts have dwelled on how this presumably internationalist institution working in the service of the world proletariat transformed itself into a slave of the Soviet Union as a tool for the advancement of Soviet national interests (Carr, 1982; Seton-Watson, 1960). The Comintern was supposed to work as an umbrella group for communist parties and organizations all over the world, to provide for mutual support and the exchange of ideas on strategy and tactics. But by 1935 it was nothing but an instrument for Stalin's dictatorship over his ideological fellows. All decisions of the congresses of the Comintern were binding. Among the 'twenty-one conditions' laid down in 1920 which member parties were forced to accept were these stipulations:

> Communist parties must support unreservedly all soviet republics in their struggle with counter-revolution, urge workers to refuse to transport arms or equipment destined for the enemies of a soviet republic, and pursue propaganda by legal or illegal means among all troops sent to fight against a soviet republic. ...They must proceed to periodic purges of their organizations in order to remove interested and petty-bourgeois elements. (quoted in Seton-Watson, 1960, p. 74)

This last sentence anticipated how the Comintern and its officials became the target of purges in the 1930s (*ibid.*, p. 171). The first provision did at times lead to surprising outcomes, as when the Comintern in 1928 issued a resolution in defence of Lithuanian independence (Kolarz, 1952, pp. 116-17). At issue was the clash of interests between the Soviet and Polish governments, the latter headed by the Polish right-wing nationalist Marshal Pilsudski, over control of Vilnius (Wilno in Polish); the Soviet position being that it belonged to Lithuania. The Comintern was also instrumental in coercing Baltic communists and thus helping to bring about the later sovietization which made the Baltic states part of the internal empire. Perhaps the Comintern's biggest role in sovietization was played in relation to the external empire, however, a topic to be addressed below.

As for micro-level actors of implementation, there was a tense interplay between colonizers and indigenous collaborators (not necessarily to be taken in the pejorative sense, given the asymmetrical balance of power). Due to *korenizatsia* and the system of *nomenklatura*, a fairly large number of new cadres, so-called *vydvyzhentsy* ('those who were promoted'), were available. The machine-tractors stations (MTS) are mentioned to illuminate the tense interplay of technical and political considerations. The concept refers not only to the numerous individual MTS's allocating machinery to collective farms, but to a state agency created in 1928 to carry out collectivization. Hence the MTS served as Stalin's task force, with a core *politotdel* of trusted party members issuing binding directives for farms and working independently of local party organizations (Fainsod, 1958/1989, pp. 280 ff.). Hugh Seton-Watson sees the heads of MTS's as 'dictators of the whole rural area' (they served some thirty farms), likening their role to that of the political commissars of Red Army units (1960, p. 158).

Most of the other sinews mentioned in Figure 3.3 need no further comment, except for GOSPLAN, the institution of economic planning which transformed the Soviet Union into a unitary economy, thus going far beyond any process of international economic integration seen ever since. From a fairly improvised system of economic monitoring, the institution of planning grew into a dreadful bureaucracy meticulously supervising absolutely all economic activity in the Soviet Union (Nove 1982, pp. 96 ff.). This totalitarian approach to state intervention converted the internal empire into virtually one single enterprise. This peculiar process of economic integration did originally proceed from the international trade philosophy of exploiting comparative advantages in a bid for regional autarky, although its distinctive feature was the liquidation of market forces. The Soviet planned economy thus worked as an international division of labour among the republics and regions, implying that there were elements of internal colonialism in the way Hechter (1975), argues, i.e. an institutionalized *cultural* division of labour. As already suggested, Uzbekistan and neighbouring republics had to embark on cotton monoculture at the expense of food production, whereas the manufacturing of textiles was assigned to other republics. But to infer from such patterns of specialization that large-scale economic exploitation took place is to jump to conclusions[5] (cf. Orlowski, 1993).

What remains is to comment on the ideological mechanisms as some of the most far-reaching, despite their verbal appearance. Among the administrative measures mentioned, Soviet law did

---

[5] What Hechter, like other Marxist materialists, seem to overlook in his understanding of colonialism is the fact that perceptions of exploitation often outweigh the reality of exploitation. As argued earlier, it is better to look upon imperialism and colonialism as political rather than economic abuse.

formulate administrative practices of operational significance. Yet one of the most important features of the Soviet imperial system was the precedence of ideology over legal and other principles, a principle which carries the Russian name of *partiinost* (i.e. biased towards the interests of the party). The Soviet Constitution of 1936, for example, contained the most noble of democratic provisions, yet it was issued at the height of terror. *Partiinost* permeated public and private life – civil society was liquidated just as much as the 'kulaks' and the enemies of the people – forcing everyone to think and behave in the interests of party and state. In this way the totalitarian state provided for censorship not only of literature and art, but in everything. The most absurd consequences were found in the field of science, where the party inflicted upon Soviet agriculture Lysenko's dubious biological theories,[6] and when the Soviet authorities insisted that jazz was born in Russia. To illuminate the direct role of *partiinost* in upholding the internal empire compare Stalin's renunciation of the right to secession, legally guaranteed by the 1923 Party Congress:

> It should be borne in mind that besides the right of nations to self-determination there is also the right of the working class to consolidate its power, and to this latter right the right of self-determination is subordinated. ...[T]his must be said bluntly – the right to self-determination cannot and must not serve as an obstacle to the exercise by the working class of its right to dictatorship. (1936, p. 168)

This amounts to a doctrine of intervention in the internal empire, parallelling the Brezhnev doctrine of limited sovereignty for the external empire that followed later.

Generally speaking, ideology served as a most tangible, if subtle tool for repression, legitimizing all sorts of political measures including genocide. The Soviet approach to exploiting ideology in the exercise of empire transformed ideology into a Kafkan weapon of terror, a mechanism of structural violence with implications reach-

---

[6] Trofim Lysenko rejected Mendel's pioneering research on heredity, arguing the primacy of environment over genetic inheritance in plants. He thus sought to prove the correctness of Ivan Michurin's theories – official Soviet doctrine from 1948 – in an attempt to grow wheat and rye farther north than their natural growth zone. It was later established that much of his research was built on falsified data and so Lysenkoism was abandoned in 1965 and Mendel's theories were reinstated.

ing just as far as other instances of structural violence identified by Galtung and other students of North-South imbalances across the globe.[7] For Soviet Marxist ideology had the effect of making terror either superfluous or legitimate. The specific concepts for the political integration of the multinational Soviet empire were the slogans of *sblizhenie* and *slianie*, of which the latter was the more radical and was therefore employed with greater caution, especially later on. It was claimed that these two processes would result in the creation of the 'Soviet people' (*sovetski narod*), yet this term was used as a common designation for the Soviet population at an early stage. It was Viacheslav Molotov, later Soviet Minister for Foreign Affairs who gave birth to the 'immortal Soviet people' in an article that appeared in 1937 (Simon, p. 173). Roman Szporluk (1986) makes the interesting observation that the idea of creating a unitary Soviet people was literally stolen from one of the prominent National Bolsheviks belonging to the bourgeois *smenavekhovshchina* group, Nikolai Ustrialov.

The internal empire as a system of foreign policy. Among the principles of ethnic tolerance listed above as the sinews of empire are the establishment of republican foreign ministries and the legalization of national armies in early 1944. Here the analysis encounters another highly dialectical side of the Soviet system, in that this provision would seem to refute anything what has been said about the unitary nature of the Soviet multinational state. The brutal fact is that the republican 'foreign ministries' were only ministries on paper, a point argued earlier to illuminate the acute organizational problems facing postcommunist countries of the internal empire when launching their new, independent foreign policies. The American scholar Vernon V. Aspaturian is one of the few to have ventured into examining the significance of republican 'foreign ministries' (1960). His analysis leaves no doubt about the manipula-

---

[7] Following Galtung (1969; 1971), structural violence is a violence that is not visible in any specific actor-to-actor relationship, but is nevertheless a 'violence' distorting the lives of millions and preventing their fulfilment of needs. What he had in mind when constructing the concept was to invent a tool for the analysis of poverty, hunger and underdevelopment in an international perspective, but this is far too narrow an approach. Besides, the concept has been castigated for being a mystification devoid of operationalization and measurement (cf. Mommsen, 1977, pp. 108-10).

tive considerations that lay behind their establishment. The timing of their instalment – on the basis of a constitutional amendment issued by the time of the second Soviet conquest of the Baltic states – was no coincidence. What Stalin had in mind was to give these new imperial dependencies, as well as the republics of the residual internal empire, an artificial legitimacy as ostensibly independent subjects of international law.

The 1944 amendment gave union republics the right to establish separate foreign offices, defence ministries and national troop formations in order to meet the provisions for UN membership. The formal right to pursue independent foreign polices was confirmed in Article 80 of the 1977 Soviet Constitution. As for the apparent military decentralization, not a single republic ever established a defence ministry or appointed a minister of defence. Similarly, nothing significant came of the apparent legalization of direct diplomatic relations between Soviet republics and foreign powers. At one point the British Ambassador to Moscow told the Soviet Foreign Minister Molotov – not in earnest – that London wanted to exchange representatives with Kiev, to which a furious Molotov retorted that Kiev was not interested in expanding diplomatic contacts (Aspaturian, 1960, p. 197).

At Dumbarton Oaks later in 1944 Molotov shocked the world by requesting that each of the sixteen Soviet republics (then including a Karelo-Finnish republic) be given a seat in the United Nations. Only Ukraine and Belorussia actually achieved this, whereas the residual USSR was represented by the Soviet Ambassador to the UN. These two republics did not pursue UN policies of their own in the Soviet era, but Ukraine's UN representation and its skilled diplomats ultimately came to serve as a springboard for real independence, as prophetically anticipated by Adam Ulam in his preface to Konstantyn Sawczuk's book on the issue (1975).[8] The Central Asian and Transcaucasian 'foreign ministries' may also have been instrumental in projecting Soviet power into Asia and the Third World in the post-Stalin era (Aspaturian, 1960, pp. 84–90). Regional party leaders occasionally used foreign policy as a platform to improve their own standing within the Soviet political hierachy by

[8] Dmitri Manuilski, a high-placed Comintern official who was appointed Ukrainian Minister of Foreign Affairs in 1944, appears to have played a role as virtual commander of the entire Soviet diplomatic staff at the UN headquarters (Sawczuk, 1975, pp. 140–5).

aping the party line or by displaying slightly more hawkish views (Hauslohner, 1981). However, this hardly qualifies as 'republican foreign policies', so the overall conclusion remains that of the irrelevance of Soviet republican foreign ministries in the formulation of Soviet foreign policy. The Soviet Ministry of Foreign Affairs (MFA) never bothered to consult or coordinate its activities with them, placing them in the position of simply having to obey instructions from above (Aspaturian, 1960, p. 151).

It would be wrong, however, to infer from this that the Soviet MFA itself was the central locus of foreign policy decision-making. As described in detail by Aspaturian elsewhere, the key forum was the party Politburo, and before that Stalin (Aspaturian, 1971, pp. 558–61). Thus *partiinost* prevailed in the field of foreign policy, although the post-Stalinist foreign policy system in particular was characterized by policy disagreements and coalition-building. The CPSU Secretariat was in charge of the *nomenklatura* covering the Foreign Ministry and the entire diplomatic service. Even for aspirants, i.e. students at the Foreign Ministry's own Diplomatic Academy and MGIMO, it took an excellent *kharakteristika* (personal dossier indicating political inclinations, used as reference for *nomenklatura* appointments) or patronage to be enrolled. Other important fora for decision-making on issues of national security were the Defence Council and the CPSU General Secretary, who always played a key role in foreign affairs. Nevertheless, Aspaturian is probably right in positing the person of Andrei Gromyko, Soviet Foreign Minister from 1957 to 1985 (an extraordinarily long tenure in the general history of diplomacy), as a foreign policy institution in his own right and moreover part of the real governing troika by the early 1980s (Shevchenko, 1985). However, when it came to supervising the external Soviet empire of Eastern Europe, other actors such as the current CPSU General Secretary, 'chief ideologue' Mikhail Suslov, and Boris Ponomarev, the junior chief ideologue and *de facto* boss of the powerful International Department of the CPSU, as well as top army officials were the more influential (*ibid.*; Tatu, 1981).

Summing up, the Soviet foreign policy system must be characterized as utterly centralist and hierarchical, with the MFA indisputably at the apex as far as the Union republics were concerned. However, the MFA was primarily a locus for implementation rather than a policy-making unit. Many authors have dwelt on the special features which Marxist-Leninist ideology added to Soviet foreign policy in the shape of a commitment to world revolution giving rise to foreign policy revisionism. While the operational Soviet motives may have been defensive, Soviet empire-building certainly falls into this revisionist category – evidently so, when the ruthless colonial approach to building the internal empire is taken into account (most foreign policy analysts do not). S. Frederick Starr's observation of the interpenetration of Tsarist Russian imperial, foreign and domestic policies can therefore be extended to the Soviet case (1978, pp. 5-7). Whereas the administrative division of labour may have been less blurred in the Soviet case, there was always a common denominator to foreign policy-making and domestic politics, namely considerations of security and upholding the Soviet order in its internal and external imperial ramifications (cf. Aspaturian, 1971, pp. 498 ff.).[9] Fear of the effect changes in the external empire might have on the internal system seems to have been decisive, for instance, in bringing about the Soviet decision to intervene in Czechoslovakia, with republican party leader Piotr Shelest of Ukraine, seconded by Piotr Masherov (Belorussia) and Antanas Snieckus (Lithuania), among the most vocal in favour of intervention (Valenta, 1984).

This brief introduction to the Soviet foreign policy system suggests a certain evolution away from the totalitarian practices of Stalinism, yet the fact remains that the institutions and ideas of Stalinism lived on for decades as atavisms propelling new instances of idiosyncratic behaviour and expansionism (cf. Snyder, 1991).

There is also a story to be told concerning the peculiar Soviet return to 'normalcy' after Stalin. First, however, the points about the internal empire are briefly recapitulated before the analysis turns to the external empire. Notwithstanding its astonishing multinational composition and formal features of federalism, the Soviet Union was a unitary state as a result of 'democratic centralism'. Local autonomy was a fiction except for the most trivial of matters, with Stalin and later the CPSU leadership as the real locus of power. The fifty states making up the United States of America, for example, enjoy greater freedoms than did their Soviet counterparts. The United States has

[9] One of E.H. Carr's points in his analysis of Comintern's degeneration is the way this organization worked in tandem with *Narkomindel* – the title of the first Soviet MFA – with only slight differences in the means employed to promote the security of the USSR (1982, p. 4).

never bothered to establish token 'foreign ministries', but on the other hand accepts republican guards corresponding to the Soviet republican 'national armies' that never materialized. The Soviet era was less of a break with the Russian empire ('the prison of the peoples') than would appear at first sight, although Soviet administration in the end did more to infuse ethnic identities than did Tsarism on the basis of its colonial *gubernia* administration. The Soviet state was also unitary at the economic level, where taut central planning ensured that the continent-sized country worked as one corporate enterprise.

The basic continuity between Soviet and Tsarist Russian imperialism lies in the political culture of empire and Russian national security cultivated by both. This became a self-serving legitimation bind between foreign and domestic policy, which facilitated the subsequent switch from focus on internal colonialism within the former Tsarist empire to external colonialism in what emerged as the external Soviet empire of Eastern Europe. Where Stalinism and Soviet internal colonialism differed is in the specific ideological tenets employed under the general rubric of sovietization as a key Soviet colonial doctrine. As it was at the same time a policy of industrialization entailing undisputed civilizational benefits such as education, Soviet colonialism was superior to its Tsarist predecessor by virtue of its modern features. In terms of degree of integration, Soviet totalitarianism is distinguished by its horrifying achievements, including a near-total elimination of civil society. Indeed, the degree of direct physical violence accompanying sovietization marks an important difference between sovietization in the internal and external empire, because of the massively genocidal nature of the former. The reaction to sovietization throughout the periphery of the internal empire was more militant, producing ever more horrifying measures in reprisal.

The preceding analysis can also be cited as evidence that Soviet imperialism and colonial practice were *sui generis*. At any rate, the German scholar Dietrich Geyer (1986) has a point when criticizing superficial theses of continuity between Soviet and Tsarist imperialism. His point about the salience of the respective international contexts is relevant. Sovietization in the external empire was thus an event moulded by the emergence of bipolarity.

Sovietization of the external empire

The course of sovietization throughout the external empire followed a somewhat different pattern than was the case in the internal empire. Except for Mongolia, which had already been sovietized mainly by Comintern agents beginning in 1921, the timing and historical circumstances were different in that the Soviet Union emerged as a victor in the Second World War. Victory was not assured from the start due *inter alia* to the excesses of sovietization which made Soviet citizens to the west prone to collaboration. The narrow margin between victory and defeat, the shock over Hitler's treachery and the recovery of Soviet power and society behind enemy lines were the likely factors behind Stalin's decision to move the lines of defence forward in another thrust of sovietization.

As for the question whether Stalin proceeded on the basis of some preconceived master-plan, the answer depends partly on the significance attributed to the Comintern as Stalin's instrument for turning foreign communists into loyal agents of sovietization in their native countries. Conventional wisdom has it that the Comintern ceased to exist upon its formal dissolution in the summer of 1943, a step taken by Stalin to signal goodwill towards his Anglo–American allies in the Second World War. But Russian historians have now confirmed a long-time suspicion among Western scholars, namely that the Comintern continued to exist and direct the work of communist parties by transforming itself into the *Otdel Mezhdunarodnoi Informatsii pri TsK VKP (b)*, the Office of International Information of the Central Committee of the All–Union Communist Party (Bolsheviks), or OMI (Lebedeva, 1993a; Kravchenko, 1946, p. 426).

As pointed out by Thomas T. Hammond in his analysis of the communist takeover in Mongolia, few if any of the Comintern and Soviet officials responsible were active in Eastern Europe twenty years later (1975, p. 141). Stalin himself played only a minor role in Mongolia, whereas he took the lead part in East European sovietization. Nevertheless, the latter basically followed the Mongolian model, down to the establishment of a formally sovereign state with the official epithet of 'people's democracy'.[10] Stalin knew about the details of the Mongolian venture and could not have failed to be

---

[10] Where no other source is indicated, the accounts of individual communist takeovers by Pavel Tigrid and others in the monograph edited by Hammond (1975) serve as sources for what follows.

impressed by its success among rank-and-file Mongolians who acquiesced in the face of what they saw as the lesser evil compared to their country's imminent annihilation by China. To return to the Comintern as the missing link in this theory, Natalia S. Lebedeva has documented the role of the Comintern in the service of Soviet interests in Poland from 1939 to 1943 and before that its role in Stalin's and the GPU's (the secret police) onslaught on the Polish Communist Party (1993b). Characteristically enough, some of the documents she uses are dated after the formal dissolution of the Comintern. In Lebedeva's assessment this is no coincidence, but reflects increased activities under the cloak of the OMI and thus testifies to the latter's role in preparing East European sovietization.

The OMI continued most of the Comintern's activities, such as running a party school where East European communists were enrolled and directing communist resistance to Nazi occupation (Lebedeva, 1993a). The OMI – which, it must be remembered, served as a branch of the Soviet Communist Party's Central Committee and had close contacts with Stalin – took care of *nomenklatura* clearances for leading East European communists (cf. Brzezinski, 1969, p. 119). Candidates for deployment at regional and local levels of administration were prepared so that they could step in once the political situation at home made it feasible (personal interview with Lebedeva). At times the OMI took the initiative itself, as when Manuilski (see note 8) recommended that the leader of the *zagran-buro* (the OMI liaison office) of the Hungarian Communist Party be replaced by Ernö Gerö, 'who has the right understanding of events in Hungary and may thus influence positively the Hungarian *zagran-buro* which has slipped into systematic support for [Admiral] Horthy' (quoted in Lebedeva, 1993b, p. 13). Between the lines one reads the OMI's difficulty in controlling its foreign agents, implying that the replacement of the Comintern by the OMI also marked a certain (involuntary) relaxation of controls.

Meanwhile, the Red Army had defeated the Germans at Stalingrad, leading to the reconquest of Soviet territory and the subsequent Soviet advance into Eastern and Central Europe. While it may be too simplistic to perceive Stalin's post-war policy as some fixed master-plan, the fact remains that his approach to waging the war and liberating Eastern Europe was one of political calculation. In contrast to the American General Patton, Stalin was anxious to liberate the capitals of Eastern Europe – Budapest, Prague, Berlin,

Vienna – while on other occasions he appeared deliberately to let down the nationalist Poles and Slovaks (Ulam, 1973, p. 598; Malcolm Mackintosh in Hammond, 1975, pp. 233 ff.). The secret protocols of the 1939 Molotov-Ribbentrop treaty had testified already to Stalin's acute interest in Eastern Europe. The Soviet massacre of some 15,000 Polish officers in Katyn in 1940 and the way this was later used by Stalin as a pretext for breaking off relations with the Polish exile government in London can be taken as evidence that later sovietization was not quite a coincidence, as can the percentage agreement between Stalin and Churchill (see note 1).

Others, including the entire group of so-called revisionist historians of the Cold War, are more prone to interpret Stalin's militancy in Eastern Europe in the light of US initiatives such as the Marshall Plan which were capable of directly challenging Soviet supremacy in Eastern Europe (Snyder, 1991, p. 220 ff.; Lundestad, 1975, p. 454 ff.). Isaac Deutscher dwells on the many contradictions in Stalin's policy in Eastern Europe, such as his draconian demands for war reparations from newly war-torn Germany, Austria, Hungary, Bulgaria and Romania which could not but undermine the communist case in these countries (1967, p. 537). Another way to argue the arbitrariness of Stalin's policy in Eastern Europe is by pointing to the 1946-8 rise of Zhdanov[11] in Soviet domestic politics as one of Stalin's militant lieutenants (Ra'anan, 1983). The role of the ensuing *Zhdanovshchina* in foreign policy, however, goes against the grain of the revisionist thesis as this was an internally generated push towards militancy, ridiculing the economist Varga's thesis of Western economic strength and his call for caution (cf. Snyder, 1991, p. 219). The implication of Ra'anan's analysis is that the Western world could have done little to prevent the shift towards aggressive, totalitarian sovietization in Eastern Europe.

As this indicates, it is possible to distinguish different periods of sovietization, as well as local variations, including outright failure.

---

[11] Andrei Zhdanov became party chief in Leningrad after the assassination of Kirov. In 1939 he became a member of the Politburo and was considered a likely successor to Stalin due to his obscurantist ideas on science and culture: Lysenkoism (see note 6) combined with vitriolic attacks on 'cosmopolitanism' in the arts, and his uncompromising attitude to issues of revolution and foreign policy ('*Zhdanovshchina*'). He died suddenly in 1948, under mysterious circumstances recalling the fate of Kirov.

In other words, the 'master-plan' was evidently one of adapting to whatever opportunities there were in relation to the Soviet goal of securing maximum security, empire and control. The years 1944–7 can be called the era of 'pluralist sovietization', characterized by rigged elections and the formation of puppet coalition governments with communists in control of the 'power ministries' of the interior and defence (except in Bulgaria, where the army was less important). The period from 1948 to 1953 was one of 'totalitarian sovietization', marked by terror and purges of non-communists and communists, in addition to the transformation of the economic and societal system along Soviet lines. This era, however, was also one in which the cracks came to the surface in the shape of Tito's defection in 1948. Arguably this is the most important factor explaining Stalin's dramatic change of gear and, ironically, it was a protest against sovietization from an ardent left-wing supporter of Zhdanov (cf. Deutscher 1967, pp. 594 ff.). Thus the Cominform – the Communist Information Bureau launched in 1947 that was to have its headquarters in Belgrade in recognition of Tito's deeds – was never allowed inside Yugoslavia, since Tito rightly suspected its Soviet representatives of infiltration (Ra'anan, 1983). The organization had to be dissolved, but then followed the purges of real and imagined 'Titoists' throughout Eastern Europe, including László Rájk, Minister of the Interior in Hungary, and Rudolf Slánsky, General Secretary of the Czechoslovak Communist Party. According to Zbigniew K. Brzezinski's seminal work (1969) on the sovietization of Eastern Europe, hundreds of thousands of party members were purged in the years around 1950 – an average of one in every four (p. 97). In Bulgaria alone more than twenty ministers were purged.

It was not that Yugoslavia constituted the jewel in the crown of the Soviet external empire – a fact that was demonstrated by Stalin's acquiescence in the face of Tito's defiance. The pride of place went to Germany, with its industrial riches, along with Poland for military strategic reasons. Yet Soviet strategy failed in the case of Germany too, in that the division of the country prevented Stalin from gaining access to the Ruhr district. The smaller eastern part of the country – the GDR – had to shoulder the war reparations alone. The Berlin blockade of 1948-9 failed, inspiring Stalin to devote his energy to consolidation (except for the role he played in supporting Kim Il Sung's attempt at the forceful reunification of Korea). Stalin's role in the Czechoslovak *coup d'état* of February 1948 is characterized by

Pavel Tigrid as an 'elegant takeover' because it had the appearance of a real, indigenous proletarian revolution in an advanced country with democratic traditions. However, judging from the revelations of Karel Kaplan, a Czech historian who gained access to the Czechoslovak party archives in 1968, the Soviet NKVD (secret police) agents and their Czechoslovak colleagues (OMI agents?) worked closely together to prepare the 1948 coup (Rupnik, 1988, pp. 100 ff.). Among other things, the Soviets were anxious to see the Czechoslovak government reject the Marshall Plan. Soviet intervention in the Romanian takeover, by contrast, was obvious and anything but elegant. The Comintern and hence Soviet connection in the Bulgarian case was also clear, as the head of the Bulgarian Communists, Georgi Dimitrov, was at the same time head of the Comintern and subsequently the leading figure in the OMI. For this reason perhaps, the Bulgarian takeover was not rushed but is an example of 'salami tactics'. It was Hungary, however, that came to be known as the ideal type of salami tactics, an expression used by no less than the party Secretary, Matyás Rákosi.

The iron curtain had definitely come down over Europe.[12] Behind it Soviet 'advisers' and their local collaborators moved swiftly to alter property relations, administrative structures and curricula, introducing censorship etc. – in short, changing the entire face of East European societies. After the successful Prague coup, sovietization hit the Czechoslovak party itself through the cadres section and Control Commission. These two bodies were in charge of repression, together with the state security agency, which in turn was directly under the supervision of Soviet advisers. Even the Czechoslovak working classes who came out in support of the coup were subject to repression. By 1950 one-third of political prisoners consisted of workers. Meanwhile, in Czechoslovakia and elsewhere a newly trained segment of local *vydvyzhentsy* were co-opted into the new state and party bureaucracy, with the proportion of newcomers reaching as high as 86 per cent in the case of the Czechoslovak officer corps (Rupnik, pp. 100–12). *Partiinost* and party control prevailed in

---

[12] Some analysts look upon Churchill's iron curtain speech of March 1946 as an offensive Western measure setting the stage for the Truman doctrine, the Marshall Plan and NATO. If anything, it was the percentage deal that was the offensive measure sealing the fate of millions of Europeans living in the eastern half of the continent. Churchill's warning of the iron curtain may have been prompted by his own feeling of responsibility for it.

the legal system, the economy and cultural life. The largey rural East European societies had to take on heavy industrial production, their constitutions read like carbon copies of the Soviet constitution and secondary schools were obliged to teach Russian. Even machine-tractor stations (MTS) were introduced during collectivization.

On the other hand, it is worth keeping in mind the features which distinguished the external from the internal empire. There was no large-scale influx of Russian rank-and-file colonizers, although advisers, military personnel and the like settled there for a while. What is more, the people's democracies of Eastern Europe were never formally incorporated into the Soviet Union as the three Baltic states were, for instance. The countries of Eastern Europe continued to function as national systems – in the plural – with governments, constitutions, armies, Soviet embassies, planning agencies and non-convertible currencies of their own. They were soviereign states with national UN representations, although of course they were what James N. Rosenau calls 'penetrated systems', i.e. characterized by direct and authoritative participation in the political process of a national system by non-members of the system (1966, p. 65). Accordingly, the political history of the East European countries following sovietization varies more than among the territorial units making up the Soviet Union. Romania came to be known as 'Maverick Romania', whereas Hungary took refuge in 'goulash communism' and Poland succeeded in abandoning collective farms. China defected altogether.

Reaction to sovietization in the external empire. Sovietization's more indirect nature in making the region a buffer-zone of Soviet satellites can be cited as a reason why reaction to sovietization followed a different pattern in the external empire. Except for a few episodes of armed resistance,[13] the populations of Eastern Europe generally acquiesced in the face of sovietization. Most analysts explain this in terms of rational choice by pointing to the presence of the Red Army. But when seeking to explain why people resorted to armed resistance in the internal empire and did not in the external empire, it is also important to mention factors such as the prestige of the

---

[13] There were some instances of armed resistance against sovietization in Poland. The clamp-down in Budapest in 1956 also caused a brief guerrilla war in which 2,500 Hungarians were killed and more than 20,000 wounded (Dunay, 1992). In 1960 some of the peasants in Romania rose in armed struggle against forced collectivization.

Soviet Union as the anti-fascist liberating power in the region. Naivety and ignorance played into the hands of Stalin.

Tito's defection was the first sign that sovietization was engendering a politically significant reaction. The subsequent wave of terror and sovietization with an iron-fist left no one with any illusions about the nature of their new regime. In 1952 – during the Korean war – Eastern Europe was literally becoming a powder keg (Ionescu, 1965, pp. 40-1). Worker unrest in Czechoslovakia spread to the GDR, climaxing in the Berlin rising in June 1953. This caused the first in a series of Soviet military interventions where tanks crushed popular resistance. The post-Stalin Soviet regime retreated and launched a new policy of moderation dubbed 'the New Course' (Brzezinski 1969, pp. 159 ff.). This opportunity was not wasted on Imre Nagy, a leading member of the Hungarian politburo who became the idol of the Hungarian people during the 1956 uprising. Before that the workers in the Polish city of Poznan went on strike, propelling into power another moderate, Wladyslaw Gomulka. These tests of strength against the Soviet patrons were fuelled by Khrushchev's secret speech on Stalin's abuses at the 20th CPSU Congress. Khrushchev felt he had to intervene in Hungary so as not to give in to the Stalinists, but the overall political climate had irreversibly changed. The last long part of communist Eastern Europe's political history was one of crisis followed by 'normalization' and new crisis: Romania's defection from socialist integration in 1962, the 1968 invasion of Czechoslovakia, worker unrest in Poland in the 1970s, culminating in the birth of Solidarity and the introduction of martial law in December 1981. Except for the brief guerrilla war in Hungary in 1956, the terminal phase of Communism in Eastern Europe was marked by non-violence: civil disobedience, 'anti-politics' and the organization of dissident groups (e.g. Charter 77).

The sinews of the external empire. At one time Stalin boasted, 'I shall shake my little finger and then there will no Tito.' This happened to be the exceptional occasion when this key sinew of empire did not have the intended effect! Joking apart, Figure 3.2 exposes the sinews of the external empire whose dreadful effect repeats the pattern from the internal empire. In the external empire, the interpenetration of party and state structures was accompanied by Soviet penetration (decreasing somewhat after Stalin's death). The

East European *nomenklatura* systems were only partly under national control in that the Kremlin reserved for itself the right to appoint general secretaries and politburos in the way the OMI did (Gati, 1987, p. 48; Schöpflin, 1986, pp. 100 ff; McCauley and Carter, 1986, p. 6). But in the 1960s and later the voice of the Kremlin was at times overruled, for instance in the case of Stefan Olszowski (Edward Gierek's closest rival in the 1970s, exiled as ambassador to the GDR) or Matyas Szürös, (a prominent Hungarian Party official who pioneered the call for an independent Hungarian foreign policy) whom the Hungarians decided to keep. According to Viacheslav Dashichev, a Soviet academic of considerable influence under Gorbachev, Moscow wanted Lubomir Strougal to take over as party secretary in Czechoslovakia in December 1987, but the Czechoslovak politburo picked Milos Jakes instead (personal interview). The residual *nomenklatura* systems worked on a national basis and were almost as extensive as those in the Soviet Union. For a short while the Prague Spring abolished the Czechoslovak *nomenklatura* system.

Another controversial dimension of Soviet penetration was the role of Soviet ambassadors as viceroys (Brzezinski 1969, pp. 118 –19). In his contacts with Tito, Stalin held that a Soviet envoy in a people's democracy had the right to gather information on all matters in the host country, including confidential matters; something Stalin considered true communist-to-communist relations despite the lack of reciprocity when it came to East European ambassadors in the Soviet capital. One ambassador serving in Warsaw from 1946 to 1953 had to be recalled because he overstepped all diplomatic etiquette in the way he treated Polish party secretary Boleslaw Bierut, whom he would summon at short notice like a clerk (cf. Bernov, 1990). Although the era of ambassadorial rule had its leyday under Stalin, the Soviet ambassador to Warsaw, for instance, continued to have direct access to the Polish party secretary thereafter (Davies, 1986, p. 39). The Polish case is special because of the role played by another 'viceroy', Konstanty Rokossowski, who was a Soviet Marshal of Polish origin and thus a genuine collaborator. He served as Polish Minister of Defence, Deputy Premier and member of the politburo in close cooperation with Bierut. Above all he served as Stalin's watch-dog (Kramer 1989/90; David Dallin 1951, pp. 5-6).

International isolation of the East European states and governments was a deliberate policy pursued by Stalin, a practice Brzezinski

Fig. 3.2. SINEWS OF EMPIRE B: INSTITUTIONAL DEVICES FOR THE INTEGRATION OF THE EXTERNAL SOVIET EMPIRE

Macro-level institutions: Stalin, later the CPSU leadership and local parties; the Comintern/OMI (Cominform); the Red Army; the CMEA and the Warsaw Pact; power ministries headed by communists; the *nomenklatura* system; international isolation and later bilateral consultations with Stalin: summitry and informal meetings; foreign policy 'coordination'; Soviet (Russian) dominance with Soviet ambassadors as viceroys; later, Soviet hegemony

Micro-level actors of implementation: Soviet advisers[14] assisted by local collaborators, MTS etc.

Practices of implementation: persuasion/pluralism; manipulation and 'salami tactics'; terror; retreat

Economic institutions: Nationalizations/public property and collectivization, economic planning by national planning agencies; CMEA cooperation, notably long-term investment projects such as pipelines for energy; price scissors; low export prices, joint stock companies

Military institutions: National armies and Soviet control via bilateral 'friendship and cooperation treaties' and treaties between East European states; the Warsaw Pact; military interventions (the possibility thereof)

Administrative mechanisms: sovietization – 'national in form, Soviet in content' – seizure of power via establishment of national communist governments and constitutional settings; efforts towards proficiency in Russian; training of diplomatic, military and security personnel in the Soviet Union or by Soviet advisers

Ideological doctrines (principles of repression): Marxism-Leninism; the leading role of the party/*partiinost*; the leading role of the CPSU and the Soviet Union; people's democracy; *splochënnost* ('bloc cohesion'), 'proletarian/socialist internationalism', the 1968 Brezhnev doctrine of 'limited sovereignty'

Principles of tolerance: the 'New Course' polycentrism/different paths to socialism; Gorbachev's abandonment of the Brezhnev doctrine

calls 'totalitarian atomization' (1969, pp. 123 ff.). Restrictions on travel between people's democracies were just as severe as those between one of these states, and a capitalist country; moreover, links

---

[14] The ratio of Soviet advisers relative to the population in the host country by far surpassed the corresponding numbers for the British empire. Tiny Albania had to receive over 3,000 Soviet advisers. According to David J. Dallin, the combined contingent of Soviet advisers throughout Eastern Europe and Asia numbered over 100,000 (including 23,000 in China; 1951 p. 19).

Dallin further observes the Soviet infiltration of the Polish army: all leading posts were given to Soviet officers whose surnames were then Polonized, four of the five military districts in Poland were under Soviet commanders and the great majority of Ministry of Defence and General Staff officials were Soviet – altogether there was a Soviet contingent numbering several thousand in military officials alone (*ibid.*, p. 5).

with communist parties abroad were broken. Stalin disliked multi-lateral gatherings with his junior party bosses, preferring to have them facing him alone. This may also explain why it was Khrush-chev and not Stalin who launched the Warsaw Pact military alliance. As for the CMEA, this organization never came to function as an international organization until after Stalin's death. The founding of the CMEA was a symbolic political act aimed at countering the establishment of the OEEC (later the OECD) to channel Marshall aid into Western Europe (Kaser, 1965). As for the terminology employed for macro-level sinews, the picture was one of unchal-lenged Soviet dominance throughout the Stalin era. Dominance was later modified by developments in the direction of hegemony in the post-Stalin era, ultimately evolving into primacy during the brief era of Gorbachev (Kramer, 1989; Skak, 1992a).

As for economic sinews other than CMEA cooperation, comment is needed on the so-called joint-stock companies functioning in the decade from 1944 to 1954. Through these companies the Soviet Union took a significant share of its junior allies' outputs – Hun-garian bauxite, Slovak oil, Czech uranium, etc. (Dallin, 1951, pp. 16 ff). Together with the war reparations and the extremely un-favourable terms of trade dictated by the soviet Union – for instance, in its coal imports from Poland – joint-stock companies would seem to qualify as a measure of genuine economic exploitation in support of Marxist understandings of imperialism.[15] These three exploitative practices amounted to a value-transfer from Eastern Europe to the Soviet Union that matches the entire Marshall aid from the USA to Western Europe, namely some $14 billion (Marer, 1984). The CMEA was instrumental in upholding a planned economic structure throughout the external empire on the basis of East European trade dependencies on the Soviet Union. In other words, it was in-strumental as a sinew of empire in the political sense. From the point of view of generating viable economies and societal prosperity,

---

[15] According to David Dallin, Anastas Mikoian, Soviet Minister of Foreign Trade in the 1940s, once briefed his officials by saying: 'You are Soviet colonizers. Economics determine politics' (1951, p. 14). As Dallin himself notes, the ministry itself worked much like a colonial ministry in charge of the economic management of the external empire through the exploitative practices just mentioned. Nonetheless, economic motives were secondary in relation to considerations of security and imperial-revolutionary prestige as key logics of empire.

however, 'socialist economic integration' was a plain disaster. Efforts at reforming CMEA cooperation were never radical enough.

Established in 1955, the Warsaw Pact played a far more important role than the CMEA as a body of control and coordination, yet the loyalty of the non-Soviet Warsaw Pact armies in the event of conflict with NATO was a constant headache (Holloway and Sharp, 1984). The senior Warsaw Pact officers received training at the Voroshilov or Frunze academies in Moscow, while the post of commander of the united forces of the Pact was always filled by a Soviet field marshal. The Political Consultative Committee (PCC), consisting of high-level governmental and party officials, served as the political decision-making body; increasingly, however, it came to serve as an *ex post facto* device for legitimizing Soviet security policy. It would therefore be an exaggeration to speak of a common foreign and security policy in the sense of operational day-to-day cooperation (Fodor, 1990, p. 97-105). The invasion of Czechoslovakia, the only joint military intervention ever undertaken, was most revealing of the real purpose of the Warsaw Pact. At the same time there was some movement towards the professionalization of military cooperation.

As in the case of the internal empire, ideological sinews were highly important as institutionalized structural violence. People's democracy was not just a constitutional epithet, but a theory legitimizing sovietization. Beginning with Yugoslavia and Albania in 1946, all East European countries adopted the title of people's democracy. But the fact that the term originated with the terminal sovietization of Mongolia in 1924 served to erode its popularity among Eastern Europeans. The Soviet idea was to launch a concept that placed Eastern Europe safely beyond the reach of bourgeois democracy and its standards, while at the same time distancing the Soviet Union from people's democracies by claiming a higher level of socialist development there, so as to uphold the right to patronize and control junior allies. The term people's democracy originally referred to a post-fascist state ruled by an anti-fascist coalition and to a state with socialist potentials. By 1947, however, following the Stalin-Zhdanov two-camp doctrine of 1946 (the doctrine of the two opposing camps, capitalism and socialism, marking the Soviet announcement of the Cold War) and the establishment of Cominform, the theory of people's democracy began to insist on the leading role of the party and loyalty to the Soviet Union (Christensen, 1978, pp. 161-94).

After Stalin's death, many people's democracies dropped the term, preferring to call themselves socialist republics.

External empire references to 'monolithic unity' often adopted the wording of *splochënnost*. The specific principle for relations between socialist parties and states were 'proletarian internationalism' and 'socialist internationalism', respectively. These terms institutionalized Soviet tutelage and were used as a general device when legitimizing the invasion of Czechoslovakia. The doctrine of peaceful coexistence guiding relations with capitalist countries explicitly referred to principles of non–interference in internal affairs and herein lies the difference from Soviet Marxist 'internationalism' (cf. *Diplomaticheskii Slovar*, 1984). The Brezhnev doctrine further argued the explicit right to intervene militarily – the right to extend 'fraternal assistance' – in fellow socialist countries when socialism was threatened. The leading role of the Soviet Union and the CPSU as a norm guiding Soviet-East European relations is found, *inter alia*, in Sanakoev and Kapchenko's monograph on socialist foreign policy. They defend it by pointing to the legacy of Comintern and the alleged 'revolutionary character' of the Soviet state (1977, p. 90). Conversely, Khrushchev's overtures towards Yugoslavia and the polycentrism brought about by the Sino-Soviet split created openings for the East Europeans as well, including new options within foreign policy.

The external empire as a system of foreign policy. As should be clear by now, the era of Stalin was one of Soviet *diktat* in every sphere, including foreign policy. In other words, the Soviet-East European system originally looked pretty much like the foreign policy system of the Soviet internal empire following the 1944 constitutional amendment that only formally legitimized republican foreign policies. However, the challenge from Tito brought a new trend. Among other things, the Soviet leadership responded by fixing the principle of state sovereignty for people's democracies as a way to demonstrate the significance of their unswerving loyalty towards Stalin's position *vis-à-vis* Tito. As a consequence, Soviet tutelage had to take on other forms than it did in the internal empire, such as providing for the training of East European diplomats at the Soviet Foreign Ministry's own Diplomatic Academy or at MGIMO. Not that the East European foreign ministries or the diplomacy of individual countries mattered much in terms of operational foreign policy-making during

Stalin's reign (Brzezinski 1969, pp. 109 ff.). But in terms of gaining organizational experience and getting to know other states and international groupings from within, the independent statehood of the countries of the external empire marks a difference. Contrary to Soviet intentions, they became less of the quasi-states they were at the outset and were thus better prepared to cope with independence than the Baltic states had been.

On the Soviet side, the real monitoring and coordinating body was not the Ministry of Foreign Affairs, but the Central Committee's Liaison Office for Relations with Ruling Communist Parties, the Central Committee's International Department and the Soviet Politburo itself. Brezhnev established his own telephone hotlines to the East European party headquarters. Party-to-party relations were what mattered most – liaisons that were gradually professionalized by the formation of foreign policy committees and departments within the East European parties too (Sanakoev and Kapchenko, 1977, p. 67; Morrison, 1978). Party-to-party consultations were mostly bilateral as long as Stalin was alive, a pattern that continued afterwards during crises. In 1972, for instance, Brezhnev summoned the Hungarian party leader Janos Kadar to Moscow to condemn his 'dangerous rightist deviationism', i.e. the cautiously liberal economic NEM (New Economic Mechanism) reform of 1968; something that would have cost Kadar his position had he not ordered a reversal of the Hungarian experiment. At other times, however, Moscow preferred multilateral fora, as was made evident during the Czechoslovak crisis of 1968. The unfolding of this drama revealed some East European leaders in favour of military intervention – Wladyslaw Gomulka of Poland and Walter Ulbricht of the GDR, not to mention the hawks on the Czechoslovak side such as Politburo member Vasil Bilak (Valenta, 1984). In less dramatic years, Brezhnev would summon his East European colleagues to his Crimea holiday resort, a court-like ritual reminiscent of the way the Tsars used to receive governors and viceroys to hear their reports and set up fashionable social gatherings. Details on these meetings are hard to come by except for the year 1977 (*Neue Zürcher Zeitung*, 17 August 1977). Yet, in this case as well as in that of the Warsaw Pact PCC, the degree of decision-making and actual operational policy coordination should not be exaggerated (Fodor, 1990). This is so despite the fact that Soviet sources insist on the significance of foreign policy coordination among the 'fraternal' countries as implementation of the treaties of friendship, cooperation and fraternal assistance (*Leninskaia politika mira i bezopasnost narodov*, 1982, p. 54).

Legitimizing Soviet decisions made in advance was what most foreign and security policy 'coordination' amounted to. Yet in the shadow of this diplomacy of rubber-stamping for the sake of placating the Soviet leadership – the gist of the regular meetings of foreign ministers – some of the small Warsaw Pact states did begin to raise their profiles in foreign policy (Kuhlmann, 1978; *Vneshniaia politika stran Varshavskogo dogovora*, 1986). The best-known example of this is Romania, which developed into a virtual non-member of the Warsaw Pact. Seen from the perspective of today's issue of postcommunist reintegration, Hungary's silent domestic and foreign policy revolution of returning to Europe proved more significant (Segal, 1992). Nevertheless, James F. Brown has a point when he states the significance of Ceausescu's defence of East European sovereignty against Khrushchevian flirtation with integration along internal empire principles of *sblizhenie* (1991, pp. 19 ff.). The common understanding between Poland and the Soviet Union on the necessity of keeping the Germans down and upholding the Oder-Neisse border also deserves mention (Morrison, 1978). At one time the Poles seem to have prevented a German-German summit otherwise approved by Moscow (*Yearbook of International Communist Affairs* 1985, pp. 307-17). Still, the Soviet-East European system was deeply hierarchical until the dawn of the brief Gorbachev era. From then on, Soviet diplomats began to negotiate in earnest with their East European colleagues – with the effect that, for instance, Hungary succeeded in modifying a PCC resolution condemning West Germany in 1989.

The external empire came to represent a far more modern version of empire than the internal empire. Sovietization here was not as genocidal, albeit roughly as brutal in its totalitarian nature. Day-to-day management of the external empire was decentralized to national units, making the system qualify as a case of 'informal empire'. This paved the way for much less violent reactions against sovietization, in contrast to the guerrilla wars within the internal empire. Relaxation of controls offered a new option of national communism, with some spin-offs to the internal empire. Because of this, however, it remains doubtful whether the Soviet Politburo really perceived the external empire as the more cost-efficient area. The

Soviet Union took on the duty of subsidizing East European economies through cheap energy deliveries, while at the same time not feeling too assured about the loyalty of its junior Warsaw Pact allies (Bunce, 1985). Most analysts agree that Eastern Europe was always a region of acute problems of regime legitimacy – more acute, in fact, than within the internal empire, with the notable exception of the Baltic republics. Tito's defection, Ceausescu's partial defection and the events of 1956 (the Hungarian revolution), 1968 (the Prague Spring) and 1981 (martial law in Poland) revealed the basic untenability of the external empire. This translated into the untenability of the internal empire. But before this aspect of the entire empire revealed itself, the area went through a period of ostensible viability.

The concentric circles of empire and Soviet doctrine

One conclusion to draw from the above account is that ideological tenets and slogans played a uniquely important instrumental role as implementation device in the process of sovietization - much in continuation of Charles Reynolds' actor-based approach to imperialism. A closer look into the workings of Soviet doctrine in order to see how the concentric circles of empire came into being and were maintained would seem warranted. As observed by Jan S. Triska and David D. Finley, and also by Zbigniew K. Brzezinski, ideology served multiple functions as both a guide to action (prescriptive function) and a tool for legitimation (descriptive function, 1968, pp. 107-48; 1969, p. 485 ff). This is also the point of departure for Robert A. Jones in his fine study of the Soviet concept of 'limited sovereignty' in a historical perspective (1990) from which the following draws. Soviet Marxism may strike the foreign observer as utterly idiosyncratic, irrational and conservative in its own way, yet it was subject to innumerable revisions and adaptations at the level of programmatic ideology as a result of developments in the surrounding milieu. In the words of Lenin, 'one and the same idea in different, concrete, historical circumstances may be, according to the case, reactionary or progressive' (quoted from Aspaturian, 1960, p. 54).

The analysis above pointed to the early erosion of the Soviet commitment to national self-determination citing Stalin's qualifications of the right to self-determination in the light of the right of the working class to consolidate its power as a precursor to the

Brezhnev doctrine. Already Lenin insisted on 'the higher value of socialism' over national self-determination and Stalin followed suit by warning the borderlands against seceding from Russia on the grounds that it was detrimental to their interests and counter-revolutionary as such regions would fall prey to imperialism (Jones, 1990, p. 41 f.). By 1921, Stalin was able to conclude: 'We have long ago abandoned the nebulous slogans of national self-determination', because the principle had 'become an empty slogan easily adaptable to the use of the imperialist' (Stalin, p. 106). Likewise, Grigori Zinoviev, the head of Comintern, claimed legitimacy for armed revolutionary interventions by declaring that 'state borders were of no greater significance as a defensive barrier than matchwood in a forest fire' (quoted from Jones, 1990, p. 32). Lev Kamenev, another leading Bolshevik, told a Ukrainian party congress that national self-determination was nothing but a weapon of the bourgeois counter-revolution against Russia (*ibid.*, p. 39). In continuation of this, early Soviet doctrines on sovereignty were rejectionist and cynical. In several textbooks on international law, *Evgeni Korovin* – the real founding father of the Brezhnev doctrine of 'limited sovereignty' legitimizing Soviet military interventions in the Soviet empire – reminded his readers that interventions had to be appraised on the basis of the situation and international experience of the Soviet Republic, without hindrance from 'juridicial fetishism' and legal dogmas such as the notion of sovereignty (p. 36). In his view, intervention was just another 'method of class struggle', 'a great instrument of progress, a surgical instrument to ease the birth labours of the new world' which he illustrated by pointing to the support rendered by the Red Army to countries in the Baltic region and the Caucasus in order to establish socialism (p. 37).

The operational significance of these legal doctrines is documented in the subjugation of the non-Russian parts of the old Tsarist empire into a an organically-bound internal empire. The bloody sovietization of the internal empire in the interwar years provides ample evidence of Bolshevik ruthlessness. The Kremlin leaders proved capable of brushing aside any consideration for self-determination not to mention human life and dignity, if this was deemed instrumental in furthering Soviet goals. Stalin argued the inevitability of the amalgamation of the Soviet republics into a single state in terms of economic circumstances, the danger of hostile intervention and the inherently international nature of Soviet power

(Jones, 1990, p. 48). Given a Soviet 'proletarian context', centralization was by definition progressive and so was expansion. The open-ended nature of the territorial make-up of the Soviet Union was further confirmed in the constitutional amendment of 1944 which appeared to turn the Soviet Union into a confederation by opening for republican foreign policies and other features of sovereignty.

In the assessment of Vernon V. Aspaturian, there is every reason to believe that future accessions were seriously contemplated by the closing of the Second World War. Aspaturian cites the remark made by Edvard Kardelj, the Yugoslav foreign minister, to the Soviet ambassador to Belgrade in December 1945: 'Our relations should be based on the prospect of Yugoslavia becoming in the future a constituent part of the USSR' (1960, p. 83). Since Yugoslavia did not share a common frontier with the USSR, this presupposed that at the very least Romania was to become Soviet territory. In his recollections Milovan Djilas reveals that as late as 1948, Soviet leaders were actually toying with the thought of reorganizing the Soviet Union by joining it with the people's democracies – the Ukraine with Hungary and Romania, and Belorussia with Poland and Czechoslovakia, while the Balkan states were to be joined with Russia (1962, p. 137). Moreover, the Soviet conquest of East Prussia (today's Kaliningrad enclave) and Ruthenia after the Second World War took place without any pretense of legality. Against the background of these facts, the real mystery is not why an East European external empire was added to the Soviet Union after 1945 but why Eastern Europe *remained* an external empire in the shape of formally sovereign nation-states. Why was it that Stalin ultimately decided on the format of concentric circles for his empire, i.e. a fully annexed inner core combined with an outer ring of states subject to only indirect rule by the centre? How come that respect for sovereignty was suddenly deemed instrumental? Through what additional doctrinal mechanisms did the Soviets ensure conformity and control in the external empire?

Robert A. Jones gives a twofold answer to the puzzle about the two-layered empire: first, balance-of-power considerations in relation to the West and secondly, perceptions of internal Soviet vulnerability to the option of forming a new unitary state (p. 51 ff.). After 1947, when the Truman doctrine had been declared, Soviet leaders may have anticipated fatal repercussions if the Soviet Union were openly to annex Eastern Europe. By masking the fact that Moscow was pulling the strings, the trappings of statehood of the people's democracies served as a protection against dramatic Western reactions. Citing Isaac Deutscher's Stalin biography, Jones further argues that Stalin may have settled for borders between the USSR and its external empire lest Western ideas infected Soviet citizens, a danger he associated with Czechs, East Germans, Poles and Hungarians (p. 53), cf.:

> Genuine contact between Russia and the people's democracies' – free travel and free exchange of ideas – could easily have become another source of ferment inside Russia. Stalin had therefore to keep in being two iron curtains, one separating Russia from her own zone of influence, the other separating that zone from the west. Public opinion in the west was more preoccupied with the latter, but it was the former that was the more impenetrable of the two. (Deutscher, 1967, p. 564)

Thus the pattern of international relations within the Soviet empire became one of mutual isolation – of totalitarian atomization in Brzezinski's apt terminology. The perceived need to establish a Soviet presence in Germany through the creation of the GDR in 1949 added another motive. The policy of establishing satellite states rather than territorial aggrandizement further provided the USSR with unwavering support for its policy in such important forums as the United Nations, to which Stalin had in vain sought admittance for all fifteen Soviet republics. Jones notices that the strategy bore fruit in that the West recognized the new vassals, unlike Manchukuo (Manchuria 1931-2) where the Stimson doctrine prevented the recognition of the Japanese puppet regime.

In the field of legal doctrine, the Soviets embraced a policy of vigorous support for the idea of sovereignty, claiming that Soviet power embodied genuine sovereignty whereas sovereignty in a bourgeois context was a sham (Jones, p. 88 ff.). Actually, a development towards a conventional legal positivist approach was discernible already in the interwar years when the need for protecting the Soviet Union against outside intervention was acutely felt and priority was given to constructing 'socialism in one country'. The fact that the Soviet Union emerged from the Second World War as one of the victors inspired a further twist to the trend of arguing the legitimacy of Soviet political practices in legal terms, however. A new theory of 'popular sovereignty' was born in 1947 – again with Korovin as midwife. In his view, only Soviet sovereignty is genuine, as the Soviet state had no antagonistic classes and displayed genuine national sovereignty, i.e. sovereignty of both the state and of its constituent nations. Conversely, bourgeois sovereignty was merely a disguise for class supremacy. Korovin's monolithic understanding of sovereignty as being proletarian supremacy represents ideology as a guidance for action in that it legitimized the sovietization of 'sovereign' territories within the Soviet orbit. When patrolling the borders of the external empire the Soviet Union was merely protecting the popular sovereignty of these countries against internal and external enemies. Any threat to communist rule was now by definition a threat to the sovereignty of the people. In the light of this self-serving conception of sovereignty reaffirmed by Korovin in 1956 in the context of the Hungarian insurrection, the later Brezhnev doctrine of 1968 ought to have surprised no one.

As for how the Soviets argued their claim to be first among equals, the already cited remarks by Stalin on the role of the Russian proletariat and Russian urban centres as the political backbone of sovietization are instructive. His perception of a more advanced stage of development of the Russian centre was simply blown up to Soviet proportions, as when Andrei Zhdanov, one of his key lieutenants in sovietizing the external empire, wrote: 'History has placed the USSR at the head of the progressive development of mankind, culture and the civilization of nations' (quoted from Jones, p. 63). In order to argue that the East European societies were, in fact, placed at a lower level of development, the Soviet ideologues went as far as inventing a syndrome of feudalism in Eastern Europe which according to the official doctrine on people's democracies had been introduced by the Nazis (Christensen, 1978, p. 191). The purpose of these absurd manoeuvres was to place the Soviet Union firmly in the role as infallible teacher for its junior allies. Its 'world-historic experience of socialist construction' was cited over and over again as was the ideological leadership of Stalin, 'the teacher and guide of all working people' (Jones, p. 65). In reality, this only repeated the old touchstone slogan of the Comintern according to which the 'touchstone for every good communist is the attitude towards the Soviet Union' – in continuation of the notorious twenty-one conditions of Comintern cited above on page 93 (cf. Jones, p. 66 ff.). The touchstone doctrine implied Soviet guidance in the international as well as the domestic affairs of socialist states as part of Leninist iron discipline. It had the advantage of having been internalized by many leading East European communists during stays in Moscow in the interwar years and the 1940s.

More specifically, Soviet ideologues stressed the decisive role of the Red Army in protecting socialism in the people's democracies (Christensen, 1978, p. 175 and 193). In the words of Nikolai Farberov, 'People in the new democracies understand that only thanks to the Soviet Army were the countries liberated', and 'They are aware that, without the help and support of the Soviet Union, they would not be able to construct socialism' (quoted from Jones, p. 64). To a Western observer this may sound like an open admission of the involuntary nature of the turn towards socialism in the external empire, but the original popularity of the Soviet liberators and subsequent brainwashing ensured that no dangerous conclusions were drawn. In addition to being forced to love their oppressors, East Europeans were instructed to look on them not as the exploiters they really were through their control of 'joint stock companies' etc. but as economic benefactors rendering 'selfless help' and 'fraternal assistance'. The catalyst for such panegyric was the Marshall Plan launched at that time, which in the Soviet perspective promised only enslavement, but nevertheless proved attractive to Eastern Europe.

As pointed out earlier, Stalin's successors abandoned his preference for informal and bilateral devices for control and opted for institutionalization and multilateralism instead. This change in approach did not alter the deeply hierarchical nature of Soviet-East European relations although I tend to agree with Mark Kramer that there was a development from Soviet dominance to hegemony as conceptualized by Hedley Bull (1989/90, p. 63). On this account it is worth remembering that when denouncing Stalin's cult of personality in the secret speech given at the 20th CPSU congress, Khrushchev did not in fact dissociate himself from Stalin's practices in the people's democracies. In the interpretation of Brzezinski, the omission of references to this field of Stalin's policy suggests that Khrushchev wanted to leave himself the opportunity of selecting those aspects of Stalinism he might find useful for managing relations with Eastern Europe (1969, p. 182). Khrushchev preferred to speak of the socialist camp in terms of 'commonwealth' (*sodruzhestvo*) rather than camp - perhaps due to the latter's unfortunate connotations of *Gulag*! - but judging from editorials in the CPSU theoretical journal *Kommunist* and elsewhere, the new commonwealth was headed by the Soviet Union just as much as the old camp of Stalin and Zhdanov had been. According to Brzezinski, it was primarily to legalize the stationing of Soviet troops in Eastern Europe that the Warsaw Pact came into being in 1955 – now that annexing the states of the external empire was out of the question (pp. 173-4). As the single most important formal commitment binding these states to the USSR, the formation of the alliance marked a new step towards turning their sovereignty into fiction. Like the Soviet constitution where provisions for exercising the much acclaimed right to secession were curiously absent, the Warsaw Pact lacked formal procedures for withdrawal or the withdrawal of Soviet forces. When signing bilateral treaties with the USSR and one another as well as the multilateral Pact, the junior allies had no real choice. For this reason, the Soviet alliance qualifies as an 'Al Capone alliance' to cite the theoretical literature on the subject (Handel, 1981, pp 127-28).

The exploitative practices of Stalin in his East European empire were replaced by real credits and subsidies, but this was accompanied by calls for centralization under the slogan of 'coordination of national economic plans within the CMEA'. Here Soviet analysts were careful to cite 'the utter importance of the Soviet economic experience', because the USSR was 'the motherland of planned economy' (Alekseev, Vikent'ev and Miroshnichenko, 1975, p. 12). Following in the footsteps of Khrushchev in his attempt to create a 'socialist division of labour', Brezhnev and his team also drew on the concept of integration to strengthen cohesion within the socialist commonwealth. As always, Soviet theoretical contributions claimed the socialist variety of the phenomenon to be the only genuine one, citing 'the harmonious joining of international and national interests' as the distinguishing feature of socialist economic integration. In this way the world socialist system (as the now truly international socialist edifice was called) had become immune to nationalism and 'national nihilism' (*ibid.*, p. 204). The doctrine of socialist internationalism – i.e. the old Comintern notion of proletarian internationalism as applied to the postwar world socialist system – turned 'the defence of the socialist achievements' into 'a sacred duty for each fraternal country and party' (Sanakoev and Kapchenko, 1977, p. 72). In the words of these two gentlemen,

In the era of the socialist commonwealth, patriotism expresses itself in the loyalty towards one's own country as well as towards the entire commonwealth (...) socialist patriotism and socialist internationalism are organically bound and presupposes the solidarity with the working class and the toilers in all countries. (p. 82).

Indeed, the crushing of the Prague spring in 1968 showed that 'extending brotherly help' meant sending one's troops into neighbouring countries for the sake of 'protecting their sovereignty'.

A new theoretical construct reaffirming the universal validity of the Soviet model towards the junior allies came into being at the 24th CPSU congress, namely Brezhnev's concept of 'developed socialism' once again arguing the case of the higher stage of development of the Soviet Union (Jones, p. 168). Developed socialism referred to the level of development immediately preceding communism, the Marxist version of the end of history. The USSR was said to have reached this stage already in the 1960s, whereas the 'fraternal states' were only to be credited with aiming for 'developed socialism' as a future target, or with having just entered it. Just as inside the Soviet Union, where the process of the ever more successful building of socialism and communism was said to imply a strengthening of 'the leading role of the party', so the era of developed socialism within the socialist commonwealth called for ever stronger party-to-party relations, as highlighted by the CPSU Central Committee on the occasion of the 25th CPSU congress in 1976:

> Naturally, the very basis of our close cooperation, its living soul and guiding organizational force remains the unshakeable combat unity of *communist parties of the socialist countries* (quoted from Sanakoev and Kapchenko, p. 68; italics in the original).

The point in this brief exposé of the doctrines of subordination within the external empire is that the approach of the Soviet centre was strikingly similar to that displayed within the internal empire. This is demonstrated in the use of the term *sblizhenie* (drawing together) for integration both within the Soviet Union and within the CMEA (cf. Jones, pp. 169-70). Notwithstanding the coming into being of the presumably unitary ethnic category of 'the Soviet people' in the 1930s, the Soviet doctrine on national relations continued in the vein of (merely) *sblizhenie*. The latter was said to precede the so-called 'blossoming' of nationalities (*rasstvet*), a slogan instrumental in upholding the illusion of national self-determination;

nevertheless the Soviets were careful to place this centrifugal trend of *rasstvet* within the allegedly dominant – and centripetal! – trend of *sblizhenie* (G. Simon, 1986, pp. 359-60). As for the assimilationist connotations of *sblizhenie*, compare the following 1980 Soviet academic contribution from the science of history:

> The governing law of the development of the Soviet people is the progressive consolidation of its unity on the basis of social equality in society and the movement of all nations and nationalities in the direction of absolute unity. (Kulichenko, quoted by G. Simon, p. 360)

In continuation of this, the aforementioned Soviet work on socialist economic integration devotes a long chapter to an empirical description of 'the development of the Soviet union republics in the direction of a unitary economic complex' implying its relevance for Soviet-East European relations. The authors further cite the guidelines ('*postanovlenia*') of the 25th anniversary of the CMEA, according to which

> The fraternal cooperation between the CMEA member countries is a powerful contribution to the realization of the policy of the communist and worker's parties aiming at their drawing together [*sblizhenie*] and close interaction in the building of socialism and communism. (Alekseev *et al.*, 1975, p. 9)

Within the internal empire, the challenge was one of crushing armed and unarmed resistance without causing an international outcry. The Stalin constitution of 1936 and other legal niceties helped – as one can see from the naïve contemporary analysis of Sidney and Beatrice Webb (1937). Within the external empire, the challenge was one of compensating for the lack of a Russian core capable of acting as a key centripetal force through subtler institutional devices. Here, the Comintern smokescreen of internationalism proved a long-term asset. As will be shown below, the post-Stalin era was one of a less traumatic and more organic relationship between centre and periphery, but not enough to make the Soviet empire last forever.

The return to 'normalcy' – and imperial decay

The preceding analysis has focused almost exclusively on the logic of power. This is a *sine qua non* when analysing relations within the Soviet empire. However, the logic of power may be subtle. One of the most interesting theses advanced in the comparative study of imperialism is that empires tend to develop into systems of bargaining – unequal bargaining, to be sure, but bargaining nevertheless (Gallagher and Robinson, 1953; Mommsen and Osterhammel, 1986, *passim*). As already suggested in the empirical analysis, this logic manifests itself in the case of Soviet imperialism. In terms of social interaction, imperialism constitutes a system of collaboration, in this instance between Russian and non-Russian communists. The crux of the matter is that there is always a price to be paid to the collaborators, something that tends to enhance their room for manoeuvre. The ups and downs in the political history of the Soviet internal and external empires thus reflect the changes in relative power and bargaining positions between centre and periphery, between the rulers and ruled.

The classic sovietological formula for the bargaining logic as far as Soviet-East European relations are concerned is James F. Brown's (1975) thesis of a dilemma between bloc cohesion and viability, concepts which easily apply to centre-periphery relations within the internal empire. There was always a trade-off between the Soviet pursuit of cohesion and viability. The fact of involuntary sovietization meant that laxity (emphasis on viability) could inspire defection, but cohesion, on the other hand, could provoke crisis and Western reaction. The logic of viability thus explains the room for manoeuvre ultimately gained by Poland under Gomulka and later by virtue of the country's strategically important position. Accordingly, the Soviet centre was placed in a permanent dilemma of systemic adaptation. As far as the internal empire is concerned, probably the most famous statement of the new pluralist, participatory bargaining logic is found in Jerry Hough's rejoinder to Merle Fainsod's totalitarian analysis *How Russia is Ruled* (1963) for which Hough deliberately chose an unexotic title: '*How the Soviet Union is Governed*' (Fainsod 1963). It was Hough who pioneered the perception of a 'return to normalcy'.

However, when it comes to capturing the rise of Soviet ethnopolitics, it is better to refer to Philip G. Roeder (1991), who stresses the role of ethnic cadres as political entrepreneurs. Soviet federal institutions and the indigenous communist cadres at their helm became instruments of ethnic assertiveness, thus dramatically changing the balance of power between centre and periphery. Brezhnev's strategy of accepting the 'mafiaization' of local élites – e.g. in the case of Sharaf Rashidov of Uzbekistan and Heidar Aliev of Azerbaijan – on condition of their loyalty towards the party and him personally only reinforces this interpretation (Remnick, 1992; Carlisle, 1991). There was a revival of medieval Russian *kormlenie* – literally 'feeding'; that is, rent-seeking. Because of the lack of democratic accountability, regional party-bosses turned their constituencies into fiefdoms for personal enrichment; a phenomenon found in Yugoslavia as well. In addition to the scandals associated with Brezhnev and his cronies, more mundane developments were also discernible at the level of federal economic management. Issues of levelling and allocating investment became increasingly complex, with instances of regional lobbying and inter-republican coalition-building – trends familiar from the CMEA (Bahry, 1987).

Central Asians lobbied against Siberian élites over the controversial Sib-Aral river diversion project, aiming at the irrigation of Central Asian wastelands by turning the flow of Siberian rivers southwards, whereas Hungarians faced not just Soviet but stiff East European resistance on issues of reform of the CMEA. National communism was flowering, as was ahistoric sovietology. William M. Reisinger (1990) went as far as characterizing Soviet-East European relations as an international regime implying role patterns similar to the Euro-American relationship. In connection with this overall 'normalization', Eastern Europe and the Western republics of the USSR began to manifest themselves as the genuine sources of modernization they were, compared to Russia (Szporluk, 1976). Eastern Europe in particular became a source of political innovation, whereas the role of the Baltic states was limited to cultural innovation following the clamp-down on the Latvian thaw in 1959.

In purely political terms, Brezhnev's strategy of muddling through appeared to be a masterpiece of systemic adaptation by way of élite co-optation in order to broaden political participation. A certain kind of corporatism also developed at the level of Soviet-East European relations. However, like all other strategies of muddling through, Brezhnev's coalition-building did little to improve systemic performance. By failing to address basic systemic deficiencies, such as the permanent crisis in Soviet agriculture and the general neglect of consumers' needs, bringing about a general degradation of health and occasional disasters, his policy contributed actively to imperial decay and subsequent collapse. Khrushchev was much bolder, as witnessed by his *sovnarkhozy* (regional economic councils) intended to decentralize economic decision-making and alter ethno-territorial allegiances. The *sovnarkhoz* principle paralleled the old Tsarist *gubernia*, which several Russian analysts today hold would have served the Soviet Union well, perhaps preventing its ultimate collapse. While continuing into imperial overstretch through expansion in the Third World, Khrushchev was the first to address the absolutely terrible housing conditions within the Soviet Union. He also tried to cut back the army's size.

Brezhnevite corporatism, by contrast, was little more than praetorian log-rolling, imperial parochialism and passing of the buck for the sole benefit of the military-industrial complex (Snyder, 1991). Brezhnev's approach to post-Stalinist adaptation prepared the way for the terminal crisis by irreversibly making the Soviet system a victim of its imperial drive. Further expansion in the Third World followed – at a time when the Soviet Union had become the world's largest importer of food. A true predicament of economic stagnation, a growing burden of empire and the soaring costs of maintaining superpower status were looming (Ericson, 1987; Bunce, 1985). The mortal sin committed by the Soviet empire, like others before it, was the obsession with security and military performance leading to a fatal neglect of issues of civil economic performance, something that ultimately undermined even its military-technological performance (Kennedy, 1988).

Convincing as they may sound, these remarks are not enough to account fully for the nature of the crisis underlying the post-Stalinist 'return to normalcy'. In order to illuminate the compelling challenge of systemic adaptation by way of system change, a brief excursus into the concept of modernization is necessary (Morse, 1976). To quote an old aphorism, sovietization amounted to Ivan the Terrible plus electrification. With the exception of countries like Czechoslovakia that were already advanced, the transformation of territories contiguous with the Soviet Union generally marked an upsurge in modernization, although this was most evidently so in the case of the non-European cultures. In its own incredibly brutal and economically misguided way, sovietization brought progress in terms of industrialization, urbanization, secularization and role differentiation – as argued by Alexander Dallin (1981). Soviet Marxist considerations of security and power were accompanied by developmental ambitions, of which the single most important was the commitment to universal education (Eisenstadt, 1992; Pye, 1990). This led to concrete achievements, but also to rising demands, thus setting the stage for the increasing need for reform that paved the way for the collapse of empire.

The outcome of the decades of Soviet imperial rule was some fairly complex societies defying crude manipulation from above – societies which developed their own kind of centrist middle-class orientations and consumerist values, bringing about a new challenge to the regime's legitimacy (Pye, 1992; Hough, 1989/90; Brown, 1991). To take one instance, the Soviet authorities unintentionally bolstered ethnicity – and, by extension, nationalist demands – by registering ethnic affiliation in the passports of Soviet citizens. European self-identification and modern television ensured that neither East Germans nor Hungarians, Czechs or Balts would compare their standards of living with Third World countries under corrupt right-wing regimes, as the Russian centre would have preferred, but with West Germany, Austria and Finland. It is against this background that socialism as a societal order and authoritarian regime-type encountered a sharp dilemma between systemic continuity and pressures for change (Senghaas, 1981).

What makes this a compelling challenge is the logic of development and social change suggested by the term modernization. Admittedly, the theoretical reasoning of modernization boils down to something rather tautological: change brings about further change by bringing about demands for change. Empirical processes of change are never as linear as suggested by this wording. The approach of modernization itself is not entirely neutral, but refers to one of the two rival paradigms within sovietology; the other being the realist approach of totalitarianism represented by Zbigniew K. Brzezinski, Martin Malia and Richard Pipes (cf. Friedrich and Brzezinski, 1965; Malia, 1990; 1992). The latter approach stresses the logic of power in a totalitarian conception of the Soviet political system and its East European offspring. Proponents of the totalitarian theory emphasize the *sui generis* monolithic nature of this system – 'the USSR Incorporated' to use Alfred G. Meyer's term (1961, cf. chapter 1, note 3). Totalitarianism proved right in arguing the anachronistic nature of the Soviet societal model. In response to Hough's thesis of a return to normalcy, totalitarianists point to the stifling of society and the fundamental lack of legitimacy. In terms of critical potential – due to its commitment to historical analysis – totalitarianism was surely second to none, as William E. Odom argues (1992).

On the other hand, totalitarianism fails to account for how the Soviet system could generate the claimed massive pressure for change from below, not to mention the rise of Gorbachev as an inside political entrepreneur who came to challenge the basic tenets of the system. Totalitarianism ignores the dimension of bargaining among *nomenklatura* élites. This is what made ethnic mobilization and national communism so powerful a weapon serving to add a new logic of bargaining between élites and their subjects (Roeder, 1991; Eisenstadt, 1992; Djilas, 1957, pp. 100-2). Totalitarianism ignores the changing balance of power between 'Reds' and 'experts' at all levels of decision-making, because of increasing complexity. In short, totalitarianism fares poorly in explaining the development away from totalitarianism towards semi–pluralist authoritarianism, a development that fundamentally changed the balance of power between the rulers and the ruled. The critics of the totalitarian approach, on their side, missed a chance to go on the offensive in their preference for revisionist ahistoric sovietology that is of too little overall relevance.[16]

As for what actually happened to the Soviet empire in its apparent heyday of viability, the key observation concerns the inherent vulnerability of authoritarian systems – be they totalitarian or authoritarian in a praetorian–oligarchic sense – because of their lack of mechanisms to correct their own mistakes. As early as 1981 – at the height of Brezhnev's 'developed socialism' – the German left-wing political scientist Dieter Senghaas was honest enough to spell out the propensity towards suicidal miscalculation of socialist authoritarian systems:

> Wherever power is monopolized, there is an imminent risk of self-isolation of leadership groups from their own societies. Precisely in a society without private ownership, the resulting social

---

[16] To quote William E. Odom, where these critics 'capture the central realities of the system, they overlap with totalitarianism, and where they emphasize other things, they neglect central realities. ...they tended to be ambiguous about the points of reference for measuring change. That ambiguity made it easier to mistake the direction of change as evolution toward a liberal system than to recognize that the old system had to collapse. ... Political decay of the old system was mistaken for political development (1992, pp. 73, 97 ff.).

distance has considerable negative consequences with respect to the effectiveness of self-steering mechanisms. Such self-isolation results in the weakening of reality-testing as shown by...socialist societies. Without participation, publicly relevant information atrophies...and motivations wither. In consequence, the basis for a down-to-earth assessment of reality by leadership groups shrinks and their chance of controlling political, economical and social processes rationally is impaired. The more they lay claim to infallibility, the more their loss of reality is translated into pathological learning. How uncertain such groups are...is revealed by the expansion of the internal security machinery and the militarization of society. (1981, p. 299)

Against the claim in much of the literature that Stalin was deeply cautious in his foreign and security policy, it is worth repeating that his folly brought him within a hair's breadth of defeat during the Second World War. Had it not been for Hitler's racial ideology, the terror and the purges unleashed upon Soviet society, including the purges of the Soviet officers' corps in the late 1930s, might have cost him dearly. Human losses and sufferings during the war were incredible – and often unnecessary. By insisting on *partiinost* – a recipe for misperception – the post-Stalinist return to 'normalcy' did nothing to correct the course, but merely altered the political logic from that of the idiosyncracies of a unitary actor to those of collective actors, that is oligarchic élites.

The collapse of the Soviet empire

When did the Soviet empire reach the point of no return in terms of missing an opportunity to check the slide towards imperial collapse? The answer from diehard totalitarianists is 'Right from the beginning'. There is no need to romanticize the character of Lenin, yet as stated earlier it would be too simplistic to say that Stalinism was pre-programmed into history. Stalinism, in turn, qualifies as the major culprit because of its crippling of society and its economy. Post-Stalinist muddling through, however, represents a decisive blunder. A combination of Khrushchev's boldness and Brezhnev's coalition-building added to the sophistication of the Gorbachev team applied at an early stage might have produced a more graceful decay. This is not to deny the surprisingly *peaceful* nature of the epochal change that followed – certainly no mean feat.

The American Sovietologist Charles Gati speculates that a shift towards Finlandization in exchange for Soviet hegemony would have been gladly accepted by the peoples of Eastern Europe if implemented before 1989 (1990, p. 192 ff.). What happened was the reverse. The 1968 invasion of Czechoslovakia conclusively ended the era of viability in Soviet-East European relations, to quote one perceptive author (Rakowska-Harmstone, 1984, p. 364). For this reason it became a point of no return in a slide towards the final collapse, as also argued by James F. Brown in his brilliant analysis of the *annus mirabilis* of 1989 (1991, pp. 23-5). Socialism was not allowed to gain a human face to bolster its legitimacy, but was forced into petrifying 'normalization'. In crisis-ridden Poland, martial law replaced the Gdansk compromise of September 1980 sanctioning power-sharing between the Polish Communist Party and Solidarity. The Brezhnev doctrine was extended to Afghanistan.

Soviet 'normalization' restored control and forced dissidents into anti-politics, but the Czechoslovak and Polish events did not go unnoticed in the Baltic republics (Vardys, 1983). 'Spill-over' – horizontally as well as vertically – represents perhaps the single most important analytical clue to understanding the dynamics of the collapse of the Soviet empire (cf. Deudney and Ikenberry, 1991, p. 250). The Baltic peoples for their part represented the weak link in the Soviet imperial edifice because of their Western identity and recent highly traumatic sovietization. The reason was their vivid memories of previous independence and injustice combined with, on the one hand, ongoing Russification measures and Lithuanian monitoring of the Polish experience; and, on the other, the lack of co-optation of Estonian and Latvian élites except for a few Russified natives. Baltic party and government authorities did not act as co-participants in decision-making, but only as lobbyists, which made the Balts inclined to conclude that they would be better off as fully independent (Szporluk, 1976; 1992).

At the level of the Soviet centre, the early 1980s were marked by increasing immobilism and diversion through foreign policy ('the second Cold War'). Gorbachev was the first Soviet leader to realize how deeply irrational the confrontation with the benign democratic West was – not least when compared to Stalin's startling naivety *vis-à-vis* Hitler. He activated the forces for change that had built up over the years in the external as well as the internal empire. The rising costs of empire and the many missed opportunities made an impatient Gorbachev attack on all fronts – vain calls for *uskorenie* (accelerated economic growth) were replaced by demands for full-scale reform (*perestroika*), accompanied by a frontal assault on *partiinost* in the shape of *glasnost,* the insights of which compelled a switch to political reform (*demokratizatsia*).

Alexander Motyl chooses to ignore the economic predicament facing the Soviet empire, but is still right in arguing – along with Ted Robert Gurr and Alexis de Tocqueville – that it was Gorbachev himself who created a revolutionary syndrome of relative deprivation by encouraging mass political participation and not being able to fulfil rising expectations (Motyl, 1990, pp. 187 ff.). At the end of the day, however, it may be the totalitarian thesis of immobilism as the cause of the Soviet demise that, curiously enough, has the final word – if Philip G. Roeder's (1993) analysis of the Red sunset is to be believed. The lesson he draws concerns the limits of political entrepreneurism – in the context of totalitarian ideologies, we may add. The leaders at the helm of the CPSU proved capable of engendering change throughout society, but the party itself could not adapt to changes. Instead, it overturned the reforms, making defection and disintegration the only possible outcome.

What is missing from the analysis so far is Gorbachev's own fatal blunder – his blind spot when it came to facing the depth of the challenge of nationalism. A few words on the hotly disputed phenomenon of nationalism seem warranted here. There are two main schools of thought, primordialism versus the mobilizationist approach, of which the latter sees ethnicity and nationalism not as *sui generis* but as one among several media for political struggle; the alternatives being class, gender, age or the like (McKay, 1982). Anthony D. Smith (1992) belongs to the primordialists insofar as he criticizes the reductionism of the latter view, including postmodernism when viewing nations and ethnic groups merely as intellectual 'constructs'. Primordialists may be right in positing nationalism as *sui generis* in that only nationalist ideologies can transform ethnicity into a distinct political force. On the other hand, nationalism – the political belief in the nation-state – is no more pre-programmed into history than are so many other phenomena, but depends on contemporary circumstances as maintained by Alexander Motyl and Ronald Grigor Suny. We need not accept the primordial Sleeping Beauty theory adopted by Zbigniew K. Brzezinski (1989/90), who depicts postcommunist nationalism as 'the long-dormant issue' waiting to be awakened (1989/90; cf. Emerson, 1960, p. 91).

As for the challenge of nationalism in the Soviet empire, this was the conjunctural outcome of primarily Soviet measures of modernization, including *korenizatsia*, post-Stalinist ethnopolitics – partly excluding the Balts – and lastly, Gorbachev's policy of *glasnost* unaccompanied by tangible reform of the centre-periphery relationship. Gorbachev's vision of economic decentralization was actually less radical than Khrushchev's (Tedstrom, 1989). At the same time he was able to ensure a new upsurge of viability towards the external East European empire, if partly by accepting *faits accomplis* (Skak, 1992a; Kramer, 1989/90; Brown, 1991).[17] Thus Gorbachev paved the way for spill-over from the external to the internal empire via the Baltic republics. Admittedly, a whole-hearted search for accommodation with the Baltic peoples might not have produced a different outcome, yet the gross insensitivity to their initial demands, which included regional economic autonomy for the benefit of *perestroika*, was striking. Other nationalities came out in support of the Baltic popular fronts, as the nationalist organizations called themselves.

Perceptions of relative deprivation were fuelled by the *glasnost* on environmental disasters – Chernobyl, the nuclear test-site of Semipalatinsk and the disappearance of the Aral Sea in Central Asia – as well as Moscow's inability to manage armed conflicts such as that in Nagorno-Karabakh. Nationalistic popular fronts modelled on the Baltic predecessors mushroomed, issuing Baltic-inspired declarations of sovereignty. In the face of this mounting challenge the CPSU grew deaf and dumb. The much-delayed Central Committee plenum aiming to redefine centre-periphery relations called for a 'strong centre to be matched by strong republics', without bothering to specify the alleged improvements in the latter's decision-making authority (*Pravda*, 17 August 1989). Instead, the CPSU leadership

---

[17] As I have argued elsewhere, Gorbachev did intervene actively in support of East European democratization during the autumn of the *annus mirabilis*, for instance by making a critical phone call to Mieczyslaw Rakowski, the Polish party leader, urging him to accept a Polish government with a communist minority, a point also made by Charles Gati (1990, pp. 168 and 187; Skak, 1992a). On the other hand, James F. Brown is right to insist that Gorbachev wanted legitimacy for socialism, not bourgeois democracy, and to argue that Gorbachev improvised rather than planned (1991, pp. 54 ff.).

issued a flat condemnation of Baltic 'extremists' who dared to organize non-violent protests commemorating the Molotov-Ribbentrop treaty. The point of no return had surely been reached. In the course of the autumn of 1989 the dominoes of the external empire fell, fuelling the subsequent fall of those of the internal empire.

An interesting discussion concerns whether the decisive nationalism was peripheral nationalism or centre nationalism, that is Russian nationalism. Baltic nationalism may have been the decisive catalyst, but Alexander Motyl (1988) perceives Ukrainian nationalism as the truly decisive non-Russian rebellion because of the Ukrainians' role as *secundus inter pares* and their country's geopolitical weight. Still others have argued Moscow's Muslim challenge – less convincingly, though. Given the role of Russia and the Russian people as *de facto* centre of the Soviet empire, a defection by Russia would be central to any domino theory. There is empirical evidence that Russian nationalism underwent a change towards conventional nation-state nationalism – RSFSR nationalism as it were – resulting in an attitude of *laissez-faire* concerning imperial subjects (Lapidus *et at.*, 1992; Szporluk, 1989). One opinion poll on attitudes towards the union showed that 65 per cent identified the union with shortages, queues and poverty, while only 3 per cent said it gave them a sense of pride in their socialist fatherland (*RFE/RL Daily Report* [49], March 11 1991). The result of the referendum on the preservation of the union was even more striking. Whereas over 90 per cent of Central Asian voters were for the preservation of the USSR, only 53.3 per cent of Russians shared this opinion – in defiance of a massive media campaign preceding the referendum (Sheehy, 1991). Gorbachev's lack of popularity probably played a key role here.[18]

Another factor behind this change in the Russian political mind appears to have been Aleksandr Solzhenitsyn's famous brochure 'How Are We to Reconstruct Russia?' (1990). Here he proposed to let go of the Baltic and all other republics – because of the imperial burden they placed upon Russia's shoulders – except for Ukraine, Belarus and northern Kazakhstan, which were to form a pan-Russian

---

[18] According to the Russian political analyst Aleksandr Tsipko, the Russians 'were guided by a desire to punish Gorbachev and the hated Communist centre...and to support Yeltsin in every way. Beyond that they couldn't care less what happened' (*Izvestia*, 1 October 1991). Tsipko is horrified by this 'diminished responsibility' on the part of rank-and-file Russians.

Union together with Russia. As stated in note 5, what matters is not the reality of unequal exchange and exploitation but perceptions thereof. Russians saw the periphery as exploiting them just as much as they were perceived as exploiters by the periphery (Pipes, 1991). Later during 1991, in the turmoil following the collapse of the August coup intended to restore the union, no less a person than Aleksandr Rutskoi was to be found arguing vehemently against any union making Russia 'a milch-cow' for others. The role of Rutskoi, Yeltsin and other 'Young Turks' of Russia at the top echelon of power, however, suggests another possibility (Rahr, 1991). The change in their attitude on the union was only a temporary trend, as it was instrumental in their private political struggle against the then Soviet President Gorbachev. This interpretation of the change in Russian nationalism at the élite level towards nation-state nationalism helps to explain the hasty coup-like dismantling of the Soviet Union in late 1991 and the equally hasty restoration of the imperial instinct among the politicians once Yeltsin and his allies were on their own at the helm of independent Russia. The August coup ushered in the final collapse of Soviet state structures – in a way this is where we stand to this very day. Lack of consolidation is what characterizes the CIS states, not least postcommunist Russia itself.

This chronological and conceptual exposé is intended to suggest the complexity of explaining the fall of the Soviet empire. It is in no way exhaustive, but suggests the present author's own position. It may be useful to summarize the more prominent approaches and theories found in the literature on the fall of the Soviet empire and comment briefly on those that have not been presented above (see figure 3.3). As the reader may have noticed I have tried to link myself to nearly all of the explanations mentioned here, not just totalitarianism. From the point of view of analytical clarity this sounds like a very frustrating outcome – a case of overdetermination, not to say explanatory overkill. Where is the mega-variable in all this? The response to this challenge is to quote from Daniel Deudney and G. John Ikenberry's now classic contribution:

> No one theory can explain the causes...of these contemporary events ... no one key fits all the locks...this inadequacy stems from the irreducible nature of the historical phenomena. Paradoxically, the shortfall of each of the theories reveals a theoretical insight, namely that these events are conjunctural: the outcome of multiple distinct processes. In the Soviet case, such large-scale logics as the

expansion of capitalism, the maturing of industrialism, the intensification of global human interaction are all evident. (1991, p. 250)

As can be concluded from these lines, the mega-variables may be something as fuzzy as 'change', 'modernization' and 'spill-over' – normally evolutionary dynamics, but revolutionary in a totalitarian context. The fact that immobilism was the only source of legitimacy of totalitarianism put it in a Catch-22 dilemma of adaptation. On this account it is tempting to borrow a metaphor from chaos theory: it only took a butterfly – Gorbachev, Mathias Rust (the dare-devil German pilot who landed a tiny Cessna plane in Red Square in 1987), Chernobyl or even Khrushchev – to set in motion the slide towards collapse (cf. Rosenau, 1990).

In retrospect, sovietization and communist totalitarianism proved the longest, most horrible and troublesome road from capitalism to capitalism, to paraphrase a standard joke from Poland. Postcommunism has succeeded in dismantling the centrally planned economy and most of the corresponding political structures, but has not finished the daunting task of constructing new, viable societies. In places like Ukraine this process has barely begun – the problem

Fig. 3.3. APPROACHES TO THE FALL OF THE SOVIET EMPIRE

Totalitarianism: Martin Malia, Zbigniew K. Brzezinski, William E. Odom; Mette Skak (point of departure for the present work)

Modernization: Daniel Deudney and G. John Ikenberry, Jerry Hough, Lucian W. Pye, George Segal *et al.*, Dieter Senghaas, Mette Skak (*ibid.*, as additional position)

Top-down approaches (the Gorbachev phenomenon; learning; etc.): Alexander Motyl, 1990; Jack Snyder, Jeff Checkel, Philip G. Roeder, 1993

Bottom-up approaches (mobilization of civil society, ethnicity): Geoffrey Hosking, Zbigniew K. Brzezinski, 1989; James F. Brown, 1991

Peripheral nationalism decisive: Martha Brill Olcott, Ronald Grigor Suny, Philip G. Roeder, 1991; Alexander Motyl, 1988; Zbigniew K. Brzezinski, 1989/90

Russian nationalism decisive: Gail W. Lapidus *et al.*, Roman Szporluk, 1989; Richard E. Pipes 1991

Imperial overstretch – the overcommitment of scarce resources through military and imperial expansion: Paul Kennedy, Valerie Bunce, Jack Snyder, Charles Wolf Jr., Richard E. Ericson, 1987

Economic crisis: Richard E. Ericson, John O'Loughlin, 1993 (argues that the drop in oil revenues was decisive); Daniel Deudney and G. John Ikenberry, Dieter Senghaas.

of anarchy is not limited to postcommunist international relations. In these circumstances it is difficult to strike the proper balance between optimism and pessimism. The logic and instinct of power argue in favour of some kind of authoritarian and imperial restoration, whereas the logic of modernization argues in favour of reintegration on the basis of Western notions of democracy and market economy. Russia has a particular option of hegemony, building on the country's size, energy resources and political culture of empire, along with domestic potentials for non-democratic outcomes and conflict. But there is another powerful logic of modernization, due to the spread of education and information conducive to middle-class aspirations of upward mobility. Most important, perhaps, is the yearning for societal stability in the population at large, and an abhorrence of extremism and war. The peaceful decolonization of the Soviet empire was and remains an accomplishment and a world historic watershed – particularly in view of the bloody decolonization at the Yugoslav fringe of empire.

4

THE FOREIGN POLICY OF
POSTCOMMUNIST RUSSIA

Postcommunist Russia is a new state in more than one sense. It resembles Tsarist Russia up to 1654, when Muscovy gained control over Ukraine, but today's Russia is bigger than that. Russia has never existed within its present borders, which are administrative RSFSR borders turned international. What distinguishes Russia from other post-communist states is the legacy of being the centre of an empire as a vastly complicating factor in Russian nation-building. The Russian state shares with other postcommunist states the problems of transition from communism and empire, such as building a market economy from scratch; dismantling the party and its power structures; nation-building in exchange for Soviet imperial internationalism; breaking the psychological syndrome of totalitarianism; providing security in an environment of new postcommunist states which lack foreign policy experience even more than Russia and, finally, adopting a policy of participation and reintegration in exchange for international isolation. This is the daunting agenda left over from the preceding seventy-four years of terror, mismanagement and decay. The only true achievement of the Soviet regime was to add general education and nuclear weapons to the country's semi-developed status.

Russia's own specific geographical, historical and cultural features only add to this challenge (see map of Russia). Despite the fact that it is 24 per cent smaller than the Soviet Union, Russia remains a continent rather than a country. The Russian Federation covers an area of over 17 million square kilometres, almost double the size of Canada, the second largest country in the world. Russia stretches from Norway in the far north-west to the Black Sea in the south-west, to China, Mongolia and North Korea in the Far East and finally serves as Alaska's and hence the United States' closest neighbour to the west. This geopolitical reach translates into innumerable cultural

137

interfaces – interfaces mirrored inside Russia in an equally breath-taking multinational cultural make-up. The country has 101 identifiable ethnic groups, a total population of some 30 million non-Russians and roughly 122 million Russians. The Russian Federation is composed of 21 republics, 52 *oblasts* (provinces) and 6 *krays* (territories), amounting to 89 territorial units, of which some lay claim to sovereignty. The threat of disintegration may have passed its peak following the compromise deal struck with Tatarstan in February 1994 – notwithstanding the inevitable long term consequences of the invasion of Chechnia in late 1994.[1] The current balance of power may be described as a weak centre surrounded by a weak periphery in terms of economic and international options. The republics inside Russia enter into international treaties and conduct their own foreign economic relations, but this does not render the Moscow level of analysis irrelevant as a key locus for Russian foreign policy-making. Russia's President Yeltsin has always defined foreign policy as his prerogative, a principle that has been fixed in the new constitution (Article 86). This is not to say that his and his Foreign Minister's course has not met with challenges and problems of implementation.

The sheer vastness of Russia's economy, combined with the depth of its crisis, explains why no Marshall Plan is forthcoming. In addition to humanitarian aid, Russia has been offered some technical assistance to bolster its own efforts, as well as macroeconomic stabilization facilities provided by the IMF (e.g. in March 1994). Russia depends on the Western world for this kind of economic relief (including debts) and conducts half of its foreign trade with the West – which is also the origin of most foreign direct investment. One source estimates a *per capita* GNP of $3,200 as of 1991; a very crude indicator of Russia's economic standing, to be sure, as income disparities are skyrocketing and inflation continues (*RFE/RL Research Report*, 7 January 1994, p. 25). As much as half of the

---

[1] Curiously, most analysts overlook the thorny problem of Kaliningrad – formerly Königsberg – when discussing potential secessionist conflicts in Russia. The geographical isolation felt in this area because of Moscow's general neglect, combined with envy towards neighbouring Poland and Lithuania over the economic assistance they receive, could translate into open secessionism. Kaliningrad is a sensitive issue not just in Moscow and Vilnius, but also in Warsaw and – by extension – in Bonn and the Scandinavian capitals (Hoff and Timmermann, 1993; *Moscow News*, no. 3, January 1994).

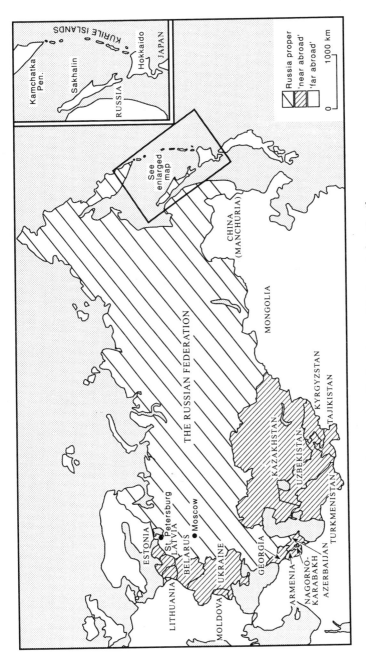

The Russian Federation, with (inset) the Kuriles

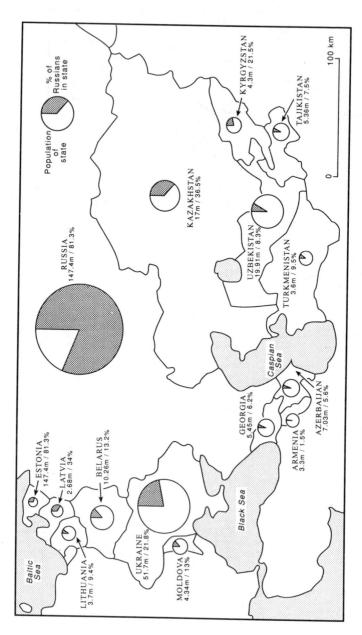

The Russian diaspora in neighbouring countries

Map labels:

% of Russians in state

Population of state

RUSSIA 147.4m / 81.3%

KAZAKHSTAN 17m / 36.5%

KYRGYZSTAN 4.3m / 21.5%

TAJIKISTAN 5.36m / 7.5%

UZBEKISTAN 19.91m / 8.3%

TURKMENISTAN 3.6m / 9.5%

GEORGIA 5.45m / 6.2%

AZERBAIJAN 7.03m / 5.6%

ARMENIA 3.3m / 1.5%

ESTONIA 147.4m / 81.3%

LATVIA 2.68m / 34%

BELARUS 10.26m / 13.2%

LITHUANIA 3.7m / 9.4%

UKRAINE 51.7m / 21.8%

MOLDOVA 4.34m / 13%

Baltic Sea

Black Sea

Caspian Sea

100 km

0

population is believed to live below the poverty level and production has been subject to a 50 per cent drop since 1991 (in the state sector). Despite progress within the fledgling private sector, the economy is in a state of paralysis, as are consumers. Mafia gangs are mushrooming because of weak or absent law enforcement and general administrative confusion. In the light of these liabilities it is of little comfort to know that Russia has more than half the world's oil and natural gas as well as large quantities of gold and many other minerals. On the other hand, Russia fares better than its CIS neighbours in terms of the resources it can mobilize and the reforms it has undertaken. As already indicated (see p. 49), Russia has a hegemonic option because of its postcommunist neighbours' economic dependence on the country, notably in the field of energy.

Despite disarmament, Russia remains Europe's and Asia's largest conventional military power and an undisputed military superpower with 1,204 ICBMs and supplementary nuclear arsenals. But the 2.1 million-strong armed forces exist on paper only as morale is exceedingly low – those drafted do not show up. Theft and corruption are widespread, as are suicides, murders and rapes. Housing problems among officers withdrawn from the external empire and the Baltic states easily breeds political extremism. Conversion of the Soviet war economy has proven difficult, partly due to the formidable problems of unemployment that threaten to follow in its footsteps. Russia is now trying to turn military production into an export asset, as reflected in the $2 billion gained from arms sales in 1993 (*NeGa*, 25 December 1993; cf. Karaganov *et al.*, 1993). But international competition is fierce. Russia's long borders – some 3,000 kilometers longer than those of the Soviet Union – represent a mixed blessing, as they may necessitate troop redeployment, e.g. to the conflict-ridden North Caucasus (as has already happened with the Chechnia invasion). For all these reasons Russia's immense military machine is no true asset except for basic functions of deterrence (Karaganov, 1993). Possible roles in regional conflict-management and peace-keeping are hampered by lack of impartiality on the part of Russia's armed forces and the activities of the paramilitary Cossacks (*Moscow News*, nos 11 and 15, 1993). Incidentally, it was not Yeltsin's original intention to build up a national Russian army; this is a side effect of the foundering of the plans for Joint CIS Armed Forces during 1992.

Finally, there is the Tsarist and Soviet foreign policy tradition as a general factor behind Russian foreign policy. In their search for role models, many Russians (including diplomats) are quite nostalgic about the Tsarist era, but the wisdom of Tsarist Russia's foreign policy is open to question (Usachev, 1993). Much pre-1917 diplomacy and military initiatives amounted to a compensation policy and diversion from domestic reform (Ulam, 1962). Tsarism committed the same fatal error of imperial overstretch as the USSR when challenging Western powers in the Balkans and Eastern powers over Korea and Manchuria in the famous Russian 'swing diplomacy' (i.e. swinging back and forth between east and west whenever it was deemed opportune). The Russo-Japanese war (1904-5) brought about the revolution of 1905 from which the country never recovered. The First World War brought total collapse. Part of this failure is, of course, attributable to the idiosyncrasies of an autocratic system which undermined the work of its own Foreign Ministry (Slusser, 1962). But the aristocratic Russian diplomats of the time were often out of touch with reality themselves. Some were good organizers, though, so the overall problem was one of disregard for professionalism. This autocratic pattern was continued by Stalin and his successors and can be said to be repeated today in a manner peculiar to postcommunist Russia (Crow, 1993a).

Tsarist Russia's policy was one of restless expansion – for defensive purposes until the conquest of Kazan in 1552, but from then on increasingly for the sake of empire-building. A similar perceived nexus between security and empire inspired Soviet foreign policy. It would be far-fetched to postulate that postcommunist Russia is on the verge of emulating this pattern of actual expansion, but the work of the Russian Security Council suggests a dangerous blurring of domestic and foreign security concerns. The head of Russian external intelligence, Evgeni Primakov, a former Soviet foreign policy figurehead, has gone as far as issuing a statement seeking to veto Eastern Europe's membership of NATO (*NeGa*, 26 November 1993). In other words, the imperial temptation is resurfacing – the syndrome of self-proclaimed protection of self-proclaimed spheres of influence abroad in more or less open disregard for the sovereignty of neighbouring states. Russia's recent role as centre of an empire may thus have left a more lasting imprint upon the country's foreign policy establishment than Gorbachev's new political thinking has done.

Russia's foreign policy situation

As a newcomer on the international arena, Russia enjoys a privileged position by having inherited the Soviet foreign policy apparatus and the USSR's permanent seat in the United Nation's Security Council. Despite the organizational confusion following Shevardnadze's resignation as Foreign Minister in late 1990 and the emergence of rival republican foreign policies, the Soviet MFA of the Gorbachev era had an image of respectability and will to reform in contrast to other ministries. As a former Soviet diplomat supportive of new political thinking, Russian Foreign Minister Andrei Kozyrev helped to transfer this respectability to his new ministry. The number of MFA employees has swollen to some 3,000, or about the same size as when it was a Soviet ministry. Suzanne Crow dwells on cutbacks and various other problems, such as Kozyrev's alleged low popularity inside the ministry – due to screening measures? (Crow, 1992a; Checkel, 1994).[2] Independent academic analysts of moderate persuasion complain about their loss of influence compared to the Shevardnadze era (Andrei Zagorski, personal interview). Seen in retrospect, the greatest deficiency was the lack of expertise on neighbouring post-Soviet republics – a lacuna in Soviet research in general. This deficiency translated into fatal vulnerability when confronted with the ongoing conflicts in the 'near abroad' and the excessive challenges to the ministry's authority in the intense domestic power struggles that unfolded.

A further factor nullifying Russia's organizational advantages was the shock of gaining independence through the breakup of the Soviet Union. Second thoughts on the wisdom of this outcome have beset the Russian political mind. As Soviet citizens, Russians profited from the nebulous confinements (i.e. the fictitious borders separating one union republic from anther) of both centre and periphery (Goble, 1993). They were 'at home' when migrating to Central Asia and when visiting relatives in the Ukraine. This has abruptly changed. Russians have become foreigners outside Russia and their country has largely been cut off from Europe. There is a feeling of

---

[2] Like the authors of the second 'Strategy for Russia' (*NeGa*, 27 May 1994), Deputy Foreign Minister Adamishin deplores the sad state of the Russian diplomatic corps. In 1993 alone 500 people left the ministry and only one out of between seven and ten MGIMO graduates would settle for a career in the ministry, partly because of low salaries (*NeGa*, 15 June 1994).

geographical isolation, not to say political abandonment by the West at a time when Russia struggles with a desperate economic situation. Rates of crime and suicide point towards anomie. Worse still is the feeling of humiliation stemming from the seemingly unnecessary slide into weakness inherited from Gorbachev. The Russian spectre of relative deprivation breeding external aggression in a repetition of the Weimar scenario haunts Europe. Russia has grown into the weak tyrant of international affairs, to cite one perceptive Russian analyst (Zubok, 1992).[3]

The challenge of Russia is tremendous for Russian decision-makers themselves. They have to somehow manage their country's basic ungovernability during this transitional era. In the field of nation-building they have to dissociate themselves from Soviet ideology and the imperial legacy, while allowing for a policy of multinational state-building in recognition of the many non-Russians living inside Russia. In addition, decision-makers cannot afford to neglect the fate of the roughly 25 million Russians or Russian-speakers now living abroad in other post-Soviet republics as ethnic minorities (they are almost majorities in Kazakhstan, Latvia and Estonia; see map). At a time when Russia has experienced an influx of several million refugees (often non-Russians) as a result of pogroms, perceptions of insecurity and economic deprivation as well as natural disasters, the problem of security for the Russian state and for the Russian diaspora – in themselves understandable and legitimate concerns – invites political manipulation. The Russian complex of humiliation plays into the hands of opportunistic forces. The country thus faces unique dilemmas in the field of nation-, state- and foreign policy-building. The problems stem from the absence of any non-imperial Russian tradition and identity to build upon. Here Russia is bereft of relevant stabilizers more than any other postcommunist state.

As a result, independent Russia is caught in an identity crisis. Losing the external empire in 1989 meant a loss of prestige; losing the internal empire means loss of identity. This has ignited a comprehensive public debate on what constitutes 'Russia' and what is its proper role in the world; its genuine 'national interest'. While this debate

---

[3] As maintained by Martin Malia, it is debatable whether Russia actually has a Weimar option, as the country's lack of resources and infrastructure suggests that it could never foster anything reminiscent of Hitlerite Germany's destructive efficiency (1994).

has not escaped either historicist mysticism or imperial revanchism, it is a necessary undertaking that springs from the era of new political thinking which sought to de-ideologize foreign policy. The Soviet era ended in a search for true 'national interests' in an attempt to break the curse of imperial overstretch (cf. Kortunov and Iziumov, 1990). Whereas the Soviet debate centred on the need for common sense and moderation, the record is more mixed in the case of the Russian successor-debate. The most remarkable development is the re-emergence of the old school of Eurasian thought inaugurated in an article by the then political adviser to President Yeltsin, Sergei Stankevich (*NeGa*, 28 March 1992; cf. Rahr, 1992). Eurasianists openly challenge new political thinking, which they prefer to call 'Atlanticism', reflecting their preoccupation with geopolitics. Both Yeltsin and his Foreign Minister, Andrei Kozyrev, used to belong to the Atlanticist school advocating a Western orientation for the sake of reintegration. The Eurasian platform therefore modelled itself on the alleged neglect of Russia's 'near abroad', China and other non-Western partners. But the operational core of the Eurasian alternative is the call for a tough stance *vis-à-vis* the post-Soviet 'near abroad', combined with a reserved attitude towards reintegration. Eurasianism may be a foreign policy orientation invented for domestic reasons in order to placate Tatars and other Turkic and Muslim peoples inside Russia, as suggested by Roman Szporluk (1992). But it is disturbing to see its proponents indulge in outlandish geopolitical determinism and observe the influence it has gained, as can be seen in actual policy developments (cf. Pozdnyakov, 1993; *NeGa*, 29 April 1993). On the other hand, compared to the unrestrained revanchism adopted towards post-Soviet neighbours and the Cold War nostalgia characterizing the outright imperialist school of though that marries 'red' and 'brown' ideologies – e.g. the position of former Russian Vice-President Aleksandr Rutskoi – Eurasianism emerges as a moderate stance (cf. Zhirinovski, 1993).

The pervasiveness of the Russian foreign policy debate and the existential crisis from which it stems make it more accurate to describe Russia's foreign policy situation as a state of mind rather than a field of activities. Russian foreign policy is also a minefield for analysts, who are careful to spell out the state of flux and the difficulties inherent in giving a factual account of foreign policy developments let alone predictions (Bluth, 1994; Dannreuther, 1993). Some give up on this and devote themselves to conceptual issues in what amounts to discourse analysis (Alexandrova, 1993b). Others focus on actors, power struggles and coalition-building or broad institutional analysis (Crow, 1993a; Malcolm, 1994; Checkel, 1992). Others still prefer to speculate on general challenges and trends (Porter, 1992).

Developments within postcommunist Russia's foreign policy

Nothing illustrates better the influence of the conceptual debate upon official Russian foreign policy than the fact that the MFA was forced into formulating a paper on its position on foreign policy, then to revise it and ultimately to yield to the Security Council, whose set of foreign policy guidelines came to be endorsed by Yeltsin as Russia's foreign policy concept ('Basic guidelines on the concept of foreign policy of the Russian Federation'). Early on, Kozyrev specified his understanding of Russia's geopolitical interests as a system of concentric circles. The first circle of interest to Russia was the future sovereign states of the internal empire, the second circle the entire northern hemisphere – Europe, North America and North-East Asia, leaving the rest of the world as a third priority (*Moscow News*, no. 43, 1990). No sooner had Russia won independence, however, before Kozyrev was swamped with demands –from parliamentarians, media and other sectors of the government –that he draft a paper on his concept of Russian foreign policy (Crow, 1992b). Kozyrev tried in vain to ridicule the campaign by making comparisons with previous party programmes and doctrines. The Foreign Ministry's draft was presented in February 1992, before Stankevich (then a State Secretary) drew up his platform. After that the ministry's concept became a political football, to use Jeff Checkel's (1994) apt expression. The ministry was inspired by CSCE norms and principles and defined Russia's national interests as the achievement of a dynamic economy, protection of human rights, democracy and integration into the world economy. The draft concept did specify as priority areas the maintenance of contacts with Russian communities in other CIS states and the Baltic states, as well as cooperation within the CIS and reintegration (*Interfax*, 21 February 1992). The draft anticipated Stankevich's criticism by proposing cooperation with certain Third World countries. In fact, as one Russian observer notes it coincided with the view on foreign policy then held by the parliamentary speaker Ruslan Khasbulatov – well renowned for his challenge to Yeltsin in the autumn of 1993 (*NeGa* 19 November 1993).

In spite of this, the head of the Russian parliament's Committee on International Affairs, Evgeni Ambartsumov, rejected the comprehensive document as 'insufficiently concrete' and demanded that the ministry come up with a new paper based on consultations with experts and parliamentarians (*ITAR-TASS*, 30 June 1992). Ambartsumov challenged the wisdom of adhering to international norms in the defence of Russians living abroad. Both he and his adviser, Andranik Migranian, proposed to turn the entire post-Soviet area into a sphere of vital Russian interests (*Rossiiskaia Gazeta*, 4 August 1992; *Izvestia*, 7 August 1992). Similarly, the 'Strategy for Russia' paper of the Council for Foreign and Defence Policy, headed by Sergei Karaganov, called for an 'enlightened post-imperial integrationist course' in relations with countries of the former internal empire, not eschewing the use of force when dealing with the threats and problems emanating from the region (*NeGa*, 19 August 1992). The MFA presented several revisions, including a final version by December, but never succeeded in gaining the parliament's consent (Crow, 1993a). Kozyrev's frustrations sparked off his innovative exercise in shock diplomacy by making a fake hardliner speech, anticipating what was in the offing if his critics got their way, at the CSCE meeting in Stockholm in December 1992.[4]

Instead Yeltsin asked the Russian Security Council, more specifically its recently established Interdepartmental Foreign Policy Commission, to draw up a concept paper. This opened the way for close cooperation with the Ministries of Defence, Foreign Economic Relations and External Intelligence, and the parliamentary committees on International Relations and External Economic Relations as well as the Foreign Ministry itself. Overall coordination and guidance were in the hands of the then head of the Security Council, Juri Skokov (*NeGa*, 29 April 1993). The Security Council's foreign

---

[4] In his fake speech, Kozyrev gave the impression that Russia had definitely swung towards the Eurasian hardliners' stance by advocating unilateral measures to protect Russian interests and by letting the world know that Russia would end its support for sanctions against the rump of Yugoslavia. He further identified the former internal empire as a post-imperial region where CSCE norms did not apply and announced that the states of this region were to be forced into a new federation or confederation (Interfax, 14 December 1992). Many of these provocations later became official policy.

policy concept has not been published, but apparently it omitted the Foreign Ministry's emphasis on 'forming a belt of neighbourliness around Russia' (cf. 'Russia's Foreign Policy Concept', 1993). The Council stipulates Russia's responsibility for the establishment of a new international order, in particular for 'creating positive mutual relations among the post-Soviet states', and stresses Russia's role as guarantor of the stability of these relations. The following are defined as threats to Russia's security and vital interests:

> Any action targeted at the territorial integrity of the Russian Federation, against the processes of integration within the CIS, any infringement upon human rights and freedoms, armed conflicts in the adjacent states or steps intended to weaken or undermine the international position [views/MS.] of Russia. (*NeGa*, 29 April 1993)

The Security Council's foreign policy concept highlights Russia's express wish for a 'worthy place' within international affairs, turning this into a precondition for its active participation in shaping a new world order. Apart from that the concept strikes a somewhat isolationist, Eurasian tone. Instead of Kozyrev's 'strategy for partnership and alliance with Western countries in an attempt to harmoniously build Russia into the international democratic community and world economic ties', the Security Council ranks relations with Western Europe below those of the former external empire of Eastern Europe, which is characterized as 'a historically founded zone of interests'. Yet the concept only seems to dwell on Russia's interest in settling the conflict in Yugoslavia at the fringe of the former empire. Relations with the EU are characterized as 'decisive', yet here the Council reveals a quite reactive approach that highlights the danger of integration without Russia. Relations with the United States are mentioned separately, but accorded less importance than the EU. While conceding the common interest in stable and secure international relations and nuclear non-proliferation in particular, the concept emphasizes possible clashes of interests with the United States. The document also urges Russia to promote balanced, stable relations with all parties in the Far East and the Pacific. The impasse in relations with China must be overcome, relations with Japan normalized and North Korea's defection from the Non-Proliferation Treaty prevented. Other parts of Asia are viewed as a possible source of instability spill-over – e.g. Afghanistan. Interests in other parts of the world are mentioned, but the absolutely dominant agenda is the post-Soviet 'near abroad' (*NeGa*, 29 April 1993). Instead of proceeding to present the Security Council's visions for this region, it is better to place them in the context of overall developments in Russia's policy towards this key target of the country's foreign policy.

Summing up, Russia's official position on foreign policy has moved from an outward-looking policy that placed reintegration on a par with considerations of establishing a belt of neighbourliness around Russia, through amicable relations to the 'near abroad', to a self-assertive inward-looking approach stressing potentials for conflicts. Russia has grown highly selective in its approach to common interests in relation to the surrounding world. The military doctrine of Russia confirms this trend in its endorsement of a *tous azimuth* threat perception; this is in itself a break with the past, however, when threats were specified as emanating solely from the capitalist world (*Izvestia*, 18 November 1993; *NeGa*, 9 June 1994). This may be as far as the Russian effort towards de-ideologizing foreign and security policy can be stretched; but certainly it is an outcome that leaves something to be desired in terms of partnership for the preservation of peace and for the sake of addressing Russia's own vital need of reintegration. 'Cold peace' is how Yeltsin himself characterizes the present state of affairs.

Russia's policy towards its postcommunist neighbours. At issue is Russia's policy towards the 'near abroad', i.e. basically the former internal empire. The point of departure is the inherent vulnerability of this regional dimension in postcommunist Russia's foreign policy. In addition to the immense difficulties in formulating a coherent policy on the basis of Russia's disorganized resources and image problem, it was this field of activity that became a political football inside Russia. But it is worth keeping in mind that some of the inconsistencies stem from President Yeltsin, who chose to inaugurate policy towards the 'near abroad' by reserving for Russia the right to (unilateral) border revisions in the aftermath of the August coup (TASS, 26 August 1991). By contrast, Kozyrev preferred to dwell on the prospects for friendship with the states of the 'near abroad' – it was he who coined the term – created by the demise of the communist empire, identifying CIS cooperation as the top priority for Russian diplomacy (*Izvestia*, 2 January 1992). In this connection Kozyrev lashed out against the irresponsible views of

Vladimir Zhirinovski and other imperial restorationists. Without denying that there were difficulties ahead, Kozyrev was adamant on the need for a non-imperial policy of intensifying military and economic cooperation. In terms of actual initiatives, however, his policy tended towards benign neglect. But given the fragile – and for Ukraine only temporary – nature of the CIS commitment, an aggressive pursuit of integration was bound to be counterproductive. 'Wait and see' was not an unwise tactic for Russia.

Yeltsin pursued the same policy of benign neglect towards the near abroad in early 1992, an approach rooted in his preference for restoring links with the Slavic neighbours at the expense of Central Asia (Rahr, 1993). Yeltsin let Iran act as mediator in the war over Nagorno-Karabakh and showed no sign of discomfort then at Turkey's appeal to Central Asians. At the time Yeltsin devoted the major part of his public diplomacy with the West to market himself and Russia as actors in international affairs, which was certainly a more rewarding undertaking than trouble-shooting in the 'near abroad'. It may be true, as suggested by the British military analyst John Lough (1993), that the Russian government and Foreign Ministry were filled with a false sense of security over developments in the 'near abroad'. After all, the CIS summit in Kiev in March 1992 was able to finalize a framework agreement on joint peace-keeping, with further progress in the offing. At the same time, the Russian MFA established a special department, headed by Deputy Foreign Minister Fodor Shelov-Kovedaev, for relations with post-Soviet states. Until then only a dozen people in the ministry were occupied with the countries of the CIS and even fewer had relevant language skills, evidently a factor conducive to Moscow's ignorance and missed opportunities in this area – as Lough insists.

At any rate, these measures did not protect Kozyrev against the gathering storm on account of his alleged neglect of the near abroad. In his response to Yeltsin's aide, Stankevich, who initiated the uproar, Kozyrev sought to adapt by stating it was necessary to insist that the inexperienced states of the 'near abroad' should adhere to principles of international law and that the human rights situation concerning Russians and Russian-speaking populations abroad should be strictly monitored (*Izvestia*, 31 March 1992). Moreover, in April 1992 he himself engaged in active diplomacy towards the 'near abroad' by visiting Armenia, Azerbaijan, Georgia, Moldova, Tadzhikistan and Turkmenistan. Unfortunately for Russia's overall priorities, his stay in the two Central Asian capitals were the more successful. Kozyrev's attempt to mediate in the war between Armenians and Azerbaijanis over Nagorno-Karabakh – then characterized by increased atrocities – failed despite his attempt to bestow legitimacy upon Russia by proposing a simultaneous Russian and CSCE peacekeeping operation at the Helsinki CSCE meeting in March (Matveev, 1992). Neither party to the conflict believed in Russia's impartiality and the conflict was not then ripe for settlement, a condition considered critical by conflict analysts (Haass, 1990). As for Moldova, Kozyrev alienated the Chisinau authorities by broaching the idea of using the 14th Army – in reality a Russian army stationed in the 'Dniestr Republic' of eastern Moldova – as a peacekeeping force in the conflict over that area, which was escalating in early 1992 (Socor, 1992). Kozyrev's action was open to only two possible interpretations. Either he was impermissibly naive – did he know nothing about the nature of the conflict and the controversial role of the 14th Army and its commander, General Lebed? – or he was aligning himself with the irresponsible hardliners.

A brief note on this Transdniestria conflict seems warranted here. Although for a while conquered by Romania in connection with the reconquest of Bessarabia, the territory of Transdniestria – i.e. today's secessionist Dniestr Republic – first became an integral part of the Moldavian Soviet republic in 1944 and came to enjoy popularity among Soviet officers as a retirement place. This is the background to the region's current reputation as a haven for pro-imperialist hardliners with a dubious secessionist case. On 1 December 1991, an overwhelming majority of the population of Transdniestria voted for the independence of their 'republic' and elected Igor Smirnov, a former Soviet general, as president. A new influx of conservative military elements followed – OMON troops, troops withdrawn from the Baltic states and Cossacks. These 'immigrants' began to attack and raid CIS units, seizing weapons, munitions and ground- to-air missiles. The Moldovan authorities who retained formal sovereignty over Transdniestria issued an ultimatum, but fighting broke out instead and there were several deaths on both sides. In other words, whatever case the secessionists may have had, they dropped any pretence at a legal approach to border revisions. Yeltsin kept silent and the Russian MFA issued a vague statement on 4 March expressing regret, but later offered to mediate together with other countries or organizations.

By the time Kozyrev came up with his idea of relying on the 14th Russian Army, Vice-President Aleksandr Rutskoi had spoken in Bendery in the self-proclaimed republic, expressing his open support of it as a republic that 'existed, exists and must exist'. This was one in a series of pilgrimages to Transdniestria by prominent Russian empire-restorationists – Albert Makashov, Zhirinovski, Viktor Alsknis, Aleksandr Nevzorov, Aleksandr Prokhanov and the entire editorial staff of the ultra-nationalistic Russian bi-weekly *Den* (Kolstø *et al.*, 1993). The supposedly neutral General Lebed called the Chisinau government 'fascist' and also came out in support of the secessionists. The Sixth Congress of (Russian) People's Deputies responded to the Dniestr Republic's appeal for diplomatic recognition by issuing a statement of support expressing concern about human rights violations in Moldova and proposing the 14th Army as a peacekeeping force. Meanwhile, Kozyrev had restored some of Moldova's confidence by announcing the establishment of formal diplomatic relations between Russia and Moldova. Prior to the Congress of People's Deputies he warned against unilateral Russian measures such as sending mercenaries (as favoured by some) on grounds that they might provoke Romania to intervene (*NeGa*, 1 April 1992). Yet this statement was symptomatic of the Foreign Ministry's loss of control over the Transdniestria crisis. *Den* was reporting in terms of 'the groaning Russian people having their blood let over their motherland can be heard as far as the Philippines' (*Den*, no. 16, April 1992). Few bothered to tell the Russian public that this was a conflict instigated by a self-appointed group of militias.[5] Russia was driven to the brink of war with Moldova – international war. This was finally realized by Yeltsin, who was quoted by Interfax as having declared: 'Don't worry, there won't be a war. We will pull back the 14th Army to Russian territory and will not permit Russia to be dragged into war' (*Financial Times*, 28 May 1992). During the ceasefire negotiations that followed, the MFA was largely by-passed as it was in the case of other conflicts and ceasefires that followed – the Ministry of Defence stepped in instead. In late June, at a time when Yeltsin was abroad and Rutskoi was touring Transdniestria, Moldovan forces

---

[5] From a strictly humanitarian point of view, Russia faced a more acute problem in the simultaneously unfolding fighting in south Ossetia, northern Georgia. In spite of the fact that Georgia did not belong to the CIS, the introduction of a CIS peacekeeping force under Russian command was arranged in an agreement between Yeltsin and Shevardnadze of 24 June 1992.

attacked Bendery. This provoked Stankevich to a frontal assault on Kozyrev and his 'wimpish foreign policy' (*Rossiiskaia Gazeta*, 23 June 1992). In the settlement that followed, a peacekeeping force consisting of Russian, Moldovan and Transdniestrian troops, including the 14th Army, was agreed upon. In a bitter response to Stankevich, Kozyrev tried to sort things out in the latest round of the Transdniestria conflict complaining about the role of the neo-Bolshevik 'war party' – thereby fanning criticism of his own person (*Izvestia*, 30 June 1992). Calls for the establishment of a separate CIS ministry – a Commonwealth Ministry – were frequently heard in a faintly disguised attempt to remove from Kozyrev whatever power he might still have over policy in the 'near abroad' (*Izvestia*, 24 July 1992). Stankevich lobbied to present himself as a candidate for the post of CIS minister, which in the event was not established at that time but in 1994. Instead, Yeltsin established the Security Council, perhaps just to provide for better coordination of policy; yet it is interesting to note that it immediately cast a vote of no confidence in Kozyrev (*NeGa*, 10 July 1992). Raising the idea of border revisions in early June could not save Kozyrev from humiliation (*Le Monde*, 7 – 8 June 1992).

In other words, the summer of 1992 was hot in more than one sense. Fedor Shelov-Kovedaev, the young first deputy prime minister placed in charge of relations with the former soviet republics in March 1992, who wrote a report on policy towards the 'near abroad' characterized by John Lough as 'lucid, perceptive and intellectually rigorous', submitted his resignation in September, frustrated at the weakening of the Foreign Ministry *inter alia* through the appointment of new hardliners to the Ministry of Defence. Meanwhile, Russian policy towards the Baltic states hardened. Under international law the Russian troops deployed in the Soviet era were to be withdrawn immediately and unconditionally, according to the wishes of the now sovereign Baltic states. But the Russian side made troop withdrawal an issue for bilateral negotiations, thereby opening the way for a phased withdrawal based on the Baltic party's fulfilment of certain conditions (*Neue Zürcher Zeitung*, 26 September 1992). In early 1992 Russia agreed in principle to regard the troops stationed in the three Baltic states as foreign, implying that a withdrawal would have to take place. But when Lithuania came up with a timetable for this in May it was completely ignored. Russia's original target was to have left by 1998, then 1997, then

1996 and finally by 1994. The fact that Yeltsin had to give a good impression at the G-7 and CSCE summits in July 1992 may be what caused him to give public assurances to the effect that the troops were to be withdrawn; something that had been left open since February (Bungs, 1993). To some extent, however, it was a Pyrrhic victory for the Balts. The Russian side began to attach tough conditions to the withdrawal – reflecting Yeltsin's greater reliance on the military and civilian hardliners. It was the Russian Ministry of Defence that drafted the agreement on withdrawal from Lithuania by 1 September 1993 which was reached in September – in itself a breakthrough, of course – thus by-passing the Foreign Ministry (Interfax, 29 October 1992). Evidently, the breakthrough was the result of incessant pressure from the Lithuanian side, including threats of internationalizing the issue by not signing the CSCE declaration in Helsinki and willingness to build apartments for military personnel in Kaliningrad, combined with the fact that the Russian presence was less of a political issue in Moscow (*NeGa*, 7 July 1992).

In spite of this, on 22 September the parliamentary Committee of International Affairs voted to annul the agreement with Vilnius and the Russian government halted the pull-out in all three countries. Nevertheless, the military personnel in Lithuania proceeded with the withdrawal (Bungs, 1993). The empire-restorationists then began specifying their strategy. During the summer the Russified Latvian Colonel Alksnis called for the issue of human rights for the large Russian minority in Latvia and Estonia to be linked to the issue of troop withdrawal. This linkage was made explicit *inter alia* in the Latvian daily *Diena*'s interview with Sergei Zotov, head of the Russian delegation in the withdrawal talks with Latvia (14 October 1992/Russian edition). He bluntly reminded the Latvians that the Russians had the guns and reiterated Yeltsin's statement on Russian TV on 6 October:

> Negotiations with Latvia are deadlocked. This is due to the gross violations of human rights in Latvia and the conditions advanced by the Latvian side which are unacceptable to Russia. If the human rights situation does not improve in the nearest future, Russia is not going to sign any treaty on the withdrawal of troops from Latvia (*ibid.*).

On 10 October, *Diena* reported that it was the Russian officers themselves who had stalled troop withdrawals – on the grounds that they felt humiliated by the way Russian arms and facilities were being handed over free of charge. This suggested once again that it was the military that had the upper hand in 'near abroad' policies, including towards the Baltic states. Thus it was the Russian Minister of Defence Pavel Grachev and his Lithuanian counterpart Audrius Butkevicius who signed the key agreements on the withdrawal from Lithuania in October.

But Yeltsin and even more so the Foreign Ministry were also losing ground to self-willed parliamentarians like Ambartsumov and Oleg Rumiantsev, the latter head of the Russian Social Democratic Party and executive secretary of the parliament's Constitutional Commission. In addition to campaigning for turning the 'near abroad', including the Baltic states, into an exclusive Russian sphere of interest, Ambartsumov pursued his own agenda in the not so near abroad of ex-Yugoslavia in tandem with Rumiantsev (Crow, 1993c). They wanted Russia to defect from the stance of the international community seeking to isolate Serbia, thereby raising Russia's profile in the Balkans in a display of traditional Russian imperial foreign policy. In the summer of 1992, when the atrocities in Bosnia-Hercegovina were recalling memories of Nazi terror in the European political mind, Ambartsumov found it worthwhile to travel with Rumiantsev to ex-Yugoslavia, something which earned him a place in the Russian delegation to the inconclusive London conference in August (*NeGa*, 2 August 1992). Ambartsumov went as far as to deny publicly the existence of Serb concentration camps, whereas Kozyrev wanted to go with the UN, the United States and the EU in condemning 'ethnic cleansing'. By December official Russian policy on Yugoslavia changed in the direction anticipated by Kozyrev in his fake CSCE speech. Russia blocked efforts to lift the arms embargo and vetoed any preparation for military intervention. Rumiantsev also played a role in bringing about the cancellation of Yeltsin's visit to Japan in September that year, an open humiliation not only of Japan but also of Yeltsin, and hence a blow to Russia's image abroad. The circumstances surrounding the cancellation are examined in more detail below.

As for Ukraine, the ostensible linchpin in Yeltsin's policy towards the 'near abroad', the year 1992 was marked by ups and downs. Kiev placed Moscow in a dilemma between offensive and defensive goals – conflicting considerations of conflict and cooperation, as it were.

On the one hand, Russia could not accept Kiev's claim to the Black Sea fleet and did not feel comfortable about Ukraine's prossession of the Crimean peninsula. Moscow was adamant that Kiev should implement the Lisbon protocol of the START-1 treaty requiring Ukraine to become a non-nuclear state. Russia was challenging and pressuring Ukraine on these issues right from the beginning. But this approach was counterproductive in relation to Russia's goals in the field of CIS policy (Solchanyk, 1993). In CIS affairs it was a Moscow priority to keep Kiev within the fold, the whole idea behind the Minsk summit on 8 December 1991 between Russia, Belarus and Ukraine, the summit *de facto* dissolving the Soviet Union. It was at the insistence of the President of Kazakhstan, Nursultan Nazarbaev, that his republic and the residual Central Asian states were accepted as co-founders of the commonwealth that came to be known as the CIS, with other republics joining. The catalyst for Russia's preoccupation with Ukraine was the republic's vote for independence on 1 December, a fact that Moscow could not come to terms with. For Russians, Ukraine was merely a western extension of Russia and moreover the historical origin of Russian statehood – *Kievskaia Rus*. Besides, Russia feared the economic and political implications of having to embrace a union with Central Asia and Armenia by itself. Although Ukraine was and remains one of the least committed CIS member states and Russia one of the most committed, Russia remains curiously hesitant when it comes to embracing Nazarbaev's many plans for turning the CIS into a tightly knit Eurasian union – for fear that it might provoke the Central Europe-oriented Ukraine to defect once and for all.[6]

If that happens, however, Nazarbaev will not be the only one to blame. As early as January 1992, the Russian parliament instructed two of its committees to examine the legality of the 1954 decision to transfer Crimea from the RSFSR to Ukraine's jurisdiction and linked this issue to the question of the Black Sea. It was Khrushchev

---

[6] Alternatively, it could cause a break-up of Ukraine into a western and eastern part; an outcome that some in Moscow expect and hope for, e.g. Andranik Migranian (*NeGa*, 12, 18 January 1994). A division of the country would mean military forces would scramble for control over nuclear weapons and a high likelihood of civil war threatening Russia itself; on top of that the economic responsibility for eastern Ukraine would fall upon Moscow. All in all, Moscow's interests are best served by not rocking the Ukrainian boat too much; something which seems to be acknowledged by Sergei Karaganov at least (personal interview).

who at that time decided to commemorate the 300th anniversary of the Treaty of Pereiaslavl by handing back Crimea to the Ukrainians – a purely symbolic gesture then, but highly important in today's context of decolonization. On 21 May the Russian parliament decided that the transfer had been faulty, an outcome which placed Yeltsin in an awkward position. On several occasions Yeltsin announced that he saw the Crimean question as an internal one for Ukraine, yet in April he dispatched none other than Vice-President Rutskoi to the Crimea hotspot. Rutskoi had published his position in an article in an open challenge to Ukrainian President Leonid Kravchuk and others 'who came to power through national careerism', thereby questioning Ukraine's legitimacy as a sovereign entity (*Pravda*, 30 January 1992). Before his Crimean audience, Rutskoi claimed that the 1954 decision had been taken as a result of a hangover or sunstroke, adding that 'such documents do not cancel out the history of Crimea' (quoted in Solchanyk, 1992).

Yeltsin's motive may have been to apply additional pressure to Kiev on the question of the Black Sea Fleet issue – an issue to which Rutskoi linked himself. Prior to Rutskoi's visit Yeltsin threatened to take the entire fleet under Russian and later CIS jurisdiction if Kiev proceeded to take control of it; something that did not deter the then Ukrainian President Leonid Kravchuk. The Russo-Ukrainian conflict is addressed below in Chapter 7, with greater emphasis on the Ukrainian side. Suffice it here to stress the cumulative effects of official and unofficial Russian policy towards Ukraine –such as when Sergei Baburin, an empire-restorationist belonging to the National Salvation Front and an influential parliamentarian, threatened Kiev's ambassador to Moscow that 'either Ukraine reunites with Russia or there will be war' (*Izvestia*, 26 May 1992). Moscow's attempts at forcing Kiev into subservience had exactly the opposite effect. Moreover, trade with Ukraine – representing 70 per cent of all post-Soviet trade – was simply a liability and had to be frozen in 1992 (*Financial Times*, 23 September 1992).

CIS cooperation, a topic that is covered in general terms in Chapter 8 below, did make some progress in 1992, as noted above. But for a while Russia settled for a bilateral approach and signed a Treaty of Friendship, Cooperation and Mutual Assistance – a wording reminiscent of past times concerning the external empire – with Kazakhstan on 25 May 1992. Similar treaties with the residual Central Asian states were also signed, except for Tadzhikistan, where internal unrest was mounting. Ukraine reacted with reserve and even relations with Belarus became strained because Russian Premier Egor Gaidar was honest enough to admit that the Russo-Belarusian bilateral treaty was a step in a confederative direction (Sheehy, 1992). With the passage of time Moscow has come to look upon relations not only with Ukraine but also with Belarus and Kazakhstan as vital –although Karaganov (1993) is more explicit on the latter point than Yeltsin. It was Karaganov who in the autumn of 1992 had spoken out on how to manipulate the issue of the Russian diaspora as a way to propel Russia into a hegemonic position in the Eurasian area, a topic to be explored in greater detail later.

I have dwelt on 1992 in order to expose the improvised and turbulent nature of Russian foreign policy towards the 'near abroad' in that formative phase. The year 1992 may be characterized as a time of tests of strength during which Kozyrev and occasionally Yeltsin had to yield, while 1993 was a year when the change in the domestic balance of power was institutionalized and from that point of view a time of greater stability. Yet the foreign and security policy implications of this shift in Russia's international orientation are by no means trivial. At issue was the institutionalization of Russia's hegemonic pretence in the 'near abroad' along the lines of the 'Monroe doctrine' as proposed by Migranian and Ambartsumov. The primary instrument for this strategy – that is, accompanying the alleged concern for the Russian diaspora – was CIS peacekeeping. In early 1993 Yeltsin began a campaign to gain an international mandate for Russian peacekeeping in the 'near abroad' and to seek international sponsorship for this purpose. The general provisions for CIS peacekeeping had been settled at the CIS summit in Kiev in March 1992, for example the precondition that the request for an operation should originate from all the conflicting sides and that a ceasefire should be in place before such deployment. As for eligibility for participation in peacekeeping, the Kiev agreement declared: 'The peacekeeping group is formed on a voluntary basis by the states that are party to this agreement with the exception of the conflicting parties' (TASS, 4 March 1992). This provision on the international nature of CIS peacekeeping is increasingly considered a cover for Russia. CIS peacekeeping actions are in essence Russian operations, based on a clear numerical dominance of Russian forces. On 28 February 1993, Yeltsin addressed the Civic Union, a party uniting Rutskoi's People's Party, Nikolai Travkin's

Democratic Party of Russia and not least Arkadyi Volski representing the powerful heavy industrial lobby – an indication that he considered the coalition an important potential ally during battles in parliament. On the subject of peacekeeping in the 'near abroad' Yeltsin said:

> Russia ... continues to have a vital interest in the cessation of all armed conflicts on the territory of the former USSR. Moreover, the world community is increasingly coming to realize our special responsibility in this difficult matter. I believe the time has come for authoritative international organizations, including the United Nations, to grant Russia special powers as guarantor of peace and stability in this region. (*ITAR-TASS*, 1 March 1993)

This was almost a verbatim recollection of Ambartsumov's thoughts on the issue when he launched the 'Monroe doctrine':

> Russia must secure from the international community the role of political and military guarantor of stability on all the territory of the USSR. It is therefore necessary to obtain the support of the G-7 countries for those functions of Russia up to the hard-currency subsidies for rapid-response forces (Russian 'blue helmets'). (*Izvestia*, 7 August 1992)

Ukraine, Latvia and Azerbaijan reacted promptly, warning that this would produce blatant violations of international law, including a legalization of the presence of Russian troops in the Baltic states, and amounted to a violation of the UN Charter (Crow, 1993d). In spite of these protests, Russia lobbied the UN. Both Kozyrev and Stankevich angrily denied suggestions that Russia's approach to CIS peacekeeping was a blueprint for neo-imperialism. But their proposal met with a very guarded international response.

Meanwhile, the Security Council's 'concept' or doctrine on Russian foreign policy had been adopted, specifying Russia's goals and interests including the claim to have 'responsibility' for the near abroad (*NeGa*, 29 April 1993). The doctrine dwells on the threat from regional conflicts in this area and from nuclear proliferation. Calling for 'a foreign policy oriented towards strengthened international cooperation for the sake of military-political stability and security', the Security Council attaches 'particular importance to preventing threats to strategic stability [the Ukrainian problem], and attempts at undermining the military might of Russia and its position in the international arms market'. The doctrine also specifies Russia's goal of becoming the only nuclear power within the CIS and urges 'protection of the outer borders of the CIS' and efforts to keep the military infrastructure intact. The doctrine calls for the 'perfection of CIS peacekeeping in the framework of integration with the participation of Russia, including peacekeeping with a UN or CSCE mandate'. According to another source on the contents of the Security Council's doctrine for foreign policy, the document specifies 'prevention of the attempts of third-party countries to exploit the existing instability in the countries of the "near abroad" for their own ends' as well as 'rejection of foreign military contingents and military bases in the ex-Soviet republics' (*Moscow News*, no. 31, 30 July 1993). In other words, military security has re-emerged as a pivotal concern, the objective being some kind of integration that includes this dimension. If anything, the Security Council tends towards including the Baltic states in its deliberations on the 'near abroad', as when stressing the uncertainties surrounding the Russian troop presence in the states of the 'near abroad' (*NeGa*, 29 April 1993).

The doctrine calls upon decision-makers to employ 'all disposable means and methods'. Russia's efforts towards recovery from the domestic crisis, the strengthening of state institutions and the effective use of foreign policy instruments are cited as important for neutralizing the perceived threats to Russia cited above (*ibid.*). As for economic relations with the 'near abroad', the 'preservation and further development of the relations of economic interaction characterizing the former Soviet Union', as well as Russian industrial export, are of primary importance. On this account the document again does not explicitly exclude the Baltic states, but proceeds to state that:

> It is a matter of principle for Russia to pursue as high a level of integration as possible in relations with the former union republics in all spheres on the basis of voluntary cooperation and mutual benefit. In case some states are not prepared to join specific proposals it is imperative to proceed by cooperating with those who are interested. (*ibid.*)

Thus the target of peacekeeping is accompanied by explicit visions of CIS integration – incidentally what the Russians call reintegration in a hint of the not so distant Soviet past.

After 1992, the number of actual peacekeeping operations grew considerably. In addition to the never withdrawn 14th Army in Transdniestria and Russian peacekeeping in south Ossetia, supposedly neutral Russian forces involved themselves in Georgia's conflict with secessionist Abkhazia. In July 1993 Russian aircraft and warships supported the assault on Sukhumi by Abkhazian rebels and in September the conflicts reached dramatic heights, with Georgian President Shevardnadze swearing not to surrender and leave Sukhumi. But the Georgian side was defeated and had to face the fact of Russia's overarching influence as an ally in the struggle against Shevardnadze's rival, Zviad Gamsakhurdia. In October 1993, at the CIS summit, Shevardnadze was bluntly told: 'If you want gas, oil, raw materials..., then join the CIS'. So Georgia joined the CIS and also signed a bilateral treaty that secured Russia five military bases in the country. The Russian military support for Shevardnadze's side ensured his victory over Gamsakhurdia within a month (Fuller, 1994). Russia was further suspected of involvement behind the scenes in neighbouring Azerbaijan where Abulfaz Elchibey fell from power and was replaced by the former party boss Heidar Aliev. After a series of humiliating defeats inflicted by the Armenians in Nagorno-Karabakh, the Azerbaijanis were suddenly able to strike back –due to Russian support? Azerbaijan's decision to join the CIS may not have been coincidental.

Russia's approach to managing Transcaucasian conflicts is essentially one of divide and rule. Given the many conflicts, mutual grievances, rivalries and general lack of political maturity in the region, this may be unavoidable. By contrast, Russian policy in Central Asia builds on a far greater degree of mutual interest as far as the non-fundamentalist élites are concerned, including the old *nomenklaturas* in Tadzhikistan and Uzbekistan. Following the reinstallation of a pro-communist government in Tadzhikistan in December 1992, the country appealed to the CIS for peacekeeping support, which was granted. Russia bore the brunt of fighting and patrolling along the border between Tadzhikistan and Afghanistan, where most of the rebels had fled to. At Kozyrev's insistence, Russia received support in the shape of token Uzbek, Kazakh and Kirgiz border patrols. The entire peacekeeping force is under Russian command and said to number 20,000 – thus vastly outnumbering the 5,000-strong Islamic Resistance fighters (*Guardian Weekly*, 10 April 1994). But Russia is wary of its role in Tadzhikistan and frustrated about the uncompromising attitude of its Tadzhik protegés.

Russia and the CIS have solemnly declared that Tadzhikistan's border with Afghanistan is also the border of the CIS, which it must defend; nevertheless, the conflict points towards the need for Russia to differentiate its interests in the CIS so as to not overcommit itself in the way its predecessor did.

It was against this background that the Security Council's work on Russia's new military doctrine ended in late 1993. Compared to earlier drafts, the final version is less expansionist and hawkish – a pattern quite opposite from what happened to the foreign policy concept (*Izvestia*, 18 November 1993). The doctrine has not been made public in full, but appears to endorse CIS peacekeeping and calls for the defence of Russia's 'vital interests', which are seen to stretch beyond the borders of Russia. But this does not imply that the Russian officers' corps is a force pushing for involvement in new conflicts, notwithstanding the case of Chechnia. The doctrine places the formation of military blocs and alliances contrary to Russia's interests among possible security threats and proposes to develop military cooperation with the states of the CIS as well as Eastern and Central Europe. Perhaps the single most controversial provision is the suggestion that states which are not signatories to the 1968 Non-Proliferation Treaty might be subject to attack by nuclear weapons – a thinly veiled warning to Ukraine, which later became a signatory.

At the CSCE meeting in Rome in early December, Russia tried in vain to gain approval for Russian peacekeeping in the CIS.[7] The CSCE is in a difficult position itself in that it must uphold the dialogue with Russia on peacekeeping and human rights so as to not let down those who are potential victims of Russian unilateralism. Accordingly, a 'gentleman's agreement' was reached in late 1993 between Kozyrev and his British colleague, Foreign Secretary Douglas Hurd, to the effect that peacekeeping has to build on respect for sovereignty and at the initiative of the governments concerned; that a parallel political process must take place; that peacekeeping requires a specific mandate and preferably has to be multinational, and finally, that there has to be a strategy for withdrawal (*Financial Times*

---

[7] Russia wanted to include the following paragraph in the final communiqué of the CSCE meeting: 'The ministers are highly impressed by the positive role played by the Russian Federation in the settlement of conflicts in the territory of the former Soviet Union, notably in Moldova, Georgia, Nagorno-Karabakh and Tadzhikistan' (*Die Zeit*, 3 December 1993).

and *Izvestia*, 14 December 1993). This last clause is a stumbling-block between Russia and the OSCE (*RFE/RL News Briefs*, 13 – 17 June 1994). Russia's reluctance to accept the authority of the UN on peacekeeping within the sphere of its 'vital interests' is disturbing. A further confirmation of the Russian 'Monroe doctrine' is found in Kozyrev's announcement at a Russian MFA conference on 'near abroad' policy held in early 1994 that the country considered it imperative not to give up its military presence and bases in the former internal empire:

> The CIS countries and the Baltic states are a region where our primary vital interests are concentrated and from whence the basic threats to these interests emerge.... We should not withdraw from regions which for centuries marked spheres of Russian interests. We should not shy away from this expression. The 'security vacuum' that is being created will inevitably be filled by forces which in many respects do not coincide with Russian interests and often they will prove outright hostile to our interests. (*NeGa*, 19 January and 12 March 1994)

On this occasion Kozyrev further made it clear that he saw the defence of the human rights of Russian-speaking citizens in the 'near abroad' as a key concern in Russian foreign policy. In the international uproar that followed Kozyrev sought to deny his words, but Russian press agencies insisted that they quoted him correctly. Incidentally, this is but one in a series of confusing episodes within Russian foreign policy where authorities contradict one another or themselves (*Financial Times*, 8 and 9-10 April 1994).[8] Sending confusing signals may be Russia's unofficial way of handling the increasingly critical Western reaction to its hard-nosed 'near abroad' policy after a period of putting 'Russia first'. At any rate some of the influential Russian foreign policy experts are publicly beginning to question the wisdom of Moscow's 'enlightened postimperial course' of bullying its neighbours. The 1994 version of the 'Strategy for Russia' issued by the Russian Council for Foreign and Defence Policy, headed by Karaganov, coined a new formula: 'leadership instead of control' (*NeGa*, 27 May 1994). The Council dismisses the coercive approach of the 'ultra-nationalists' as a threat to stability.

---

[8] In July 1993 the Russian parliament laid claim to Sevastopol, the navy headquarters of Crimea, a decision that was immediately denounced by Yeltsin, who felt 'ashamed'.

In contrast to Migranian, the Council avoids the terminology of 'near abroad' and reiterates Kozyrev's concept of good neighbourliness with reference to the Baltic states. Another prominent voice is that of Aleksei Arbatov, who strongly criticizes the 'infantile imperialism' of Russia (*NeGa*, 24 June 1994).

These critical notes to Russia's self-assertive foreign policy are to be placed in the context of a new Russian campaign of seeking to convert the CIS into an international organization – i.e. as a legal subject within international law. In continuation of the foreign policy concept envisioning economic and military integration within the CIS, high-level Russian officers proposed in 1994 to form a military alliance, first with CIS members and later, perhaps, with the Baltic states too. The source for this is an interview with Lt.-Gen. Leonid Ivashov, Secretary of the CIS Council of Defence Ministers. As observed by the Russian journalist interviewing him, this idea amounts to a new 'Warsaw Pact' on the territory of the former internal empire in a repetition of Moscow's old policy towards the external empire (*NeGa*, 17 May 1994). Moscow's heightened CIS policy reflects the institutional shortcomings of the CIS in general; shortcomings which have become painfully clear in connection with NATO's offer of a 'Partnership for Peace' (PfP). The popularity of this concept among CIS members – most of whom signed up before Russia – caused frowns in Moscow, where it is perceived as a challenge to CIS integration (*NeGa*, 7 April 1994). This was the background to the Russian '16+9 formula': the goal of forming a bilateral partnership between what would then be two military alliances. Another controversial development is Russia's economic union with Belarus in concordance with Moscow's original preferences in the 'near abroad'.

Except for former Yugoslavia, the no longer so near abroad of Eastern Europe was originally placed low on independent Russia's list of foreign policy priorities.[9] Without doubt this reflects the fact that this former outer ring of the Soviet empire consists of mostly less vulnerable states placed further away from Russia due to the establishment of new post-Soviet buffer-states. The first version of the 'Strategy for Russia' acknowledged the need to prevent Eastern Europe from joining any system of collective security that excluded

[9] Among other things, Yeltsin cancelled planned trips to Bulgaria and Romania in December 1991 and generally showed little enthusiasm for the former external empire at that time.

Russia (*NeGa*, 19 August 1992). But the authors went on to argue East and Central Europe's irrelevance in Russian foreign policy, due to the region's lack of resources to invest in the rebirth of Russia. They singled out Poland for its strategic significance to Russia and somewhat surprisingly added Bulgaria and Slovakia. In stark contrast to this contribution, the Security Council's concept of Russian foreign policy insists on the significance of Eastern Europe. The Russian military doctrine even speculates on possibilities of military cooperation. Behind this ostensible upgrading of policy towards the former external empire lies changing Russian perceptions of the future of East-Central Europe.

Originally, Russia only worried about Central Europe's functions as a buffer cutting it off from Western Europe, the nightmare being that this might happen in conjunction with Ukraine and the Baltic states in a deliberate attempt to construct a *cordon sanitaire* excluding Russia (*NeGa*, 13 February 1992).[10] Senior officials in Moscow have warned the Visegrad countries against forming a political union, let alone a military coalition with Ukraine on the grounds that both Ukraine and Belarus fall within the Russian sphere of influence (*The Economist*, 15 May 1993). Later on, as the Visegrad countries' approach to reintegration sharpened, Russia's attitude shifted to fear that the region might actually abandon its present buffer status and become part of the EU and NATO. At the outset, however, Russia sent exactly the opposite signal. During Yeltsin's visit to Poland in August 1993, he assured President Walesa that Russia would not object to Poland's joining NATO. Their joint declaration characterized this as 'a decision taken by a sovereign Poland in the interests of overall European integration that does not go against the interests of other states including Russia' (ITAR-TASS, 25 August 1993). Afterwards Kozyrev had to correct his superior by saying that such a development would be conditional upon a fundamental transformation of NATO and the entire European security architecture, in line with his thoughts on the nexus between Russia, NATO and Eastern Europe advanced earlier (Kozyrev, 1993).

Nevertheless, the previous benign neglect of the external empire

[10] Moscow's hypersensitivity about consultations and cooperation between the Baltic and Ukrainian foreign ministries is rooted in fear of the revival of the Polish Marshal Pilsudski's concept of a confederation stretching from the Baltic to the Black Sea.

was now replaced by fence-mending as Yeltsin visited not only Poland, but also the Czech Republic and Slovakia in September 1993. The idea was to demonstrate Russia's respect for their independence and willingness to strengthen bilateral cooperation (de Weydenthal, 1993). But as neither party has shown much interest in formulating a viable new framework for closer cooperation, Russia's bid for influence in the Visegrad region is not too convincing.[11] Early on, the reformist Soviet Union and subsequently Russia lost the confidence of the Poles by delaying the troop withdrawal from Poland at a time when troops were hastily retreating from Hungary and Czechoslovakia. Hungary did host an official visit by Yeltsin in November 1992, when he sought to heal the wounds of 1956 (*Neue Zürcher Zeitung*, 12 November 1992). But the Russian parliament for a long time stalled the ratification of the December 1991 bilateral treaty between the two countries because of its wording on the 1956 insurrection. More than anything else, however, it is Russia's stiff opposition to an eastward expansion of NATO, as made explicit in the autumn of 1993 and repeated many times since, along with the other neo-imperial tones in Russian foreign policy that have soured relations between the former centre and its external empire.[12] Thus, in early 1994 Yeltsin proposed that NATO and Russia should yield to Eastern Europe security guarantees followed by reminders from Russian MFA officials, including Kozyrev, that the region remained in Russia's sphere of vital interests (*Summary of World Broadcasts*, 14 January 1994).

Russia's policy of reintegration. The whole irony about the political uproar on account of Kozyrev's and Yeltsin's initial approach to postcommunist Russia's foreign policy is that at the end of the day their basic priorities are shared by the major part of Russia's political élite. This is particularly so when we turn to the topic of reintegration (Skak, 1993b). According to one Russian opinion poll, it is a

[11] Not without justification, Russia pins its hopes on EU protectionism as a way to revive close economic cooperation with Eastern Europe; see Pichugin (1994).

[12] Earlier (see p. 68) I have dealt with Russia's ambiguous policy of suggesting approval of NATO membership for Slovakia, Bulgaria and Hungary. Nevertheless, during an official visit to Sofia, Vladimir Shumeiko, chairman of the upper house of the Russian parliament, expressed discontent that Bulgaria signed a PfP, warning that the country was still dependent on Russian spare parts for its weaponry (*RFE/RL News Briefs*, 13-17 June 1994).

minority – 45 per cent – who declare themselves Slavophiles, that is preferring Russia to follow its own model of development, whereas a majority of 52 per cent place themselves in the camp of Westernizers. When presented with the question 'Towards which country or region should Russia orient itself with a view to develop long-term good-neighbourly relations and close economic cooperation?', as many as 47 per cent of the Russian foreign policy-making élite (including parliamentarians) answered Western Europe and 11 per cent the United States, whereas 8 per cent preferred Eastern Europe, 7 per cent China and only 5 per cent the CIS (Popov, 1994). As a further example of the basic inconsistency bordering on schizophrenia of the calls to focus on the 'near abroad', presumably at the expense of the 'far abroad' one can cite the views of one of the semi-hardliners Vladimir Lukin who said, while still Russian ambassador to the United States, that Russia should devote more attention to its 'friends in the near abroad' than to its 'partners' in the 'far abroad' by way of integration (*Segodnia*, 3 Sept. 1993). However, Lukin panicked on learning the reaction of the 'far abroad' to his country's invasion of Chechnia, and said that Russia's international prestige had reached an all-time low, even compared to the Brezhnev years of stagnation when it was at least feared if not respected (*ibid.*, 11 January 1995). In particular he regarded the EU's suspension of its partnership with Russia and of Russia's entry to the Council of Europe as ominous.

Upon closer examination, Kozyrev's original vision of reintegration appears less subservient towards the West than his critics would have us believe. Kozyrev did commit himself to the new political thinking, hailing the developed countries of the West as the real allies of Russia. He described Moscow's strategy of gaining international recognition as one of 'joining the world economy to get help to satisfy Russia's domestic needs' (*Izvestia*, 2 January 1992). But he went on to say that Russia was no poor little brother obediently following the directives of a rich, malevolent West wanting to buy it out. The sole approach needed was one of common sense, where the success indicator of foreign policy would be the improvement of standards of living for the Russian people (*ibid.*). On 31 January 1992, Yeltsin made his first speech to the UN Security Council, announcing the end of confrontation with the West and declaring democracy, human rights and high legal standards to be the three pillars of Russian foreign policy. Yeltsin characterized the United

States and the West as 'not just partners, but rather allies'. At that time it fell to Kozyrev to remind the world that 'Russia is destined to be a great power' (interview on Russian TV, 3 March 1992). Conversely, it was the then Speaker of the Russian parliament, Ruslan Khasbulatov, who reminded Kozyrev that real greatness is determined by the status of a country's citizens, its quality of life, and not by the size of its territory (Matveev, 1992).

In fact, Kozyrev appears to have found inspiration in Andrei Kortunov, a most respectable Russian political scientist who pointed to France and de Gaulle as role models for Russia (*Moscow News*, no. 36, 1990). In its new political game with the West, Kortunov advised Russia to balance between the centres of power: 'The strategic task of the 1990s is to start cooperation with all the "centres of strength", without turning into an economic and political appendage of any one of them' (*ibid.*). This point was picked up by Yeltsin in his speech to the US Congress: 'In joining the world community we wish to preserve our identity, our own image and history' (ITAR-TASS, 17 June 1992). Similarly, Kozyrev outlined his approach to reintegration in terms of 'joining the club of the most dynamically developing democratic states in order to take a worthy position as predetermined by our history and geography' (*NeGa*, 1 April 1992). More specifically, Kozyrev wanted Russia to focus its reintegration diplomacy on the countries making up the G-7 (*Izvestia*, 31 March 1992). According to Kozyrev, it was no coincidence that Yeltsin's first visits abroad were to important G-7 capitals – Paris, London, Washington, Bonn and Tokyo – as well as Beijing. In addition to helping Russia gain access to the IMF and provide economic support for the domestic transition – aid diplomacy, as it were – Moscow courted the G-7 with the explicit aim of ultimately becoming a member of the group:

> Without doubt, due to her possession of vast natural, human, scientific and technical resources, the Russian Federation meets the requirements needed for taking its seat in the club of the most advanced countries of the world worthy of a great power. In my view this is simply the idea behind the transformation of Russia, [the gist of] her strategic interest in the modern world and the essence of her domestic and foreign policy concept. (Kozyrev in *Izvestia*, 31 March 1992)

There seems to be near-total consensus within the Russian foreign policy opinion-making élite on the expediency of this goal as a cornerstone of Russia's strategy for reintegration (personal interviews with Karaganov and Zagorski). G-7 membership would represent a real victory in the popular quest for Russian greatpowerhood. The political culture of empire of the Russian political élite thus turns the quest for rank and greatpowerhood into the essence of the country's reintegration policy.[13] The G-7 for its part is wary of extending membership to the destabilizing rather than stabilizing Russian economy. Until recently, the formula for Russia's participation in G-7 summitry was 'G-7 plus one' rather than G-8. In the lead-up to the G-7 summit in Naples in the summer of 1994, Kozyrev changed tactics, demanding merely 'political membership' denying that Russia had any wish to join the global macroeconomic talks (*NeGa*, 23 February 1994). Furthermore, Russia's G-7 diplomacy is telling for its intergovernmental approach to cooperation with the West, along the lines of the classic European concert from 1815 to the Crimean war – the era of the Holy Alliance that suited Tsarist Russia so well (Seton-Watson, 1967). Intergovernmentalism was de Gaulle's line on European integration too and today there are frequent calls for a Russian 'neo-Gaullism' – not least on the undercurrent of Russia's foreign policy concept (*NeGa*, 24 May 1994; 29 April 1993).

Russia's approach to membership of essentially Western multilateral fora other than the G-7 is less clear-cut. To be sure, Moscow was very enthusiastic about the establishment of the NACC as a framework for cooperation with NATO and went as far as publicly airing its interest in full NATO membership at the inaugural session of NACC (*Financial Times*, 21 December 1991). The guarded Western response to this prospect explains much of Russia's opposition to NATO's eastward expansion, which it is understood would not include Russia – not for the time being at least. For its part Russia may thus calculate that the only way to force the West into taking its reintegration seriously is by vetoing Eastern Europe's reintegration. Some analysts believe that this pattern will repeat itself once the Visegrad countries enter the EU as full members. At any rate, Karaganov insists that Russia's muting of its quest for EU membership does not imply that the goal has been abandoned

---

[13] Thus Karaganov dismissed Yeltsin spokesman Viacheslav Kostikov's otherwise surprising proposal of making Russia's adherence to a PfP conditional upon G-7 membership for Russia as a kite flown solely *for domestic purposes* (*Financial Times* and *International Herald Tribune*, 9-10 April 1994).

(personal interview). Thus Russian Prime Minister Viktor Chernomyrdin used the occasion when Hungary submitted its official application for EU membership to announce that Russia planned to submit its application in 1994 as well (Reuter, 1 April 1994). The fact that the application was never sent does not turn it into an 'April Fool' in overall significance. With or without EU membership, the point is that Chernomyrdin's bold EU approach may reflect voter preferences. According to a Eurobarometer survey of late 1992, as many as 70 per cent of Russian respondents living on the western side of the Urals support the idea of Russia becoming a member of the EU (*Central and Eastern Eurobarometer*, no. 3, 1993).

For the time being, however, Russia's relationship with the EU will be determined by the agreement on partnership and cooperation signed at the European Council at Corfu on 24 June 1994 – the implementation of which has become subject to delay due to the bloody events in Chechnia. Negotiations dragged on for two years as France dug its heels in on the issue of Russian aluminium and uranium exports. Significantly, the EU agreement was not subject to noteworthy politicization inside Russia. Like most other postcommunist countries, Russia was sceptical about the EU's Pact on Stability in Europe originally proposed by French Premier Edouard Balladur, but acquiesced (*Le Monde*, 28 May 1994; see Chapter 7 below). Now that several postcommunist countries have become full members of the Council of Europe, including Estonia (much to Russia's dismay), Moscow is pushing for membership of this forum, where the country has a special guest status (Agence Europe, 8 May 1992; *NeGa*, 8 October 1993; 20 April 1994). The vehement reaction of the Russian MFA and Vladimir Lukin to the postponements of Russia's entry to this forum shows the importance Russia attaches to the Council of Europe. By contrast OSCE membership has been extended to virtually everybody, including the Central Asian states – at Kozyrev's behest – making this forum less relevant as a platform for Russia's ambitions. Yet Moscow considers the OSCE as a vehicle for campaigning against NATO's expansion. This was seen in Russia's vain calls for placing NATO and the CIS under OSCE supremacy. Russia has also consented to a modest strengthening of the OSCE. Russia stands outside the so-called consultation forum of the West European Union that embraces nine postcommunist countries, including Estonia, Latvia and Lithuania. Till recently, Russia appeared to take less interest in the WEU, but in

December 1994 it proposed that the WEU establish a joint consultative council, apparently to anticipate the WEU possibly gaining greater significance. Russia has concluded a treaty with the OECD that will earn it access to the organization's economic expertise and general prestige (*Moscow News*, no. 23, 1994).

Postcommunist Russia continued Gorbachev's policy of opening the 'European house' by approaching the individual inhabitants to seek their support. As argued on p. 47 above, this strategy amounts to a search for reintegration patrons (Skak, 1991b; 1992b). Insofar as only great powers and multilateral fora will match Russia's need for material assistance, this corresponds nicely with the intergovernmental vision of great power concerts. Like several Visegrad countries, Yeltsin began by courting France and was received with pomp and circumstance in February 1992. However, his appeal for cuts in the French *force de frappe* as a way to add new impetus to nuclear disarmament among CIS countries fell on deaf ears – something that has been attributed to amateurish preparation (AFP, 7 February 1992; Matveev, 1992). Germany counts as the single most important reintegration patron, shouldering over half of all economic assistance to Russia as well as foreign direct investment, a fact readily acknowledged by the Russians (cf. Timmermann, 1993). Moscow has sought to reciprocate by expressing its support for Bonn's ambition of gaining a permanent seat at the UN Security Council (*Frankfurter Allgemeine Zeitung*, 6 October 1992). Nevertheless, a certain donor burn-out has gripped Bonn, along with a more sceptical attitude towards Russian security policy. This was coupled with a keen interest in opening NATO to the Visegrad countries, thus challenging Russian interests. Despite Yeltsin's usual enthusiasm, his visit to Bonn in May 1994 was a less unequivocal success, although German Chancellor Helmut Kohl was forthcoming on the issue of transforming the G-7 to G-8 (*International Herald Tribune*, 14 May 1994). The bilateral relationship with the United States continues to enjoy a special position in Moscow's foreign policy as a manifestation of Russia's great power status. At one time, Russia even wanted to join Washington's Strategic Defense Initiative (SDI). Yet. as noted earlier, Moscow's foreign policy concept more than suggests a parting of the ways, except for the common interest in avoiding nuclear proliferation, where Moscow needs Washington to manage the game with Kiev. As with Bonn, Moscow's brutality in

Chechnia served to undermine the position of the 'Russia First' faction in Washington.

Few, however, would deny the fact of paradigmatic change in Russia's international outlook. Inasmuch as partnership with the West used to be ideological anathema, this new rhetoric cannot be discounted as empty. It is all the more sad, then, that something as innocent as NATO's PfP offer could stir controversy inside the country. The idea of NATO partnership was a Russian just as much as a Western quest (Kozyrev, 1993). Initially, the PfP was embraced by the Russian foreign policy élite as the compromise it was concerning NATO-Visegrad relations. Russia was to sign the PfP framework agreement in the spring of 1994, but parliamentarian opposition prevented this. The allegedly moderate former ambassador to the United States, Vladimir Lukin, as chairman of the International Affairs Committee of the *Duma*, spoke of PfP in terms of the 'rape of Russia' (*RFE/RL News Briefs*, 14-18 March 1994). According to Andramik Migranian, a PfP threatens the isolation of Russia and limits its room for manoeuvre in foreign policy; others have spoken of an unequal marriage (*NeGa*, 15 March 1994).[14] It was not until 22 June 1994 that Russia signed the PfP framework –after having secured for itself 'no surprises' in terms of states of the former Soviet empire being granted NATO membership and an undefined say on other NATO issues, reflecting its special status compared to other PfP signatories. One may look upon the domestic turmoil surrounding this outcome as the result of pressure from the home front in Russia's international game with NATO. But in view of Moscow's inability to prevent the extension of the PfP framework to the CIS, it is hard not to look upon the temporary rejection of PfP as pure idiosyncracy.

Explaining foreign policy developments in Russia

As a first analytical step, it is worth reflecting on the relevance of the institutional approach to understanding Russian foreign policy. After all, there are certain recurrent themes and continuities which

[14] Along with Lukin, Marshal Evgeni Shaposhnikov warned that the strengthening of NATO through the PfP programme could lead Russia into confrontation with China; on the other hand, a failure to sign could leave Russia isolated (*RFE/RL News Briefs*, 6-10 June 1994).

could be said to reflect normative orientations amidst all the stir. As already shown, the principle of observing human rights has gained an almost sacrosanct status in the Russian foreign policy discourse. Concern for the human rights of Russians is the common denominator of contributions from both nationalists and cosmopolitans. The Norwegian historian Pål Kolstø (1993) warns against taking this lightly as merely a pretext for meddling in the internal affairs of neighbouring countries. It is the state on whose territory a given ethnic minority lives that carries responsibility for their protection; nonetheless, the fate of minorities is a legitimate concern for the international community and hence also for Russia.

But it would be utterly naive to take the Russian concern for human rights at face value, The fact that the country has chosen to align itself with Hungary, which is equally insistent on the minority issue for obvious reasons[15] but has not aligned with, e.g., Ukraine, another country with minorities abroad, does not remove suspicion concerning hidden agendas – on the contrary. To substantiate their case, Russian think-tanks such as the Gorbachev Foundation have prepared studies arguing that there is a massive exodus of Russians from non-Russian republics because of discrimination and ethnic violence (*NeGa*, 7 September 1993). But their analyses tend to simplify matters. Russian emigration is part of a long-term trend that began decades before the present political upheaval. Economic motives loom large in this, although it may be reinforced by feelings of insecurity (Halbach, 1994). What is more, the Russian campaign for protecting ethnic brethren abroad has been directed at the Baltic states, where the physical threat to the security of Russians is much less evident than elsewhere in the former Soviet Union. As far as the Baltic states are concerned, it is broadly recognized that the Russians arrived as a force of occupation, which makes it difficult to speak of a minority problem in the conventional sense. International organizations have failed to find evidence of violation of human rights – as distinct from civil and political rights. Yet Moscow continues to claim gross discrimination or even apartheid in the practice of the Baltic states.

Most disturbing is the fact that semi-official papers on Russian

---

[15] Russia and Hungary issued a joint 'Declaration on the principles guiding the cooperation between the Republic of Hungary and the Russian Federation regarding the guarantee of rights of national minorities' in November 1992. See also Chapter 6.

foreign policy as well as individual contributions by prominent Russian political scientists reveal an openly cynical attitude on the human rights issue (G. Simon, 1994). The 1992 version of the 'Strategy for Russia' argued Moscow's interest in emphasizing the Russian diaspora throughout the former Soviet empire as a political, economic and social 'trump card' of substantial weight (*NeGa*, 19 August 1992). Karaganov has developed this thought further in an all-embracing neo-imperial concept:

> I believe that the basis for the Russian foreign policy concept in relation to the Russian-speaking population must be the concept of protecting rights and minority rights on the territory of all of the former Soviet Union.... The Russian speaking population is ... a powerful asset for Russia.... We must do everything to keep a Russian-speaking population in the regions ... we have to have levers of influence in a long-term perspective.... Russia has to initiate large-scale economic expansion and investment exploiting the huge debts accumulated by most republics, concentrate firms, own them to build a powerful economic and political enclave forming the core of our political influence.... We have to continue the training of the elites of the former republics in Russia so that these elites will be close to us.... We have to strengthen the role of Russians in the officers' corps and continue the training of the future military elites in Russian military academies. (1992)

In addition to harping on the theme of human rights in Latvia and Estonia, Karaganov proposes using economic sanctions and/or, if necessary, force towards the 'near abroad'. His views can only strengthen suspicions about the Russian minorities as a virtual fifth column, thus contributing to a worsening of their safety. Karaganov is not that primitive, yet the statement quoted here casts serious doubts on his further proposal of dividing the OSCE into two zones.

Admittedly, the fact that human rights are part of Russia's larger strategy could be said to prove the role of international norms and institutions. But Moscow's highly selective approach serves as a warning not to exaggerate the institutional logic behind its foreign policy (cf. Checkel, 1992; 1994; Dannreuther, 1993). Russia appears tempted by the possibility of looking upon the Dniestr Republic from the vantage point of national self-determination, but balks at this notion when applied to the Russian Federation, which includes the Kaliningrad exclave. As one of the world's two leading nuclear powers, Russia has a self-evident interest in upholding a regime of nuclear non-proliferation. Indeed, it is the self-identification as a great power that provides the key institutional logic behind the country's international conduct. Russia's tendency to aligning itself with Serbia is less a gesture of Slavic brotherhood – in that case a most selective brotherhood – than it is part of the aim of becoming a necessary partner in the great-power concert on former Yugoslavia.[16] Russia has persistently called for an international conference to solve the nuclear crisis on the Korean peninsula and is keen to continue to have a say on Middle East affairs – or even African affairs (*NeGa*, 22 September 1993). As pointed out earlier, Moscow's great-power ambition may drive it into foreign policy overstretch. But for the outside world it is exactly this ambition that might become an avenue for tempering Russian unilateralism – e.g. within peacekeeping. At any rate, the country fears international isolation and needs the world more than the world needs it.

This points towards the condition of interdependence as a pivotal argument of many institutionalists. References to interdependence and the security dilemma have almost gone out of fashion in the Russian foreign policy debate, together with new political thinking – geopolitics takes the pride of place instead.[17] A partial exception to this can be found in the Russian deliberations on CIS cooperation, which focus on interdependence as a means to further cooperation and integration and as an end itself. Yet the fact remains that CIS interdependence is both lopsided and underdeveloped. It is a function of bilateral energy dependency upon Russia more than anything else. Truly multilateral and multi-level interdependencies – e.g. links between private companies or citizen-to-citizen contacts – are underdeveloped, as are the CIS structures of decision-making and implementation. This overarching problem of a low institutionaliza-

[16] Russia has played a more moderating role in former Yugoslavia than these lines may suggest; something that has earned the government accusations from Belgrade belligerents that it is acting as a fifth column (*NeGa*, 23 April 1994). Moscow's Serb protegés reciprocated by humiliating Russia during the siege of Gorazde. As in the case of Israel and the United States – often cited as a role model for Russia in its relationship with Serbia – it is frequently the tail that wags the dog.

[17] In the same vein as former Russian Ambassador to Washington Vladimir Lukin, Alexei Bogaturov argues the United States' interest in Russia on account of its potential as a stabilizer for the entire Eurasian area, capable of keeping the lid on international turbulence (1993).

tion of cooperation, in turn, compels a closer look at the argument of institutionalism. If turned upside down in this way, institutionalism does offer a plausible explanation of the ups and downs in the external conduct of the new Russian state. Once again, the argument focuses on the lack of stabilizers.

The realist balance-of-power perspective. Like other non-consolidated states, postcommunist Russia's policy develops in a tentative, *ad hoc* fashion that would seem to reflect the logic of power more than anything else. Russian decision-makers appear more prone to perceive the outside world in terms of conflict, clashes of interest and zero-sum than through the lenses of mutual interest and common approaches – e.g. Andranik Migranian (*NeGa*, 12 and 18 January 1994). His thinking in terms of spheres of influence, windows of opportunity and power vacuums has gained an astonishing degree of respectability (cf. *NeGa*, 10 March 1994). In continuation of this new outlook bordering on a 'fortress Russia' perception, unilateralism has come to be seen as both legitimate and necessary. Aleksei Arbatov, Viacheslav Dashichev and Vitali Portnikov, the foreign policy columnist of *Nezavisimaia Gazeta*, are among the few to speak out on these trends (*NeGa*, 5 Oct. 1994). Arbatov warns against a repetition of the Afghanistan scenario as the misguided attempt to check a perceived power vacuum it was (*NeGa*, 24 June 1994). However, others conclude that the 'near abroad' is a power vacuum towards which Russia cannot afford benign neglect (Karaganov, 1993). Ednan Agaev, adviser to Kozyrev, admits that cooperation is profitable for Russia and the West alike. But he goes on to argue a strictly realist approach to international relations:

> It stands to reason that in their relations with us the Western nations pursue their own interests. ... they already want to reduce the resurgent Russia's possible sphere of influence.... Therefore the aid they render us will be carefully rationed. We are entering a world of cut-throat rivalry... we have to stand up for our interests.... There is no need for the Byzantine sophistry inherent in Soviet diplomacy with its first communist and then universal human slogans. We should openly announce our national interests, declaring that they are of paramount importance to us and that we will work to secure their realization – thus securing the respect of our international partners. (*Moscow News*, no. 18, 1992)

To be sure, it is possible to interpret these hawkish tones in two ways. First, we can regard Russia's policy towards its neighbours as guided by defensive motives. This is how the British analyst Roland Dannreuther comments on Russia's new assertiveness:

> This does not presage another round of imperial expansion. Rather it is a policy of retrenchment, seeking to ensure that there is no further unravelling of the Russian state. It also reflects a conscious decision to attempt to regain the initiative in promoting Russian security and economic interests in countries like those in Central Asia and the Persian Gulf. However, this new assertiveness will still not fundamentally change the shift in the balance of power to the new countries of Central Asia and their immediate neighbours to the south. Certainly, Russia cannot be discounted as a powerful actor wielding for some time predominant influence in Central Asia, but this should not obscure the underlying reality that Russia is engaged in a process of withdrawal from the Muslim world which is unlikely to be reversed. (1993, p. 94)

It would, indeed, be foolhardy to deny that Russia has vital geopolitical and economic interests in relation to its immediate neighbours –interests ranging from the well-being of the Russian minorities abroad, to the availability of ice-free ports in the Baltic and Black Sea, to transport and communications, and a security interest in preventing the immediate neighbours from joining alliances that are hostile to Russia. Dannreuther's analysis focuses on Moscow's sensitivity to security threats from the south, a perception shared by Aleksei Arbatov (1993). One scenario feared by Russian analysts is the spill-over of Muslim fundamentalism from Central Asia via Kazakhstan to Tatarstan and Bashkortostan, thereby splitting Russia proper along the Volga river. But in view of all these vulnerabilities and legitimate security concerns, Russia's heavy-handed treatment of Kazakhstan and other 'near abroad' states becomes all the more puzzling.

Here the second – offensive – interpretation offers itself, an approach that highlights the revisionist, intimidatory nature of Russian foreign policy and thus takes seriously the neo-imperial threat emanating from the country (G. Simon, 1994). In the analysis of Renée de Nevers, Russia pursues a *three-pronged strategy* in the CIS. First, one of genuine *peacekeeping*, as seen in Tadzhikistan where it successfully brought an end to hostilities. Secondly, a strategy of *province-making* or establishing forward-based positions, e.g. to secure Russian interests in the Balkans; this is how General Lebed sees the role of the 14th Army in Transdniestria, a sign that it may prove difficult to implement the withdrawal planned for 1997. Finally, there is a strategy of *peace-prevention*, de Nevers' term for Russia's role in Nagorno-Karabakh, which seems carefully calculated to prevent Turkey from gaining a foothold in Transcaucasia through peace between Armenia and Azerbaijan, which could boost the Turkish concept of Black Sea cooperation (1994, pp. 54–5). The offensive interpretation marks a balance-of-power approach that focuses on windows of opportunity, as when Migranian offers the following explanation for Russia's adoption of a more assertive line during the crisis in Transdniestria: 'after the Western countries refrained from serious protests to Russia, the Foreign Ministry's position began to change in the direction of unconditional defence of the Dniester republic' (*NeGa*, 12 January 1994). Another example of this kind of reasoning is found in an observation made by Lukin: 'the change of president [in the United States] ... is to the benefit of our diplomacy. During the transitional period there is an opportunity within the framework of diplomatic decency to adjust our overall course... which has suffered from an excess of pro-American romanticism' (quoted in Crow, 1994a). Suzanne Crow is not alone in arguing the responsibility of the international community when seeking to draw attention to these Russian views (cf. Lynch, 1994). In her assessment, the change in Russian foreign policy is a change by default – that is, brought about by Western inertia and willingness to grant Russia its strategic wishes (Crow, 1993b).

The domestic logic of power. Arguably, the single most important window of opportunity is the one represented by the institutional void on Russia's home front. The balance-of-power perspective must therefore be carried on to the domestic scene, as already suggested in the many hints to actors and their mutual rivalries. The only way to give a satisfactory explanation for the truly irrational traits of postcommunist Russia's foreign policy – such as the obsession with the supposed dangers of a NATO expansion at the expense of a much more probable security threat from China, as pointed out by de Nevers – is to take a closer look at the labile decision-making structure. The zeal with which parliamentarians, extra-parliamentarians,

Foreign Ministry officials and non-Foreign Ministry officials, opinion-makers and journalists have embraced the field of foreign policy bears no relation to the lack of enthusiasm for supposedly 'vital' foreign policy issues among Russian citizens. As Geoffrey Hosking reminds us, the mass desertions of the Russian peasant soldiers during the First World War is but one example of a healthy indifference towards the imperial ambitions of the Russian political élite; an indifference repeated in the war in Chechnia, as revealed in opinion polls (*The Independent,* 7 January 1995; cf. *Segodnia,* 23 February 1995). In the words of one frustrated Western diplomat in Moscow: 'Russia's ideal foreign policy now would be not to have one at all' (*Financial Times,* 3 February 1994). What is more, the Eurasian neo-imperial tide in Russian foreign policy contradicts the opera-tional foreign priorities of the Russian élite itself, as pointed out earlier. The Russian officers, for instance, are wary of getting entrenched in armed conflicts all over Eurasia. In other words, by turning foreign policy into high politics the Russian foreign policy-making élite is manipulating the interests of the Russian people as well as its own interests.

How is this paradoxical outcome to be explained? The answer is by a mixture of idiographic and nomothetic determinants, that is through the interplay of the unique legacy of a political culture of empire at the élite level and the contemporary institutional void brought about by the transition from communism to postcom-munism. As already revealed, the reasoning here borrows from the American political scientist Jack Snyder (1991), who describes how empires – be it pre-Second World War Japan and Germany or the Soviet Union – become victims of their own imperial drive. In times of upheaval, parochial revisionist orientations may gain the upper hand through the reckless pursuit of 'national interests' out of an 'innocent' pursuit of power in the domestic game of *kto-kogo.* This may lead not only to expansion, but to overexpansion or 'overstretch' – a syndrome characterized by rising costs and diminishing returns (Kennedy, 1989; Bunce, 1985; Ericson, 1987; Wolf, 1987; cf. *NeGa,* 27 May 1994). The reason is that imperial and military interests tend to be more concentrated and better organized – i.e. more powerful – than anti-imperial and anti-militarist trends among taxpayers and consumers (Snyder, 1991, p. 44). In other words, the game is biased in favour of praetorian forces, who in the specific context of postcommunist Russia feel they need to distance themselves from

Gorbachev's political legacy. The short term costs associated with reorienting Russia's foreign policy is passed on to groups outside the praetorian coalition – the MFA, which has had to face up to *faits accomplis* – whereas long-term social costs remain uncalculated because of the highly parochial perspectives of the groups in the log-rolling coalition (*ibid.*).

Let us briefly recapitulate some of the main developments and actors. In theory, Russia has a 'presidential' foreign policy in that Article 86 of the new constitution attributes to the president a 'guiding role' in foreign policy (*rukovodstvo*; 'Konstitutsia Rossiiskoi Federatsii', 1993). At the outset Yeltsin did try to raise his profile in matters of foreign policy, in continuance of his previous line of outsmarting Gorbachev on new political thinking. But the onslaught on Kozyrev and the Foreign Ministry made him recede into the background. Like Kozyrev (who was not an MP then), Yeltsin lacked a political basis and this made the policy inherently vulnerable. It was this factor more than actual blunders in the 'near abroad' that presented the temptation to outside interference – against the background of a volatile, unrewarding external environment for foreign policy-making. Meanwhile, Kozyrev tried to weather the storm by posing as executor of the presidential foreign policy while occasionally adapting to the neo-imperial currents. Part of the fury directed against Kozyrev – e.g. on the part of his rivals for office as minister, such as Stankevich – may be due to his international reputation and skills. But there were occasional leaks of classified material from his inferiors and things clearly got out of the ministry's control, as when Kozyrev complained about unauthorized arms transfers to the Dniestr Republic: 'Why are the military leaders deciding the most important political issues?' (*Izvestia*, 1 July 1992). The example of the troop withdrawals from the Baltic states showed that the Ministry of Defence became involved on Kozyrev's authority. A likely motive for Kozyrev transforming himself into a hardliner may thus have been to seize control back from the military, as maintained by Flora Lewis (*International Herald Tribune*, 2 February 1994). Kozyrev's strategy of turning his ministry into a 'power ministry' has had some success, although tending to make him part of the problem rather than its solution when it comes to Russia's co-existence with its neighbours.

But Yeltsin surely also became involved by relegating work on Russia's foreign policy concept to the then newly established

Security Council. The stir caused by the concept provided a key vehicle for praetorian forces eager to display their ostensible concern for Russia's national interests. As for the Security Council, its role in foreign policy appears to have climaxed with its work on the foreign policy concept in 1992-3 when the politically ambitious Juri Skokov was its secretary. Afterwards it devoted itself mostly to domestic security issues and conversion, where the military clearly has a say. Not that the role of the Security Council is trivial; on the contrary, it seems to have been a key decision-making forum behind the Chechnia invasion, in addition to such people as presidential adviser Korzhakov. The bias towards domestic issues is illustrated by the personality of its new secretary, Oleg Lobov, an economist (personal interviews). In view of the Security Council's limited interest in foreign policy, it is ironic that Skokov managed to formalize its role in foreign policy by designing a new mechanism for decision-making and coordination through its Interdepartmental Foreign Policy Commission. Instead of Kozyrev's emphasis on good neighbourliness, Russia has settled for a somewhat isolationist 'fortress Russia' foreign policy doctrine. Yeltsin's use of the Security Council to weather the storm over foreign policy, in turn, was part of a larger and successful strategy of courting the so-called power ministries, which unfortunately did not include the MFA (Rahr, 1993b; Yasmann, 1994; Crow, 1993a). Given these bodies' tendency to entertain militarist positions rather than the opposite, this illustrates how power tends to be concentrated around these views in great powers and would-be great powers.

The reason why Yeltsin had to change his tactics centres on the eternal struggles with the Russian parliament – struggles mainly rooted in domestic power motives, but often involving foreign policy (as if reforming Russia was not a more pressing issue).[18] One leading figure in 1992 was the head of the Supreme Soviet's (parliament's) Committee on International Affairs, Ambartsumov – simultaneously a member of the Presidential Council and mooted as a possible replacement for Kozyrev – seconded by Rumiantsev and Khasbulatov. In addition to providing aggressive parliamentary opposition to Kozyrev, Ambartsumov pursued his own agenda

[18] One reason why foreign policy was chosen as a battlefield may have been dissatisfaction with Yeltsin's *eminence grise*, Gennadi Burbulis, a rising star in charge of day-to-day control of the MFA (Crow, 1993a). Burbulis held liberal, moderate views.

vis-à-vis Yugoslavia, as Vice-President Rutskoi had done in Transdniestria and Crimea. Rutskoi's switch to spearheading the political opposition in Russia, in turn, is most revealing of the volatility of political loyalties in postcommunist Russia. It ended in the bloody showdown of early October 1993, yet it may be premature to conclude that Rutskoi's political career has reached its zenith. However, during 1994 the maverick General Lebed rose to pre-eminence as another contender for power. As for other curiosities within the supposedly presidential circles of power, one should mention Migranian in his capacity as adviser to both Ambartsumov and Yeltsin, in addition to his membership of the foreign policy forum Club 93. It is a club that includes another influential and capable but semi-hawkish presidential adviser, namely Karagnov, and has been attributed with having a most manipulative role at the apex of power in Russian politics (Meier, 1994). Maksim Meier describes the forum as one that excludes 'extremists' – whether pro-western liberals like former Prime Minister Gaidar or Zhirinovski at the opposite pole or, before them, Stanislav Shatalin, author of the (never implemented) 500 days' programme of reform in the Gorbachev era – and attracts political scientists united in their ambition for power and influence. Then there is Karaganov's own club, the Council for Foreign and Defence Policy, established with the explicit goal of forming a strong centrist foreign policy platform by issuing first one and then a second 'Strategy for Russia' – in defiance of the MFA.

Until recently Zhirinovski was counted among the extra-parliamentarian outsiders, but this is no longer so. Most analysts appear to exaggerate the danger represented by Zhirinovskii and in this way underestimate the power of others. The new parliament – the *Duma* – will continue to make its voice heard in this field, notwithstanding the institutionalization of presidential foreign policy (Adams, 1994). Finally, there are the real extra-parliamentarian outsiders, such as the Cossacks who have on several occasions taken security policy in their own hands – e.g. through intervention in Transdniestria. The danger of warlordism they represent is only amplified by the fact that Cossacks are not exclusively Russian –there are equally self-willed Ukrainian Cossacks (Gehrmann, 1994). The Russian Cossacks see themselves as defenders of the Russian state, but do not accept its external borders fixed by the founding summit of the CIS in Alma-Ata in late December 1991

(*NeGa*, 18 February 1994). Cossack interventions in Tadzhikistan and Kyrgyzstan, not to mention Kazakhstan, and the Caucasus, could spell disaster. Equally disturbing are the many signs of President Yeltsin's loss of control over his presidential apparatus, leading to the re-emergence of Byzantine Kremlin power schemes, climaxing in the muddled decision to invade Chechnia. However, neither Yeltsin's nor Chernomyrdin's influence over foreign policy is necessarily conducive to moderation.

Admittedly, this sketch of actors and influences may have over-emphasized the volatility of the domestic framework of Russian foreign policy decision-making. After all, Kozyrev is still there, securing a measure of continuity if, however, through a startling change in tenor. But as rightly observed by Suzanne Crow (1993a), Russian foreign policy is a far cry from mainstream 'bureaucratic politics' as envisioned by Western political scientists. What must be taken into consideration are the turbulent conditions of democratization implying norms of openness and participation which mix with unfortunate lack of ground rules, lack of a stable balance of power between the legislative and executive power and an immature political culture inviting reckless institutional and personal rivalries. Policy-making in postcommunist Russia is quite another world from that of routine budget struggles. As a final analytical step, this point will be illustrated by a case study of one controversial decision in postcommunist Russia's foreign policy, applying the approaches listed in Figure 2.2 above (see page 60).

The cancellation of Yeltsin's visit to Japan in 1992

The rational actor perspective. So far, the analysis has omitted Russia's substantial interests in the Far East, which compel it to develop at least a *modus vivendi* with China, Japan and (South) Korea and if possible a close economic and political relationship with these countries. Put in these general terms, this is an insight shared by the entire Russian foreign policy élite (Blank, 1993). At an early stage the Russian government took diplomatic initiatives in the region. In March 1992 Kozyrev travelled to Beijing, Seoul and Tokyo to prepare visits by Yeltsin in all three capitals later that year, but nothing came of the visit to Japan. It was due to start on 13 September, but was cancelled abruptly on the 9th – at a time when Russian limousines had been flown in and all preparations had been made. The cancellation took the Japanese and the Russian MFA totally by surprise (*Moscow News*, no. 38, 1992; Akaha, 1993, p. 176; personal interviews with Russian and Japanese diplomats in Moscow). In view of Japan's central position as a prospective economic partner and Moscow's need for its political support to realize the goal of gaining G-7 membership it is difficult, indeed, to explain the cancellation in terms of careful calculus and rational choice. To be sure, there was the delicate and still unsolved issue of the southern Kuriles, dubbed the Northern Territories by the Japanese – the small islands of Etorofu, Kunashiri, Shikotan and Habomais which are claimed by Japan (see map, facing p. 139). For this reason no peace treaty has been concluded with Japan since the Second World War. (For further historical and legal analysis of the dispute, see Stephan, 1974; de Villafranca, 1993).

Given Yeltsin's declared will to proceed on the principles of 'justice and legality', implying an outcome in Japan's favour, combined with the softening of the Japanese position since May 1992 there was reason to believe that the visit would take place – even if there would be no sensational results. By the summer of 1992 Yeltsin had stronger motives for going to Japan than for not going. Germany had publicly aired its frustration at having to shoulder the lion's share of international economic assistance to Russia at the Washington conference in January 1992. This made it all the more urgent for Moscow to seek alternative sources of assistance, among which Japan was certainly one of the most prospective. It might be counterargued that the Japanese had shown little interest in boosting economic relations – and that there was no guarantee they would change their reserved attitude towards investing in the Russian economy (cf. *NeGa*, 7 July 1992). But there is no conclusive evidence that this kind of calculation motivated Yeltsin; if it did he probably would have cancelled the visit much earlier, thus avoiding the scandal. What is more, after the cancellation of the visit the Japanese Minister of Foreign Affairs, Watanabe, revealed that Tokyo had told Moscow in advance that a Russian reconfirmation of the 1956 Declaration and an agreement to discuss the future of Etorofu and Kunashiri would have been enough to unleash 'full-scale' Japanese assistance, hitherto withheld (de Villafranca, 1993). This Declaration committed the Soviet Union – and by extension Russia – to transfer to Japan the two southernmost islands of Shikotan and Habomais in the event of a peace treaty. As for the theory that

Yeltsin may have counted on Washington, Bonn and Brussels to make Tokyo contribute its fair share of international help to Russia without Moscow having to take direct steps *vis-à-vis* Tokyo, this still does not explain the sudden nature of the decision not to go – with the humiliation of Russia it entailed (*NeGa*, 10 September 1992).

In other words it is the sudden cancellation of the visit by Yeltsin that turns the whole affair into a mystery for rational actor analysis. Against the proposition that Yeltsin may have been worried about the attitude of the residents of the Kuriles, by mid-1992 opinions were actually coming round to an increasing willingness to accept Japanese suzerainty, which indicated a growing impatience over Moscow's manipulations and neglect (Skak, 1993a; *Independent*, 2 July 1992; *The Times*, 21 July 1992; *Financial Times*, 6 August 1992).[19] Locals were so frustrated about supplies and facilities at the utterly inhospitable isles that, for instance, half of the inhabitants of Shikotan were interested in a takeover by Japan in the spring of 1992 (Szajkowski, 1993a, p. 250). This is in stark contrast to the outcome of the March 1991 referendum, when between 70.2 per cent of the Kunashiri and Habomais citizens and 81.3 per cent of the Shikotan and Etorofu citizens in a 90 per cent turnout voted against the return of the islands to Japan (Glaubitz, 1994). In late 1992 the mood changed again into opposition to Japanese suzerainty (*International Herald Tribune*, 30 November 1992). Yeltsin did not seem concerned about the strategic value of the islands, or their resources as reported by one Japanese analyst: rich fishing grounds along with tin, zinc, lead, copper etc. in the area seaward of the islands, in addition to titanium sand, sulphur and metal sulphide deposits of particular importance for Russia (Akaha, 1993, p. 168). Another frequently heard Russian argument is that renouncing the islands would have repercussions on other territorial issues – involving China, Estonia and Germany or Lithuania (Kaliningrad). If Yeltsin did weigh all this as arguments for not going, why is it that he was prepared to go until the very last?

The organizational process and the bureaucratic politics perspective. Graham Allison's (1971) organizational model focuses on inertia and routines ('standard operating procedures' or SOPs) within ministries and the

[19] An organization of Kurile residents – '*Zemliak*' – wanting the islands to be transferred to Japan without compensation was founded in the summer of 1992 (Szajkowski, 1993a).

like when seeking to explain foreign policy outcomes. In contrast to the rational actor model which has as its ideal type the individual utility- or power-maximizing statesman – in this case Yeltsin – the organizational model points towards dynamics within groups, especially administrative cultures. Insofar as the cancellation of the Tokyo visit was no standard procedure but an open break with all planning and diplomatic etiquette, it would seem a waste of time to apply this model. Judging from the analysis of Stephen Blank (1993), the MFA was absolutely convinced that the Kuriles issue alone precluded massive Japanese investment in Russia. The ministry's positive expectations of the outcome of the visit would imply a strong preference for it to take place almost at any cost. Or would it? According to the Russian analyst Aleksei Pushkov, what happened was:

> Back in March when Kozyrev was on a visit to Japan, the Foreign Ministry made it clear to the Japanese side that the dispute about the islands could be settled in principle. On the other hand, by the summer the Foreign Ministry officials had assumed a tougher stand for fear of being accused of 'betraying the national interests'. This ambiguity could not but lead to such an outcome. (*Moscow News*, no. 38, 1992)

What is suggested here is that even some ministry officials ended up having a hidden agenda of cancellation if necessary – Kozyrev included, because of the ferocious attacks on him during the summer causing Yeltsin to dissociate himself from him amidst calls for his resignation (*Financial Times*, 18 August 1992). Significantly, after the cancellation Kozyrev sought to put a bold face on it by declaring himself 'satisfied that the political logic got the upper hand.... I concluded that we were not ready to make the visit as productive as it should be' (*Moscow News*, no. 38, 1992).

In any event, however, it would be grossly misleading to portray the MFA as the sole instigator of the cancellation. Other bureaucratic actors and their political game have to be considered in a further 'bureaucratic' or 'governmental politics' analysis. As Blank sees it, 'the rivals were represented by the MFA, reformers and new thinkers in the government, and the Japanologists in major research institutes on the one hand, and the [Ministry of Defence] and its partisans on the other' (1993, p. 149). The military would prefer a Far Eastern policy focused on China rather than Japan and in this it has many supporters (Skak, 1993a). Military circles were openly dissatisfied with Yeltsin's announcement in May to the effect that Russia would withdraw all its troops – 7,000 – from the Kuriles by 1994 as part of an MFA initiative (Foye, 1992). Defence Minister Pavel Grachev told a press conference on 19 May that the geostrategic interests of the army dictated that there would be no military withdrawal; a position that hardened as new hardliners were added to his ministry in June. The Russian officers saw the Kuriles as a vital link in the Russian Far Eastern defence system, notably the defence of the strategic nuclear fleet and as an outlet into the Pacific Ocean (*Krasnaia Zvezda*, 22 July 1992; Foye, 1992). The General Staff circulated its evaluation of the consequences of a transfer of the islands to Japan to Russian parliamentarians as ammunition in the parliamentary hearing on the topic scheduled for late July (*NeGa*, 30 July 1992). This document took a bellicose tone, depicting Russia's military presence as a deterrent against a Japanese seizure of the Kuriles by force. The military did not bother to mention the miserable state of its facilities there, as pointed out by *Komsomolskaia Pravda* (Skak 1993a). On other occasions, the Russians have to some extent admitted the Kuriles' military insignificance (*Moscow News*, no. 43, 1992; Glaubitz, 1994).

To conclude, the top officials of the Russian Army did intervene and for their part displayed SOPs in the shape of Cold War attitudes. But the military was not alone, as implied by Blank. There is still the role of the then newly established Security Council to consider. The German scholar Joachim Glaubitz is convinced that it was a session in this forum which took the decision to cancel and cites *Izvestia*'s coverage (11 September 1992). Kozyrev more than suggested interference by the Security Council in the interview with *Moscow News* cited earlier. According to him 'the *apparat*' – minus Yeltsin's personal aides – tried to meddle. He dismissed the official explanation for the cancellation – that Japan could not guarantee Yeltsin's security – as 'childish', and elaborated:

> There's acute struggle in this sphere, I mean getting access to the President ... I know they are trying to get on my nerves ... I believe that a true patriot cannot but lament the fact that we are currently unable to establish normal relations with Japan. ... these people would gladly take up the security issue to create another image – that the president is afraid to do what Gorbachev had done, i.e. to visit Japan. (*Moscow News*, no. 38, 1992)

One of the Security Council's five voting members was Rutskoi, who was pursuing his own foreign policy in this case. The culprit within the Security Council could very well have been Rutskoi had it not been for the fact that he may not have been present at all during the decisive meeting on 9 September (*NeGa*, 11 September 1992). Admittedly, one very prominent source who was present at the meeting, namely Foreign Minister Kozyrev, implies that Rutskoi was present, at the same time as claiming that it was he, Barannikov (Minister of Security) and Skokov who suddenly demanded the cancellation of the visit, allegedly because of insufficient Japanese security preparations (*Segodnia*, 17 Jan. 1995). Several sources highlight the role of Skokov, including the then Governor of Sakhalin, Valentin Fodorov, another curious actor in the drama (personal interviews, cf. Foye, 1993). The Russian journalist Vera Kuznetsova cites Japanese sources according to which Yeltsin's aide, Juri Petrov, also played a role in the cancellation of the visit – he is also mentioned by Kozyrev (*NeGa*, 11 September 1992). Petrov's motive, like Skokov's, may have been personal rivalry with Burbulis, who together with Skokov and Petrov was in charge of the practical preparations. Petrov himself explained his role by citing instructions from the security services (implying Barannikov). Burbulis was reluctant to make the President and his *apparat* appear as the decision-making locus, implying that it was acting under pressure (Crow, 1993a, p. 26). In other words, the bureaucratic politics model in the exotic empirical version presented here does carry the analysis forward. But throughout there have also been hints concerning the role of outsiders in relation to these decision-making fora.

The dramatic actor model. The dramatic actor model invented by Peter Calvert (1986) is the opposite pole of the rational actor model in that it focuses on foreign policy decisions as diversions from domestic problems – as public theatre rather than the pursuit of interests in relation to the external world. An implicit premise in the model is that foreign policy decisions taken by dramatic actors have to have some popularity or prestige – or else they won't work. Given the politicization of the visit to Japan, it could, of course, be argued that the cancellation would satisfy some circles; hence that the whole affair was motivated by Yeltsin's wish to appear as a stubborn defender of Russian national interests. To be sure, Yeltsin may ultimately have decided that it was necessary not to go in order to give exactly this impression. But again, the scandal surrounding the cancellation militates against this. True dramatic actors are good at giving the appearance of control, but neither Ambartsumov, Kozyrev nor Pushkov approved of the impromptu way the visit was called off. Yeltsin himself was moody afterwards. The real dramatic actor was not Yeltsin, but somebody else.

One such person may have been Valentin Fodorov, who might be said to have had a motive for diversion. His ill-fated attempts to attract investments to Sakhalin and the Far Eastern region aroused the suspicion of Yeltsin and Khasbulatov; besides, Fodorov took care to let it be known publicly that he pressed for a cancellation of the visit (personal interviews in Moscow; *Frankfurter Allgemeine Zeitung*, 24 August 1992). Fodorov led the campaign against Deputy Foreign Minister Georgi Kunadze – a moderate willing to negotiate a cession of the Kuriles – by insinuating that he was a 'criminal' in the service of Japanese interests, and wrote several letters to Yeltsin warning against the 'pro-Japanese lobbies' in the MFA. Fodorov may be the one who started the rumours about a secret MFA plan to hand over the islands to Japan almost without compensation – $100 million according to Ambartsumov (personal interview; Foye, 1992 and 1993). No one, including Fodorov, seems ever to have seen the alleged plan, but the rumour was instrumental in whipping up public opinion and rousing the parliament into action. The final word on the issue therefore goes to the praetorian model.

The praetorian model. As should be clear by now, what was intended as a cordial visit aimed at breathing new life into the strategically important Russo-Japanese relationship produced a public uproar and an unintended diplomatic scandal. Various forces outside and inside the government mobilized themselves in an allegedly patriotic campaign against the handover of the Kuriles and against the state visit. The Russian political summer of 1992 was hot indeed, as seen in the hysteria surrounding the distribution of an explanatory brochure by the Japanese embassy in Moscow (*Japan's Northern Territories*, 1992; Skak, 1993a). The conservative media whipped up emotions and rumours, as did nationalist circles in Japan at a time when the political process between Japan and Russia was gaining momentum.[20] Japan declared its flexibility on the 'modality' of the

[20] According to Russian sources, the Japanese communists were among the most

solution, provided Russia recognized in principle the Japanese right to the Kuriles. This made the Russian governmental committee preparing the visit look into the 1956 model (*JiJi-Press-Newswire*, 6 and 22 July 1992). But the false rumours of an 'unconditional surrender' hurt the process badly. A group of fifty-two parliamentarians and non-parliamentarians wrote an open letter to Yeltsin demanding that he consult the parliament. In open contradiction of its own demand for a referendum on the Kuriles, the letter further claimed that a review of Second World War territorial outcomes could lead to a Third World War and that it was immoral to deprive Russia of part of its territory (Reuters, 15 July 1992). No one seemed to appreciate the fact that Yeltsin and his aides were applying pressure upon Japan themselves.

Rumiantsev in particular had thrust himself into the issue with open calls for a cancellation of the visit – for the sake of torpedoing the presidential foreign policy, it seems (*NeGa*, 29 and 30 July 1992; *Izvestia*, 29 July 1992). He was entrusted with the task of preparing a legal memorandum on the issue for the parliamentary hearing in late July and was accused by several Russian legal experts of giving a biased presentation of legal facts, e.g. casting doubt on the binding nature of the 1956 Declaration (*NeGa*, 30 June 1992). He took the initiative at the closed parliamentary hearing, which was only 'closed' in the sense that among its fifty-two participants there were just fifteen MPs, while the rest included prominent Sakhalin politicians eager to contribute in the struggle against the 'samurais' (*NeGa*, 30 July 1992). Rumiantsev's memorandum boiled down to a call to let parliament issue the directives to the MFA and to instruct the President to consult parliament (*NeGa*, 25 July 1992). In spite of the extreme tension between parliamentarians and MFA officials at the closed hearing, *Izvestia* was much less alarmist than *Nezavisimaia Gazeta* on the prospects for the visit; an assessment shared by the American analyst de Villafranca (cf. *Izvestia* 29 July 1992 and *NeGa*, 30 July; deVillafranca, 1993, p. 621). Indeed, by August it was as if the crisis had climaxed. Tokyo may have been too adamant on the territorial issue for Moscow to respond, but Watanabe did try to convey the message of Japan's flexibility to the very last (*Izvestia*, 8 September 1992). The semi-official excuse for the cancellation of

---

opportunistic in their desperate bid for votes. They did not shy away from demanding a takeover of all of the Kuriles, adding 'Why not Kamchatka?' (*NeGa*, 30 July 1992).

the visit – public opinion in Russia – was not too convincing. The All-Russian Committee for the Defence of the Kuriles, including notables like Nina Andreeva, a prominent Stalinist, staged a 'mass protest action' on 10 September in Moscow – a mass protest numbering 100 people (*NeGa*, 12 September 1992). Indeed, Ambartsumov's explanation for the cancellation is quite revealing of the kind of manipulations at work. He attributed it to the MFA's 'uncoordinated policy' and its 'impolite' behaviour towards Japan (Crow, 1993c). In this context he counts among the more reasonable and balanced actors (personal interview).

Epilogue. Yet another proposed visit to Japan was cancelled in early May 1993 though with less of a scandal. It was not until October 1993 that Yeltsin went to Tokyo on a state visit – immediately after the military showdown with the parliamentary opposition, as if he wanted to demonstrate his grip on power (cf. Foye, 1993). In view of the success of the 1993 visit against the background of a more tactful Japanese approach, including a more forthcoming attitude on economic assistance, it is tempting to dismiss the 1992 affair as essentially a victory for Russia and its interests. This may be so. But the damage done in terms of weakening Russia from within was considerable. In the assessment of Aleksei Arbatov, the 1992 crisis constitutes a real turning point in Russian foreign policy:

> The cancellation of the summit at the very last moment, and the incomprehensible official explanations of this erratic step, were the first time that Boris Yeltsin yielded so obviously to the nationalists' massive political campaign (1993, p. 24).

The outcome of the 1992 turmoil over policy towards Japan only added to Russia's praetorian syndrome. Moscow was deprived of whatever opportunity there might have been *vis-à-vis* Tokyo and thus wasted precious time. The visit appears to have been designed as part of a greater exercise in classic Russian swing diplomacy, intended to avoid lop-sided dependence on the United States and Europe. When extolling the significance of his visit to India in January 1993, Yeltsin clearly would have liked to add Japan to his list of diplomatic successes: 'The recent series of state visits to South Korea, China, and now to India is indicative of the fact that we are moving away from a Western emphasis' (Russian TV, quoted in Crow, 1993a, p. 76).

The emerging pattern in postcommunist Russia's foreign policy reiterates the concentric circles of empire in a curious way. Instead of the previous *Pax Sovietica* and in an effort to alleviate the inherent anarchy in postcommunist international relations, Russia seeks to establish a layered sphere of influence around itself.[21] The country continues to view itself as the centre in CIS relations and further seeks to claim exclusive influence in the Baltic states by declaring them part of the 'near abroad'. Finally, Russia has sought to gain certain veto powers in relation to Eastern Europe, which used to constitute the external empire. The operational goal is not to re-establish the Soviet Union, but rather to turn the previous internal empire into something resembling the old external empire on the basis of a formal military alliance or the like – a new Warsaw Pact as it were – and to turn the CIS into an international organization that is also of economic significance. Although the international community has failed to give Moscow the go-ahead to act as gendarme which it wants, its policy is not without success. To depict the Russian political mind as anti-Western is misleading, rather the Russians want to have their cake (empire) and eat it too (reintegration). In the field of reintegration Russia differs from other postcommunist states in its reluctance to sign a PfP and to focus on acceptance of its great power status – hence the obsession with gaining G-7 membership. Moscow may note with satisfaction the success of transforming the G-7 into a G-8 as far as the political talks at the Naples summit of 1994 are concerned. As for what looked like another milestone, the Partnership and Cooperation Agreement concluded with the EU in the summer of 1994, the ratification has been suspended because of events in Chechnia together with Russia's membership of the Council of Europe.

Zbigniew K. Brzezinski insists that Russia cannot be both an empire and a democracy. Yet the country may prove to have the option of muddling through as a semi–empire and semi–democracy.

[21] The conception of a layered sphere of influence is modelled on the layered buffer concept advanced by Buzan *et al.* (1990, pp. 177 ff.) in somewhat idyllic terms as a future option of the former internal and external empire. What the authors have in mind is something akin to the so-called Nordic Balance, i.e. a pattern stretching from Finlandization to formal neutrality in Sweden and full NATO membership in Norway, Denmark and Iceland. Finland's eagerness to gain NATO membership in the post-Cold War era is indicative of the limits to this idyll. A strategy of Finlandization is Andrei Kortunov's clue to Russia's position regarding its former empire (*Moscow News*, no. 3, 24 January 1994).

It is the eternal problem of balance between cohesion and viability that crops up here in Russia's relations with its 'near abroad' and to its own resources and aspirations. Semi-democracy and semi-empire may be no disastrous outcome, but neither does it spell stability and for Russia's immediate neighbours it smells of a great power backyard. In Dimitri Furman's analysis Russia follows a dualistic foreign policy: for the Western 'far abroad' it dresses in a dinner jacket, while for the 'near abroad' it dons a flak jacket and rolls up the sleeves – and by-passes its own MFA (Teague, p. 11). Russia's decision-making environment is far more volatile than that of other postcommunist states. It is rooted in the power vacuum created by the dissolution of the CPSU which – for lack of institutionalization of the level of the executive and the political parties – causes power to concentrate around arbitrary lobbies and strong personalities. This pattern of politics exists in most other postcommunist states bereft of their one-party rule, but nowhere as ominously as in Russia.

The new Russian state further suffers from a lack of stabilizers in the shape of a non-imperial past, which, coupled with institutional weakness, threatens imperial overstretch. Since 1992, an unholy alliance of empire-restorationists, bewildered democrats and cynics have successfully checked Russia's return to foreign and security policy normalcy – so successfully that some of them are beginning to show regrets (*NeGa*, 27 May 1994). Portraying Kozyrev's and Yeltsin's opponents in these negative terms is by no means to suggest that there were no flaws or weaknesses in Yeltsin's and Kozyrev's original strategy. The point is that domestic criticism was mostly misguided, unfair and rich in hidden agendas. To the extent that there is consensus around centrist positions at present, I do not share the optimistic assessments of its inherent stability as held by some analysts. Things may grow even worse (Lepingwell *et al.*, 1994). Neither, however, do I share the pessimistic view that European culture and democracy are alien to Russia. Russia's aspiration of a return to European normalcy is what makes it worth warning about praetorian manipulations and crude power politics internally as well as externally. The pervasive logic of power, in turn, is a reason for not exaggerating the institutional logic behind Russia foreign policy although progress is undeniable even here.

5

THE FOREIGN POLICY OF POSTCOMMUNIST LITHUANIA

Along with its Baltic neighbours to the north, Lithuania is unique among the former states of the internal Soviet empire in having experienced independence as a sovereign state earlier this century.[1] On 16 February 1918, Lithuania declared its independence and was recognized by Soviet Russia in 1920, but was annexed by the Soviet Union in the summer of 1940 as a result of the Soviet-German non-aggression pact of 1939. Lithuanian parliamentary democracy did not survive the coup of 1926 when Antanas Smetona was installed as president, but his rule was more civilized than his authoritarian nationalism would suggest (Lieven, 1993, pp. 66 ff.). Accordingly, like their Baltic fellows, Lithuanians tend to look upon the interwar years with some nostalgia, while the reverse is true for the subsequent period under Soviet rule. As described in Chapter 3, sovietization was incredibly brutal and brought about a protracted guerrilla struggle (cf. Vardys, 1965, pp. 85-108). But thanks to this, as well as to Lithuania's fewer industrial facilities as the most rural of the Baltic states, the influx of Russian settlers to work in the factories was never as massive as in Latvia and Estonia. Today Lithuanians constitute 79.8 per cent of the country's population, Russians make up only 9.4 per cent and Poles 7.6 per cent; something that provides for a more manageable relationship with Russia than is the case further to the north.

---

[1] For a most entertaining and reasonably up-to-date introduction to the political history and culture of the Baltic states, see Lieven (1993). On interwar Lithuania, see e.g. Rauch (1974). In addition to Misiunas and Taagepera (1993), there is Vardys (1965) on Soviet Lithuania. In the brief introduction to Lithuanian political culture and history that follows I have omitted the fascinating topic of Lithuanian art – wooden totem poles along the highway and in the backyards of Vilnius; mustard-coloured wooden village houses with exquisite wooden carvings on the roof, etc. – as having only a faint bearing on the country's foreign policy.

The Soviet era also brought some leeway to Lithuania thanks to the adroitness of party Secretary Antanas Snieckus, a native communist in office since 1930. He used the opportunity of Khrushchev's thaw to Lithuanize the party and to bring in younger experts at the expense of older 'Reds' (Misiunas and Taagepera, 1993, pp. 146 ff.). Algirdas Brazauskas, Lithuania's current President and last communist party Secretary, continued the Snieckus tradition of pursuing Lithuanian economic and cultural interests *vis-à-vis* Moscow as much as possible. In a pioneering move, Brazauskas' party split off from the CPSU in late 1989. Whatever popularity he enjoys is rooted in this image of pragmatism and political savvy. Conversely, Vytautas Landsbergis, who led the Lithuanian struggle for independence and served as head of state (parliamentary Speaker) from 1990 to 1992, models his political vision on interwar Lithuania and Smetona (Lieven, 1993, p. 68). This points to one common trait shared by Landsbergis and Brazauskas as well as their fellow Lithuanians, namely a certain parochialism reinforced by isolation under Soviet rule. As pointed out by Anatol Lieven, Soviet rule brought a strange mixture of industrial modernity and kitsch, thereby cultivating the rejection of modernity inherent in the peasant political culture of the Baltic societies[2] (*ibid.*, p. 126 ff.). Now that state sovereignty has been achieved, giving rise to the new challenge of reintegration, a culture clash between the romantic Lithuanian nationalism of yesterday and the mundane realities of today is inevitable, as can be seen in the eclipse of Landsbergis' political star. To be sure, there are no Eurasian undertones in the way Lithuanians see themselves in relation to Europe – as in Russia. Yet, according to one indigenous scholar, Lithuanians are mostly 'incompetent, ignorant, and not interested in the problems of Europe' (Jurgaitiené, 1993, p. 37). This assessment may be too negative when considering the fact that as much as 86 per cent of the population has declared itself in favour of EU membership – a higher proportion than in Estonia (79 per cent) and Latvia (72 per cent; *Central and Eastern Eurobarometer*,

---

[2] In 1991 Lithuanian Foreign Minister Algirdas Saudargas was quoted as saying that Western democracy is 'sham' and that true democracy stems from the heart of a nation (Lieven, 1993 p. 391, n. 15). This view is reminiscent of both Solzhenitsyn and Havel, who want politicians to display 'high moral standards'. In this all three gentlemen display a common misunderstanding of democracy as embodying 'good politics'. Democracy's only *raison d'être* is as a safeguard against 'evil politics', by offering a procedure for the orderly change of government.

no. 3, 1993). Be that as it may, the unfortunate point of departure for Lithuania is its backwardness in relation to, if not alienation from, contemporary Europe – and a lack of qualified people to help the country catch up. It is to be hoped that this will be outweighed by the observation of Lieven, namely that underneath the flamboyant rhetoric Lithuanians are moderate pragmatists – not least the ordinary people (1993, p. 25).

The true source of pride for Lithuanian nationalists is medieval Lithuania rather than the 1920s and 1930s. In contrast to Latvia and Estonia which were subject to conquest and colonization from an early time, Lithuania managed to establish itself as an independent great power, later in union with Poland. At its peak, Lithuanian power stretched from the Baltic to the Black Sea and from the outskirts of Moscow to Poland – a past greatness inspiring daydreams among youngsters to this very day. While still pagan, Lithuania gathered strength in the thirteenth century and joined hands with Poland in 1386 through dynastic marriage. That same year, Lithuania converted to Christianity as the last European state to do so. In 1410, the combined armies of Poland and Lithuania defeated the Teutonic Order at Grünwald. The Union of Lublin of 1569 diminished Lithuanian autonomy, however, and gave rise to Polonization. Worse still, Lithuania came to share the fate of Poland, namely anarchy, political decay and annexation by the Russian empire in 1795. Today, Lithuanians speak with bitterness about the historical influence of Poland. Catholicism is not as strong as it used to be and is tinged with pagan traits. The strained relationship between Lithuanians and Poles is further due to Poland's annexation of the multinational Vilnius region in 1920 (see map), forcing Lithuania to move its capital to Kaunas. Following Lieven, the loss of the highly cosmopolitan city of Vilnius with its rich Jewish culture partly explains the tendency towards myopia in Lithuanian political culture (1993, p. 60). On the other hand, progress in the field of reform may be more evenly distributed in Lithuania than elsewhere as a result of its strong commercial provincial centres – e.g. Klaipeda with its international harbour. But the international community and the Lithuanian polity would probably be well advised to take seriously the threat from Lithuanian ultra-right forces, reiterating the old 'Kaunas faction', in continuance of the rural anti-capitalist mentality fearing Popper's open society featuring pluralism – political and economic competition based on rational critical discourse (*ibid.*, pp. 73 ff.).

The merging of paramilitary groups and mafia gangs, reflecting the growth of organized crime in Lithuania, is another ominous trend.

These critical remarks should not be taken to suggest that Lithuania is eternally lagging behind its neighbours to the north, particularly not when it comes to foreign and security policy. Consensus prevails on the need to balance relations with Russia through reintegration as the way to make the de-sovietization of society irreversible. Except for marginal groups, everybody acknowledges Lithuania's limited room for manoeuvre in international affairs in contrast with the position in the thirteenth century, when the country was able to check the power of the then tiny Russia. With an area of 65,200 square kilometres, Lithuania qualifies as a small state – much the same size as Latvia. Lithuania is more densely populated than Latvia and Estonia, though, as it has 3.7 million inhabitants. The country enjoys a favourable geopolitical location in terms of maritime access to the West and remoteness in relation to Russia (except for Kaliningrad) because of the position of Belarus, but the significance of this buffer may diminish. Lithuania lacks mineral resources and is dependent on energy from Russia, although it is seeking additional suppliers. Generally speaking, industry is not competitive but has to be modernized throughout. Much the same could be said about agriculture. The economic transition will be very painful, with slow progress – shock therapy or not. The lack of enthusiasm among Lithuanians themselves shows that this is broadly understood – if anything, the danger is one of too pessimistic an outlook. But in view of the sharp drop in production – by a total of some 70 per cent between 1992 and 1993 – and subsequent pauperization of much of the population, this is very understandable. In 1989 Western estimates put the country's GNP *per capita* at $5,880, a figure that failed to reflect the miserable purchasing power by then, however. More instructive is the index of Lithuania's level of development in relation to a Soviet average of 100 units, where its score would be 118 units. Contrary to what might have been expected, the current left-wing government of the Lithuanian Democratic Labour Party (LDLP) has not halted reform, but is struggling *inter alia* with parliamentary opposition to its privatization scheme. As a result of the introduction of the national currency, the *litas*, on 25 June 1993, inflation had dropped to 5-6 per cent per month by January 1995. In 1994, for the first time in five years, there was modest economic growth.

Lithuania's resources in the military sphere are not rich either. At present there is an active force of 9,800 (including a paramilitary border guard) and a reserve force of 11,000 men – a token military presence compared to Russia's (International Institute of Strategic Studies, 1993). The Lithuanian Army may be more motivated than any invading troops would be, but it needs munitions badly, down to the most trivial of items. None of the NATO countries have been very forthcoming in supplying weapons and military equipment; neither has neutral Sweden, otherwise known as a prominent international arms merchant. The military strategy of all three Baltic states boils down to mounting brief formal resistance to·underline the will to resist and then to retreat into the forests to wage a guerrilla struggle. The key element in this strategy would be the reporting of international media, creating public outrage in the West – known as CNN-defence after the US cable television network. Indeed, this is the only strategy possible given the present force levels and actual threats, for instance in the event of a crisis in the heavily militarized Kaliningrad exclave. Still, Lieven voices some doubts concerning the purpose behind the size of the Lithuanian armed forces, apart from reflecting the country's self-image (1993, p. 321). Plans for the army foresee a force of 30,000 men, including the Home Guard – this is higher than the corresponding targets of Estonia and Latvia. For the time being, however, it would be absurd indeed to dramatize Lithuania's military power. The nation's real resources are those of a typical small state, such as the ability to concentrate on issues because they are limited in number – e.g. by being adamant on the question of troop withdrawal. Despite all evidence on the infantile disorders of Lithuanian diplomacy, negotiators and political leaders alike have demonstrated sufficient tactical skills to prove their value as a resource for security policy. Moreover, as a formerly independent nation-state (though not mono-ethnic) with strong links to Europe, the Lithuanian polity has a much clearer sense of direction than has its Russian counterpart, with the result that there is less harmful factional strife. This has created not only a basic foreign policy consensus, but a degree of continuity in foreign policy as well.

Developments within postcommunist Lithuania's foreign policy

At the outset – i.e. upon the declaration of independence on 11 March 1990 – Lithuanian diplomacy faced the not so simple task of gaining international recognition of the newly free state (Trapans, 1991). Moscow responded with an economic blockade and no one responded with diplomatic recognition except for Iceland. The step taken by the Lithuanian popular front *Sajudis* was pioneering and received the strongest support from the Latvian and Estonian popular fronts, which were adopting the same strategy. All three also wanted to restore links with the Scandinavian states and were offered 'information offices' in Stockholm and Copenhagen in addition to moral support. The Baltic foreign ministers were accepted as guests at the CSCE conference in Copenhagen in June 1990, but then, in the wake of the August 1991 coup in Moscow, things changed at breakneck speed. Foreign diplomats swamped Vilnius in a scramble to display solidarity. The agenda of Lithuanian diplomacy changed overnight. Instead of a heroic struggle for independence came dull administration. For a while the improvised 'diplomacy' of Balts travelling abroad coexisted with desperate attempts by hastily recruited youngsters to cope with the demands of the situation – in what has kindly been termed 'pluralistic' decision-making (Fagelund Knudsen, 1992). For one thing, it did not occur to the Vilnius authorities to appoint an administrative MFA director to relieve the foreign minister of administrative work so that he could concentrate on policy matters (information from a Western diplomat).

Landsbergis' foreign policy focused exclusively on the withdrawal of Russian troops because of its real and symbolic significance for Lithuania's sovereignty. His strategy of reintegration was never very elaborate, except for the basic idea of returning to Europe. Nevertheless, Lithuania joined the IMF on 29 April 1992 and stepped up activities in international fora as well as bilaterally. The foreign policy of the *Sajudis* government worked reasonably well under the circumstances, with relations with Poland the most notable blunder. Among other reasons, this outcome can be attributed to Landsbergis' own nationalist prejudice and arrogance towards the Polish minority in Lithuania (Lieven, 1993, pp. 166 ff.). In spite of this and other flaws, no doubt Landsbergis' bold foreign policy enjoyed genuine legitimacy with the Lithuanian public. In early 1992 the Pentagon issued a report on post-Cold War hotspots across the globe. It envisioned a Russian invasion of Lithuania as a likely catalyst for a conflict involving NATO; not the most likely scenario, thus revealing Western circles' ignorance of Baltic realities at the time.[3] But Landsbergis appeared on TV with a stiff upper lip, urging the Americans to guarantee Lithuania's energy supplies now that the United States had officially declared its interest in upholding Lithuania's freedom (*NeGa*, 25 February 1992). Prime Minister Vagnorius followed suit, specifying Lithuanian economic needs. *Vis-à-vis* the Russians, Landsbergis could not resist the temptation casually to suggest Lithuania's option of reviving the medieval *cordon sanitaire* from the Baltic to the Black Sea and to point to possible extensions to the Visegrad countries, thus playing on the Russians' nightmare of new powerful Pilsudskis able to deny them access to the West (*NeGa*, 1 July 1992).

Brazauskas' foreign policy is more cautious – perhaps unnecessarily so, as Lieven holds – but to some extent it qualifies as the consolidation of the Landsbergis line and not really as a departure from it except in the field of relations with neighbouring states. On 28 January 1993, following the LDLP landslide victory in the parliamentary elections, *Tiesa* (the LDLP daily) published Brazauskas' platform for the presidential elections, which stressed pragmatism in foreign policy, the protection of state interests and peaceful coexistence with all neighbouring states (*RFE/RL News Briefs*, 25-9 January 1993). In his inaugural speech as President of Lithuania, Brazauskas stressed the need to balance relations between East and West; to secure a Russian troop withdrawal on schedule; gradually to diminish dependence on Eastern energy and Eastern markets, and actively to participate in European and international structures. 'I can only envision a future for Lithuania in Europe', he added (*NeGa*, 27 February 1993). Speaking to the UN General Assembly on 28 September, Brazauskas called upon the international community to give effective economic assistance to former communist states to ensure that they would not succumb to 'nostalgia for a pseudo-socialist past that would be unacceptable to all of us' – thereby challenging stereotypes about himself (*RFE/RL News Briefs*, 27 September – 1 October 1993). More explicitly than their predecessor, the LDLP government and Brazauskas have renounced territorial claims on any of their neighbouring states (Girnius, 1993a).

[3] One cannot escape the suspicion, though, that this Pentagon report with its arbitrary conception of conflict scenarios in the Baltic was somehow conducive to persuading the Russians to withdraw their troops from Lithuania on schedule.

LDLP enjoys a solid parliamentary majority – 75 out of 140 seats. The limited influence on policy exerted by opposition parliamentarians which these figures imply may be what has demoralized them into abandoning their promises of acting as a 'constructive opposition' (Girnius, 1993b). With or without constructive opposition the parliament, *Seimas*, serves as an important public forum for foreign policy debates, as demonstrated during the live broadcast of the session on 22 December 1993 when Brazauskas specified his regional priorities:

(1) increasing cooperation between the Baltic states and the Nordic Council;
(2) closer integration into the economic, political, cultural and defence structure of Europe; and
(3) normal relations with neighbouring states.

Commenting on item 3, Brazauskas denied that there was tension in Russo-Lithuanian relations and further proposed to invite foreign experts to help settle the problems of military transit from Kaliningrad through Lithuania (*RFE/RL News Briefs*, 11-24 December 1993). The pragmatism suggested by these remarks is taken by the opposition led by Landsbergis as a sign that Brazauskas is 'soft' *vis-à-vis* Moscow. Whatever differences there are between the two men however, these often seem to be differences in temper and style, not necessarily of substance. The incongruence between Brazauskas' professed policy of reintegration and domestic reform measures would seem to suggest a more noble cause were it not for the fact that these kind of issues never attracted Landsbergis. In other words, the bottom line is that there has been a fair degree of foreign policy consensus and continuity between the first Lithuanian government and the second. The opposition leader Landsbergis comes out as more impatient to see Lithuania entering NATO than Brazauskas, who in turn is critical of the idea of a limited eastward expansion of NATO. This has been taken by some analysts as a measure to placate Russia – a misreading of the signals (Girnius in *Transition*, vol. 1, no. 1, 1995). When all is said and done in terms of Landsbergis' grievances towards the present government, foreign policy appears to be one of the less divisive issues in Lithuanian politics. One indicator for this is Audrius Butkevicius' readiness to continue as Minister of Defence, thus helping to ensure continuity in the critical troop withdrawal issue. Butkevicius' own thoughts on Lithuania's foreign and security policy are recommended as intelligible reading (1993).

Lithuania's policy towards its postcommunist neighbours. Although Lithuania does not border directly on Russia, except for Kaliningrad, relations with Moscow remain among the more troublesome. Early on – prematurely so in the opinion of his Baltic colleagues – Landsbergis decided on a policy of pressing for the full withdrawal of troops, the sooner the better (Girnius, 1992). He presented this view on 5 October 1991 at a session of the Baltic Council, a forum the three Baltic states established for themselves. Originally, the Lithuanian side did not even know the exact number of Russian troops on their territory and could not prevent reinforcements from being flown in as they did not have control of their airspace. Another problem was knowing with whom to negotiate as long as the Russian parliament had not ratified the treaty recognizing Lithuania as an independent state; this finally happened on 17 January 1992. A high-level Russian delegation held a meeting on this in Vilnius with an equally high-standing Lithuanian delegation shortly afterwards, a meeting that took place in a friendly atmosphere. In the communiqué that followed, the Russian side committed itself to resolve the question of withdrawal 'by honoring the independence and state sovereignty of the Republic of Lithuania' (*ibid*). But nothing much more happened until May, when the Russian military authorities revealed that they wanted to include economic and humanitarian issues in the agreement. The Lithuanian government specified its willingness to let officers stay if they resigned from the Russian Army and to assist in the re-housing of military personnel elsewhere. But the foot-dragging Russian approach caused Vilnius to change tactics. On 8 June 1992 the parliament passed a *constitutional amendment* declaring that Lithuania would

> ...never, under any circumstances, join any new political, military, economic, or other unions or alliances being formed on the basis of the former USSR.... On the territory of the Republic of Lithuania there can be no military bases or army units of Russia, the Commonwealth of Independent States, or its member states. (quoted in Girnius, 1992)

In addition to the deadlock in Russo-Lithuanian talks, the Lithuanians were disturbed by the Russian invention of the term 'near abroad' to include the Baltic states, implying a continued Russian military presence (*ibid.*). Subsequently, the Russians came up with data on manpower and weaponry. By 30 June the Lithuanian side produced what looked like a reasonable timetable for the withdrawal however, the Russians chose to ignore it. In order to refute Moscow's claims that a majority of Lithuanians did not want the troops to leave, a referendum was held to establish whether or not voters wanted them to go unconditionally by the end of 1992 and pay compensation for the damage done since 1940. As many as 91 per cent of the votes cast said 'yes', corresponding to almost 70 per cent of all eligible voters (*ibid.*). Without doubt this all put pressure on the Russian side, but, as stated above (pp. 151-2) the upcoming G-7 and CSCE summits were equally helpful in making Moscow commit itself to the withdrawal. No doubt Landsbergis' threat not to sign the final communiqué of the CSCE summit ('Helsinki-2') also played a part (*NeGa*, 7 July 1992). But what really set things in motion was a Lithuanian initiative on 6 September, when Deputy Foreign Minister Valdemaras Katkus met with the commander of Russia's Baltic Fleet, Vladimir Egorov. On this occasion the Lithuanian side offered to build housing in Kaliningrad for 10,000 officers, in exchange for two Russian torpedo-boats and two small anti-submarine vessels. Two days afterwards, on 8 September 1992, Lithuanian Defence Minister Butkevicius and his Russian counterpart Grachev met in Kremlin and agreed on a timetable according to which all Russian troops were to leave by 31 August 1993 (Bungs, 1993).

As described in the previous chapter, this agreement was destined to become a political football inside Russia. The period leading up to the deadline for the withdrawal was not without its war of attrition – or political confusion in Moscow, to cite Butkevicius' friendly interpretation. Among other things, in January 1993 Russia demanded that Lithuania should change its negotiating team – probably hoping to profit from the electoral victory of the ostensibly less staunch Brazauskas and at the very least to cause internal friction (Girnius, 1993a). Brazauskas was indeed more pragmatic and less intransigent towards Moscow. While allowing for the possibility that he was, as rumour had it, over-zealous about changing provisions in the inter-state treaty then being negotiated, so as to get things moving by the summer of 1993, Brazauskas' approach was partly attributable to his broader foreign policy agenda, but partly also to his critics' lack of realism. On 23 June 1993 the Lithuanian Christian

Democratic Party sent him a memorandum, urging him to resist efforts to bring Lithuania back into the Russian sphere of influence further insisting on the need to receive compensation from Russia for the damage done by the Soviet military since 1940 (Girnius, 1993a). It was the June 1992 referendum that fixed the principle of compensation, giving a populist twist in the direction of humiliating Russia. In any case, the Lithuanian government was bound by this principle, although it was wise enough never to specify any amount. On 22 August, amidst mounting debate in the Lithuanian media and among the opposition, together with signs of frustration over the Lithuanian negotiating team's narrow lines of competence and rumours in the Russian media that Lithuania's demand for compensation ran as high as $146 billion, Moscow broke off negotiations. Afterwards, a spokesman for Brazauskas denied the Russian allegations, noting that Lithuania sought compensation only as a matter of principle (*RFE/RL News Briefs*, 23-7 August 1993). Nevertheless, Moscow flatly rejected Brazauskas' proposal of inviting a third party to help settle the problems, and a Yeltsin spokesman further declined any economic responsibility for the Stalin era, which had also made Russia suffer (AFP, 23 August 1993). Saulius Girnius may have a valid point when reproaching the Lithuanian government in the following terms:

> By failing to explain adequately to the public what they believed to be the advantages of greater flexibility in negotiations with Russia Gylys [the Foreign Minister] and other Lithuanian officials had inadvertently aroused widespread fears about a possible sellout of Lithuanian interests (1993a, p. 27).

Yet he may be closer to the truth when exposing how both sides undermined the talks:

> Compromise had become impossible. Brazauskas could not offer any concessions without risking his political career. Likewise, Russia could not back down and resume the troop withdrawal in light of the numerous warnings it had issued over Lithuania's alleged intransigence (*ibid.*).

In view of the hardening of Russia's policy as a result of the new foreign policy doctrine and its claim to act as police officer in an unspecified 'near abroad' in early 1993, it would have been foolhardy for Lithuania to proceed unswervingly with demands for compensation at a time when it badly needed Moscow's will to negotiate to keep up the deadline for its military retreat. This was not appreciated by the Lithuanian public, and probably not by Landsbergis either judging from his proposal of 5 April to urge Russia to let its troops leave ahead of schedule; something which Povilas Gylys found ill-advised and 'provocative' (*RFE/RL News Briefs*, 5-8 April 1993). Misunderstandings about concessions from the Lithuanian side hampered the efforts of Butkevicius, for instance when he inquired about the possibility of purchasing Russian military equipment at a meeting with Grachev in May. Butkevicius later explained that Lithuania just wanted to reserve for itself the right to buy Russian arms, as Poland and the Czech Republic had done before it (Girnius, 1993a). To this day there is no evidence of major arms deals with Russia, but if there were this would reflect common economic sense. In the meantime Lithuania has received Czech surplus weapons worth $66,000 (*RFE/RL News Briefs*, 18 – 22 October 1993). Grachev's idea of creating a Lithuanian-Russian helicopter- and tank repair facility in Kaunas was subsequently dropped 'for political reasons' by the Lithuanians. His offer of training Lithuanian officers at the military academies in Kaliningrad and Riazan in Russia was accepted, but before that – in December 1992 – Butkevicius visited China with the explicit aim of strengthening military cooperation, indicating a strong Lithuanian determination to ensure it was not dependent on just one power (Wacker, 1994, p. 37; cf. Butkevicius, 1993).

Significantly, two days after the Russian suspension of talks the crisis was abating and the Russian troops withdrawn on schedule. To be sure, since then Russo-Lithuanian relations have hardened, but as far as economic relations are concerned this may be due less to interference on behalf of Russian military hawks than to autonomous decisions or technical problems in Russian energy-supplying firms such as *Lentransgaz* of St Petersburg. Lithuania is caught in a triangular drama of mounting debts on the part of Kaliningrad stemming from Lithuania's deliveries of electricity and transport, and its own debts to *Lentransgaz*, which cannot be swopped. Vilnius' success in achieving military withdrawal under conditions of energy-dependence on Russia and the need for improved access to the less demanding Eastern markets speaks volumes about the collapse of the Soviet monolith. But the Russian side still has the option of linkage, which it is using to press the

Lithuanian side into signing a special transit agreement for Kaliningrad. Till recently Russia blocked the introduction of an MFN-regime in mutual trade which would raise the competitiveness of Lithuanian products – virtually nil now – on the Russian market. The Lithuanian side reciprocated by re-instating the old transit regime, which made Kaliningrad a less thorny issue (*Segodnia*, 20 January 1995). Vilnius has legitimate concerns over the possible – uncontrollable – transfer of weaponry or drugs in case a new transit regime is agreed upon, but from a Russian point of view the Lithuanians are pursuing several agendas, including some of a less noble nature.

Lithuanians refer to Kaliningrad as *Karaliaucius* – 'little Lithuania' – as it used to be part of the Lithuanian empire. At one time when he was Ambassador to the United States, Stazys Lozoraitis (who later ran for the presidency in Lithuania) raised the claim to the region in public at a press briefing: 'Some day, perhaps not tomorrow, Karaliaucius might become part of Lithuania. ... we must approach the situation much more energetically than before.' (Reuters, 1 March 1992). This represented a major *faux pas* and has not been repeated by government officials since then. Yet Lithuanian nationalistic hotheads like Young Lithuania continue to pursue the idea, thus raising the suspicion of even moderate Russians (*Moscow News*, no. 3, 24 January 1994). Should Lithuania ever take over Kaliningrad, it would lose one of the few advantages it enjoys by virtue of its minuscule Russian minority. This is realized by the large majority of Lithuanian politicians, but some of them resort to the alternative option of pursing independence for Kaliningrad as a fourth Baltic state (*Die Zukunft des Gebiets Kaliningrad*, 1993). In early 1994 the parliamentary Speaker Ceslovas Jursenas called for Kaliningrad's secession; a call which was substantiated by legal considerations put forward by Romualdas Ozolas, another prominent opposition politician (*Information*, 8 February 1994). Thus, in a very unfortunate way, nationalist zeal mixes with highly legitimate concerns over the threat to Lithuania's security constituted by this militarized region –the likely outcome being failure on the part of the international community to address the problems concerning Lithuanians. In continuation of the semi-official policy of seeking to stimulate Kaliningrad's autonomy *vis-à-vis* Moscow, Lithuania concluded a free-trade agreement with the region, which was later annulled by Moscow (*RFE/RL News Briefs*, 6-10 December 1993). Whatever unilateral steps Vilnius may have taken, such as upgrading controls and transit fees for passage through Lithuania to and from Kaliningrad, they are attributable to pressure from the opposition; a factor overlooked by Girnius when he notices the worsening of relations with Russia since Landsbergis's time (1993a; cf. *NeGa*, 6 March 1994; *Segodnia*, 20 January 1995).

As for Poland, in spite of substantial differences between Landsbergis and Brazauskas in their approach to relations with Warsaw, this issue was never politicized to the extent that relations with Russia have been. As stated above, Landsbergis' failure to improve relations with Poland qualifies as a major shortcoming in his foreign policy. Indeed, this illustrates Lithuanian parochialism. The first government was trapped in obsolete enemy images of Poland, thereby depriving itself of the option of exploiting postcommunist Warsaw's commitment to a dynamic Eastern policy (Burant, 1993). The point that Poland wanted to replace the primitive chauvinism of the Pilsudski era with a much more modern outlook was wasted on Lithuanian nationalists, who are stuck in the groove themselves. The two factors bedevilling the relationship are, firstly, the seizure of Vilnius and the eastern strip of Lithuania in 1920, making Lithuanian nationalists eternally suspicious of possible 'Polish aggression'; and, second, the Polish minority in Lithuania, whom the Lithuanians tend to consider 'Polonized Lithuanians', thus making them valuable as a source of pressure to be applied on Lithuania by Moscow. True enough, the Poles sided with the Putschists in Moscow in August 1991, but this was after waiting in vain for the Lithuanian authorities to accommodate to some of their not very outrageous demands.[4] Their behaviour towards the head of state may have been boorish, as Lieven argues, but Landsbergis reciprocated equally childishly, thus missing a precious opportunity – as Lieven also insists (p. 170). Without doubt, the views of the intelligentsia in Poland regarding their ethnic brethren in Lithuania were similar to those of Landsbergis. But when the Lithuanian authorities decided to suspend the authority of the Salcininkai district council's presidium and later dissolved the popularly elected councils in this and the Vilnius district (along with similar measures in the ethnic Russian settlement of Snieckus), the Warsaw

[4] Lieven's analysis of the background of present Polish-Lithuanian tension (1993, pp. 158-73) is most illuminating, if not as scientific as Voytek Zubek's (1993). Zubek analyses the issue from a perception of deliberate Lithuanization policies on the part of the Lithuanian state. The change of government and policies is missing from his analysis, however.

government felt that it could not stand idly by. On 19 September 1991, Polish Foreign Minister Krzyzstof Skubiszewski declared that his country would not interfere in Lithania's internal affairs, but neither would it 'remain inactive with regard to certain moves in relations to the Polish minority in Lithuania. ... We simply demand rights for them' (quoted in Burant, 1993, p. 403).

In late November 1991 Butkevicius repeated the (mis-)perception that Vilnius continued to be disputed territory between the two countries. In mid-December Landsbergis received a letter from Polish President Lech Walesa deploring the near-crisis in Polish-Lithuanian relations. Nevertheless, Warsaw did not suspend diplomatic activities *vis-à-vis* Lithuania, calculating that an agreement fixing European norms and legal standards would be the best way to proceed. A declaration of friendship and cooperation was initialled in early 1992, but relations remained frozen until the summer, when the Lithuanian parliament fixed a date for elections in the Polish districts. But even then the normalization process became bogged down – allegedly because of Warsaw's dissatisfaction with Vilnius's failure to honour the provisions set by Poland for progress on the planned state treaty, but in reality because of Polish furor over Lithuanian insistence on a formal condemnation of the 1920 aggression in the preamble. It was not until the summer of 1993 that real progress occurred, following the change in government, but this time without reprisals from the opposition. In the meantime it had become painfully clear to Vilnius that it needs Poland as a gateway to Europe and that Lithuania and Poland have a common interest in the *Via Baltica* motorway project linking Helsinki with Warsaw through all three Baltic states (Girnius, 1993a). Poles and Lithuanians were eager to open a new border crossing at Kalvarija–Budziski, (only the second, in spite of a 110-km. long common border) for the planned motorway. As for the state treaty, the two sides agreed to drop any mention of the 1920 incident, leaving the way open for it to be concluded the following year, on 26 April 1994. On 15 June 1993, Lithuania and Poland signed a military agreement and, subsequently Polish Minister of Defence Onyszkiewicz donated armoured transport vehicles and other military equipment to Lithuania in commemoration of the Polish-Lithuanian victory at Grünwald in 1410. When Walesa visited Vilnius to sign the state treaty he used the occasion to stress that affirmations of ethnic identity should go hand in hand with loyalty to the state in which one resides.

Brazauskas reciprocated with a lack of tact, re-stating the Lithuanian point of view about Vilnius and acknowledging that in this his Polish partners 'might not agree', yet he continued by calling for reconciliation – to which the Polish side reacted with irritation (*RFE/RL News Briefs*, 25 – 9 April 1994). There is still some way to go in the relationship between the two countries.[5]

Turning to relations with Lithuania's two Baltic neighbours to the north, at first glance things appear to have run much more smoothly. Mutual support and solidarity were part and parcel of the three countries' struggle for independence, because of their common political history – first, as sovereign states in the interwar era and, second, as subjects of the internal Soviet empire following their annexation in 1940. There are close similarities between the Latvian language and Lithuanian – which is, incidentally, the oldest Indo-European languages still spoken – but apart from that the cultures, histories, geo- and ethnopolitics of the three countries differ. All three pay lip-service to the idea of Baltic cooperation, but since Estonia's right-centrist government began to speed up reforms and was followed in this by the Latvian government, a certain aloofness *vis-à-vis* Lithuania has been discernible. Brazauskas has been fairly isolated in his calls for converting the Baltic Council into a more structured forum modelled on the Nordic Council (*NeGa*, 1 April, 1994). On the other hand, Brazauskas may prove to have the last laugh. Baltic cooperation has gained some momentum lately due *inter alia* to developments in Russia. This is not least because the December 1993 elections in Russia, which suddenly brought to prominence Vladimir Wolfovich ('Adolfovich', as the Russian joke goes) Zhirinovski, had an electrifying effect upon Baltic cooperation. But even before this, Grachev's unilateral suspension of military withdrawals in the spring of 1993 created an upsurge in Baltic cohesion. There has been more frequent coordination of policy positions, e.g. in jointly applying pressure on the Western powers to advance Baltic membership of NATO, as seen in Paris in early 1995 (*Segodnia*, 3 February 1995). Without doubt, Latvia appreciated the joint position of Estonia and Lithuania – both full members of the Council of Europe – on the need to accept Latvia as a member

---

[5] On the other hand, Brazauskas' later visits to Poland point towards a maturing inter-state relationship. Among other things he proposed the establishment of a joint Polish-Lithuanian peace-keeping battalion and joint control of air space and Sea borders (*OMRI Daily Digest*, 20 February 1995).

of that forum before Russia, as it did on 10 February 1995 (*RFE/RL News Briefs*, 5-8 April 1994). Estonia and Lithuania hold the same line on energy imports from Russia too, but the establishment of a joint Baltic peacekeeping force – BALTBAT – and a free-trade regime is of greater future significance. Estonia, Latvia and Lithuania also share reservations on the Nordic initiative of appointing a human rights commissioner within the framework of the larger Council of Baltic Sea States (CBSS; see *RFE/RL News Briefs*, 15-19 March 1994). In the meantime the outside world – represented by the then chairman of the European Parliament Egon Klepsch – has come to appreciate Lithuania's potential as an 'active mediator' in the Baltic region (*ibid.*, 30 May-3 June 1994).

For a long time, relations with Belarus were bogged down, due *inter alia* to the sloppy demarcation of the 724-km. long border – according to Vilnius; 609-km. according to Minsk – as a remnant of Stalin's era (Reuters, 8 March 1992). To make matters worse, the Belarusian government openly laid claim to Vilnius and the Vilnius region on several occasions in 1991 and 1992. At one time this was raised by Minister of Foreign Affairs Pietr Krawchanka during talks with no less than the EC Vice-President, Commissioner Frans Andriessen (Agence Europe, 26 February 1992). These demands were not welcome news in Lithuania, but somehow it handled this affair much more gracefully than relations with Poland – where territorial claims are imagined, not real. The then Belarusian parliamentary chairman Stanislau Shushkevich's dismissal of the claims as a 'joke' may have helped to soothe tempers in Vilnius as it played into the slightly paternalistic attitude of Lithuanians towards Belarusians, echoing Warsaw's attitude towards Vilnius. In any case, Belarus is not a gateway to Europe for Lithuania – hence Vilnius was better able to bear the lack of a breakthrough in its relations with Belarus than Minsk. This is likely to have been a factor behind the two countries' recent normalization of their relations with the signing of a treaty on good-neighbourly cooperation and border demarcation (*OMRI Daily Digest*, 7 February 1995). When the LDLP government took over, Brazauskas reminded Shushkevich of Lithuania's commitment never to become a member of the CIS – to which Belarus belongs (*RFE/RL News Briefs*, 10-23 December, 1992). Mutual dialogue was resumed in 1993 but no progress was made on the border issue, which blocked implementation of an otherwise promising mutual free-trade agreement (excluding agricultural products) signed in the spring. The Russo-Belarusian economic union and the outcome of the 1994 parliamentary elections in Belarus could spell the end of the independent Belarusian state, but this conclusion may be premature. Lithuania further worries about the regional security implications of Russo-Ukrainian tensions and wants the West to pay far more attention to this conflict (*ibid.*, 30 May-6 June 1994). Simultaneously, the Lithuanian MFA and Brazauskas issued an official declaration calling on both Russia and Ukraine to show responsibility and restraint in the conflict over the Crimea (*NeGa*, 25 May, 1994). The statement confirmed Lithuania's January 1994 Treaty of Friendship and Cooperation with Ukraine, in which it recognizes Ukraine's territorial integrity.

Lithuania's policy of reintegration. As can be inferred from this analysis, Lithuania's pursuit of reintegration with the Western world is motivated above all by the search for security in the volatile context of postcommunism (cf. pp. 30-47 above). The search for export outlets and alternative sources for imports certainly plays a part in this, but the essential issue for Lithuanians is to uphold sovereignty in its relations with Russia. Binding commitments in relation to the Western world are increasingly seen as the best way to protect sovereignty and make the domestic transition from communism irreversible. Some analysts perceive Lithuania's policy of reintegration as more subdued than Estonia's and Latvia's (Friis Hansen and Østergaard Jørgensen, 1993). Yet in January 1994 Lithuania surprised the world by filing what amounts to an official request to become a full member of NATO – only the second of the postcommunist states to have done so (the first was Albania). In so doing, however, Lithuania displayed a subtler approach than Albania by requesting NATO to send a fact-finding mission to investigate whether the country meets membership requirements (Brazauskas, 1994). Brazauskas was careful not to cite specific threats (e.g. the ominous turn of development in Russia at the time), or Lithuania's need for hard security guarantees, but presented the matter in the context of Lithuania's aspirations for reintegration:

> On behalf of the Republic of Lithuania, I hereby assert that Lithuania adheres to the values and commitments contained in the North Atlantic treaty and seeks to contribute to the security

of the North Atlantic area by joining [NATO]. The Republic of Lithuania fully realizes the scope of obligations that arise by virtue of membership in [NATO] and is undertaking relevant domestic legal and organizational steps to implement them. Therefore, on behalf of the Republic of Lithuania I would like to invite a fact-finding mission from [NATO] and to express my conviction that the results of that mission will affirm the progress that the Republic of Lithuania is making toward meeting the require-ments necessary for the enhancement of security in the North Atlantic area. Lithuania's position on NATO membership is not directed against neighbouring states or any other European countries. There should be a place for each of them in the new security structures of our continent. We regard favourably the [PfP]. As in the past, we support close cooperation among the Baltic States in all areas, including defense, as well as the advan-cement of security and stability throughout the Baltic Sea region. (*ibid.*)

The application for NATO membership represents a departure from earlier positions. At the outset, two of *Sajudis'* factions favoured formal neutrality as the orientation of security policy, whereas Landsbergis merely wanted 'autonomy', reflecting both parochialism and international political realities at the time (*International Herald Tribune*, 15 April 1989). In the following year, Lithuania went as far as offering Moscow that it would become a member of the Warsaw Pact in exchange for state sovereignty. When Landsbergis visited NATO headquarters in Brussels in the autumn of 1992 he expressed his belief in the fruitfulness of deepening cooperation between NATO and the Baltic states, but stressed that the real safeguard against the emerging security vacuum in the Baltic states would be the national military build-up in the Baltic states. 'We are bound to build entirely our own defensive forces in the end', he said (Landsber-gis, 1992). He expressed his appreciation for NATO, but did not raise the issue of membership. He merely wanted NATO to send observers to monitor the Russian troop withdrawal (*ibid.*; Reuters, 23 September 1992). In other words, contrary to what most would expect, Landsbergis pursued a more ambiguous policy towards NATO when he was in power than his leftist successor; an outcome to be discussed further below. Lithuania joined the PfP framework imme-diately after Romania, the first postcommunist country to sign such an agreement. Brazauskas used the opportunity to reiterate the goal of full NATO membership.[6] Ever greater integration into European political, economic and defence systems is singled out as the focus of current Lithuanian foreign policy, according to the 1995 annual address by Brazauskas to the *Seimas* (*OMRI Daily Digest*, 22 February 1995).

Lithuania is not yet in a position to apply for EU membership, but, as cited earlier, as many as 86 per cent of Lithuanians are in favour of full EU membership. Among the three Baltic states Lithuania is the main beneficiary of PHARE assistance (over 200 million Ecu; PHARE projects, 1993; *RFE/RL News Briefs*, 22-6 March 1993). On 31 January 1992 Lithuania initialled a so-called first-generation trade agreement with the EU, i.e. an agreement providing for an MFN-regime except for coal, steel, and textiles (*RFE/RL Research Report*, 14 February 1992). In January 1994 the Lithuanian MFA sent the European Council a letter urging it to prepare a negotiation mandate for the European Commission so that negotiations on an association agreement with Lithuania could begin. The letter stated that this 'would be of great importance for the future prosperity of Lithuania, as well as for the stability and security of the whole Baltic region' (*Agence Europe*, 20 January 1994). Lithuania does not pursue an EU policy on its own, but together with Estonia and Latvia. Inspired by the example of the Visegrad countries, the three Baltic states met in Jurmala (Latvia) in mid-1993 to issue a joint appeal to the European Council, which was due to meet in Copenhagen to open negotiations on Europe Agreements of Association by the end of 1993 (*ibid.*, 3 June 1993). It was the Copenhagen European Council meeting that opened the prospect of future EU membership for Lithuania among others. From mid-1994 preparations for a Europe Agreement on association were speeded up so that it could be signed by mid-1995. The EU member states are interested in a political dialogue similar to that

[6] In June 1993 Lithuania took part in the annual NATO naval exercises in the Baltic Sea, together with Poland and the Nordic neutrals. Estonia and Latvia participated as observers, whereas Russia had to withdraw for lack of funds for docking fees. As mentioned earlier, the Baltic states are establishing a joint peacekeeping battalion, planned to have a Lithuanian commander, a Latvian deputy and an Estonian chief of staff in a rotating leadership. This is intended as a PfP activity with English as the language of command (*RFE/RL News Briefs*, 22-6 November 1993; 14-18 February 1994).

envisioned for the Visegrad countries to be able to influence policy towards Russian and other minorities. Lithuania has signed a comprehensive fisheries agreement with the EU in 1993 (*ibid.*, 30 December 1993). The three Baltic states' progress towards establishing a free-trade regime among themselves, except for agricultural produce, has to be placed in the context of EU policy, as free trade is a precondition for joining the internal market as a consequence of EU association.[7]

Like Russia's policy of reintegration, the Lithuanian variety is marked by a development towards giving priority to the more exclusive fora at the expense of the OSCE. But it is worth remembering that the Baltic states tend to be less cynical about the OSCE than other postcommunist states which is probably a reflection of the Nordic pro-OSCE influence upon them. In addition, the OSCE was helpful in the Baltic states' quest to gain an independent say in international affairs, and influential in their reorientation away from Russia – which to some extent they have in common with Ukraine (Trapans, 1991; Butkevicius, 1993). Early on, however, Lithuania expressed the ambition of joining the Council of Europe as a symbol of its democratic recovery. At a press conference in Vilnius on 12 November 1992, the Lithuanian ambassador to the EC (EU) and NATO noted that his country would already have been admitted to the Council of Europe had the European Parliament not decided to tie its membership to that of Estonia and Latvia – which had been delayed owing to their 'inflexible laws on citizenship' (with few exceptions Russians in Lithuania have received citizenship; *RFE/RL Research Report*, vol. 1, no. 47, 27 November 1992). Lithuania was accepted as a full member ahead of the two others on 14 May 1993 with the support of no less than Russia – the second major foreign policy victory that year (second only to Russia's military withdrawal). A year later, Brazauskas addressed the parliamentary forum of the Council of Europe and took care to stress Lithuania's unswerving European orientation: 'Lithuania is placed in the centre of Europe and cannot be its province. One of the most important achievements following independence on 11 March 1990 is the revived hope of joining Europe' (*NeGa*, 20 April 1994). Brazauskas added that it was

---

[7] One reason why the process towards Baltic EU association is gaining momentum is that the Nordic EFTA countries will have to annul the free-trade agreements concluded bilaterally between them and the Baltic states following the entry of Finland and Sweden into the EU.

his country's ambition not just to profit from Europe, but to prove its utility and interest to Europe as well. As shown above, Lithuania has attracted some interest as a force capable of alleviating tension between Estonia and Latvia, on the one hand, and Russia, on the other – though these are somewhat exaggerated hopes, perhaps. On the pending issue of Russia's membership of the Council of Europe, Brazauskas has said that

> ...once Moscow abstains from the concept of the 'near abroad', once the Russian governmental authorities distance themselves from certain parliamentarians and political groups which clash with the legal foundations of the Baltic states and their inde-pendence – then a positive decision of the part of the Council of Europe concerning the acceptance of Russia's membership moves closer. (Quoted from *NeGa, ibid.*)

Brazauskas further touched on the over-militarized region of Kaliningrad as the number one problem in relations between Moscow and Vilnius. He announced Lithuania's intention to stage 'yet another cavalry charge on Europe', namely to conclude an agreement of EU association in 1994 – as 'an expression of support for our reforms' (*ibid.*). Apart from seeking to attract international attention to Lithuania's specific problems – a typical small-state approach, although used by Russia as well – he acknowledged that the primary function of the Council of Europe is to monitor the observance of human rights by European states.

Lithuania is thus raising its profile in the field of reintegration. As head of state, Brazauskas has devoted nearly all of his visits abroad to the West, beginning with visits to Denmark and Iceland in March 1993. This trip was partly of symbolic importance as these two countries were the first to recognize Lithuania's independence (or, in Denmark's case, to re-confirm it), but as the only Nordic EU member till recently, Denmark is no insignificant reintegration-patron for Lithuania. Together with Germany, Denmark has been instrumental in persuading the EU countries to step up economic aid to the Baltic region and prepare Europe Agreements with the Baltic states. Further, the two countries' foreign ministers launched the CBSS in March 1992 – encompassing Denmark, Estonia, Finland, Germany, Latvia, Lithuania, Norway, Poland, Russia and Sweden. Lithuania has concluded a military cooperation agreement with Denmark, providing for the training of officers (some fifty persons altogether) for the Baltic peacekeeping battalion (see note 5, *RFE/RL News Briefs*, 7-11 March 1994; *Politiken* 8 March 1994). One outcome of this is the deployment of a Lithuanian platoon in Croatia serving with the Danish peacekeeping force. Relations with Germany are of greater significance, though, *inter alia* because of German direct investments[8] (cf. *Frankfurter Allgemeine Zeitung*, 29 February 1992; 28 October 1993). Through their joint efforts via the Nordic Council, the Nordic countries form a kind of collective reintegration-patron for Lithuania, together with Germany. Bilateral economic relations have gained some momentum because of the free-trade agreements with Sweden and Finland. Relations with Great Britain and France are also important, not least because of the military cooperation pacts signed between France and all three Baltic states opening the way for the training of Lithuanian officers in France and joint military exercises; similar agreements have been signed with the WEU (*RFE/RL News Briefs*, 9-13 May 1994). Together with the two other Baltic states, Lithuania is becoming an associate partner of the WEU, although several WEU and EU members demand some kind of Finlandization as a precondition for their eventual full membership. Over half of Lithuania's foreign trade is with Western countries, even if Russia continues to be the single most important trading partner. As the above analysis has shown, this Western orientation is not limited to the field of economics, but encompasses security and overall political visions; nevertheless, this profile is mainly a product of the post-Landsbergis era.

Explaining foreign policy developments in Lithuania

As stated earlier, there is basic consensus among Lithuanian politicians on the country's European orientation, resulting in a fair degree of foreign policy stability. Developments are therefore better described in terms of a sharpened reintegration profile than of paradigmatic change. If anything, change should be conceptualized as a move towards 'institutionalism' and interdependence in recognition of the inherent security benefits for a state of Lithuania's size

[8] In January 1923 Lithuania seized Memel (Klaipeda) from Germany, but neither this nor Lithuanian interwar scepticism towards Germany – only tempered by fear of Poland – is an issue between the two countries today. Contrary to its attitude towards Poland, Lithuania acknowledges Germany's change for the better.

of becoming firmly embedded in a web of international cooperation of its own choice. Landsbergis' strategy may be characterized as re-nationalization of security policy, whereas Brazauskas' is one of internationalization – in other words, a promising departure from the legacy of parochialism in Lithuanian political culture. In continuance of this, the allegedly left-wing government displays a more liberal approach than its predecessor did on certain aspects of economic restructuring. As for the notoriously fashionable notion of environmental security, Lithuanians fully realize its potential for drawing economic attention from the Nordic countries and the EU, for instance by dwelling on environmental hazards in connection with the transit of goods to and from Kaliningrad (Butkevicius, 1993). The sloppy safety precautions at the Ignalina nuclear power plant are a real headache, representing a powerful option for committing richer neighbours to cooperation. Brazauskas' attitude towards Baltic cooperation is another expression of the institutional trend in Lithuanian foreign policy, the most striking example being the Lithuanian contribution to international peacekeeping, mirroring the Nordic commitment to UN operations in recognition of milieu goals (Wolfers, pp. 73-4; cf. p. 44 above). The free-trade regime between Estonia, Latvia and Lithuania introduced on 1 April 1994 provides another example. Yet it would be futile to interpret Lithuania's foreign policy solely from the vantage point of upholding norms and institutions in recognition of complex interdependence. The norms and principles of international law and diplomatic interaction are multiple and hence not unambiguous. In relation to China, Lithuania has settled for the standards of non-interference and mutual respect for sovereignty instead of human rights – as the latter would cause China to balk (Wacker; *Summary of World Broadcasts/*Far East, 16 November 1993).

Evidently, Lithuania's motives for seeking cooperation with China as well as other non-Russian superstates are rooted in the reverse logic of power, expressing Lithuania's strategy of seeking to balance itself between dependence on powers to the maximum extent possible.[9] Brazauskas' own catch-phrase for his vision of Lithuania's role in international affairs is that of the 'bridge between

[9] Another example of this strategy of balancing is the military cooperation agreement concluded with the Czech Republic, which provides for cooperation in drafting military doctrines and in the training of officers (*RFE/RL News Briefs*, 11-15 October 1993).

East and West' (*NeGa*, 18 June 1993). Admittedly, through the glasses of a diehard institutionalist the commitment to 'bridge-building' is nothing but a manifestation of institutional logics. Given the security context of Lithuania, this may just as well be a polite way to reject Russian attempts to include Lithuania in its sphere of influence. The hyper-sensitivity displayed by Brazauskas and his ministers over Russian claims to have special security interests in the Baltic region – e.g. on the occasion of signing the PfP – underscores exactly that. When Brazauskas approached NATO to express his country's interest in joining the alliance, his Foreign Minister sent a letter to US Secretary of State Warren Christopher expressing Lithuania's desire for cooperation in the field of national security and defence and urging greater US investment in Lithuania. Gylys' explained this step by recalling that although Russian troops had left Lithuania, it was still in a 'security vacuum'. He described the continued deployment of Russian troops elsewhere in the region as 'destabilizing' and dubbed Russia's treatment of the Baltic states as 'near abroad' 'unacceptable' (*RFE/RL News Briefs*, 27 December 1993-4 January 1994). When appearing at a joint Press Conference with his Baltic colleagues in Paris on 1 February 1995, Gylys told his audience that he preferred a 'cold peace' to a Cold War – which, if one reads between the lines, would place Lithuania in the Russian sphere (*Segodnia*, 3 February 1995). In other words, upon closer examination the Lithuanian political élite appears to have adopted a more offensive institutionalist strategy of publicly crying wolf; an institutionalism rooted in perceived realities of power. Indeed, the primary catalyst behind Baltic cooperation was and remains a perceived deterioration in Moscow's policy towards the three countries.

In the phraseology of adaptive foreign policy, Lithuania's strategy is one of seeking to avoid being pushed into so-called acquiescent adaptation, that is accepting the position of being in the sphere of influence of a great power in exchange for, say, welfare benefits or simple survival ('pilot fish behaviour'; Bjøl, 1971). Proceeding from the fact of its economic and security dependence, Lithuania seeks to exploit whatever alternative commitments there are in a determined effort to give itself some room for manoeuvre; something that qualifies as a strategy of 'balancing adaptation' (Petersen, 1977). To quote the former Defence Minister:

Thus, in Lithuania we have lived under the constant influence of two power blocs – Eastern and Western. The struggle between them for dominance was in conflict with our interest as it impeded the development of our culture and economy. Only the status of an independent state will enable us to protect the interests of our people. That is why the main objective of our policy is to seek a balance in our relations with East and West, preserving a maximum of independence. (Butkevicius, 1993, p. 8)

His review of threats surrounding Lithuania concentrates wholly on threats from Russia (such as authoritarianism and nationalism) and the other volatile post-Soviet states, strongly suggesting that the parlance of balancing relations is a diplomatic nicety rather than substantial. The proud announcement by Brazauskas of the security perspectives inherent in Lithuania's EU association – 'this would mean that we are entering the sphere of influence of the European Union' – only reinforces this interpretation (*Lithuanian Weekly*, 20 January–2 February 1995). Given Lithuanian pride, it is doubtful whether the country would accept a future lop-sided security and economic dependence on the West if perceived as detrimental to its interests. For the foreseeable future the challenge is to distance lithuania from Russia in security terms while upholding economic links to Russian firms. This is so difficult because Russia itself is not pursuing a genuine policy of balancing adaptation, but is prone to dominant adaptation, that is a foreign policy which above all adapts to pressures from the domestic environment, as described in the preceding chapter.[10] In this Lithuania controls few levers, except for the lack of a Russian minority and, conversely, the option of playing various 'disaster cards' *vis-à-vis* the West – the more firmly embedded the Western economic and political interests, the more efficient are the disaster cards. In addition Lithuania seeks to turn a brave face towards Russia by repeating every now and then that it would not object to Russia's joining NATO or becoming an associate member of the EU.

True, the above analysis is biased in that it proceeds on the implicit premise of rationality, careful analysis and optimal decision-making. While the thesis of a sharpening of Lithuania's foreign policy profile

---

[10] Dominant adaptation is an option reserved for the true top-dogs of the international scene, as it implies the will and the capacity to change the external environment instead of adapting to it. The fatal implications for, in this instance Russia's, neighbours are self-evident.

against the background of a reasonable degree of stability and consensus would seem to hold water, the account may have given a euphemistic picture – out of the simple desire to provide the reader with some benchmarks. Admittedly, the material behind the analysis is somewhat patchy, reflecting the tentative and inchoate nature of Lithuanian foreign and security policy. What is more, Lithuania's external behaviour is not devoid of features of domestic adaptation, including 'adaptation' to the organizational disorder of postcommunism. Several authors note the lack of coordination between various actors and bureaucracies – the President and his advisers (e.g. J. Paleckis) versus the MFA, versus the Ministry of Defence, versus the negotiating team appointed to hold talks with Russia on the troop withdrawal, versus the *Seimas* Foreign Affairs Committee (Østergaard Jørgensen, 1994). The Minister of Foreign Affairs, for instance, is not a member of the State Defence Council – whereas Kozyrev is a member of the Security Council of Russia. Procedures are often invented *ad hoc*, implying few SOPs capable of serving as administrative stabilizers. Another legacy from the Soviet era is excessive specialization and departmentalization, e.g. within the MFA (*ibid.*). Nothing better illustrates the lack of diplomatic cadres than Brazauskas' vain attempt to sack Lozoraitis as Ambassador to the United States. On top of the embarrassing Karaliaucius incident, motives of revenge – not just on the part of Brazauskas – seem to have been part of this. In the end Brazauskas could find no suitable replacement for Lozoraitis and had to ask him to continue his duties. As in Russia, the new Lithuanian constitution provides for a 'presidential foreign policy', whereas the responsibility for implementing foreign policy rests with the MFA. In contrast to Yeltsin, however, Brazauskas is firmly in control of foreign policy because of his strong political basis – the LDLP – the biggest and best organized party in Lithuania. As for the problem of coordination, a new interdepartmental body has been set up to alleviate this (*ibid.*).

It is no coincidence that the strongest criticism of foreign policy– whether regarding organizational or conceptual weakness – is voiced outside the government, namely by the opposition. Landsbergis recurrently accuses the government of wanting to bring Lithuania back into Moscow's fold. More than anything else, however, his fierce attacks have to be viewed in connection with Landsbergis' personal frustration over his failure to become Lithuania's first president and his increasing marginalization in Lithuanian politics. The principle of a strong presidency was his, and much of the constitution with its provisions for a presidential foreign policy was aimed at him. But the sudden change to an explicitly NATO-oriented policy does raise the issue of praetorian decision-making as a theoretical possibility. This is the explanation favoured by Moscow as the reason for the deplorable state of affairs in Russo-Lithuanian relations. The Russian media depict Brazauskas as being under strong pressure from Lithuanian right-wingers and Social Democrats – who are said to overreact to dubious statements from Russian parliamentarians (*NeGa*, 1 February 1994; 30 December 1993). What this explanation overlooks is the strong parliamentary majority behind Brazauskas, suggesting that whatever policy the Lithuanian government follows it is basically one of its own. Nevertheless, there is little doubt that Brazauskas believes in the virtue of bridge-building on the domestic scene as part of the duty of being president. To German interlocutors, Landsbergis insisted on one occasion that the Lithuanian opposition and government are *jointly* pursuing the goal of NATO membership (*Frankfurter Allgemeine Zeitung*, 28 October 1993). However, this does not imply that Brazauskas was forced to apply for NATO membership in the way Yeltsin was forced to cancel his 1992 visit to Japan.

A case can be made for positing Brazauskas as a dramatic actor using foreign policy as a diversion from reform. Everybody expected Brazauskas to direct his energies to the field of economic and social policy, but he picked foreign policy instead (Girnius, 1994). Some analysts see Brazauskas as paying for his weak domestic measures through foreign policy – by adopting the foreign policy of his predecessor so as to protect himself against criticism. There is a grain of truth in this interpretation. As for possible external dramatic actor motives, Lithuania was experiencing a certain image problem at the time of the NATO initiative, as evidenced by Tallinn's reservations towards Vilnius. The step had not been coordinated with Latvia and Estonia (whose MFA reacted rather coolly; see AP, 5 January 1994). On the other hand, it would be unfair to portray Brazauskas as purely opportunistic in this. For a small, dependent state like Lithuania, external relations are critical and, generally speaking, Brazauskas has concentrated on substantial rather than populist issues in defiance of the opportunistic dramatic actor model. The way the popular but probably unrealistic demands for financial compensation from Russia have been quietly put aside is significant. The diplomatic breakthrough in relation to Warsaw challenged Lithuanian prejudices of Polish plots to recapture Vilnius, a field where Landsbergis gave in to nationalistic urges, thereby betraying important Lithuanian interests. By contrast, Brazauskas is pragmatic and flexible – to the extent of being able to identify himself with an unreservedly pro-Western orientation.

As for Allison's model of organizational process, it would be far-fetched to argue that the approach to NATO grew out of firmly entrenched SOPs in the MFA or the Ministry of Defence, as the decision marked a *volte face* in security policy. One may speculate that this initiative can in some way be traced back to Lithuanian emigrant diplomats such as the Ambassador to Washington, Lozoraitis, who according to Lieven pushed Landsbergis into the declaration of independence in March 1990 – much to the surprise of Lithuanians (Lieven, 1993, p. 235 ff.). It is a matter of fact, however, that once they learned about the Lithuanian initiative, Western diplomats advised the government to request a fact-finding mission to investigate Lithuania's preparedness for NATO membership rather than simply sending an application (personal interview). As for the bureaucratic politics perspective, the new Minister of Defence, Linas Linkevicius, and armed forces commander Jonas Andriskevicius held talks in Brussels with NATO General Secretary Manfred Wörner in November 1993 where they confirmed Lithuania's interest in closer cooperation with NATO and eventual membership (*RFE/RL News Briefs*, 22-6 November 1993). In so doing, however, they were hardly pursing an agenda of their own. Rather, this reflected a change of mind in the entire decision-making stratum –in effect uniting Landsbergis and Brazauskas. This, in turn, suggests that the best explanation can be found within the rational actor framework.

The Polish analyst Marek Garztecki provides a typical example of this kind of reasoning (1994). According to him, Russia may rattle its sabres about NATO, but it will never attack a member. As Garztecki sees things, the Lithuanian leaders knew exactly what were the dangers and the benefits of making a NATO membership application – Brazauskas, 'an old communist hand himself, understands perfectly [that] in a few years time Lithuania will be either a part of Russia or the West' (1994, p. 79). This exposition of the case may be too crude, however. Lithuania was beginning to have second thoughts about the vagueness of its security policy orientation as a result of the ominous signs in Russia's 'near abroad' policy – so far Garztecki is right in taking seriously the wish to join NATO. Strobe Talbott, United States Deputy Secretary of State in charge of relations with the postcommunist world, responded to the request by saying that NATO was not ready to accept new members (AFP, 6 January 1994). Russian spokesmen said Yeltsin was alarmed and dubbed the Lithuanian motives unconvincing, citing the Russian military doctrine. While the Baltic states were not a Russian sphere of influence, the region was part of the 'near abroad' and represented a sphere of Moscow's vital interests, the Russian MFA declared (*RFE/RL News Briefs*, 27 December 1993-4 January 1994). On the face of it, Lithuania would seem to have achieved nothing but increased tensions by sending its letter.

But the way the application was designed shows that the Lithuanian authorities realized that membership was not imminent. Rather, the initiative has to be understood in the context of the lead-up to the NATO summit of early 1994, where the alliance was to design a new policy towards the postcommunist world that moved beyond NACC. All of Central Europe was campaigning to place itself on NATO's agenda as future members. Poland and the other Visegrad countries were the most vocal, demanding a far more radical approach than a simple PfP. They were so successful in this that most of NATO forgot about the Baltic states as a region of more imminent crisis. Given the Russian troop withdrawal from Lithuania, the country ran less of a risk than the two other Baltic states by explicitly lining up for NATO membership as a way of attracting the alliance's attention. To some extent, then, what Lithuania did was to use its greater freedom of manoeuvre to act as solicitor for the entire region. Afterwards both Latvia and Estonia did express support for the move, with Estonian President Meri saying that he understood Lithuania's urgency and would follow with interest how NATO reacted (*ibid.*). The full wording of Talbott's response reveals that the initiative actually had the effect of putting the Baltic region on NATO's agenda: 'Naturally, we understand the desire of the Baltic and eastern European states to become members of the alliance' (AFP, 6 January 1994).

As one of the few analysts who systematically monitors Lithuanian developments, it is interesting to compare the Radio Free Europe/Radio Liberty and now OMRI journalist Saulius Girnius' analysis of

Lithuanian foreign policy published in September 1993 with his annual review of 1993 (1993a; 1994). His first contribution criticizes Brazauskas and the LDLP government for having lost whatever goodwill Vilnius enjoyed in Moscow under Landsbergis and for having delivered little but a worsening of the crisis in Lithuania. His second analysis strikes a more balanced tone, as if realizing that not all of the blame is to be placed at Brazauskas' door. What has to be taken into account is the fact that when Brazauskas took over, Moscow was institutionalizing its hard-nosed policy towards the 'near abroad', with the result that there was much less room for manoeuvre for Vilnius – notwithstanding the troop withdrawal. Given these circumstances, Brazauskas and the LDLP government have been innovative and reasonably efficient in the way they used and improved Lithuania's access to the West. Some may object that this analysis is still too superficial in the way it has sidestepped the political crisis in Lithuanian society at large – witness the lower ratings scored on trust in the government and future expectations compared to Estonia and Latvia. To be sure, Lithuania is hampered by poor performance on the part of its leadership and an even worse showing by the opposition, leading to apathy.

On balance, however, Lithuania appears to be muddling through in the direction of recovery rather than being on the verge of an explosion. To some extent, the situation resembles that of Slovakia – also a rural country with strong nationalist traditions, making it poorly equipped for pursuing a policy of its own in the contemporary European context. But in both countries a healthy process of learning is going on. The real significance of the coming to power of Brazauskas and LDLP is the rejection of chauvinist nationalism which it marks – no mean feat indeed (Lieven, 1993, p. 383). This brings us to the final case of Hungary, where a similar development is found.

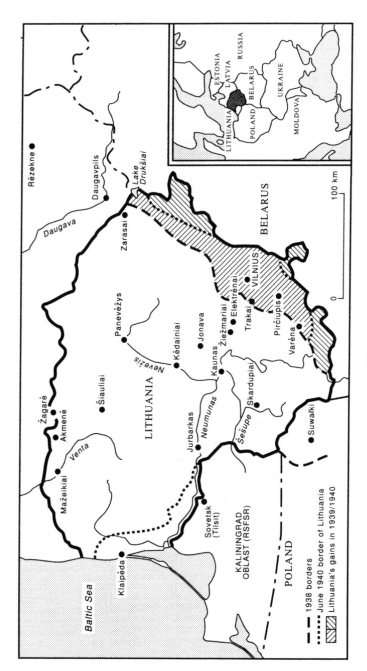

Lithuania

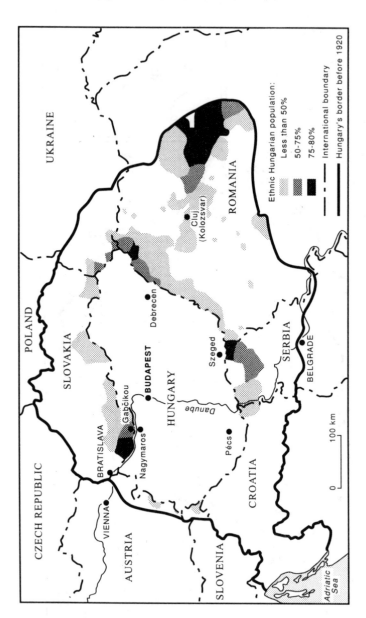

Hungary

6

THE FOREIGN POLICY OF
POSTCOMMUNIST HUNGARY

On 23 October 1989, Hungary was again proclaimed a republic –
without the epithet 'socialist'. Free elections were held in 1990,
bringing to power a non-socialist government. As one of the
well-established and well-known countries of the former Soviet
external empire, Hungary would seem to need no further introduction.[1] It has a reputation as a Central European anchor of stability
and prosperity, in contrast to its Balkan neighbours. Generally
speaking, this stereotype holds true. But appearances are deceptive.
The return to power of the former Communist Party – now the
Hungarian Socialist Party (HSP) – as a result of the 1994 general
elections, shows that the country merits further analysis. The organizational legacy of the pre-1989 era is a state apparatus that is
already in place and a professional élite with a good knowledge of
the West. Parliamentary democracy – including the Constitutional
Court – works reasonably well in Hungary, but the postcommunist
state has a more mixed record of economic reform and foreign policy
performance than is often perceived. As a Central European success
story, Hungary has been overtaken by the Czech Republic and by
Poland's economic growth. As for foreign and security policy, some
of the country's problems were caused by events beyond its control,
such as the eruption of a gruesome war in former Yugoslavia. But
there are endogenous factors as well. While it may be true that the

---

[1] English-language materials on Hungary are not as sparse as on Lithuania, so just
a few references will do. Although outdated – and hopelessly out of fashion in its
admiration for Karoly Grosz – Paul Lendvai's monograph (1988) is recommendable.
For a thorough review of the political history of Hungary in the twentieth century,
see Hanak and Held, 1992. On the transition from communism, see Bozoki *et al.*
Although slightly biased in its admiration for the Antall government, Joseph C.
Kun's monograph on Hungarian foreign policy is useful, not least because of its
historical content (1993).

extremist forces in Hungary – such as the anti-Semitic and utterly revisionist writer Istvan Csurka – are marginal forces, Hungarian nationalism is a force to be reckoned with ('The Politics of Intolerance', 1994, pp. 55-61; Lendvai, 1988). This is not to say that Hungarian nationalism is clearly revisionist in its foreign policy implications –certainly not mainstream Hungarian nationalism, as the 1994 elections showed (Lomax, 1994). However, the point should be made that Hungarian perceptions often act as a barrier to dialogue with neighbours.

The leading party of the then ruling coalition in Hungary, the Hungarian Democratic Forum (HDF), did ultimately expel Csurka from its ranks in mid-1993, but the ideology of the HDF is based on Hungarian nationalism and a strong commitment to Christian and traditional values. To some extent, the country is caught in the same kind of political vacuum as Lithuania – suspended between nationalist conservatism on the one hand and modernity with a socialist face on the other, thus lacking powerful liberal-centrist forces. The problem with the HDF conservatism is basically the same as with Landsbergis' Homeland Union. Forty years as a subject of the Soviet external empire isolated non-socialists in Hungary from the modernizing trends in West European political life, with the result that even sophisticated Hungary is stuck with a legacy of pre-modern conservatism. As demonstrated by the Hungarian-British analyst George Schöpflin, the Hungarian conservative mind-set is essentially populist, anti-urban, anti-liberal and very often also anti-Semitic – in a phrase hostile towards the open society (1992).[2] This kind of anachronistic conservatism did not necessarily serve the country well, although the HDF must be credited for having implemented the basic transition from communism and bringing about an irreversible return to Europe. On balance the HSP would seem to have a better case when presenting itself as a modern political party – not least in view of the role of the Hungarian reform-communists in providing for the transition from communism (Bozoki et al., 1992). At any rate, the Social-Liberal government puts issues of re-integration higher on the agenda relative to the issue of Hungarians living abroad than its predecessor (personal interviews with Hungarian MFA officials and others).

[2] When it held the reins of power, the HDF proved very uncomfortable about the workings of a free press and tried to control Hungarian radio and TV in the so-called media war.

The issue of Hungarian minorities casts a baleful influence over Hungary's relations with neighbouring postcommunist states, although the latter tend to over-react in their proclaimed fear of Hungarian irredentism. The reason why this is so is rooted in the period following the Trianon peace of 1920. As junior partner in the Austo-Hungarian dual monarchy, Hungary was on the losing side in the First World War. The Treaty of Trianon deprived Hungary of two-thirds of its territory and a similar share of its population, Hungarians as well as non-Hungarians, to parts of what became Czechoslovakia, Yugoslavia and Romania, etc. (see map). The declared principle behind this new geopolitical configuration was Wilsonian national self-determination, but the victorious *Entente* powers applied it selectively, partly in order to crush the power of Hungary. This traumatized the nation for generations to come – so much so that the Hungarian government aligned itself with Hitler in Nazi Germany's attack on Yugoslavia in 1941. Hungary became one of the Axis powers. Hungarians believed in Hitler's victory and in the subsequent recovery of territories lost. Needless to say, this cost the country dearly. Because of the Trianon treaty and the political follies it led to, it is not the interwar period which is the main source of pride for Hungarian nationalism; except perhaps for the country's dictator, Admiral Miklós Horthy, and the civilized authoritarianism he practised. There is little doubt that Horthy's Christian nationalism (cum anti-Semitism) served as a role model for the late HDF leader and Prime Minister Joszef Antall, the right-wing authoritarian leader of interwar Lithuania, as Smetona does for Landsbergis.

Still, the Hungarian revisionism of the interwar period – which created the key rationale for the Little *entente* uniting Romania, Yugoslavia and Czechoslovakia, backed by France – provides only a partial explanation for the built-in tension between Hungary and its neighbours. The Central European wave of nationalism in 1848 had spread further to the east and to the south, causing a temporary paralysis of Vienna's power. Because of its exclusiveness, nationalism cemented mutual suspicion and brought armed struggle between Hungarians on the one hand, and Serbs, Croats and Romanians on the other. With the help of Russian military intervention, Vienna managed to crush the Hungarian bid for independence, but later had to give in and let Hungary determine its internal affairs in the *Ausgleich* ('compromise') of 1867. Unfortunately, the *Ausgleich* did not inspire Hungarians to similar generosity towards their non-Hungarian subjects. Nationality policies continued in the liberal vein of the Habsburgs, providing in theory for the usage of local languages by the authorities, but the reality was one of harsh assimilation, in this case 'Magyarization'. The Nationalities Law of 1868, for instance, laid down that all citizens of Hungary, whatever their nationality, constituted politically 'a single nation, the indivisible Hungarian nation'. Not surprisingly, the equally nationalist non-Hungarian peoples demanded independence, but in response the government committed the gross political blunder of failing to arrange a compromise with the Czechs in 1870 and the Croats and Romanians, to quote the contribution of Hanak and Held (1992, p. 167). In other words, the non-Hungarian minorities' memory of Hungarian rule is one of repression. On the positive side, the latter half of the nineteenth century brought economic progress and integration in a historical precedent of the EU's internal market. Hungarians therefore tend to look upon this time as a truly golden era. Another glorious era was from the year 1000, when the first Hungarian King, Istvan (Stephen), accepted Christianity, up till the Battle of Mohacs in 1526, when the invading Turks defeated Hungary. It was in the medieval period that Slovakia and Croatia fell under Hungarian rule, later joined by Moravia, Silesia, Styria and Lower Austria.

As this suggests, like Lithuania and Russia Hungary used to be a great power, an additional factor that bedevils perceptions of Budapest's intentions in neighbouring countries on top of their hosting Hungarian minorities as the result of Trianon. The neighbours do not take Hungary's conversion into a small state at face value, despite the fact that no political authority in the country dares question the present borders which date from Trianon, and despite the lack of a serious constituency behind a strongly nationalist, let alone revisionist foreign policy, as the 1994 elections made clear. Budapest's concern for the fate of Hungarians living abroad (estimated at 3,266 million people altogether) is simply misunderstood when posited as a vehicle for revisionism (see e.g. *International Herald Tribune*, 26 January 1993). This is not to say that there are no ambiguities or follies in the Hungarian stance on the minorities issue – Hungarians manifest a dangerously selective memory when arguing the injustices done to their nation – only that we should see it in perspective. The Western stereotype of a Hungarian – as an aristocratic, melancholic intellectual with sombre visions of the future – is in fact closer to reality than the Eastern image of a flamboyant nationalist bent on revanchism. In a typical defeatist vein, the historian Laszlo Lengyel depicts Hungary as prey to the forces of history and the great powers (1990; *Népszabadság*, 10, 13 and 14 April 1993). One overarching source of this defeatism which must not be forgotten was sovietization, including the terrible events of 1956 which once again put Hungary in the role of loser. During Kadar's otherwise gentle reign, the issue of the Hungarian minorities was taboo in the face of openly assimilationist policies in Romania, thus fuelling Hungarian frustrations. In other words, the human drama of the Hungarian diaspora cannot be taken lightly.

Geography has not placed postcommunist Hungary in an enviable position. The country has been sandwiched between two collapsing federations, those of Czechoslovakia and Yugoslavia, adding to the danger of nationalist anger turning against Hungarian residents in Slovakia and Vojvodina (Serbia). The war in former Yugoslavia has had a most tangible effect upon the Hungarian state in terms of refugees – at one time numbering as many as 100,000 in the country – and economic losses due to sanctions against Serbia and Montenegro (estimated at $1.2 billion) and on top of that a cessation of deliveries of natural gas through the Adria pipeline. On the other hand, the proximity of Austria promises to draw Hungary closer into the West European orbit, which Budapest so ardently desires. Hungary's economic potential lies within agriculture, industries and services – due less to mineral riches than to its infrastructure and consumer sector, developed above the average of ex-CMEA countries. Hungary has recently established a car industry and is the largest recipient of foreign direct investments in postcommunist Europe. Trade with Russia is recovering and Hungary ranks as Moscow's sixth or seventh most important economic partner. But in contrast to the Czech Republic, Hungary has not recovered from the recession that hit the region when the CMEA and the Soviet market collapsed, adding to the domestic travails of transition. Inflation, trade and budget deficits, together with rising debt, continue to characterize Hungary (Okolicsanyi, 1994). Growth is sluggish, and the government balks at implementing the painful measures that are needed. Western sources put Hungarian GNP *per capita* at $3,300, but Hungarian sources cite a more credible figure of $5,500 − 6,000 − i.e. including private sector activities (*Népszabadság*, 14 April 1993).

One factor − among many − in the sluggish Hungarian growth is the $800 million debt owed to Russia, which the two countries have agreed to swop for 28 MIG-29 interceptor jets and an unresolved number of air-defence missiles (*RFE/RL, New Briefs*, 10–21 January 1994). Hungarian officers still receive training in Russian military academies. A triangular swap between Russia, Germany and Hungary has also been arranged, resulting in a major transfer of free spare parts from the former GDR Army to Hungary. But generally speaking, the situation in the Hungarian armed forces is characterized by cutbacks as a result of the CFE treaty − from a standing army of 105,000 men before 1989 to 78,000 now (plus 195,000 reservists; International Institute of Strategic Studies 1985-6, 1993-4). The national security doctrine does not identify an enemy, although unofficially Hungary perceives Russia as a potential threat. What worries Hungary in relation to Serbia is not outright attack, but reprisals against Hungarians, for instance their being deployed to the front-line in disproportionate numbers − as has actually happened. In the event of conflict-escalation, Hungary is counting on international intervention and has adopted a non-alarmist tone; on the other hand, in the long term Budapest wants to escape the present perceived security vacuum. Apart from this, Hungary attaches great importance to economic security and to preventive measures such as regional cooperation and bilateral military CSBMs; a field where progress is steady in spite of the thorny minority issue.

Developments within postcommunist Hungary's foreign policy

As in the case of Lithuania and Russia, the first most important task of postcommunist Hungary was to formulate basic foreign and security policy interests anew so that they matched domestic change. Hungary was still a member of the Warsaw Pact in 1990, but wanted to leave and switch to neutrality instead. Thus on June 26 the National Assembly instructed the government to begin talks on Hungary's withdrawal from the pact by the end of 1991, although few believed that it would be able to survive for long. Another pressing need was to secure the withdrawal of the Soviet troops − some 2,500 men − by 30 June 1991, as stipulated in the agreement signed on 10 March 1990 by the then HSP government (Barany, 1990). These measures of disengagement in relation to the former hegemon paved the way for Hungary's courting of Western fora of cooperation as its real foreign policy priority. Particular attention was devoted to the EC, which launched the Europe Agreements to accommodate Hungary and other Central European postcommunist states. Relations with individual Western countries were intensified, whereas Hungary experienced only scant success in establishing a dialogue with its postcommunist neighbours – due *inter alia* to its withdrawal from the Gabcikovo-Nagymaros project with Czechoslovakia in 1989 (Reisch, 1990). Nevertheless, Hungary was a founding member of several promising initiatives of regional cooperation in Central Europe.

These sweeping changes in foreign policy cannot solely be attributed to the HDF-led coalition that came to power as a result of the elections of spring 1990. Hungary's aspirations for a return to Europe through closer cooperation with the EC, through the CSCE process and some kind of Danubian cooperation, can be traced back to Kadar and the post-Kadar years in particular (*ibid.*; Skak, 1991a). Hungary had already concluded a first-generation trade agreement with the EC in September 1988. The present constitution came into being through a series of amendments in October 1989, among which was this provision: 'The Republic of Hungary feels responsibility for all Hungarians living beyond the country's frontiers, and assists them in cherishing their relations to Hungary' (Constitution of the Republic of Hungary, section 6, art. 3). This reopening of the minorities issue as part of Hungarian foreign and security policy combined with the reintegration overtures provided for a good deal of continuity between Hungary's last communist and first postcommunist governments. To some extent, the agenda had been formulated in advance, leaving the new government with few options other than pursuing its goals all the more vigorously and unambiguously. In the field of reintegration the Antall government was notable for adopting a policy of seeking full membership of Western fora – the EU, NATO, etc. – thus leaving earlier visions of neutrality behind. On the issue of minorities, Antall declared in August 1990 that he considered himself 'in spirit' prime minister of all 15 million Hungarians throughout the world, a statement which produced a sharp reaction from Czechoslovakia and Romania (Oltay, 1992).

Hungarian Minister of Defence Lajos Für went even further when speaking at a mass rally in Miskolc in early 1992:

> The security of the Hungarian nation has a particular, special feature and condition that I may say characterizes only us Hungarians. Namely, that the Hungarian nation here in the Carpathian basin does not only mean the Republic of Hungary. The Hungarian nation...means a language nation. A nation one third of which, with the dictated peace of Trianon, got into minority status. It is an indispensable part and element of the observance of the nation's security that the whole Hungarian nation be safeguarded here in the Carpathian basin. The Hungarian government and the Hungarian parliament, any Hungarian [politician] has to do everything, has to use every legitimate, diplomatic means now in this transitory period in order [to ensure] that the endangered status of our minorities would come to an end; the conditions for the survival of our minorities could be guaranteed by them and us. (quoted from Dunay, 1992)

Neither this statement nor Antall's were intended to signal military protection and intervention by Hungary, let alone border revisions. Für's remarks were hardly noticed in Hungary, but caused quite a stir in Czechoslovakia and Romania. Yet a comparison of this kind of Hungarian statement with similar Russian utterances on how and why to project Russians in the 'near abroad' will reveal a much cleaner record on the part of Hungary (see p. 172 above). Whereas some of the more hawkish Moscow spokesmen have no qualms about placing their countrymen abroad in the role of fifth columnists, such slips are anathema in Hungary. Nevertheless, the wisdom of the approach of the Antall government can be questioned and, indeed, has been questioned in the lead-up to the 1994 elections as is shown below.

Continuity notwithstanding, 1990 marked the opening of a new chapter in the history of Hungarian foreign policy. On 6 November 1990 Hungary became the first postcommunist country to enter the Council of Europe – the seal of the country's democratization. Because of the unfolding war in Yugoslavia, the so-called Pentagonal (later renamed the Central European Initiative, or CEI) was showing signs of weakness, but in return Visegrad cooperation (launched in February 1991) gained some momentum. In December 1991 Hungary signed a Europe Agreement of Association with the

EC and in December 1992 the soon-to-be Visegrad quadrangle initialled a mutual free-trade agreement in preparation for the EU internal market. In February 1993 the so-called Carpathian Euro-region was established as a framework for sub-regional economic and cultural cooperation between eastern Poland, eastern Hungary and western Ukraine, with eastern Slovakia as observer for the time being. A free-trade agreement with the seven EFTA countries was signed on 29 March 1993, to take effect on 1 July. On 1 February 1993 the EU Association Agreement came into force and on 8 February Hungary signed a PfP agreement with NATO. But these remarkable achievements were accompanied by the lack of a break-through in Slovak-Hungarian and Romanian-Hungarian bilateral relations and increasing tension with Serbia over Vojvodina. The Hungarian public reacted with increasing nervousness to the con-tinuing hostilities in ex-Yugoslavia, fuelled by the EU's exclusive-ness after the Maastricht crisis (*Népszabadság*, 7 March 1992, 15 June 1993; *Frankfurter Allgemeine Zeitung*, 27 April 1993).

The looming problems in Hungary's relations with its neighbours created cracks in the otherwise unique consensus on basic foreign and security policy goals among the six parliamentary parties in 1993 –4. As already indicated, the upcoming elections reinforced this development. Virtually all politicians agree on the primacy of seeking Hungary's full integration into Euro-Atlantic structures, the importance of fostering regional cooperation and good bilateral relations with neighbours on the basis of monitoring the situation of the Hungarian diaspora. Where opinions differ is on the finer details of the sensitive border and minorities policy (Reisch, 1994a). The opposition at the time, notably that of the HSP, whose chairman Gyula Horn for a long time chaired the parliamentary Foreign Relations Committee, was always critical about the nationalist zeal displayed by Antall – an outdated, ideological nationalism ac-cording to Horn (*Népszabadság*, 19 April 1993). Hungary's political impotence in the face of the victimization of Hungarians in Voj-vodina brutally exposed Budapest's dilemma. In Romania and Slovakia political leaders proved adept at misreading Hungarian signals, thus confirming the eternal security dilemma between states. The threat of a new '*Little entente*' uniting an aggressive Serbia with an equally unpredictable Romania and a chauvinist Slovakia was looming on the horizon (*Frankfurter Allgemeine Zeitung*, 5 May 1992). The opposition found further vindication in Hungary's growing image problems in the West, as reflected in a report published by the International Institute of Strategic Studies in London identifying Hungary as a destabilizing factor as a result of the open questioning by Csurka (see above, p. 224) of the Trianon borders and his call for *Lebensraum* (*Népszabadság*, 22 May 1993). The row surrounding the ratification of the Hungarian–Ukrainian inter-state treaty shows how slippery the road of Antall's nationalism was. The opposition was unanimous in its support for the treaty, whereas Antall's own party was deeply divided, resulting in the hitherto unprecedented number of thirty-nine votes against. The bone of contention was a clause precluding forever territorial demands raised against Ukraine by Hungary, or *vice versa*. The radical nationalists based their hostility to the clause on the precedent it would set for Slovakia and Romania (*Neue Zürcher Zeitung*, 14 May 1993).

The parliamentary consensus did survive the voting on the guidelines for Hungary's security policy – with only one vote against – on 2 March 1993; guidelines which reject any changes to borders brought about by force but turn guarantees for the basic rights of Hungarian minorities into a precondition for establishing good relations with neighbouring countries.[3] This nexus, however, was later questioned by the opposition, made up of the Alliance of Free Democrats (the AFD), the Alliance of Young Democrats and HSP. The opposition was careful not to dissociate itself from concern for the minorities as a humanitarian priority, but the AFD wants greater attention paid to the improvement of inter-state relations on the basis of a more explicit Hungarian commitment to maintain (present) borders (Reisch, 1993c). In the eyes of the opposition, the HDF government's excessive preoccupation with the minorities issue has contributed little to the improvement of their situation and may in fact have worsened it. In an interview with Radio Budapest on 3 January 1993, Antall declared it was governmental policy to aid Hungarians living abroad through their elected representatives on the assumption that 'they know best what can be done to improve

---

[3] The passage reads: 'Our conduct must reflect the principle that we view the assurance of the rights of the Hungarian minorities as a fundamental requirement for the desirable neighbourly relations with neighbouring countries. In resolving this question we reject both the alteration by force of existing borders and artificial alteration of the ethnic consistency of the population by any means, not only in the Carpathian Basin, but in the whole Central and Eastern European region,' ('Basic Principles of the Security Policy of the Republic of Hungary', 1993).

their rights' (*RFE/RL News Briefs*, 28 December 1992-8 January 1993). It may be argued that by letting the Hungarian diaspora determine official Hungarian policy in this way Antall deprived himself of critical room for manoeuvre. In effect he put himself at the mercy of interest organizations, who are by definition biased in their views and approaches.[4] The HSP, by contrast, sought to raise its profile through its commitment to 'historical reconciliation' although inter-state treaties were still missing (*RFE/RL News Briefs*, 18-22 April 1994). HSP leader Horn, Hungary's current Prime Minister, paid official visits to Romania and Slovakia prior to the elections, during which he announced the new approach, something that earned him angry reactions from the government which felt he undermined its negotiating position (*CTK Business News*, 22 April 1994).

Despite the heated controversies prior to the 1994 elections, foreign policy is scarcely likely to change dramatically under the new HSP-ADF government formed after the landslide victory of the HSP.[5] By disassociating itself from the Procrustean bed of conservative nationalism offering pragmatism and 'professionalism', the new government clearly seeks to gain some leeway for itself. There is an unmistakable change of tone, for instance when the Foreign Minister designate László Kovács called on minorities to 'live and succeed where they were born' and announced his government's intention to avoid 'any kind of pressure on neighbouring countries', wishing to avoid 'lecturing' as well as 'ambiguous statements or hints' (MTI, 12 and 13 July 1994). Horn explicitly declined to declare himself prime minister of the 15 million Hungarians, that is including the diaspora. But the negotiations between Horn and his Romanian and Slovak counterparts show that the parties are often divided on the same issues as before. Alfred A. Reisch rightly points

[4] The potential dangers of letting Hungarian state policy be dictated by the parties of Hungarians abroad are illuminated by the criticism of Slovakia's insistence on border guarantees by the chairman of the Hungarian Coexistence Movement on the basis of hair-splitting legal arguments without addressing the legitimate – and maybe justified – Slovak concerns (*CTK-Business News*, 3 May 1994).

[5] The HSP gained 54.1 per cent of votes cast and thus enjoys an absolute majority in the National Assembly, with 209 out of 386 seats. The HDF, by contrast, lost 32 per cent of its seats and now occupies thirty-eight seats. Despite the fact that the AFD was also among the losers receiving only sixty-nine seats in the parliament and losing twenty-one, the HSP wanted to form a coalition government to demonstrate its commitment to centrist-leftism ('professionalism' in HSP parlance).

to the contradictions in the twin HSP goals of signing state treaties with Romania and Slovakia and striving to achieve minority rights (including autonomy), which those countries continue to reject (1994a, p. 47). One of AFD's prominent politicians, now State Secretary in the MFA, István Szent-Ivanyi was not too happy about Horn's opportunist way of suggesting quick fixes to what was and remains an important political issue in Hungary and neighbouring countries (MTI, 13 July 1994). On the other hand, with Slovakia and Romania becoming more unequivocal in their commitment to reintegration, new impetus was added to the process of negotiating inter-state treaties before the deadline for the European Stability Pact by 21 March 1995. Hungary and Slovakia did enter an interstate treaty on 19 March in Paris, which raises the possibility of autonomy for the Hungarians living in southern Slovakia discreetly by means of a reference to Council of Europe recommendation no. 1201 (Treaty on Good Neighbourliness..., 1995).

Hungary's policy towards its postcommunist neighbours. It is worth repeating that Hungary's troubled relationship with some of its neighbours cannot solely be blamed on the country's previous government. Budapest is caught in a real dilemma of how to prevent an uncontrollable influx of Hungarians fleeing intolerant polities without being branded as meddling in internal affairs. But its solution to this dilemma, to trade guarantees against border revisions in exchange for minority rights (including administrative autonomy)[6]

[6] That there is such a policy was confirmed by Foreign Minister Geza Jeszenszky, who in an interview in *Uj Magyarország* came up with the following curious formulation: 'inasmuch as our neighbours recognize and guarantee the rights, equality and state-creating character of Hungarians living beyond our borders, then we can seek formulations that confirm the territorial decrees of the [Trianon] peace treaty and the validity of the Helsinki Final Acts. But the two cannot be separated' (MTI, 5 August 1993). This approach of trading border guarantees for minority rights has been confirmed by the Foreign Minister designate, László Kovács, who said that 'concluding a basic treaty exclusively on the inviolability of borders has always been out of the question' (MTI, 13 July 1994).

The Hungarian policy of seeking administrative autonomy was motivated by Geza Entz, the Hungarian State Secretary for Hungarians abroad, on the grounds that Slovak and Romanian authorities face a choice between autonomy and civil strife, including 'massacres' and 'ethnic cleansing' that would force people to leave the country and lead to uncontrolled migration within the region (*International Herald Tribune*, 26 January 1993). The omission of Serbia as a target of this warning – undoubtedly for fear of the violent repression of Hungarians living there –

has failed to allay the fears of neighbours anxious that autonomy would be the first step in a dismemberment scenario. The formula has worked in the case of Ukraine, though – less because of a deep-seated Ukrainian commitment to securing the rights of ethnic minorities than because of the small size of the Hungarian minority (some 200,000) when expressed as a share of the total population (0.4 per cent), combined with Ukraine's need for good relations to Hungary as a gateway to Europe (*Népszabadság*, 22 and 23 May 1992). During the then Ukrainian President Kravchuk's visit to Budapest in May 1991, a joint declaration on the collective rights of minorities was made,[7] leading to the inter-state treaty renouncing border revisions; an arrangement hailed by Hungary as a model for relations with other countries. But the Ukrainian parliament has not accepted administrative autonomy for that part of *Zakarpatskaia Oblast* ('Kárpatálja' in Hungarian) where the Hungarian minority is concentrated and, interestingly, Hungary has chosen not to press the issue (Reisch, 1993a). What motivates Budapest in this surprising display of pragmatism may be that it does not wish to become a party to the Russian pressure upon Ukraine, in recognition of the need to uphold Ukraine as a buffer between Hungary and a resurgent Russia. In spite of Ukraine's economic mismanagement, the two countries have several economic treaties (covering e.g. agriculture). Apart from promoting cooperation with Ukraine within the framework of the Carpathian Euro-region, Budapest advocates Ukraine's closer affiliation with the CEI. Hungary has entered into several military cooperation agreements with Ukraine and has a military attaché in Kiev.

Hungary's relationship with Romania represents much more of a headache – for both parties. As observed by Reisch, the pattern is one of good relations between Hungary and countries with insignificant Hungarian minorities – Ukraine, Slovenia, Croatia and Austria – and troubled relations where Hungarian minorities are large – Romania, Serbia and Slovakia. By far the biggest Hungarian minority is in Romania – 2 million people (1.6 million according to Romanian

---

combined with the explicit references to genocidal Serbian practices, cannot but have infuriated the Slovak and Romanian governments and confirmed their conviction that their Hungarian counterpart has no sense of proportion.

[7] See 'Declaration on the Principles of Co-operation between the Republic of Hungary and the Ukrainian Soviet Socialist Republic in Guaranteeing the Rights of the National Minorities', Budapest, 31 May 1991.

sources, or 7.1 per cent of the total population). Although Romania's irredentist case in relation to Moldova ought to inspire understanding for the Hungarian concern for ethnic fellows in Transylvania (*Erdely* in Hungarian), this is not so in practice. Pal Dunay, a Hungarian political scientist, blames his own government for having failed to use the unique opportunities created by the violent showdown in Romania in late 1989, when Hungary acted swiftly in providing humanitarian aid and is rumoured to have helped to tilt the scales in favour of the anti-Ceausescu forces. Dunay certainly has a point when criticizing the Antall government for its refusal to include a clause in the planned inter-state treaty whereby Hungary renounces border revisions.[8] But he underestimates the fact that Bucharest continues to be the captive of ultra-nationalistic forces such as the Party of Romanian National Unity which provides parliamentary support for the government and whose chairman, Gheorghe Funar, is Mayor of Cluj. Budapest has asked in vain for the reopening of the Hungarian consulate and the Hungarian university in Cluj (*Kolozsvár* in Hungarian), while the Romanian press frequently features anti-Hungarian copy.

However, the negotiation of the Europe Agreement with the EU in 1993 appears to have opened Romanian decision-makers' eyes to the option of bringing an end to Romanian isolation through reintegration with positive spin-offs for Hungarian-Romanian relations. In September that year Hungarian Foreign Minister Geza Jeszenszky paid an official visit to Romania – the first since December 1989, when then Foreign Minister Horn visited the country – signifying renewed dialogue, although this fell short of a breakthrough (Ionescu and Reisch, 1993). The visit took place two weeks before the Council of Europe was to decide on Romania's acceptance as a member. Apparently Romania feared a repetition of the situation in June 1993, when Hungary abstained from voting on Slovakia's membership to show its dissatisfaction with Slovakia's treatment of Hungarians. Barely a week after the visit by Jeszenszky, then Foreign Minister, the Foreign Relations Committee of the Hungarian National Assembly – chaired by Laszlo Kovács of the

---

[8] The position of the Antall government was that Hungary's adherence to the Helsinki accords of 1975 and the Paris Charter of 1975 makes such bilateral border guarantees redundant; a view that may have its legal merits – but why then has Hungary accepted such a clause in the treaty with Ukraine? (see the interview with Jeszenszky in *Népszabadság*, 5 June 1993).

HSP – recommended that the government should vote in favour of Romania's acceptance on the grounds that it was in the interest of both Hungary and Hungarians in Romania that Romania be integrated into the EU and – as a first step – admitted to the Council of Europe (*RFE/RL News Briefs*, 20-4 September 1993). It took quite an effort on the part of the Foreign Relations Committee to dissuade Jeszenszky from vetoing both Slovakia'a and Romania's admittance to the Council of Europe and instead to abstain from voting (*Frankfurter Allgemeine Zeitung*, 24 November 1993). Yet even France reminded its erstwhile ally that non-compliance with the Council's human-rights norms might result in Romania again being suspended from the forum. Hungary's critical attitude towards Romania thus enjoys substantial Western backing, as further indicated by a rather critical report on Romania submitted by two Council of Europe officials – to which the Romanian MFA responded in mid-1994. On the other hand, Romania's position, emphasizing the obligations of minorities towards the state in which they live, is not without its merits and as it happens corresponds closely to Lithuania's stance on its Polish minority. Early in 1995 there was tension not only between Funar and the Hungarian organizations but between him and the Bucharest government as well. On the Hungarian side, the parliamentary debate on foreign policy on 22 February showed an inclination to compromise on the issue of cultural autonomy on the part of the AFD (*OMRI Daily Digests*). Cooperation between the Romanian and Hungarian Ministries of Defence is proceeding smoothly, as can be seen in the pioneering Hungaro-Romanian Open Skies treaty of May 1991, in addition to the military cooperation treaty of November 1990.

From a humanitarian point of view, Serbia, with its 400,000 Hungarians living in Vojvodina (*Vajdaság* in Hungarian), or 22 per cent of the Serbian population, marks an even more dreadful case than that of Romania as a consequence of the unleashing of the genocidal urge in the post-Yugoslav struggle for power. As a result some 35,000 Vojvodina Hungarians fled to Hungary, many of whom were sheltered by private citizens. Budapest is far more cautious towards Belgrade than other neighbouring capitals – to the point of being tempted to break the ranks of the international ostracization of Serbia and Montenegro. In 1993 Defence Minister Für announced his opposition to a 'hermetic isolation' of Serbia and in early 1994 the Hungarian government announced that it would normalize relations with Serbia (*Népszabadság*, 5 April 1993; *International Herald Tribune*, 7 February 1994). On 9 February Jeszenszky said his country would be the first to welcome the lifting of sanctions and termed them 'bankrupt'; nevertheless, he promised the parliamentary Foreign Relations Committee that his government would make no unilateral moves on this (*RFE/RL News Briefs*, 7 – 11 February 1994). Jeszenszky further said that the pressure upon the Hungarian minority had eased. Hungary did not allow the overflight of NATO's AWACS *en route* to Bosnia to strike Serbian positions around Sarajevo, although it permitted this during the entire no-fly zone operation. These signs of waivering towards former Yugoslavia have been criticized inside Hungary as detrimental to the country's NATO policy (Reisch, 1994). Meanwhile, Budapest has strengthened relations with Albania and tacitly sides with the Kosovars in their struggle with the Belgrade authorities – as Kosovo shared the fate of Vojvodina when it had its autonomy suspended in 1988 by the Belgrade authorities. But the key consideration in Hungary's policy towards its southern neighbours is not to become involved in the fighting. Measured by this standard Budapest has been successful, as Dunay (1992) argues.

As stated above, relations with Croatia, Slovenia and Austria may be categorized as harmonious – the same applies to the Czech Republic. Despite the fact that Croatia was subject to Magyarization policies under the Austro-Hungarian dual monarchy, the country does want to return to Europe via Central Europe and through friendship with Hungary, as does Slovenia. One incident causing strain in Hungaro-Serbian relations was a Hungarian shipment of arms to Croatia in October 1990. Croatia and Slovenia have signed the Ukrainian-Hungarian agreement on minority rights (see note 6) and there is a free-trade agreement with Slovenia. Relations with Slovenia and Austria include military cooperation. Relations with Czechoslovakia used to be strained because of the large Hungarian minority in Slovakia, but the 'Velvet Divorce' has been conducive to a thaw in Hungaro-Czech relations – except for Prague's irritation about what it considers Budapest's undue attempts to solicit its support in the rows with Bratislava (Slovakia). Prague has emerged as a rival to Budapest in the quest for the most convincing reform performance; something that is tacitly recognized by Hungarians when they lump Hungary, Slovenia and the Czech Republic together as the most promising candidates for full EU membership (*Népszabadság*, 14 April 1993).

Relations with Slovakia have been bedeviled *inter alia* by Slovakia's lack of international experience and by Prime Minister Vladimir Meciar's personality.[9] But the vote of no confidence against him and his cabinet in March 1994, and the reappraisal of the environmental hazards associated with the Gabcikovo-Nagymaros hydro-electric power and water management project coupled with the change of government in Hungary, offer new opportunities for a breakthrough in Hungaro-Slovak relations – notwithstanding the re-election of Meciar as head of government in late 1994. In the course of 1993, Slovak-Hungarian cooperation gained some momentum, as exemplified by the military cooperation accord of 4 October which could lead to the training of Slovak officers at Hungarian military academies. The crucial role of the fourteen Hungarian deputies in the Slovak 150-member parliament may help to explain this – a situation parallelling that of the Turkish minority in Bulgarian politics. Slovakia's need to obtain acceptance by the Council of Europe as a sovereign state has also been conducive to improving relations. Slovakia has a Hungarian minority of 600,000 people, or more than 11 per cent of the population, but in spite of that the Slovak Constitution employs monoethnic parlance: 'We, the Slovak people...' (although the preamble ends with the phrase 'We, the citizens of the Slovak Republic...'). The reluctance of the Slovak authorities to allow bilingual signs and Hungarian names would seem to confirm suspicions of assimilationist policies, but the Council of Europe and the staff of the CSCE's High Commissioner for Minorities, Max van der Stoel, represent an important third party – as witness the apparently undramatic conclusions reached by the CSCE in early 1994 on the actual measures of disorientation and inter-ethnic co-existence. The role of Vladimir Meciar as a stumbling block is indicated by Slovak and Hungarian unison assessments of a fresh start in mutual relations once the government of former Foreign Minister Jozef Moravcik took over (*RFE/RL News Briefs* 14-18, 21-5 March and 20-4 June 1994). True enough, the Hun-

---

[9] Some might disapprove of this personalized view of inter-state dynamics, but Meciar's style is deliberately provocative and as such a factor of some weight. On the eve of Slovakia's independence he declared the Hungarian minority to be assimilated, claiming that few felt part of the Hungarian nation (*RFE/RL News Briefs*, 28 December 1992-8 January 1993).

garian MFA spokesman Janos Herman characterized Slovakia's insistence on a clause on the inviolability of borders in the planned inter-state treaty 'tiring and incomprehensible' (*Summary of World Broadcasts*, 14 April 1994). But it may prove significant that the Presidents of Slovakia (Michal Kovac) and Hungary (Arpad Göncz) issued a joint statement where they pledged to work together for 'historical reconciliation' when they met with United States President Bill Clinton in mid-1994 because neither of them is liable to be replaced through a parliamentary election (*RFE/RL News Briefs*, 20-4 June 1994). As in the case of Romania before the 21 March 1995 deadline of the European Stability Pact, the atmosphere in Slovak-Hungarian relations was hectic due, *inter alia*, to gentle pressure from third parties such as US President Clinton and Max van der Stoel of the CSCE for the conclusion of the treaty by this date.

Till recently, the Gabcikovo-Nagymaros dam complex on the river Danube represented a notorious stumbling bloc in Slovak-Hungarian relations and before that in Czechoslovak-Hungarian relations. As a project launched in 1977, this has come to symbolize communist megalomania. When Slovakia took over in 1993 foreigners saw it as a dubious manifestation of Slovak nationalism – the Aswan disaster of Central Europe, as it were. But Slovakia's poor showing in the international uproar may be less the result of actual environmental degradation caused by the diversion of waters than its lack of experience in waging a public relations war (Fischer, 1993). Notwithstanding the fact that Hungary violated the 1977 treaty, odds were always in Budapest's favour because of the worldwide popularity of environmental concerns. This was Hungary's official motive for cancelling its participation in the project and for campaigning against Slovakia for proceeding with its part of the dam in a revised scheme (the so-called C-option). Hungary was very skilful in manipulating the public image of its Slovak counterpart as concrete communists turned concrete nationalists, as when Minister without Portfolio Ferenc Madl commented on his inconclusive talks in April 1991 by saying that he had been 'knocking his head against a brick wall' (quoted in Martin, 1991). To be sure, at that time the Hungarian side was genuinely alarmed, anticipating a dramatic drop in drinking-water supplies for Budapest and north-western Hungary affecting millions of people and devastation of the Szigetköz nature reserve. Conversely, the Slovak side held that it was too late to abandon the project for economic reasons; moreover, Slovakia needed electricity from the planned power plant to reduce pollution from the use of coal and to lessen its dependence on the Bohunice and Mochovce nuclear power plants which Austria would like to see closed down. Mindful of the 1965 floods which destroyed 55,000 homes, Slovakia further argues that it needs the dam to prevent a similar disaster through regulation of the Danube.

What Hungary did was to stop work on Nagymaros and the Dunakiliti dam on 31 October 1989, when only 10 per cent had been completed whereas 90 per cent of the then Czechoslovak part of the work was finished. The C-option provides for completing the project solely on Slovak territory through the use of the Hrusov reservoir. On 24 October 1992 Slovak water managers blocked the Danube to divert it to the Gabcikovo power plant, only to be stopped a few days later because of fierce protests from Hungary and the international community (MTI, 2 November, 1992). In January 1993 the EC intervened, anxious about the security risks of further escalation of the conflict. It persuaded both parties to bring their dispute to the International Court of Justice in the Hague and applied a stick-and-carrot approach towards Slovakia, which currently receives 10 per cent of its electricity supplies from Gabcikovo. But contrary to all expectations, the Gabcikovo diversion has proved beneficial for the environment in Slovakia's wetlands (*New Scientist*, 16 July and 17 September 1994). The Slovak side has altered its project in order to quell environmental fears by diverting some of the Danube waters back into the wetlands, thereby reviving branches of the Danube which have been dry for 30 years. As a result, the international campaign against the project led by the World Wide Fund for Nature has cooled off and apologies have been forwarded to Slovak scientists, including Igor Mucha, a hydrologist representing Bratislava in the trilateral commission set up by the EU. Gabcikovo could become a tourist asset for Slovakia!

Relations between the two parties improved in the course of 1994, as acknowledged by Slovak officials (TASR, 8 April 1994; *CTK-Business News* 15 April 1994; TASR May 13 1994). On 2 July Horn declared that his government wanted to approach the Gabcikovo-Nagymaros conflict 'without any prejudices', albeit maintaining that environmental issues must remain decisive and that an expert solution and then a political one must be found as a step towards an inter-state treaty (*Népszabadság*, 2 July, 1994). He also promised to consult the Hungarians in Slovakia before submitting the treaty for ratification in the Hungarian National Assembly. As stated earlier, Hungary is fairly enthusiastic about multilateral cooperation with its postcommunist neighbours as a way to deepen dialogue and bolster mutual interests and commitments. The CEI has proved less important for Budapest, not least because of suspicion about Hungary's chairmanship of its minorities committee. Hungary and the Czech Republic were united in their support for Slovakia's admittance to the Visegrad framework, with Hungary in the role of advocating greater political cooperation and the Czech Republic giving priority to implementing the CEFTA free-trade agreement (MTI, 4 February 1993; *Népszabadság*, 5 October 1992). Presidential meetings such as the gathering in Litomysl (the Czech Republic) in April 1994, in which Germany also took part, serve as additional CSBMs; in 1995 Hungary hosted the meeting. As for the Russo-Hungarian declaration of mutual support on minority issues in international fora (see Chapter 4, note 15), it has at best proved of limited use for Hungary, tainting as it does its image of being motivated purely by humanitarian concerns in its pursuit of minority issues because of foreign policy developments in Russia meanwhile (personal interviews with Hungarian civil servants, cf. *Népszabadság*, 7 April 1993). However, there is a delicate situation in relation to the Estonians, the Finno-Ugric brethren of Hungarians. At one time Jeszenszky reminded Estonia of the need to guarantee certain rights to the Russian minority in the country, while Antall and his Estonian counterpart Mart Laar came to the conclusion that there should be legislation to protect 'historical minorities' who have lived in a country for a long time (MTI, 28 January 1993; *Népszabadság*, 7 April 1993).

Hungary's policy of reintegration. The Hungarian ´deliberations on reintegration have long traditions dating back to the pre-1989 era and are therefore among the more articulate even for the Visegrad countries (cf. Skak, 1993c). On p. 43 above, the political scientist Attila Agh was quoted on his thoughts on reintegration as a means of making the changes in the domestic system irreversible. In a similar vein Jeszenszky has more than once urged the West to open itself up to the postcommunist East: 'Full membership in institutions that provide political, economic and military security – organizations like the Council of Europe, the European Community and NATO – is essential for consolidating Central and Eastern Europe'

(*International Herald Tribune*, 22 October 1992). This membership policy marks the Antall government's innovation in reintegration policy, but the parliamentary consensus behind the guidelines for Hungary's security policy is a reminder of the overwhelming legitimacy which it enjoys. The membership policy is confirmed in the 'Basic principles of the security policy of the Republic of Hungary' of 1993, which adds the WEU to the list of reintegration targets. On the significance of EU membership the document reads: 'Hungary's security will ultimately be determined by our membership of the European Community' – in other words, non-military measures constitute security policy and, conversely, military cooperation is held to have broader political and institutional significance in continuance of the broad analytical approach to reintegration advanced in the present work. Hungary is anxious to become involved in the common foreign and security policy of the EU and appreciates recent overtures in that direction – which act partly as a yardstick for Hungary's 'return to Europe'. But EU policy is very much a question of market access, as a consequence of Hungary's dependence on agricultural exports and the diverse effects of the collapse of the Soviet market (Skak, 1993c; Tovias 1991).

In this respect a rude awakening is in the offing for Hungarian farmers, not just because of the protectionist clauses in Hungary's Europe Agreement, whose trade provisions have been in force for some time. During the first year of Hungarian EU-cooperation under this new agreement, the Hungarian side proved unable to boost its exports by more than 10 per cent. By contrast, EU farmers who enjoy generous CAP subsidies were able to increase their exports to Hungary by 54 per cent, thereby creating a large trade deficit for Hungary (*Népszabadság*, 17 April 1993; cf. Galinos, 1994). Hungarian exports were hampered by EU precautions against foot-and-mouth disease, but even without such safeguards Hungarian agriculture will need restructuring if it is to face up to European competition. This sobering experience will hardly lessen the Hungarian determination ultimately to join the EU as a full member, as only this will put EU and Hungarian exporters on an equal footing, although the CAP may have to be dismantled by then. As a secondary step in preparing for EU membership, Budapest has concluded a free trade agreement with EFTA – only to find that Austria strikes just as tough a bargain as the EU. Before its EU entry, Austria represented the third biggest export market for Hungary

(*New Zürcher Zeitung*, 29 February 1991; *Népszabadság*, 8 April 1993). In December 1993 Hungary applied for OECD membership as another 'crucial milestone' of economic and institutional reintegration (*RFE/RL News Briefs*, 21-5 February 1994).

Hungary has been ahead of other former CMEA countries in orienting its trade towards the EU market – 25 per cent of the total by 1989 and 50 per cent by 1992, although at that time Poland surpassed Hungary. Hungarians used to be very enthusiastic about joining the EU, with 83 per cent coming out in favour by late 1992 (*Central and Eastern Eurobarometer*, no. 3, 1993). But representatives of the Hungarian policy-making élite complain about growing apathy towards the EU (*Népszabadság*, 11 May 1994). The outgoing government remained faithful to its promise of making Hungary the first postcommunist country formally to apply for EU membership on 1 April 1994. This, however, followed a vote in the National Assembly where 233 MPs voted for and none against in another striking display of foreign policy consensus (*RFE/RL News Briefs*, 21-5 March 1994). The then State Secretary in the International Economic Relations Ministry, Endre Juhász, announced that he expected admission talks to begin in 1997 (MTI, 20 April 1994). HDF Prime Minister Peter Boross – installed after Antall's death – admitted the serious challenges for Hungary in bringing its economy up to EU standards; a problem Gyula Horn often dwelt on as opposition leader (*Népszabadság*, 19 April 1993). Indeed, the HSP likes to expose what it sees as HDF's undue haste and naivety in its EU policy. The HSP wants the question of Hungary's membership of the EU and NATO settled by referendum. The AFD and HSP are united in their emphasis on careful preparation, for instance in the field of harmonizing laws where Horn sees Austria as a prospective reintegration-patron; nevertheless, one cannot escape the conclusion that the HSP is, in fact, slightly less enthusiastic about its EU and NATO membership policy than its coalition partner is.

Many Western observers were caught by surprise over the increased courting of NATO in 1993 by postcommunist countries wanting hard security guarantees and membership. This gave birth to the theory of NATO as a substitute reintegration target now that the EC had revealed itself as protectionist and self-contained towards the East in the crisis over the ratification of the Maastricht Treaty. The Hungarian security guidelines lend some credibility to this hypothesis. After having established the primacy of seeking EU membership for reasons of security policy, the document goes on to state: 'In addition we are firmly striving to achieve membership of the [NATO] as soon as possible – in our view even prior to attaining membership status in the European Community' ('*Basic Principles*', 1993). But Hungary's approach to NATO dates back earlier than this. The then Foreign Minister Horn caused quite a stir when he suggested in early 1990 that the Warsaw Pact countries might as well join NATO's political and other branches or even pursue 'common membership' (Reisch, 1993b). Hungarians never wanted to change or dismantle NATO, in contrast to the Czech dissidents who signed Charter 77, which was the backbone of postcommunist Czechoslovakia's first government. When explaining the NATO policy of Hungary, however, one also has to take into consideration the formation of the Visegrad triangle and the need not to be seen by the Soviet Union as a new military alliance. For tactical reasons the forum had to launch itself as a framework for joint Europeanization, but very soon this rationale took on operational significance as a cohesive force for the new forum. Later still, the participants' mutual suspicions that they might work as a brake on one another's return to Europe compelled this development. The Cracow summit of 1991 had already heralded the joint pursuit of closer cooperation with NATO (*Népszabadság*, 7 October 1991). The war in Yugoslavia served as a specific catalyst for Hungary's search for security guarantees which it had been denied (*RFE/RL News Briefs*, 14-21 May 1993). Nevertheless, Hungary's PfP relationship with NATO – which Serbia does not have – may entail more than meets the eye; according to Jeszenszky: 'It's a relationship of trust that may turn into protection without specification in any agreement. For instance, the Soviet Union had its submarines plough Swedish waters, but could go no farther than that because the seas fringing Sweden enjoyed undeclared NATO protection' (*Hungarian Observer*, May 1994, p. 10). This interpretation may not be off the mark, judging from the response of German Federal Chancellor Helmut Kohl to Antall's request for closer links to NATO: 'Even if Hungary does not become a NATO member in the near future, it should feel its security is provided for' (MTI, 23 June 1993). Hungary's cooperation with NATO in connection with the no-fly zone in Bosnia may not have been without impact in this connection. In my assessment, it is a misreading of Hungarian signals when Western analysts insist that Hungary reacted with disappointment to the PfP formula (Reisch, 1994b). Certainly, Hungary will not feel content until it acquires the status of a full-fledged NATO member, but its approach to PfP was 'to fill it with real content' (*RFE/RL News Briefs*, 27 December 1993-4 January 1994). Hungary clearly appreciates the opportunity for joint exercises with NATO military forces as 'a signal to the Hungarian people that the security of Central Europe is important to the United States and its allies' (*ibid.*, 10-21 January 1994). Later that year Budapest welcomed British Prime Minister John Major's and Kohl's offer to hold joint British-German-Hungarian peacekeeping exercises on Hungarian soil in 1995; exercises which were to be planned by NATO bodies, thereby manifesting Hungary's emerging integration into NATO's military structure (MTI, 28 April 1994). Meanwhile, on a par with the other countries of the WEU's so-called consultation forum, Hungary has been extended associate partner membership of this forum, thus filling in the missing link in its strategy of seeking expanding cooperation with the triangle of the EU, WEU and NATO.

As may be inferred from the references to the CSCE (OSCE) and the Council of Europe as a third party between Hungary and its neighbours in minority disputes and as a further option for blocking their reintegration, Budapest does attach importance to these two fora. Together they represent 'an important framework for our security policy endeavours both in defining human rights and in gaining their acceptance and application', to quote the 'Basic Principles' of Hungary's security policy once again. In the autumn of 1994 Hungary took over from Italy the rotating chairmanship of the CSCE. To some extent, Hungary has left behind its bilateral approach to seeking minority guarantees and has switched to a policy of seeking to have them enshrined as binding norms at the international level via the OSCE and the Council of Europe. Hungary's quest for seeking collective minority rights has not met with unconditional approval on the part of Western countries, however – something that causes a certain frustration in Budapest (*Neue Zürcher Zeitung*, 9 February 1995). Over-institutionalization of minority rights could very well erode the fragile stability of the postcommunist states and become a lever for militancy, a problem Hungarians tend to overlook.

Germany is Hungary's chief Europeanization patron – as for many other countries. Bonn still remembers Gyula Horn's contribution to German unification by letting East Germans use Hungary as an escape route to West Germany in August 1989, when the GDR was on the verge of collapse. German officials as well as Hungarians speak of an excellent ('*hervorragend*') relationship, as reflected in the German-Hungarian inter-state treaty of 6 February 1992 which employs slightly more definite wording in its clause on Germany's help for Hungary's aim of EU membership when compared to the treaty with Czechoslovakia (Majaros, 1993). Both Jeszenszky and Horn have cited former German Foreign Minister Hans-Dietrich Genscher as their role model. Nevertheless, in June 1991 Genscher showed signs of annoyance over Antall's attempts to promote Hungary to 'front runner' among the postcommunist states by pushing for its entry into the EC ahead of others at one time mentioning January 1995 as an entry date (Skak, 1993c). This is one likely reason why Hungary changed to pursuing a policy of joint Europeanization together with its Visegrad partners, to the point where Hungary and Poland are now alone in upholding the virtue of a joint position. In response Kohl recently reassured Budapest that 'without Hungary the EU remains only a torso' (*Frankfurter Allgemeine Zeitung*, 19 July 1994). Kohl welcomed Hungary's application for EU membership – in a move that had been coordinated with Poland, which filed its application at the same time – characterizing it as a 'wise' decision, but also reminded Budapest that it would have to make the necessary preparations itself to fulfil entry criteria (Reuters, 21 April 1994; *RFE/RL News Briefs*, 28 February – 4 March 1994). German-Hungarian relations are not confined to economic cooperation – although this is of key importance to Budapest – but encompasses military cooperation as well. This is not a unique phenomenon, yet Hungary stands out among the Visegrad countries in its fairly relaxed attitude to German unification. The German-Hungarian relationship is not the only bilateral relationship with Western powers worth mentioning, but without doubt it is the most significant.[10]

---

[10] For a while Italy promised to become a partner of some significance via the CEI, but as it foundered Hungary-Italian economic cooperation appears to have receded somewhat into the background. As a member of the EU Austria will again become more important than Italy for Hungary.

Explaining foreign policy developments in Hungary

The basic thesis in the above analysis is that the foreign policy of postcommunist Hungary displays a large measure of stability in its overall patterns and problems. The change of government will hardly bring about a radical reorientation, but very likely a change of style marking the further maturing of the country's political élite. To some extent Antall's conservative government displayed the same trends of nationalist parochialism seen during Landsbergis' period in power in Lithuania and – *mutatis mutandis* – in postcommunist Russia. At the same time the outgoing Hungarian government must be credited for its strong commitment to institutional logics. Proceeding from the premise of Hungary's limited powers and acute need of international *Einbindung* as the only solution to the instability of transition, Antall and his team formulated a strategy of reintegration through full membership and participation. Jeszenszky's belief in the virtue of *Einbindung* came to the fore in connection with the preparation of the German-Hungarian inter-state Treaty of Friendly Cooperation and European Partnership when he proposed to 'bind the entire continent into a network of treaties' (*Frankfurter Allgemeine Zeitung*, 20 December 1991). Indeed, the Hungarian quest for *Einbindung* represents more than a superficial parallel to Germany in relation to which the principle of *Einbindung* marks the acceptance of realist balance-of-power thinking on the need to 'keep Germany down'. Given Hungary's perceived potential as a regional hegemon through aggressive irredentism in the eyes of its neighbours, the only way for the country to gain legitimacy is by pursuing its goals through international forums, thus committing itself to internationally accepted solutions and renouncing national unilateralism.

The overarching normative aspiration in Budapest's policy towards its neighbours is the pursuit of collective rights for Hungarian minorities, including the pursuit of their administrative autonomy. In relation to this, principles of non-interference and inviolability of borders take the back seat or, rather, they are viewed as bargaining chips to raise the stakes in a generous policy towards minorities. The Hungarian reaction to the EU project of the European Pact on Stability is quite revealing. Whereas most other postcommunist countries at whom the initiative was targeted wryly accepted it, Budapest displayed a more business-like approach making clear the need to involve national minorities and their representatives in the

EU-sponsored bilateral negotiations elaborating the specific contents of the Stability Pact (Jeszenszky, 1994). Hungary rightly perceived the initiative as another opportunity to fix the rights of minorities in an arrangement that was sponsored by the EU and hence endowed with international legitimacy (*Frankfurter Allgemeine Zeitung*, 18 November 1993). But the Hungarian considerations of *Einbindung* and willingness to enter a process of bargaining also point in the direction of the logic of power behind Budapest's policy. It is not at all unlikely that the incoming government's hints of a new order of priorities in which the protection of Hungarian minorities no longer enjoys primacy over normalization of state-to-state relations are the direct result of the Balladur plan for the Stability Pact, forcing Hungary to adapt – given the absolute primacy of reintegration through ever closer links to the EU. In this perspective, the development within Hungarian foreign policy qualifies as a case of acquiescent adaptation to the pole represented by the EU (cf. Mouritzen, 1993).

However, it is also tempting to invoke the concept of 'maladaptation' as a way to emphasize the evident shortcomings in the former Hungarian government's approach to its neighbours. On several occasions Hungary may be said to have overstated its case, neglecting the legitimate concerns of some of its neighbours – notably so in the case of Slovakia. The fact that the Antall government was tempted by the option of blocking Slovakia's and Romania's entry into the Council of Europe is suggestive of Budapest's will to step out of its role of a cowed small state and exercise power. On the other hand, it would be jumping to conclusions to brand Hungary's conduct – and for that matter the conduct of the three Baltic states *vis-à-vis* Russia – improper playing with fire, that is maladaptation. There is every reason to believe that Hungary's outcry against what it perceives as an infringement upon legitimate rights and the accompanying international publicity have had a sobering effect upon governments; conversely, that failure to draw attention to perceived problems would have yielded nothing.

Some might find it suspicious that institutionalist Hungary adheres to the doctrine of deterrence through a national army that is 'leaner but meaner', to use Pentagon parlance ('Basic principles...'; Basic Principles of National Defence in the Republic of Hungary', 1993). More than anything else, however, this qualifies as evidence of Hungary's conviction that it is placed in a security vacuum which temporarily has to be filled by the individual defence efforts of the governments in the region until NATO steps in (*Frankfurter Allgemeine Zeitung*, 18 November 1993). The very terminology of vacuum is suggestive of the healthy dose of balance-of-power thinking in the Hungarian élite, as also confirmed by the overtures made towards some of the countries at odds with Romania, Serbia and Russia, respectively: Moldova, Albania, Ukraine and Turkey.

It is also possible to interpret the weaknesses, strengths and developments in Hungarian foreign policy as determined by the domestic balance of power, organizational shortcomings or *vice versa*. The general hypothesis is that formerly external empire states like Hungary were at an advantage when faced with the challenge of becoming truly sovereign states through the international and organizational experience gained during sovietization, notably prior to the collapse of the Soviet order. Broadly speaking this perception holds true – not least because of the continuing role of the old Hungarian élite as ministerial officials and decision-makers (e.g. the respected Minister of International Economic Relations during the Antall regime, Béla Kádár, who is independent of party). As emphasized by one of the ministry's two State Secretaries, Tamás Katona, the HSP caretaker government of Miklós Nemeth handed over an MFA that was in good shape (in contrast to some other ministries; *Népszabadság*, 30 December 1990). In his assessment, it was mainly thanks to the earlier efforts of Nemeth and Horn that the new Hungarian government was able to achieve swift progress in relation to the EC. Nevertheless, the Antall government felt it necessary to recall fourteen ambassadors and to streamline the ministry and its staff to match the demands of reintegration and a rapidly changing European environment (Reisch, 1992). Among the Budapest-based staff, some 20 per cent of MGIMO graduates decided to stay; unfortunately, among those who left were some of the best qualified people who preferred more lucrative jobs in the private sector, thus exemplifying the general organizational problems facing postcommunist states (see above, pp. 26–30).

Judging from the remarks of the other MFA State Secretary, János Martonyi, Hungarian foreign policy has been marred by problems of coordination, notably in Brussels where the Hungarian representation had to be upgraded with EC and NATO experts (*Népszabadság*, 8 June 1992). The problem appears to be rooted in the old Soviet-era over-specialized ministries, including an MFA that is unsuited for managing international economic relations and an integrated security agenda. The declared personnel policy of the HDF government was to apply professional rather than political criteria, but as suggested in the introduction the personality and ideology of the leading HDF politicians, including Jeszenszky – a historian – also represented serious drawbacks. According to himself, when serving as Foreign Minister Jeszenszky meticulously monitored all ministerial correspondence and edited papers written in English; a painstaking style of management that hardly qualifies as modern (*Hungarian Observer*, May 1994). During the election campaign the incoming government sought to proclaim its alleged professional approach; it has since announced a further streamlining of the MFA and its ambassadorial staff and missions abroad, including the Hungarian embassy in Brussels (*Magyar Hírláp*, 27 and 29 June 1994; MTI, 13 and 21 July 1994). Among other things, the MFA is to take on responsibility for economic diplomacy and is to have a stronger EU section. It stands to reason, however, that a good deal of both the former HDF-led government's and the incoming HSP-AFD government's perceived need of organizational shake-ups can be attributed to electoral considerations. One should not underestimate the MFA's and its staff's capacity for adaptation, or its role as administrative stabilizer of foreign policy. More than anything else it may be in this respect that Hungary's organizational features 'explain' foreign policy, in this case evidencing a fairly stable pattern.

In Hungary foreign policy is not a presidential prerogative, in contrast to the situation of Russia and Lithuania. In reality, however, the Hungarian President Arpád Göncz has played a certain modifying role in foreign policy because of his moral prestige abroad as a former dissident. At one time the parliamentary Foreign Relations Committee clashed with the government over his right to dissociate himself from governmental policy. It turned out that Göncz always coordinated his visits and speeches with the MFA (Reisch, 1993d). Another evident factor of moderation, particularly on questions relating to neighbouring countries, is the Foreign Relations Committee. The work of this Hungarian body confirms that parliamentary inputs may be fruitful and not just an extension of petty squabbles undermining the legitimacy of democracy, as has been the case in Russia. Parliamentarians and government often work in tandem in the promotion of Hungarian interests abroad, and the Hungarian Foreign Relations Committee has regular consultations with its Austrian and Slovak counterparts (MTI, 18 July 1993). Admittedly, the fact that the HSP daily (until recently) *Népszabadság* reported on the work of this HSP-chaired parliamentary body in a matter-of-fact fashion has to be taken with a grain of salt. But the coverage of one session devoted to discussing the political crisis in Russia, for instance, was most informative and conveyed the impression of a serious forum (*Népszabadság*, 7 April 1993). Yet another foreign affairs committee has been founded, the parliamentary Committee on European Integration Affairs. The European Commission plans to work on the draft scheme for Hungary's entry negotiations with this new body (MTI, 4 July 1994). In due course the Hungarian Committee on European Integration Affairs could grow into something like the Market Committee of the Danish *Folketing* (parliament), dubbed the thirteenth EU member by former Commission chairman Jacques Delors. Apart from that the Hungarian constitution places the government, i.e. the Council of Ministers, in the position of determining foreign policy for the time being with Kovacs and Horn, with MFA State Secretary Istvan Szent-Ivanyi of the AFD in change of operational foreign policy-making. At times the former Foreign Relations Committee chaired by the HSP complained about the government's failure to consult it prior to making decisions. The incoming government has therefore promised to provide for greater parliamentary participation in foreign policy-making.

Even so, Hungarian politics is not without its irrational features, a case in point being the controversy with Czechoslovakia and subsequently with Slovakia over the Gabcikovo-Nagymaros project. On the one hand, the rational-actor perspective cannot be dismissed altogether – i.e. the hypothesis that a cost-benefit calculation on the environmental hazards associated with the dam provides the real explanation for Hungary's cancellation of its participation in the project. The threatened degradation of fresh-water supplies to Budapest and north-western Hungary represented a problem which few politicians could afford to ignore. On the other hand, it would be impermissibly naive to preclude the influence of other factors that point away from rational-actor decision-making. The fact that this concerns a non-routine decision to cancel a project does not necessarily rule out the perspective of organizational process, or that of bureaucratic politics. As pointed out by the Norwegian political scientist Janne Haaland Matlary, the Hungarian Ministry of the

Environment was literally born in the struggle against the project, thereby turning the cancellation of Hungary's participation into the *raison d'être* for this organizational and bureaucratic actor. In her words, the conclusions of the expert report by the National Office for Environmental Protection and Nature Conservation – the precursor of the Ministry of Environment – tended to disfavour the dam (Haaland Matlary 1993, p. 14).

Given the popularity of the decision to call off Hungarian participation, it is also instructive to apply the perspective of the opportunistic dramatic actor to the two Hungarian governments involved. Hungary's October 1989 decision to cancel its participation marked a *volte face* on the part of the Hungarian communists, who had just then decided to rename themselves socialists, dropping the W for 'Workers' in HSWP. Growing popular protests against the project had led thirty-two MPs to demand a referendum on the issue in 1988, but the then ruling HSWP (Communist Party) wanted to proceed with construction, leading to a collection of 120,000 signatures against one-party rule. In 1989 the strategy of the Hungarian reform communists changed to a bid to spearhead the country's abandonment of communism. All of a sudden they were in dire need of popularity and legitimacy in the forthcoming free elections. In the analysis of Peter Martin, they 'did not want to risk alienating a large segment of the population over a costly and increasingly unpopular issue that was not crucial to their plans for establishing a multiparty democratic system' (1991, p. 8).

Much the same could be said about the Antall government's policy of continuing the struggle against the project and protesting at the Slovak party's unilateral diversion of the Danube in the autumn of 1992. Yet there is a further twist of lack of credibility on the part of this actor: the government's support for domestic environmental reform has not been strong since the 1990 elections, and the Hungarian public does not put environmental concerns at the top of the political agenda (Fischer, 1993, p. 11). Similarly, Haaland Matlary observes that the environmental NGOs lost political significance after 1990 and today less than 1 per cent of Hungarian GNP is allocated to environmental purposes. Thus it would be unfair to criticize only Slovakia for having speculated in the nuisance value of upholding past positions *vis-à-vis* its neighbour in this controversy. Just as the dam played a role in Slovak nation- building, so Hungarian opposition to the dam was instrumental in postcommunist Hungary's nation-building.

The role of environmental NGOs, in turn, points towards the praetorian perspective of manipulation by strong pressure groups rather than governmental decision-making. One of the most important was the Danube Circle, formed in the early 1980s, which distributed a *samizdat* newsletter and was awarded an 'alternative Nobel Prize' in 1985. In 1986 it organized a 'human chain' of over 100,000 protesters from Hungary and Austria and in 1988 the organization was legalized. Austrian 'Greens' cooperated closely with it and later the WWF and International Rivers Network joined the protest. But, as already stated, the role of interest groups climaxed in 1989, implying that the praetorian model provides only a partial explanation.[11] Rather, analysts must consider the coincidence of overlapping situational factors – as envisioned in the garbage-can model – by applying more than one explanatory framework, as briefly sketched here.

Despite this last exposition of some of the more curious dimensions in Hungary's foreign policy, the country stands out among the three cases examined as having a more mature foreign policy and a better consolidated pattern of foreign policy behaviour. The chances are that some of the lacunae in the foreign policy of Hungary's first postcommunist government will be attended to now; on the other hand, the new government is anxious to play down any expectation of swift breakthroughs. This may be taken as evidence of the legitimacy of the foreign policy pursued by the outgoing conservative government, and not least of the fact of its perceived viability in the face of nasty dilemmas in relation to some postcommunist neighbours. The foreign policy credo of the AFD partner in the new ruling coalition is to proceed step by step – in the field of reintegra-

[11] The Hungarian media's evocative way of reporting on the Gabcikovo – *Bös* in Hungarian – also helped to institutionalize the public outcry against the project. One example is Tibor Kis' editorial in *Népszabadság* of 20 May 1992, featuring biased rhetoric such as: 'Slovak concrete lobby', 'Danube-saurus', 'hydro-monster' etc. The reader may feel that I am stretching Huntington's praetorian model a bit too far when making it synonymous with grassroots activism and critical media. But my point remains that processes of transition characterized by this kind of militant political mobilization could lead to the more archetypical military praetorianism – although it is unlikely in this case.

tion policy too. The prospects are that referenda will decide Hungary's entry to the EU and NATO. The voting could prove close, notably on Hungary's membership of NATO as Hungarians are known to be in doubt about joining this alliance. The era of re-nationalization of security policy may not be entirely over, but on the other hand, the outcome of the recent election is encouraging for the rejection of chauvinist nationalism it suggests, thus parallelling political developments in Lithuania.

7

POSTCOMMUNISM'S
INTERNATIONAL RELATIONS

This part of the analysis must begin with a disclaimer. What follows is not a detailed mapping of the web of international relations of individual postcommunist states – which would be a hopeless undertaking anyway, and not at all necessary for identifying important trends and problems. After the in-depth studies of postcommunist foreign policy at the level of individual countries – each representing an ideal type within the concentric circles of the Soviet empire – it is time now for an overview of the international interaction between the countries and peoples in the region in order to examine the thesis of the development from empire to anarchy. The present chapter thus marks a departure from the state level of analysis, instead adopting bilateral and multilateral approaches. The first part of the analysis concerns the problems.

Conflict in the postcommunist world

Both Western and Eastern media indulge themselves by dwelling on the twin themes of conflict and crisis in the postcommunist world. This is not just a reflection of the old truth that bad news is good news for journalists; unfortunately it is very much the reality. The publication of an encyclopedia of conflicts, disputes and hotspots throughout the postcommunist world is most revealing of the kind of challenges created by the decolonization of the Soviet empire. After having digested the figure of over 274 conflicts – potential as well as actual in the postcommunist world presented by the editor of the encyclopedia, few would deny the pervasiveness of conflict in this region (Szajkowski, 1993a). But circumstances and the potential for the eruption of armed struggle differ vastly across cases. An assessment of the depth of the problem of conflict calls for a closer examination of dissimilar cases – that of war (former Yugoslavia) and that of peaceful conflict-resolution (Czechs and Slovaks) –in order to discuss implications for latent cases of war such as Russia versus Ukraine. Before that, however, I should like to take issue with a common misperception of the phenomenon of conflict in the postcommunist world and elsewhere.

After long period of neglect, concepts like ethnicity, nationalism and ethnic conflict have gained a hitherto unseen popularity. The previous 'struggle against imperialism' stereotype of conflict-analysis has been replaced by the new stereotype of 'ancient hatred' in continuation of the primordial understanding of ethnic phenomena – the wounded *Volksgeist* sweeping back like a bent twig (Berlin, 1991). This 'Sleeping Beauty' theory of ethnic conflict, however, overlooks the fact that the eruption of ethnic conflict is very much tied up with the context, as is the eruption of violence. To cite the classic contribution of Lewis A. Coser, conflicts are about scarce resources in one sense or another – material wealth, jobs, water, territory, security, power, etc. (1956, p. 8). Human life is rich in scarcity so to speak, implying that conflicts are embedded in all sorts of social interaction. The clash and accommodation of interests provide for change. What is important in this connection is that ethnic and national mobilization serves as a convenient medium for the pursuit of ordinary political interests. Nationalists often believe in their own myths, but analysts have to be able to look beyond them or else they end up as anthropologists going native. This is not to deny the virtue of empathy and the hermeneutic method of understanding as an analytical first step. More often than not, however, a closer examination of specific cases of armed ethnic struggle will lead to conclusions along the lines of Bogdan Szajkowski's concerning the conflict between Azerbaijan and Armenian secessionists in Nagorno-Karabakh:

> The main problem has never been religion or ethnicity, rather, it is the lack of democracy and the lack of political maturity on both sides. The present tragedy in the region could have been avoided and the Karabakh problem solved peacefully, if both sides had tried to reach a solution through democratic means and through mutual agreement and understanding. (1993a, p. 241)

Given the pervasiveness of conflict under postcommunism it is tempting to coin a theory of postcommunist conflict based on the collapse of communism. The overriding contextual factor might be exactly that – the collapse of *Pax Sovietica* and central control. Sovietization worked as a brake on unfolding processes of nation-building in Eastern Europe, retarding a process which might have been finished by now. There is much to be said for this theory except for the fact that conflict does not limit itself to the postcommunist world. Most other violent conflicts are concentrated in the weak states of the Third World a factor pointing towards institutional weakness and unconsolidated power structures as the general preconditions – in this instance the fact of transition from communism. The pervasiveness of nationalist mobilization in the terminal phase of communism and after has further to be understood against the background of the hypocritical doctrine of internationalism serving as a sinew of the deeply authoritarian Soviet empire. This had the effect of turning nationalism into a powerful protest ideology on a par with environmentalism and democratic pluralism. At the same time postcommunist nationalism – or tribalism, to use Popper's word for it – expresses the reaction against an emerging open society. The attraction of nationalism stems from the sense of direction and comfort it provides for individuals in times of upheaval through its reliance on historicist mythology (cf. Schöpflin, 1991b). This makes nationalism an instrument for enemies of the open society. This critical Popperian approach to nationalistic collectivism – in effect replacing one totalitarianism with another – is essential in order to grasp the hidden agendas and manipulations typical of many nationalist leaders. Warlords often masquerade as nationalists and freedom-fighters, an indication that modern nationalism only adds to the arsenal of organized crime. While primordialists may be right to argue that ethnic hatred willingly let itself be mobilized in Yugoslavia as a circumstance working *a priori*, the critical factor was and remains the deliberate, ruthless manipulation of this element by political actors.

It was the British weekly *The Economist* that first came up with the idea of juxtaposing the case of Yugoslavia with that of Czecho-slovakia (5-11 September, 1992; cf. Bookman, 1994). Among the four tests for violence advanced is that of would-be borders: do they tend to create an ethnic muddle or not? This factor certainly marks a difference between the Yugoslav case, where present borders created an ethnic patchwork later modified through the gruesome practice of ethnic cleansing, and Czechoslovakia, where the conversion of internal borders to international borders resulted in manageable diaspora problems. Quite a few of the perhaps half million Slovaks living in the Czech Republic want Czech citizenship, while Slovakia houses only about 40,000 Czechs (Fischer, 1994). This, however, could be taken as evidence of the importance of cultural factors otherwise dismissed by *The Economist*. The lack of aggressive anti-Slovak nationalism in the Czech part of the country and the willingness to find viable solutions – a velvet divorce – was a factor of immense importance. There was no ignition of intolerance creating acute security dilemmas at the level of individuals leading to the well-known dreadful consequences. Although the Czech expulsion of Sudeten Germans in the aftermath of the Second World War qualifies as ethnic cleansing, it is not without justification that ever since 1968 Czech political culture has earned a reputation for being non-violent and pragmatic, with 'the Good Soldier Svejk' as role model. The implication for cases like the Russo-Ukrainian conflict may not be that sombre. It is not difficult to find Russian nationalists laying claim to Crimea, but the Russian government pursues a cautious line – as when Yeltsin phoned Ukrainian President Kravchuk at the height of the crisis, assuring him that no forceful measures against Crimea would be necessary and that he considered Crimea a sovereign republic *within* Ukraine (*NeGa*, 24 May 1994). Notorious hardliners such as Migranian avoid hints of military action in a strategy marketed as letting fall what cannot stand on its own feet; yet in its own way this is a stance conducive to institutionalizing the present coexistence. Of course, it is the Russian diaspora in the Crimea and all over eastern Ukraine and its perception of relative deprivation that hold the key to the future. But the election of Leonid Kuchma as President of Ukraine in the spring of 1994 promises accommodation of the demand for closer cooperation with Russia without necessarily putting an end to Ukrainian independence, which would be a certain recipe for disaster by mobilizing militant Ukrainian nationalism in the western half of the country (Umbach, 1994). By early 1995 there were signs that at long last Ukraine will address the issue of economic reform promising a decrease in frustration over hardships and hence in ethnic tension.

Is there a recent memory of ethnic slaughter? This is the second test for violence advanced by *The Economist*. Again, this is a case where the Yugoslav situation certainly differs from those of the Czechs and Slovaks and the Russians and Ukrainians. The appalling atrocities committed by Croats against Serbs, by nationalists against communists and *vice versa* within the same ethnic group during the Second World War is a living memory for the entire older stratum of the population. But contrary to what is held by *The Economist*, this need not be so decisive a catalyst for violence provided there is some sort of institutionalized coming to terms with the past – *Vergangenheitsbewältigung* in German, a term used for mental de-Nazification. Tito's formula of 'bratsvo i jedinstvo' (brotherhood and unity) prevented precisely that by tabooing an honest discussion of the past since this would have disrupted his own legitimacy. His reign may have had a human face, but his Yugoslavia was no democracy. To return to the case of Ukraine versus Russia, might not the legacy of the incorporation of Ukraine into Russia under the 1654 Treaty of Pereiaslavl and memories of subjugation under Soviet Russia in 1920, the terrible famine during collectivization and the subsequent guerilla war against the Soviet power structure instigate fratricidal war between Russians and Ukrainians? Nothing of the kind can be excluded, but given the decisive role of the Soviet-Russian centre – in contrast to rank-and-file Russians – in the repression of Ukraine it is not a likely scenario. Russians entertain a paternalistic attitude towards Ukrainians, but they do not perceive them as an existential threat the way Serbs, Croats and Yugoslav Muslims perceive one another. In other words the catalyst for citizen-to-citizen violence is not that strong (cf. Posen, 1993). The conflict is basically political – mainly a struggle among élites over Ukraine's international orientation and the future of Crimea, the Black Sea Fleet and Ukraine's strategic nuclear arms.

The third factor concerns whether a hegemonic scenario is unfolding, pushing in the direction of armed conflict. Certainly, perceptions of a threat from a Greater Serbia and Serbian fears of German as well as Turkish-Albanian conspiracies, in addition to innumerable counter-conspiracies and ententes – e.g. the Belgrade-Moscow-Athens axis – have probably served as an additional determinant of violence. *The Economist* is wrong in assuming that this factor is lacking in Central Europe, however. Czech perceptions of German hegemony might equally well have triggered attempts to keep Slovakia in the fold through coercion. Likewise, Slovak fears of an imminent Hungarian reconquest of Slovakia ought to have served as a disincentive for Bratislava's challenging of Prague. Curiously enough, these enemy images were cast aside in the velvet divorce in a process that concentrated on the bilateral relationship between the Czech and Slovak halves of Czechoslovakia. The same logic of 'subsidiarity' – i.e. conflict-resolution at the immediate bilateral level – might also have prevailed in Karabagi-Azeri and Serbo-Croat relations, but it did not. In the case of Ukraine versus Russia, subsidiarity would seem to be to no avail in the face of Russia's undisputed hegemony in terms of military and energy weapons at its disposal. But Yeltsin's disinclination to internationalize the dispute over Crimea through Russian intervention is conducive to maintaining subsidiarity in this tricky case.

Finally, *The Economist* attributes great significance to the continuing role of communists in the power structure of the country – a criterion where Serbia is notable for the continuing role of the old party and military *nomenklatura*, as are Croatia and other parts of former Yugoslavia. By contrast, Czechoslovak *'Lustrace'* – i.e. screening – provided for a cleaner break with the past, whereas the picture is more mixed in Russia and outright 'Serbo-Croatian' in the case of Ukraine. But are former communists by necessity more hawkish in the role of nationalists than other nationalists are? The analysis in Chapters 5 and 6 can be taken as evidence that reform communists may in fact pursue less prejudiced policies than conservative nationalists. Former party bosses such as Shevardnadze (Georgia) and Aliev (Azerbaijan) display more realism and pragmatism than do their nationalist predecessors. Saparmurad Niazov of Turkmenistan, Karimov of Uzbekistan and Nazarbaev of Kazakhstan believe their interest lies in cooling inter-ethnic and religious tensions rather than the opposite, in contrast to e.g. Slobodan Milosevic, Franjo Tudjman (of Croatia) and Meciar. Personalities differ and as pointed out in the deliberations on the phenomenon of imperialism in Chapter 3, it takes a ruthless actor to turn ethnicity into political dynamite. In other words, the four factors advanced may not be the only and truly decisive ones.

One frequently cited factor behind the escalation of conflict in former Yugoslavia is the hasty international recognition of Croatia and Bosnia by Western powers before the problem of minority rights had been adequately addressed. In the words of the British journalist Misha Glenny:

> This is not merely a pragmatic response to problems in Yugoslavia – national and ethnic minorities provide a highly sensitive detonator of war during a period of immense political instability. The failure to solve the problems surrounding minorities, which

by definition question territorial integrity, is behind the fighting in Croatia, Bosnia, Moldova – Transdniestr[ia] and Nagorno-Karabakh. (1992, p. 100)

But if this is really so, then how is it that the issue of the Hungarian minorities in Slovakia did not initiate a bloody civil war – or that this was not the outcome of the uncertainties surrounding minorities in other newly free Soviet republics such as Russia? There is no denying the importance of minority problems as a catalyst for conflict (Georgia offers another example); but the fact that it is possible to cite cases where conflicts appear to have been avoided erodes the analytical value of this factor as a root cause. Meciar lacked the qualities of true statesmanship just as much as his colleagues in former Yugoslavia, so the answer to the question why Yugoslavia could not escape the slide into civil war must be found elsewhere.

For a start, we may return to the pre-theory of the concentric circles of empire and Yugoslavia's position at the fringe of the Soviet empire. Following his rupture with Stalin in 1948, Tito became one of the founding fathers of the Non-Aligned Movement while also seeking closer economic cooperation with the West. Yugoslavia acquired a special status in the OECD and joined the GATT, the IMF and the World Bank before any of the CMEA countries. Already in 1970 the EC constituted the most important trading partner for Yugoslavia – with a 35 per cent share of total trade. Yugoslavia was thus in a position to have been the first formerly planned economy to become a full EC member[1] – had it not been for the collapse of communism throughout the Warsaw Pact region in 1989. All of a sudden, Yugoslavia lost its *raison d'être* as an actor in the international system and to make matters worse, the international system lost its interest in Yugoslavia because of what was happening in the rapidly eroding Soviet empire. The freedom of manoeuvre enjoyed by Yugoslavia was always premised on the perceived need not to rock the boat at home so as to not invite Soviet intervention. Accordingly, Yugoslavia died not when Tito died in 1980 – when bipolarity was still alive – but in 1989-90 when

---

[1] In retrospect it appears that the EC's failure to lump Yugoslavia together with Spain, Portugal and Greece as post-authoritarian countries worthy of external nursing through the extension of membership of the Community represents a fatal blunder of European cooperation. With Gorbachev's coming to power there was little chance that the Brezhnev doctrine would apply; moreover, by 1986 EC integration measures were mainly economic.

bipolarity yielded to national self-determination in the trail-blazing German unification. The Central European wave of democratization, marketization and national liberation called the bluff of Titoist internationalism-cum-authoritarianism and economic self-management as the source of cohesion. Preoccupied as it was with monitoring events in Central Europe, the World left Yugoslavia at the mercy of its infernal domestic dynamics. In Czechoslovakia, conversely, the proximity of Russia and recent experience with the Brezhnev doctrine combined with gentle EC pressure to reach viable solutions gave way to restraint and pragmatism. In both Ukraine and Russia the possession of nuclear arms and the recognition of the geopolitical implications of a military showdown help to inspire less irresponsible behaviour at the élite level.

Accordingly, the broader structural context of conflicts matter. In this respect the Yugoslav case warrants further elaboration of local determinants. Tito cut the Gordian knot of inter-ethnic animosity through an ingenious consociational system operating at the federal level – dominance of Serbs by Croats and others – and repeated at the republican and lower levels in the reverse order – i.e. dominance of Croats by Serbs; a system that provided for a progressive feudalization of the federal state (Djilas, 1957; Gow, 1991). Economic mismanagement brought indebtedness, hyper-inflation and spectacular scandals such as the billion-dollar fraud of *Agrokomerc*, the firm launched by one of post-Yugoslavia's many free-wheeling warlords, Fikret Abdic of the Bihac enclave (north-western Bosnia). Monetary discipline at the federal level collapsed as Belgrade began to pay off Serbian pensioners and workers with money stolen from the central bank before the 1990 elections – nearly $2 billion (*Neue Zörcher Zeitung*, 8 February 1991). More important still was the progressive Serbianization of the federal army and the mushrooming of private militias and armed mobsters continuing the Second World War tradition of decentralized defence (Gow, 1993). As rebels without a cause, they were only too happy to turn to nationalism. This provided for the reliance of the federal army on paramilitary forces 'beyond its control' to do the dirty work in return for generous supplies of weapons and other forms of support. As revealed by the British military analyst James Gow (1993), the role of the armed forces was crucial in the country's war of dissolution, more specifically through their assistance to Serbian groups in Croatia and Bosnia from 1990 onwards, including the provision of arms. In other words, the federal army took sides and prepared for ethnic cleansing – which began in August 1991 – and for conquests in Bosnia *before* the republic declared its independence. Gow concludes that this questions the importance attached to the EC and United States' recognition of Bosnia as the main trigger of violence. Indeed, while there is much to be said for the amateurism, cowardice and hidden agendas with which the international community – the EC, the individual great powers and the UN – has handled the crisis of Yugoslavia and most other conflicts in the postcommunist world, the bottom line remains that it is for states themselves to prove their viability through the exercise of prudence. Clearly, this holds true for multinational federations as well.

Yugoslavia may offer an extreme case of New Medievalism (cf. Bull, 1977, pp. 254 ff.), but the mushrooming of militant nationalistic and paramilitary groups in both Ukraine and Russia – e.g. Cossacks and the Ukrainian National Self-Defence Organization (UNA-UNSO) – is a deeply disturbing factor (Gehrmann 1992, 1994; Umbach, 1993, 1994; *Neue Zürcher Zeitung*, 4 May 1994). Unfortunately, this is not sufficiently reflected in the analysis of the British scholar John Morrison, probably the reason why he settles for a conclusion couched in guarded optimism (1993). Notwithstanding the way the Ukrainian and Russian governments have lashed out at one another, their manipulations of the conflict are vastly preferable to dynamics at grass-roots level. The implication is that newly free states should be encouraged to enforce a ban on all sorts of paramilitary groups – something which Ukraine has, in fact, tried to do – in exchange for a reasonable build-up of national defence and police forces. The Czechoslovak case differs enormously from those of the Russo-Ukrainian and Yugoslav cases in terms of centralized control through a stable federal system, a key factor, we may now conclude, in why it was possible to arrange a negotiated divorce mediated by the disparate personalities of Klaus and Meciar. The Czechoslovak case can be cited as yet another evidence that the former position within the concentric circles of the Soviet empire matters.

This case is also interesting for its surprising distribution of roles among secessionists and centralists. At the outset Slovakia represented the secessionist party, although this was never articulated as such. Since 1990 Slovakia was pursuing independence, among other things through the establishment of its own Ministry of International

Relations. Slovakia's increasing attacks on Prague for its alleged paternalism and unbalanced allocation of resources looked like the prelude to undisguised secessionism, but nobody in Slovakia wanted exactly that. The declared aim of the Slovaks, according to Meciar, was to arrive at a more balanced relationship through a confederation, but Slovak positions paralyzed the Federal Assembly and hence Czechoslovak decision-making (Pehe, 1992). The Slovak side wrongly anticipated that the Prague centre wanted to preserve the federation at any cost, but the Slovaks' open dissatisfaction with it led Klaus to conclude that it was better to let go of Czechoslovakia; moreover, he rightly calculated that the Bohemian and Moravian parts of the country would more swiftly catch up with Western Europe on their own. Once Meciar revealed his ambition of making Slovakia a subject of international law, he crossed the Rubicon (personal interview with Vladimir Handl, a Czech analyst). This was what gave the Prague centre the pretext to secede from its Slovak periphery in a scenario reminiscent of Russia's and the other Soviet Slavic republics' secession from Central Asia and Transcaucasia. Given this distribution of preferences in the periphery and the centre it was, in fact, conducive to peaceful conflict-resolution that the Czech part of the country held as much as 80 per cent of the military assets. At this time of writing there are still some unresolved issues left from the velvet divorce, but this has not hindered an overall improvement in the Czech-Slovak relationship.

Postcommunist regional cooperation

Another pervasive feature of postcommunist international relations is the opposite of conflict, more specifically the proliferation of schemes of regional cooperation (Skak, 1991b, pp. 65-76). However, except for empirical analyses in, for instance, Radio Free Europe/Radio Liberty's research reports, the subject has drawn precious little attention from the academic community.[2] This is

---

[2] English-language contributions on Barents Sea cooperation and CBSS are sparse, but the reader may consult Uspensky and Komissarov (1993) and the 'Declaration of the Conference of Foreign Ministers of the Baltic Sea States', Copenhagen, 5–6 March 1992 and the 'Terms of Reference for the Council of Baltic Sea States' (available through the Danish MFA, Copenhagen).

On Black Sea cooperation, see Connelly (1994) and Kovalski *et al.* (1993). On Carpathian cooperation, see e.g. de Weydenthal (1994). Zagorski (1994) offers a

quite paradoxical in view of the popularity which the study of international cooperation enjoys these days (Groom and Taylor, 1994; Milner, 1992). Most political science contributions aim at theoretical discussions of incentives and disincentives for cooperation and the like and cannot be blamed for lacking comprehensive empirical description. But the empirical examples cited to illustrate the difficulties and dynamics of multilateral cooperation are excessively ethnocentric. At present, at least the following frameworks – regional as well as sub-regional local community cooperation – can be cited (the list does not claim to be exhaustive):

—*Barents Sea Cooperation* (Denmark, Iceland, Finland, Norway, Russia, Sweden)
—the *Baltic Council* (Estonia, Latvia and Lithuania)
—*Black Sea Economic Cooperation* (Albania, Armenia, Azerbaijan, Bulgaria, Georgia, Greece, Moldova, Romania, Russia, Turkey, Ukraine)
—the *Carpathian Euro-region* (eastern Poland and Hungary, western Ukraine and eastern Slovakia as observer)
—the *Central European Initiative*, or CEI (Austria, Bosnia, Croatia, the Czech Republic, Hungary, Italy, Macedonia, Poland, Slovakia, Slovenia; plus Bulgaria, Belarus, Romania and Ukraine as associate members)
—the *Commonwealth of Independent States*, or CIS (Armenia, Azerbaijan, Belarus, Georgia, Kazakhstan, Kyrgyzstan, Moldova, Russia, Tadzhikistan, Turkmenistan, Ukraine, Uzbekistan)
—the *Council of Baltic Sea States*, CBSS (Denmark, Estonia, Finland, Germany, Latvia, Lithuania, Norway, Poland, Russia, Sweden; plus a representative from the European Commission)
—*Economic Cooperation Organization*, or ECO (Afghanistan, Azerbaijan, Iran, Kazakhstan, Kyrgyzstan, Pakistan, Tadzhikistan, Turkey, Turkmenistan, Uzbekistan)
—the *Union of Kazakhstan, Kyrgyzstan and Uzbekistan*
—the *Visegrad group* (the Czech Republic, Hungary, Poland and Slovakia)

---

good supplement to the extensive coverage of CIS cooperation by Radio Free Europe/Radio Liberty and OMRI. Reisch (1993e) may be supplemented by the 'Central European Initiative and Hungary' (1993) collection of materials. On Visegrad cooperation, see Tökes (1991) and Vachudova (1993).

Apart from the ECO, which was launched in 1965 – without gaining much momentum – all these regional schemes are of recent origin. It was the collapse of the Soviet empire which paved the way for them, implying that any theory of the particular phenomenon of postcommunist regional cooperation must adopt a historical approach, as indicated in the very terminology. Given the modest results which these regional schemes have yielded so far – very little, indeed, when compared to long-standing and economically strong frameworks like the EU – it may be tempting to dismiss them as irrelevant for the study of international cooperation. However, the timing of their emergence and their striking popularity as expressed in their quantitative growth defies their insignificance. Some are more embryonic than others and as all are more or less fragile structures it may be unwise – or premature – to enforce John G. Stoessinger's demanding definition of regionalism upon them. In his view, regionalism requires three or more states whose goal it is to form a distinct political unity (1969, p. 302). While this definition matches Russia's ambitions in relation to the CIS, it is highly problematic to posit the formation of a political unity as the shared goal of other CIS countries. The same qualifications concerning the level of ambition would have to be made in connection with Visegrad cooperation and the Baltic Council, as they are seen by the participants as secondary in relation to the long-term goal of joining the EU and NATO. But depending on how narrowly the concept of distinct political unity is defined – and in this respect Stoessinger shows little concern when discussing the Council of Europe on a par with the EC and NATO – the regional arrangements of post-communism do partly qualify as regionalism. Most of them do if regionalism is defined in common-sense terms as the perception of cultural affinity or a geographically focused interest in relation to neighbouring countries. There can be little doubt that the Visegrad concept aimed at strengthening the Central European front-runner identity of the participants through the exclusion of Balkan countries. Similarly, the popularity of the suspiciously Hanseatic CBSS among Balts, Poles and Russians stems from the access to Scandinavia and the richer parts of Europe it promises, confirming claims to European-hood and facilitating economic recovery. If reintegration may be characterized as the 'politics of belonging' for postcommunist countries caught in the problem of abandonment from the preceding communist autarky, then postcommunist regionalism qualifies as the politics of belonging writ small.

The close correlation between the collapse of the Soviet empire and the emergence of postcommunist regional arrangements invites realist theorizing along the lines of balance of power and abhorrence of a vacuum. There is much to be said for this explanation of the phenomenon, in particular if we turn to Russia and the CIS. As pointed out in Chapter 4, Russia fears the increasing influence of third countries such as the United States, Germany, France, Turkey and Iran in the post-Soviet sphere. This prompted Moscow to abandon its initially luke-warm attitude towards the CIS and vigorously to support CIS integration instead (Zagorski, 1994). As for the CEI, it was very much German unification and fear of excessive German influence in Central Europe that prompted Italy to launch the initiative at the Venice summit in August 1990 (dubbed the Pentagonal by then; de Michelis, 1990). Before that Havel convened a Central European summit in Bratislava as the predecessor of Visegrad cooperation, also with an eye to the unification of Germans which the Czechs fear most of all the peoples in the region. The Soviet intervention in Riga and Vilnius in January 1991 had an electrifying effect on what were to become the Visegrad states following their inaugural gathering in the small Hungarian town of that name on 15 February 1991. Given Turkey's vision of strengthening its influence in the Black Sea region through this concept, it is safe to assume that some of the other participants became involved in order to monitor and if necessary check exactly that – e.g. Russia, Greece, Armenia and Bulgaria. As pointed out by Daniel A. Connelly (1994) and confirmed by Russian studies of Black Sea cooperation, the framework is conceived as a competitor to the CIS. Black Sea cooperation offers an alternative to the Russia-dominated concept for the south-western CIS countries and provides them with direct links to the peaceful Balkan states (Kovalskii *et al.*, 1993, pp. 17–18). In addition to the bilateral links between Russia and Turkey, Ukraine and Turkey are strengthening mutual cooperation, as are Georgia and Turkey; similarly, Bulgaria and Armenia are reaching out to one another.

In other words, the record of postcommunist regional arrangements would seem to confirm Arnold Wolfers' contention that the most potent incentive for international cooperation is the perception of a (common) threat rather than the desire to improve relations within the group (1962, p. 27). The qualification of the perceived commonality of threats indicated by the brackets, however, serves to underline the fact that motives for participation may vary greatly across countries, not to mention domestic groups and actors. As can be seen by the example of Black Sea cooperation, some countries may perceive Turkey and others Russia as the threat against which multilateral cooperation opens the possibility of entering the lion's den in the comfortable company of others. This is probably the best way to explain the Baltic countries' acceptance of Russia's membership of the CBSS, which in turn gives Moscow a chance to monitor human rights[3] in the Baltic states as well as their reintegration. Moreover, as indicated by the Russian enthusiasm for this concept, the CBSS provides Russia with some of the direct access to Western Europe which it lost in the creation of buffer-states to the west after the demise of the Soviet Union (Uspensky and Kommissarov, 1993). This, in turn, suggests that the perception of benefits is no insignificant determinant of postcommunist regional cooperation. Greece's announcement before the decision to place the Black Sea foreign trade and investment bank in Thessaloniki that it would seek EC funding seems to have been decisive in persuading Bulgaria and Turkey that it was better placed there; in any case, the bank will have a Turkish chairman and a Bulgarian deputy chairman (Connelly, 1994). Few postcommunist countries have much to offer in the way of economic resources and they rightly anticipate foreign investors will be more attracted to investing in their countries if they can create the impression that investors will gain access to a larger and potentially dynamic region. Thus postcommunist regionalism has its virtue in the political signals of future interdependence and stability through shared interests it is sending out, however vague such prospects may be.

But it is not just the external signalling which is important in this respect. As will be recalled, the basic thesis of the present work is that as an act of national liberation the transition from communism

---

[3] Recently the CBSS appointed a human rights commissioner modelled on the similar institution of the CSCE – the 'Commissioner of the CBSS on Democratic Institutions and Human Rights, including the Rights of Persons Belonging to Minorities', at present the former Danish Minister of Justice, Ole Espersen. The quiet Russo-Nordic-Baltic diplomacy on the situation of Russians in the Baltic states within the CBSS has somewhat dampened tension among Russia and Estonia and Latvia.

has the effect of inducing the perennial security dilemma, even in inter-state relations among friends and even more so between potential enemies. Given the fact that postcommunist states are generally finding it more difficult to establish a relationship of trust and cooperation in relation to postcommunist neighbours than to countries belonging to NATO, for example, we should, in fact, expect energies to be devoted to resolving this security problem. This is where regional cooperation comes into the picture, irrespective of whether or not it has an explicit dimension of military cooperation. Provided that the CBSS gains some momentum as a short-cut to Europe and economic recovery for the postcommunist members, it could have tremendous spin-offs in the shape of a Russo-Baltic *détente*; the same applies to Black Sea cooperation concerning Greece and Turkey, not to mention Armenia and Azerbaijan (who have to sit next to another during sessions because of the alphabetical order). Indeed, one compelling reason why postcommunist regional structures merit the attention of security analysts is because of their contribution to creating islets of order, regularity and stability – peace in parts as it were, to quote Joseph S. Nye's classic contribution (1971; Stoessinger 1969, pp. 302-34).[4] The apparent widespread belief in the virtue of international co-operation and rejection of autarky found in postcommunist states would perhaps seem to refute the relevance of seeking independence in the first place, but here it is worth recalling John Zametica's point about the availability of choices as the true meaning of sovereignty (1992, p. 76).

Even so there may be an element of imposition in postcommunist regional cooperation – evidently so in the case of CIS cooperation. The overriding fact of Russian hegemony has so far prevented the non-Russian countries from exploiting what was really their option within this framework, namely to turn it into a scheme for keeping Russia down through the introduction of supranational decision-

---

[4] Admittedly, Nye is cautious when drawing conclusions from his in-depth empirical study of the EC, the OAS, OAU and Arab League: 'we did find some modest evidence...about regional organizations helping to create islands of peace in world politics. Micro-regional organizations have helped to create a web of functional links, which has improved the nature of relationships among the members [...but] contrary to its doctrines, regional organization does not provide a master key to a peaceful world order. Regional organizations merely contribute small but useful pieces to the puzzle of peace' (1971, pp. 198 ff.)

making. Most of the south-western CIS countries have committed the same error as Ukraine:

> By choosing to op out, Ukraine has appeared increasingly marginalized and unable to find allies among the other remaining members. Its neighbour Belarus in particular has moved closer to Russia and Kazakhstan. After complaining for most of 1992 that the CIS was ineffectual because none of its decisions was implemented, Ukraine found itself in the awkward position of resisting efforts to give it more powers by introducing a new charter. ...The risk for Kiev is that it may be manoeuvred into the 'slow lane' of a two-speed community where it will get the worst of both worlds: it would be unable to block moves by other member states towards closer integration, but would also be unable to pay the crippling economic price of complete withdrawal, such as a switch to trade in hard currency and higher tariffs. (John Morrison, 1993, p. 690)

The case of the non-Russian members of CIS thus illustrates the eternal prisoners' dilemma of international cooperation.

The case of Russia's hegemony among the CIS countries further illustrates the weaknesses of imposed as opposed to negotiated cooperation (Milner, 1992). As is shown in Chapter 4, the domestic dynamics behind Russia's foreign policy could once again push the country into imperial overstretch for the sake of preventing defections. As long as Moscow maintains a neo-imperial understanding of its role in the 'near abroad', it is hard to see how it can avoid the residual CIS members' free-riding, as was made painfully clear in Grachev's vain calls to his CIS partners to commit themselves to a peacekeeping force in Abkhazia in the summer of 1994. Russia's problems in striking a balance in its relationship with its postcommunist neighbours are unique. They are also rooted in their perception of the country as successor to the role of centre rather than a new option of cooperation pointing towards reintegration. This is where the Russian case differs from other instances of hegemonic leadership. Germany's role as *de facto* hegemon in the CBSS is hardly noticed as a problem by the postcommunist participants, whereas the other Scandinavian capitals originally reacted somewhat coolly to this joint initiative by the Danish Foreign Minister Uffe Ellemann-Jensen and his German counterpart, Hans-Dietrich Genscher. Likewise, Turkey's controversial role in post-Cold War international affairs tends to work more as a magnet than as a deterrent for the countries in the region. The element of hegemonic leadership in the CEI, by contrast, wore off when Italy's Foreign Minister Gianni de Michelis left the scene, thereby worsening the crisis created by the war in Yugoslavia. The implication of these deliberations would seem to be that the weakness of Visegrad and Baltic cooperation (among Estonia, Latvia and Lithuania) is due to the lack of hegemonic leadership by Western reintegration patrons. This may indeed be true, although the dimension of imposed cooperation is still there in the shape of the EU pressure for free trade among postcommunist countries and other steps in preparation for reintegration.

The gist of postcommunist regional cooperation from the point of view of international peace and security may be the stabilizing function through the multiplication of identities – the extra layers of belonging and communities they represent (Buzan *et al.*, 1990, p. 220). The multiple incentives – negative as well as positive – that may motivate actors to participate in multilateral cooperation adds a quality of discretion and quiet diplomacy to these fora which may facilitate mutual dialogue. Up till now, the lack of transparency in EU cooperation has proven one of its great strengths. Indeed, the blurring of conflict through the deliberate expansion of agendas, opening the way for complex horsetrading and overlapping interests is a well-established tactic of conflict-resolution, a case in point being the Maastricht Treaty. What is really significant about postcommunist regional schemes is that they may provide postcommunist foreign policy and international relations with some mundane tasks as a healthy counterweight to the lofty struggle for the defence of the nation. Still, the tangible results of this new trend in international cooperation remain limited. The CEI limps along, although it is worth noting that the Czech Premier, Klaus, is upgrading his interest in it as a key political forum in Central Europe and wants his Visegrad partners to concentrate on the implementation of their mutual free-trade agreement, CEFTA (see also *Frankfurter Allgemeine Zeitung*, 18 July 1994). The recently launched Central Asian union of Kazakhstan, Kyrgyzstan and Uzbekistan appears to have drawn some interest from the EU, and then there is the EU direct representation in the CBSS helping to bolster this framework. The real importance' of CBSS, however, may lie in the many decentralized activities rather than intergovernmental cooperation; an approach found in the Carpathian Euro-region which it is hoped will prove capable of bringing some depth to the conspicuous breadth characterizing many systems of postcommunist regional cooperation, such as the CEI.

Post-Cold War East-West relations

Until now, the politics of reintegration have been addressed solely from the angle of the newly free postcommunist states. But in order to apply a truly multilateral perspective to the post-Cold War East-West relationship it is necessary to consider the stakes involved from a Western perspective as well – the dilemmas of the new *Ostpolitik*, as it were (Andersen and Skak, 1993). It is commonplace to lament the replacement of the fixed enemy and conflict structure of bipolarity with the limitless and confusing 'risks' of post-bipolarity. Yet it takes only a cursory reading of newspapers to realize that postcommunism has brought a kind of fixed threat – in the shape of the Eastern quest for participation in the Western economic and security order. First the EC/EU and now NATO and the WEU have been caught in the dilemma of how to respond to the pressure for full membership on the part of their former CMEA and Warsaw Pact counterparts. From the perspective of the Western national actors involved, the issue is one of opening up one's own markets and channelling economic resources eastward in exchange for an expected growth in Eastern purchasing power. As far as military security is concerned, it is a question of committing national defence resources – including human lives – to the defence of fragile post-communist states in exchange for a lower threshold of general instability and conflict in this region and hence a general rise in Western security. Game theorists will look in vain here for an accurate calculation of the costs, benefits and risks sketched. The point is the insecurity surrounding the assessment of pros and cons as a determinant of the Western foot-dragging response to the collapse of communism – when due allowance is made for conventional factors of vested economic interests, general inertia and outdated approaches.

From a systemic perspective, the challenge of postcommunist participation concerns the absorptive capacity of international fora – more specifically, how to combine efficiency with geographic range. Within the EU this classic dilemma is conceptualized by the trade-off between integration in-depth and in-breadth. Even before the collapse of communism, the EC faced demanding tasks of simultaneous expansion and increasing integration. The paradigmatic change of 1989 has left it with an outright daunting agenda of institutional reform. The Babylonian confusion of languages illustrates the intricacies of expansion. When there were only twelve EU members, interpreters had to juggle with sixty-six bilateral language combinations, whereas in a fully expanded EU the number would rise to 231. One analyst, Renaud Dehousse, summarizes the very real political problems of 'widening' as follows:

> The wider the number of partners involved, and the more diverse their interests, the more difficult it will be for them to reach a consensus on a large number of issues. ... There is a real risk that the Community plane will be prevented from taking off because of an excess of passengers. (1991, pp. 7-11)

Nevertheless, Dehousse warns against automatically putting considerations of 'deepening' above 'widening' in the EU's response to the Eastern demand for participation:

> It suffices here to recall the important part adhesion to the community played in the consolidation of democratic processes in countries like Greece, Spain, and Portugal. Excessive concern for institutional values should not blind us to this kind of strategic thinking. (*ibid*)

The conviction that the EU – as well as NATO – can and should open itself to integration of the postcommunist countries is the tacit premise of this writing. Doing otherwise would be to mock the strides made towards establishing additional open societies in Europe, in other words a mockery of core Western values of freedom and participation. By no means should this reintegration credo be taken as nullifying the need for proper adaptation and preparation by the post-communist states themselves; something they tend to overlook in their pre-occupation with the international diplomacy of re-integration.

In 1996 the EU members will have to make some hard decisions on the sensitive topic of decision-making. They may adopt federalist solutions, such as the construction of a two-chamber European Parliament. But former EU Commissioner Henning Christophersen displayed just the right attitude: 'Surely we can manage the Inner Market, the implementation of the Union, and expansion 'at a time'

(*Information*, 22-3 June 1991). The reason why the EU and NATO are singled out here stems from their institutional clout and the combined economic and military power they represent. Together they make up a supreme lever of *Einbindung* and multi-faceted security in the face of the many conflicts in postcommunist Europe, as pointed out by one leading ideologue of the German Social Democrats, Peter Glotz (*Die Zeit*, 24 August 1990).

Theoretically speaking, the collapse of communism left NATO with an absolutely open agenda, implying that the organization should be well equipped to meet the challenge of participation. But here the notorious problem of how to meet the challenge of Russia's participation plays into the hands of those doubting the need to continue NATO cooperation and current Russian campaigning to place NATO, CIS, EU, WEU and the Council of Europe under the jurisdiction of the OSCE. Not that this proposal will generate much enthusiasm in the West, but it reflects the fact that the difficult search for a viable post-Cold War European security architecture continues to occupy the mind. Although things look brighter now in terms of clearer priorities and the beginning of attempts to link the EU and NATO via the WEU, we should not expect the dust from the institutional debate sparked off by 1989 to settle this side of the millennium. In addition to the continuous danger of Western introversion, the lesson from the post-Yugoslavian wars is that we are left with not interlocking but 'interblocking institutions', to quote the apt phrase of the German analyst Heinz Kramer (1993).

The Western dilemma concerning reintegration of the postcommunist East may be conceptualized in terms of entrapment and abandonment, as if it were a national actor entering an international alliance. There is a danger of overcommitment in a way that would jeopardize security and hence a danger of entrapment: 'many NATO members regard the region to their east as a security nightmare –fraught with complex religious, political, economic and ethnic rivalries – for which they would prefer not to assume responsibility' (J. Simon, 1993, p. 21). As will be remembered, Article 5 commits NATO members to consider an attack on any NATO member an attack on the entire alliance. The evident lack of political maturity and experience seen in many postcommunist countries makes the question of hard security guarantees most controversial. As for economic entrapment, Jack Snyder likens the integration of poorly reformed post-Soviet economies into Western markets to 'a leap into the dark' (1990/1, p. 139). The dilemma of post-Cold War *Ostpolitik* arises from the fact that the inherent risks in excluding the postcommunist region from reintegration are equally high. They entail the danger of Western abandonment through its loss of a stabilizing influence and of general political influence in the East:

> The world sails dangerously if it allows momentous changes without moving early to agree on the rights and responsibilities of all in the new world. Eastern Europe and the Soviet Union will be a magnet for outside interference, and a possible wellspring of general conflict, unless the main NATO powers and the Soviet Union promptly agree on the rights of all powers in the Eastern region. (*ibid.*, p. 136)

Like Glotz, Snyder rightly calls for an *Ostpolitik* focused on the institutional logic of *Einbindung* to solve the imbalances of power inherent in the transition from communism and Soviet empire as the only short-term solution to Eastern security vacuums. Mercifully, there is a further consideration of *Einbindung* pushing Western *Ostpolitik* in exactly this direction. What I am hinting at is the perennial problem of Germany, whose unification cannot but strengthen the determination of France, Great Britain and other European powers 'to keep Germany down'. For geographic reasons, the key to Bonn's willingness to let itself be bound by NATO and the EU lies in the perceived efficiency of the *Ostpolitik* of these two fora, in other words in Germany's confidence in its great power partners' commitment to *Ostpolitik*. The German Defence Minister, Volker Rühe, has more than once called for NATO's eastward expansion, and the German EU chairmanship of 1994 autumn placed closer cooperation with the postcommunist candidates for full EU membership very high on the agenda. Attempts to prevent Germany from speeding up *Ostpolitik* could backfire in a dramatic way, as when the German-American neo-realist Mearsheimer argued the case for Germany going nuclear. The dilemma for NATO (and by extension the EU) is that given the choice the Visegrad countries would happily settle for bilateral security guarantees from Germany if no offers from NATO and the EU are forthcoming (Frost, 1993; J. Simon, 1993). In other words, the non-German West runs a double security risk of abandoning itself it it opts for reticence towards the postcommunist East, leading to German perceptions of abandonment.

One indication that this nexus is being realized is the growing engagement of France – otherwise known as one of the most foot-dragging powers on issues of *Ostpolitik*, one example being defence cooperation in the so-called 'Weimar Triangle' of France, Germany and Poland (*Frankfurter Allgemeine Zeitung*, 6 and 7 March 1994). That there is a clear element of German arm-twisting of the French in this arrangement is revealed by French Defence Minister François Leotard's remark that Poland's difficulties in joining NATO pale in comparison with the process of French-German reconciliation (*RFE/RL News Briefs*, 18-22 July 1994). Likewise, Britain is co-operating with Germany in relation to third countries – *inter alia* in order to monitor Germany, one suspects. From the point of view of the prospective postcommunist NATO members, these multi-lateral contacts represent a valuable gradual incorporation into the alliance's military structure. Thus Poland's PfP and its bilateral military cooperation agreements with Germany and Denmark allow for joint triangular manoeuvres (*Frankfurter Allgemeine Zeitung*, 30-1 January 1994).

These examples of the implementation of PfPs have been in-cluded to show that these treaties do, in fact, open the road to NATO membership. The principle of letting each country define the level of ambition of its PfP with NATO corresponds with the principle of self-selection advanced by the American security analyst Jeffrey Simon as the way to minimize risks – a necessary precaution – while gradually expanding the circle of NATO members (cf. *International Herald Tribune*, 10 January 1994; 'Declaration of the Heads of State ...' 1994). Contrary to what critics say, PfP's are a path to membership – through the back door, as it were, namely by gradually expanding participation in military cooperation at a pace determined by the resources and interests of each country (personal interviews with NATO officials). Some might object that joint peacekeeping (cf. Lithuania taking part in Danish peacekeeping in Croatia) is irrelevant in view of the Eastern demand for security guarantees, but this is not necessarily true. For the Western world it is a way to test the depth of the alleged commitment to principles of collective security and safeguarding European peace and stability – allegiances which for obvious reasons cannot be considered tested through former Warsaw Pact membership.

This is not the place to review in detail all the economic dimensions of Western post-Cold War *Ostpolitik* as briefly sketched pp. 51-2, above (cf. H. Kramer, 1993; Skak, 1991b, pp. 51 ff.). The EU members can be blamed for pursuing a reactive, inward-looking *Ostpolitik* instead of exercising leadership, as Kramer argues. But it is as if the EU is recovering from the Maastricht crisis with positive spin-offs for *Ostpolitik*, as witness the European Council in Copenhagen (Agence Europe, 22 July 1993). From the perspective of reintegration the Europe Agreements and the membership perspective they offer are the most significant. But the entire spectrum of activities qualifies as a comprehensive partnership structure that begins to reach into the CIS starting with the partnership agreements with Ukraine and Russia. Kramer is very pessimistic about the actual acceptance of postcommunist members, citing the vague preambles of the Europe Agreements. Admittedly, nothing can be taken for granted.[5] The entry into the EU of the richer European countries with a vested interest in opening the EU to the east – namely Austria, Finland and Sweden – would seem to add a new *Ostpolitik* momentum to the 1996 intergovernmental EU conference. For better or worse, it has proved notoriously difficult to predict political developments in the Community, as demonstrated in a depressing fashion by the Danish 'no' in the first Maastricht referendum. What can be concluded is that there is every reason to continue to call attention to the problem of abandonment and the solution in terms of *Einbindung*.

To illustrate the thesis of a revival of EU *Ostpolitik*, a brief excursion into the EU project on the Pact on Stability in Europe is warranted. Originally coined by the French Premier Edouard Balladur – indicating the activization of French *Ostpolitik* – it has be-

[5] The British economist Richard Baldwin (1994) has tried to estimate the costs of incorporating the Visegrad economies into the EU; he puts it at some 20-40 billion ecu, corresponding to a very steep rise in member countries' contributions to the structural funds. The problems represented by these countries are their large population (which could turn them into very lucrative markets, provided there is a rise in purchasing power), the current low *per capita* incomes (far below even that of Portugal) and their heavy concentration on agriculture – less obviously true for the Czech and Slovak Republics, though.

On the other hand, economists Jim Rollo and Alasdair Smith (1993) point out that sensitive products occupy only a small a fraction of the EU labour force; in other words that protectionism on behalf of the production of agricultural goods, steel, coal and textiles is really giving in to narrow lobbies in complete disregard of European consumers. It is estimated that a total liberalization of agricultural exports would give the EU a net gain of 2.1 billion ecu and postcommunist Eastern Europe a net gain of 2 billion ecu (1993).

come part and parcel of the EU's strategy in relation to the nine prospective members of the EU among the postcommunist countries – Bulgaria, the Czech Republic, Estonia, Hungary, Latvia, Lithuania, Poland, Romania and Slovakia – and as a likely number ten, Slovenia ('Concluding Document of the Inaugural Conference...', 1994). The idea is to force the development of good neighbourly relations among future postcommunist EU members through bilateral or regional talks on outstanding border and minority issues – during which the EU is offering to act as moderator. The French have agreed to tone down the prospects for actual border revisions following resistance from Poland. The specific agreements and arrangements resulting from these talks, e.g. Hungary's inter-state treaties with Romania and Slovakia, are to be included in the Stability Pact as a precondition, it is understood, of the EU's willingness to extend membership eastward. As such the initiative bears witness to the comprehensive concept of security at the heart of the Community's understanding of economic integration. However, it is not the EU but the OSCE and the Council of Europe that are to be entrusted with the task of monitoring agreements. The fact that the Baltic countries are included in the EU proposal testifies to the 'return to Europe' of this group of states. Thus two regional blocs of negotiations took place in the period up till 21 March 1995: the Baltic region, i.e. Estonia, Latvia, Lithuania, Poland and Russia (where the EU appears to have been successful in persuading Russia to accept this multilateral formal for settling minority problems); and the Central European and Balkan region, covering the residual countries but excluding Greece's disputes with Macedonia, Albania and with Turkey over Cyprus. The post-Yugoslavian complex of problems are entirely excluded (as falling under the aegis of UN), as are ongoing conflicts in the CIS. In other words, the ambition lies in the field of conflict-prevention rather than conflict-resolution, as emphasized in Kohl's and Balladur's joint marketing of the idea (*Frankfurter Allgemeine Zeitung* and *Le Monde*, 27 May 1994).

This narrow scope forms the basis of much of the criticism of the initiative, but this is really wide off the mark when taking into account the widespread wisdom after the Yugoslav events that they ought to and could have been prevented. The lukewarm reception by Czechs, Russians and Poles is also no convincing indicator of weaknesses in the concept. As mentioned in Chapter 6, Hungary saw the Stability Pact as an opportunity to resolve minority problems and in this way improve its relations with neighbouring states. The programme declaration of the Slovak caretaker government actually welcomed the initiative as a measure furthering the integration of Central Europe into the EU ('Den slovakiske regerings pro-gramerklæring', 13 April 1994). In a strong defence of diplomatic discretion, the *Financial Times* expresses fear that the initiative will rock the boat too much (26 May 1994). But in view of the rather indelicate approach to minority and border issues displayed by many politicians in postcommunist states, this overly cautious commentary closes its eyes to the fact that the boat is already rocking and could do with some imposed stabilization.

There are elements in the new East-West relationship worthy of consideration, such as the WEU consultation forum encompassing the same countries as the EU member-aspirants of the Stability Pact. The efforts of the Council of Europe as a safeguard for civil society and a mediating force in ethnic disputes together with the OSCE are not that minuscule. The great power concert on Yugoslavia, dubbed the contact group, could help to socialize Russia into more far-sighted behaviour. In due course it could grow into the European Security Council sometimes called for. Despite foot-dragging, in the West as in the East the bottom line is one of paradigmatic change –both in terms of problems as well as solutions devised.

8

FROM EMPIRE TO ANARCHY?

What has been written so far can be taken as evidence, first, that the now defunct Soviet international order constituted an empire and, secondly, that it has been replaced by a functional anarchy of sovereign states. Further, it is the basic contention of the pre-theory of concentric circles of empire that the former Soviet internal empire – the Soviet Union proper – has been converted into something akin to the quasi-states that were the result of decolonization in Africa and much of Asia due to the lack of institutional preparation for sovereignty. Concerning the residual Warsaw Pact states and Mongolia, making up the external Soviet empire, it is assumed they will be transformed into viable sovereign states. Both these findings have to be modified, however. While it may be true to speak of functional anarchy in the case of postcommunist international relations, as with international relations in general there are startling differences in the degree of anarchy and conflict across postcommunist countries and regions. It is tempting to apply Zbigniew K. Brzezinski's classic concept of the Arc of Crisis to the entire postcommunist region as the geopolitical consequence of transition from communism – due to power vacuums etc. But in reality there are islands of peace and relative stability in Central Europe and elsewhere, whereas the Arc of Armed Struggle limits itself to the fringe of empire (former Yugoslavia), Transdniestria, Caucasus, the Transcaucasian states and Tadzhikistan. The Russian Federation represents a case of internal as well as external anarchy; but even Russia can boast signs of consolidation. In other words, it is absolutely vital to be sensitive to actual developments and to assess dangers accurately when studying postcommunism.

For this reason I settled for the method of case studies as the way to make an in-depth analysis of foreign policy in the newly free postcommunist states, another motive being to test the actual distribution of quasi-states and states. There is a further theoretical consideration in this. While there is no need to deny the conceptual richness and valuable insights from systemic analysis – be it neo-realist reasoning on polarity and international distribution of power, or institutionalist conceptions of interdependence, norms and other power modifiers – the varying dynamics of postcommunist states require analysis at the level of the state and below. Equally important is the comparative principle of analysing more than one case so as to contribute to the cumulative study of systemic transition and decolonization and their foreign policy outcomes. The field of foreign policy offers itself as the real arena for closer examination of international relations and international-national linkages. It is a field which is open to the study of actual – that is perceived – security dilemmas and peacefulness as it is to the study of ideologies and their operational codes. The format of national studies thus adds flesh and blood to the general deliberations and concepts advanced for studies of postcommunist foreign policy in Chapters 1 and 2.

What postcommunist countries have in common is the challenge of nation-building – most acutely so for countries in the internal empire, not least the former imperial centre, Russia – while at the same time managing the security dilemma. A second task is the diplomacy of aid and reintegration, of which the latter, fortunately, tends to alleviate security dilemmas through *Einbindung*. *Einbindung* is also instrumental in overcoming domestic insecurity; two important reasons why the notions of non-alignment and neutrality are to be considered more harmful than helpful. The perception of abandonment – the fear of standing outside European cooperation – as a threat is one of the distinguishing features throughout the postcommunist world in this process of decolonization, in contrast to Afro-Asian decolonization where the threat-perception was one of neo-colonial entrapment. As stated in chapter 7, the postcommunist embrace of reintegration and notions of regional cooperation does not render sovereignty irrelevant, particularly not in view of the terrible repression under sovietization, as described in chapter 3. The political history of sovietization containing a review of sinews of empire, as well as internal and external empire foreign policy systems, are included in the analysis as further nomothetic determinants of today's postcommunist foreign policy.

The point is the distribution of centre and periphery identities produced by the recent imperial past. The problem of Russia and its neighbours concerns the odds in favour of a return to Russian self-identification as the centre in a neo-imperial scenario, as seen in the explicit Russian references to the Monroe doctrine. The danger of praetorianism – through the re-emergence of Cossacks, among other things – adds to the probability of this scenario. The case study of the Russian decision to cancel Yeltsin's visit to Japan in 1992 illustrates the praetorian trends in Moscow's foreign policy decision-making. The aggressive campaign against Kozyrev's alleged lack of profile offers another example of the manipulation of Russian foreign policy by domestic forces in their bid for power. But there is a ray of hope in the emerging recognition among influential Russian analysts that the country risks imperial overstretch – e.g. through peacekeeping commitments – and international isolation if the course of foreign policy is not checked. The Chechnia adventure could prove fatal for empire-restorationists. The common problem faced by the non-Russian quasi-states of the internal empire is their lack of foreign policy experience and occasionally excessive perception of interest-conflicts in relation to Russia as an outcome of their identity as a newly free periphery. In other words, the non-Russian former internal empire is not devoid of hyper-sensitivity in the shape of perceptions of entrapment by Moscow, although the flames of this have surely been fanned by Russian politicians and actors themselves.

The analysis of Lithuanian foreign policy underscores the differences among the post-Soviet quasi-states. While clearly constituting a functional quasi-state at the outset, having no people with relevant diplomatic qualifications, no national defence and precious little in the way of contemporary centrist political forces, Lithuania as an actor in the international system has been subject to a healthy learning process. The more limited colonization by Russian settlers and cultural-historical differences compared with the other two Baltic states have been conducive to less prejudiced Lithuanian policies towards Russia once Brazauskas came to power. The fact that his more forthcoming attitude towards Moscow has been to no avail cannot be taken as evidence of the weaknesses of Brazauskas' foreign policy, as it coincided with the strengthening of Russian hawks. Disillusionment over Russia, in turn, has pushed Lithuania in the direction of a more unambiguous and efficient policy of reintegration, as witnessed by the trail-blazing application for NATO membership. Where the Baltic states differ from their non-Baltic fellows in the former Soviet Union is in their record of past independence – even if this can be counterproductive when taken as an infallible source of know-how. What the Baltic region lacks in professionalism – including adequate knowledge of current European realities – it makes up for through its determination to become part of Europe in much the same way the countries of the external empire do. The performance of the Baltic states would seem to support Gertrude Schroeder's contention (see pp. 53 ff., above) that the viability of states is a function of goal-oriented behaviour rather than resource endowment. Ukraine's slide into chaos in spite of a wealth of resources compared to the Baltic states shows the validity of this point. Yet the fact that the three Baltic states have gained a competitive edge in their commitment to domestic reform does not imply that there is no room for improvement in Lithuania, or even in Hungary. What has to be taken into account is the international attention enjoyed by Lithuania and Hungary in contrast to, say, tiny Moldova which, however, does not fare badly when measured by its commitment to survive as a sovereign unit and its resulting magnanimity towards ethnic minorities.[1]

The expectation that the external Soviet empire will smoothly develop into well-functioning states therefore has to be qualified somewhat. To be sure, from an institutional point of view the very gradual transition in Hungary left the country with important stabilizers, as can be seen in the way the parliamentary Foreign Relations Committee modified nationalist trends in foreign policy. But the politically powerful non-socialist ideologies in the country tend towards anachronism in their unbalanced preoccupation with issues relating to the Hungarian diaspora; one reason – albeit not the main one – why the HDF was voted out of power in 1994. It is possible to interpret this pattern as a confirmation of the pre-theory of empire which anticipates that the countries of the external empire will prefer to pick contemporary or pre-Soviet problems as opposed to clashes of interest with the former centre. Depending on one's own inclination, the overriding issue of the Hungarians abroad may be taken as a contemporary human rights problem or as a leap into the past. While it stands to reason that the level of sophistication in Hungarian foreign policy is higher than in Slovak foreign policy, the case of the Gabcikovo-Nagymaros dam shows that, just as much

---

[1] The Council of Europe has objected to Moldova's plans for Gagauz autonomy on the grounds that they carry autonomy too far (*RFE/RL News Briefs*, 5-8 July 1994).

as this project was instrumental in the nation-building of the fledgling Slovak state, Hungarian opposition to it was instrumental in Hungarian postcommunist nation-building. Despite such slips into dramatic actor behaviour bordering on praetorianism, the process of development in Hungary qualifies as a case of maturing and not just learning.

All in all then, the admittedly brief history of postcommunism, its respective foreign policies and international relations tells a story that is different to that of the decolonization in the Third World and what followed. It may be premature to speak of security communities, but anarchy is becoming more mature in some corners of the postcommunist space – and here I am not just referring to the trends of a neo-imperial order around Russia. Leaving aside cultural factors, the decisive difference is the more active involvement of the West in monitoring the postcommunist process of systemic transformation and nurturing recovery. Originally, there was a fairly generous flow of aid to Africa, but without much thought for the proper use of these transfers. The principle of conditionality – the demands for pluralism, market economy and human rights – is undisguised in economic assistance to the postcommunist countries and explicit in the latest Europe Agreements. For better or worse, this helps to impose order and bring about a swift socialization into West European inter-state and intra-state norms. Another key factor is the nature of colonization, in this instance the imposition of Soviet power. European colonization of the Third World was by no means a tea-party, but during the first half of the twentieth century repression receded into the background before the abandonment of the colonial system. Stalinist totalitarianism, by contrast, climaxed at that time. The forceful rule of Europeans by Europeans within the multinational Soviet empire blossomed in an era of alleged transition from authoritarianism with explicit reference to Europe. Adding insult to injury, the Soviet masters insisted that their brutality spelled freedom. The anachronism, humiliation and threat-perceptions inherent in this create quite another resolve concerning reintegration, even if there are discouraging signs of popular apathy and disillusionment.

In other words there is reason to take issue with the pessimistic generalizations of authors writing on the evils of self-determination and failing and failed states (Etzioni, 1992-3; Helman and Ratner, 1992-3; Halbach, 1994). If Georgia and some other states in the postcommunist Arc of Crisis do really constitute 'failing states', as suggested by the involuntary inclusion of Georgia into the CIS, this is due to obvious, avoidable follies on behalf of Georgian nationalist leaders. Failing states in the context of postcommunism are the exception that proves the rule of mostly viable states. It is reductionist to depict self-determination movements in general as undermining the potential for democratic development in non-democratic states. The quest for independence in the context of communism has to be placed in the larger context of reintegration – namely as a reaction to autarky, isolationism and lack of democracy. Even Amitai Etzioni admits to the utterly foot-dragging response of Soviet authorities in the Gorbachev era to legitimate demands for decentralization. This lack of responsiveness – also demonstrated during the superficial 'return to normalcy' of Khrushchev and Brezhnev, as described in Chapter 3 – caused Soviet imperial overstretch. The Soviet empire, like the European colonial empires, simply ceased to be viable in a development that further pulled the carpet under multinational Yugoslavia. Against this background it is absurd to see self-determination as the culprit. The blame lies in the failure to realize and live up to responsibilities which, to be sure, justifies a critical attitude towards nationalists before and after the acquisition of sovereignty.

It is my impression from several years of studying postcommunist foreign policy that most governments take foreign policy seriously in terms of interests and options. There are trends towards stability and consensus in some of the smaller states, whereas Russia is an example of foreign policy as a deeply divisive issue, resulting in an excessive preoccupation with this field of activity at the expense of implementation of reform. Against these findings, some might object that by proceeding on the basis of the unspectacular category of foreign policy the present contribution has a built-in bias towards normalcy. Instead of wallowing in catastrophes and conflicts, the comparative study of foreign policy compels analysis of current interaction in relation to the external world. This tends to impose regularity, rationality and 'decisions' where there are none. To the extent that this objection is valid it has a bearing upon social science in general. What is more, through the systematic application of Graham T. Allison's classic models of decision-making and two additional models of foreign policy decision-making in new states on a specific event in the foreign policy of Russia, Lithuania and

Hungary, the present work does test the limits of rationality in postcommunist foreign policy in a closer examination of actual dynamics at work.

There is a section devoted to discussing conflicts in the postcommunist world in Chapter 7's overview of postcommunist international relations. When comparing the post-Yugoslav wars to the peaceful conflict-resolution between Czechs and Slovaks, one cannot but conclude that the eruption of armed conflict is very much bound up in a particular political context and not at all a historical or social necessity. This raises the unpleasant question of responsibility which, to be sure, points in many directions. Interestingly, the additional case of the Russo-Ukrainian conflict shows that there is more responsibility at the élite level than is often perceived. The real problem here, as in Yugoslavia, is the decentralization of security policy through the proliferation of paramilitary groups as a medium for virulent nationalism. Surely, this is the reverse side of the coin of the mobilization of postcommunist civil society in the general development towards an open, pluralistic society. In view of the danger of a slide into warlordism, postcommunist governments should be encouraged to ban paramilitary groups and fight organized crime. Pages 265-73 above discussed the multiple determinants and motives of actors behind the post-1989 wave of schemes for regional cooperation involving postcommunist states or sub-regions. Hegemonic leadership and the perceived need to check the power of hegemons play a prominent role, thus confirming realist approaches to international relations – although there is more to it than that. Generally speaking, however, the efforts in the field of reintegration have greater impact than regional cooperation even if the two trends may be mutually supportive.

This brings me to the final topic of the post-Cold War East-West relationship and policy implications in general. The pressure for participation from postcommunist countries places the Western world in a peculiar dilemma between entrapment and abandonment. The perennial problem of Germany may help to tilt the scales towards full reintegration of the newly free states in the eastern half of Europe. This may still leave Moscow and the world with the problem of Russia. The only way to solve this problem is by placing the ball in the country's own court by formulating functional criteria for entry into international organizations and avoiding geographical criteria. And why not? – a prosperous, democratic Russia could be an enormous asset as a member of the EU, notably from the point of view of those fond of stressing the Union's role as an actor in a global competitive game involving the United States, Japan and other Asian powers. Most postcommunist governments reacted unenthusiastically to the Stability Pact launched by the EU, but the project could signal new efforts at full reintegration, as seen in the circle of countries targeted for settling mutual outstanding issues. At any rate it counts as an ambitious venture in the field of CSBMs. Similarly, NATO's PfP initiative may be more of a step in the right direction than is often perceived. As for the perennial question of the European security architecture, it is imperative to uphold whatever institutional clout there is (e.g. within NATO) and give up the search for fancy new pan-European solutions.[2] Much more important than playing with acronyms is the one task of inducing *Ostpolitik* with an operational content.

To some extent this implies a return to the Harmel formula of deterrence and *détente* coined by NATO in 1967. It is often said that there are no enemies to target in the post-Cold War environment, only risks. This is only partly true. In 1943, at the height of Nazi totalitarianism, Karl Popper developed his thoughts on the enemies of the open society as a shorthand for threats to democratic pluralism and societal stability. The postcommunist world is rich in ideologies, movements and actors embodying this kind of threat, which are also found in the consolidated democracies of the West. It takes a highly multifaceted security policy to manage this type of threat, such as determined and visionary efforts at reintegration and active encouragement of CSBMs, including regional cooperation involving postcommunist states. Caution may be warranted in relation to the CIS because of the neo-imperial undertones of Russia's visions for this framework, but there is a need to encourage closer cooperation notably at the level below governments – such as cooperation among private companies in order to create post-*nomenklatura* structures of vested interests across countries. Altogether, these measures may be subsumed under the heading of *détente* or preventive measures. As for deterrence in the narrow sense, the armed struggle for power in former Yugoslavia is a reminder of the continued relevance of strong

[2] In connection with the many proposals for dismantling the allegedly obsolete organizations born in the Cold War, it is curious to see how few bother to argue the abolishment of the Council of Europe – which is just as much a child of the Cold War as NATO.

structures of international crisis management and willingness to undertake military intervention if necessary. But there is an important addition to the formula of deterrence and *détente*. It is still imperative to approach the new foreign policy partners of the postcommunist East in the spirit of empathy counselled by Peter Calvert, remembering that they are often at a disadvantage in the defence of their interests. Perhaps the single most important policy prescription for Easterners and Westerners alike is to temper pessimism.

BIBLIOGRAPHY

Abbreviations

BIOst – Berichte des Bundesinstitus für ostwissenschaftliche und internationale Studien

Jan S. Adams (1994). 'Who Will Make Russia's Foreign Policy in 1994?', *RFE/RL Research Report*, vol. 3, no. 6 (11 Feb.), pp. 36–40.

AFP.

Agence Europe (Brussels).

Mikhail Agursky (1987). *The Third Rome: National Bolshevism in the USSR.* Boulder, CO: Westview.

Tsuneo Akaha (1993). 'The Politics of Japanese-Soviet/Russian Economic Relations', pp. 161–84 in Tsuneo Akaha and Frank Langdon (eds) *Japan in the Posthegemonic World.* Boulder, CO: Lynne Rienner.

A.M. Alekseev, A.I. Vikent'ev and B.P. Miroshnichenko (1975). *Sotsialisticheskaia integratsia i eë preimushchestva pered kapitalisticheskoi.* Moscow: Nauka.

Olga Alexandrova (1993a). 'Perzeptionen der auswärtigen Sicherheit in der Ukraine', *BIOst*, no. 40.

——— (1993b). 'Entwicklung der aussenpolitischen Konzeptionen Russlands', *BIOst*, no. 13.

Graham T. Allison (1971). *Essence of Decision: Explaining the Cuban Missile Crisis.* Boston, MA: Little Brown.

Michael Andersen and Mette Skak (1993). 'The New Western Ostpolitik: Challenges, Current State and Issues'. Paper presented to the ECPR Joint Session of Workshops, Leiden (2–8 Apr.).

AP.

Alexei G. Arbatov (1993). 'Russia's Foreign Policy Alternatives', *International Security*, vol. 18, no. 2 (Fall), pp. 5–43.

John A. Armstrong (1992). 'Nationalism in the Former Soviet Empire', *Problems of Communism*, vol. XLI (Jan.–Apr.), pp. 121–33.

Vernon V. Aspaturian (1960). *The Union Republics in Soviet Diplomacy: A Study of Federalism in the Service of Soviet Foreign Policy.* Geneva: Publications de l'Institut Universitaire de Hautes Etudes Internationales, no. 36.

——(1971). *Process and Power in Soviet Foreign Policy*. Boston, MA: Little, Brown.

Edward E. Azar and Chung-In Moon (eds) (1988). *National Security in the Third World: The Management of Internal and External Threats*. Cambridge University Press.

Donna Bahry (1987). *Outside Moscow: Power, Politics, and Budgetary Policy in the Soviet Republics*. New York: Columbia University Press.

Richard E. Baldwin (1994). *Towards an Integrated Europe*. London: Centre for Economic Policy Research.

Zoltan D. Barany (1990). 'Not a Smooth Ride: Soviet Troop Withdrawals from Hungary', *Report on Eastern Europe*, 15 June, pp. 20–33.

Michael Barratt Brown (1974). *The Economics of Imperialism*. Harmondsworth: Penguin.

'Basic Principles of National Defence in the Republic of Hungary' (1993). *Fact Sheets on Hungary*. Budapest: Ministry of Foreign Affairs.

'Basic principles of the Security Policy of the Republic of Hungary' (1993). *Fact Sheets on Hungary*. Budapest: Ministry of Foreign Affairs.

Isaiah Berlin (1991). 'Two Concepts of Nationalism: An Interview with Isaiah Berlin', *New York Review of Books*, 21 Nov.

Yuri Bernov (1990). 'Poland in the 1950s', *International Affairs* (Moscow) (Feb.), pp. 122–32.

Alain Besançon (1986). 'Nationalism and Bolshevism in the USSR', pp. 1–13, in Robert Conquest (ed.) *The Last Empire: Nationality and the Soviet Future*. Stanford, CA: Hoover Institution Press.

Beyond Assistance (1992). Report of the IEWS Task Force on Western Assistance to Transition in the Czech and Slovak Federal Republic, Hungary and Poland (May). New York and Prague: Institute for East-West Studies, European Studies Center.

Seweryn Bialer (1984). 'Socialist stagnation and Communist Encirclement', *Adelphi Paper*, no. 189 (Spring), pp. 13–30.

Erling Bjøl (1971). 'The Small State in International Politics', pp. 29–37 in August Schou and Arne Olav Brundtland (eds) *Small States in International Relations*. Stockholm: Almquist & Wiksell/New York: John Wiley.

Stephen Blank (1993). 'Diplomacy at an Impasse: Russia and Japan in a New Asia', *Korean Journal of Defense Analysis*, vol. 5, no. 1 (summer), pp. 141–64.

Christoph Bluth (1994). 'Russia and European Security', *The World Today* (Apr.), pp. 73–6.

Alexei Bogaturov (1993). 'The Eurasian Support of World Stability', *International Affairs* (Moscow) (Feb.), pp. 32–44.

Milica Z. Bookman (1994). 'War and Peace: The Divergent Breakups of Yugoslavia and Czechoslovakia', *Journal of Peace Research*, vol. 31, no. 2, pp. 175–87.

András Bozóki et al. (eds) (1992). *Postcommunist Transition: Emerging Pluralism in Hungary*. London: Pinter/New York: St Martin's Press.

Algirdas Brazauskas (1994). *Letter to His Excellency Manfred Woerner* (4 Jan.).

George W. Breslauer and Philip E. Tetlock (eds) (1991). *Learning in U.S. and Soviet Foreign Policy*. Boulder, CO: Westview.

James F. Brown (1975). 'Relations between the Soviet Union and Its Eastern European Allies: A Survey'. *Rand Report*, no. R-1742-PR, Santa Monica, CA.

—— (1991). *Surge to Freedom: The End of Communist Rule in Eastern Europe*. Twickenham: Adamantine Press.

Zbigniew K. Brzezinski (1969). *The Soviet Bloc: Unity and Conflict*, revised and enlarged edn. Cambridge, MA: Harvard University Press.

—— (1989). *The Grand Failure: The Birth and Death of Communism in the Twentieth Century*. New York: Charles Scribner's & Sons.

—— (1989/90). 'Post-Communist Nationalism', *Foreign Affairs*, vol. 68 (Winter), no. 5, pp. 1–25.

Hedley Bull (1977). *The Anarchical Society: A Study of Order in World Politics*. London: Macmillan.

Valerie Bunce (1985). 'The Empire Strikes Back: The Transformation of the Eastern Bloc from a Soviet Asset to a Soviet Liability', *International Organization*, vol. 39, no. 1 (Winter), pp. 1–46.

Dzintra Bungs (1993). 'Progress on Withdrawal from the Baltic States', *RFE/RL Research Report*, vol. 2, no. 25 (18 June), pp. 50–9.

Stephen R. Burant (1993). 'International Relations in a Regional Context: Poland and Its Eastern Neighbours – Lithuania, Belarus, Ukraine', *Europe-Asia Studies (formerly Soviet Studies)*, vol. 45, no. 3, pp. 392–418.

Audrius Butkevicius (1993). 'The Baltic Region in Post-Cold War Europe', *NATO Review* (Feb.), pp. 7–11.

Barry Buzan (1983). *People, States and Fear: The Nationl Security Problem in International Relations*. Brighton: Wheatsheaf.

—— et al. (1990). *The European Security Order Recast: Scenarios for the Post-Cold War Era*. London: Pinter.

Peter Calvert (1986). *The Foreign Policy of the New States*. Brighton: Wheatsheaf.

Donald S. Carlisle (1991). 'Uzbekistan and the Uzbeks', *Problems of Communism*, vol. XXXX (Sept.–Oct.), pp. 23–44.

E.H. Carr (1982). *The Twilight of Comintern, 1930–1935*. London: Macmillan.

Central and Eastern Eurobarometer (1993). no. 3 (Feb.), Brussels: Commission of the European Communities.

'Central European Initiative and Hungary' (1993). (Interview with Prime Minister József Antall + CEI documentary materials) Budapest, ambassador A. Szabo (May).

Jeff Checkel (1992). 'Russian Foreign Policy: Back to the Future?', *RFE/RL Research Report*, vol. 1, no. 41, (16 Oct.), pp. 15–29.

———— (1993). 'Ideas, Institutions, and the Gorbachev Foreign Policy Revolution', *World Politics*, vol. 45 (Jan.), pp. 271–300.

———— (1994). 'Structures, Institutions and Process: Russia's Changing Foreign Policy'. Paper for the workshop on 'The Influence of Foreign Policy Priorities and Decisionmaking on Russian Foreign Policy, Johns Hopkins School of Advanced International Studies and the University of Maryland, mimeo (Mar.).

John Chipman (1993). 'Managing the Politics of Parochialism', *Survival*, vol. 35, no. 1 (Spring), pp. 143–70.

Johnny Christensen (1978). *Ideologi og begivenheder: Den sovjetiske udenrigspolitik i stalinismens efterkrigsfase*. Aarhus: Arkona.

Christopher Clapham (ed.) (1977). *Foreign Policy Making in Developing States: A Comparative Approach*. Farnborough, Hants: Saxon House.

Michael Clarke and Brian White (eds) (1989). *Understanding Foreign Policy: The Foreign Policy Systems Approach*. Aldershot: Edward Elgar.

Michael D. Cohen, James G. March, and Johan P. Olsen (1972). 'A Garbage Can Model of Organizational Choice', *Administrative Science Quarterly*, vol. 17, pp. 1–25.

'Concluding Document of the Inaugural Conference for a Pact on Stability in Europe' (1994).

Daniel A. Connelly (1994). 'Black Sea Economic Cooperation', *RFE/RL Research Report*, vol. 3, no. 26 (1 July), pp. 31–8.

'The Constitution of the Republic of Hungary' (1989). Budapest.

Lewis A. Coser (1956). *The Functions of Social Conflict*. Glencoe, IL: Free Press.

Suzanne Crow (1992a). 'Personnel Changes in the Russian Foreign Ministry', *RFE/RL Research Report*, vol. 1, no. 16, (17 Apr.), pp. 18–22.

————(1992b), 'Competing Blueprints for Russian Foreign Policy', *RFE/RL Research Report*, vol. 1, no. 50 (18 Dec.), pp. 45–50.

———— (1993a). *The Making of Foreign Policy in Russia under Yeltsin*. Munich/Washington, DC: RFE/RL Studies.

———— (1993b). 'Russia Asserts its Strategic Agenda', *RFE/RL Research Report*, vol. 2, no. 50 (17 Dec.), pp. 1–8.

———— (1993c). 'Ambartsumov's Influence on Russian Foreign Policy', *RFE/RL Research Report*, vol. 2, no. 19 (7 May), pp. 36–41.

———— (1993d). 'Russia Seeks Leadership in Regional Peacekeeping', *RFE/RL Research Report*, vol. 2, no. 15 (9 Apr.), pp. 28–32.

———— (1994). 'Why Has Russian Foreign Policy Changed?', *RFE/RL Research Report*, vol. 3, no. 18 (6 May), pp. 1–6.

CTK-Business News (Prague).

Alexander Dallin (1981). 'The Domestic Sources of Soviet Foreign Policy', pp. 335–408 in Seweryn Bialer (ed.) *The Domestic Context of Soviet Foreign Policy*. Boulder, CO: Westview.

David J. Dallin (1951). *The New Soviet Empire*. New Haven, CT: Yale University Press.

Roland Dannreuther (1993). 'Russia, Central Asia and the Persian Gulf', *Survival*, vol. 35, no. 4 (Winter), pp. 92–112.

Norman Davies (1986). *Heart of Europe: A Short History of Poland*. Oxford University Press.

'Declaration of the Conference of Foreign Ministers of the Baltic Sea States', Copenhagen, 5–6 March 1992. Reprinted in *Dansk Udenrigspolitisk Årbog 1992*. Copenhagen: DJØF.

'Declaration of the Heads of State and Government Participating in the Meeting of the North Atlantic Council held at NATO Headquarters, Brussels, on 10–11 January 1994' [Declaration on PfP]. Press Communiqué M-1(94)3.

'Declaration on the Principles Guiding the Cooperation between the Republic of Hungary and the Russian Federation Regarding the Guarantees of the Rights of National Minorities', 11 Nov. 1992.

'Declaration on the Principles of Co-operation between the Republic of Hungary and the Ukrainian Soviet Socialist Republic in Guaranteeing the Rights of National Minorities', 31 May 1991.

Renaud Dehousse (1991). 'Pan-European Integration: The Institutional Constraints – an EC view'. European Security. A SNU-EUI seminar at European University Institute, Florence, Mar. 1991. Copenhagen: *SNU Papers*.

Den (a Moscow biweekly).

Daniel Deudney and G. John Ikenberry (1991). 'Soviet Reform and the End of the Cold War: Explaining Large-Scale Historical Change', *Review of International Studies*, vol. 17, no. 3 (July), pp. 225–50.

Karl Deutsch *et al.* (1957). *Political Community in the North Atlantic Area: International Organization in the Light of Historical Experience*. New York: Greenwood Press.

Isaac Deutscher (1967). *Stalin. A Political Biography*. 2nd edn. London, New York/Toronto: Oxford University Press.

C.J. Dick, J.F. Dunn and J.B. Lough (1993). 'Potential Sources of Conflict in Post-Communist Europe', *European Security*, vol. 2, no. 3 (Autumn), pp. 386–406.

Diena (a Riga daily – Russian-language edition).

Diplomaticheskii Slovar' I-III (1984–6). Moscow: Nauka.

Milovan Djilas (1957). *The New Class: An Analysis of the Communist System*. London: Thames & Hudson.

——— (1962). *Conversations with Stalin*. Harmondsworth: Penguin.

Pál Dunay (1992). 'Stability and Instability in Europe: The Contribution of Hungary'. Paper presented to the ECPR Standing Group on

International Relations' Inaugural Pan-European Conference, Heidelberg, 16–20 Sept.

John F. Dunn (1992). 'Hard Times in Russia Foster Conspiracy Theories', *RFE/RL Research Report*, vol. 1, no. 46 (20 Nov.), pp. 24–9.

Maurice A. East (1973). 'Foreign Policy-Making in Small States: Some Theoretic Observations Based on a Study of the Uganda Ministry of Foreign Affairs'. *Policy Sciences*, vol. 4, no. 4 (Dec.), pp. 491–508.

Eastern Europe and the Commonwealth of Independent States 1992. (1992). London: Europa Publishers.

The Economist.

S. N. Eisenstadt (1963). *The Political System of Empires: The Rise and the Fall of the Historical Bureaucratic Societies.* Glencoe: Free Press.

—— (1992). 'Center-Periphery Relations in the Soviet Empire: Some Interpretive Observations', pp. 205–23 in Alexander J. Motyl (ed.), *Thinking Theoretically about Soviet Nationalities: History and Comparison in the Study of the USSR.* New York: Columbia University Press.

Carol R. Ember, Melvin Ember and Bruce Russett (1992). 'Peace between Participatory Polities: A Cross-cultural Test of the "Democracies Rarely Fight Each Other" Hypothesis', *World Politics*, no. 4 (July), pp. 573–99.

Rupert Emerson (1960). *From Empire to Nation: The Rise to Self-assertion of Asian and African Peoples.* Cambridge, MA: Harvard University Press.

Richard E. Ericson (1987). 'The Soviet Economic Predicament', pp. 95–120 in Henry S. Rowen and Charles Wolf Jr. (eds) *The Future of the Soviet Empire.* London: Macmillan.

Amitai Etzioni (1992–3). 'The Evils of Self-determination', *Foreign Policy*, no. 89 (Winter), pp. 21–35.

The European.

Olav Fagelund Knudsen (1992). 'Strandstater med erosjonsproblemer: De baltiske staters utenrikspolitik', *Internasjonal Politikk*, no. 50, pp. 159–75.

Merle Fainsod (1958/89). *Smolensk under Soviet Rule.* Boston, MA: Unwin Hyman.

——(1963).*How Russia is Ruled.* rev. edn, Cambridge, MA: Harvard University Press.

Ib Faurby (1976). 'Premises, Promises and Problems of Comparative Foreign Policy', *Cooperation and Conflict*, vol. 11, no. 3, pp. 139–62.

Financial Times.

Sharon Fischer (1993), 'The Gabcikovo-Nagymaros Dam Controversy Continues', *RFE/RL Research Report*, vol. 2, no. 37 (17 Sept.), pp. 7–12.

—— (1994). 'Czech-Slovak Relations Two Years after the Elections', *RFE/RL Research Report*, vol. 3, no. 27 (8 July), pp. 9–17.

Frederic J. Fleron Jr. and Erik P. Hoffmann (eds) (1993). *Post-communist Studies and Political Science: Methodology and Empirical Theory in Sovietology.* Boulder, CO: Westview.

Neil Fodor (1990). *The Warsaw Treaty Organization: A Political and Organizational Analysis*. London: Macmillan.

Stephen Foye (1992). 'The Struggle over Russia's Kuril Islands Policy', *RFE/RL Research Report*, vol. 1, no. 36 (11 Sept.), pp. 34–40.

—— (1993). 'Russo-Japanese Relations: Still Travelling a Rocky Road', *RFE/RL Research Report*, vol. 2, no. 44 (5 Nov.), pp. 27–34.

Joseph Frankel (1963). *The Making of Foreign Policy*. Oxford University Press.

Frankfurter Allgemeine Zeitung.

Lawrence Freedman (1976). 'Logic, Politics and Foreign Policy Processes: A Critique of the Bureaucratic Politics Model', *International Affairs*, no. 3 (July), pp. 434–49.

Carl J. Friedrich and Zbigniew K. Brzezinski (1965). *Totalitarian Dictatorship and Autocracy*. 2nd edn. Cambridge, MA: Harvard University Press.

Tina Friis Hansen and Finn Østergaard Jørgensen (1993). 'De baltiske lande: På vej mod Europa?', *Politica*, vol. 25, no. 4, pp. 431–41.

Howard E. Frost (1993). 'Eastern Europe's Search for Security', *Orbis*, vol. 37, no. 1 (Winter), pp. 37–53.

Elizabeth Fuller (1994). 'The Transcaucasus: War, Turmoil, Economic Collapse', *RFE/RL Research Report*, vol. 3, no. 1 (7 Jan.), pp. 51–8.

Alexis Galinos (1994). 'Central Europe and the EU: Prospects for Closer Integration', *RFE/RL Research Report*, vol. 3, no. 29 (22 July), pp. 19–25.

John Gallagher and Ronald Robinson (1953). 'The Imperialism of Free Trade', *Economic History Review*, 2nd series, vol. VI, no 1, pp. 1–15.

Johan Galtung (1969). 'Violence, Peace, and Peace Research', *Journal of Peace Research*, no. 6, pp. 167–91.

—— (1971). 'A Structural Theory of Imperialism', *Journal of Peace Research*, vol. 8, no. 2, pp. 81–117.

Marek Garztecki (1994). 'Poland's Western Dilemma', *The World Today* (Apr.), pp. 77–9.

Charles Gati (1986). *Hungary and the Soviet Bloc*. Durham, NC: Duke University Press.

—— (1987). 'The Unsettled Condition of Eastern Europe', pp. 41–52 in Harry S. Rowen and Charles Wolf Jr. (eds) *The Future of the Soviet Empire*. London: Macmillan.

—— (1990). *The Bloc that Failed: Soviet-East European Relations in Transition*. London: I.B. Tauris.

Udo Gehrmann (1992). 'Das Kosakentum in Russland zu Beginn der neunziger Jahre: historische Traditionen und Zukunftsvisionen', *BIOst*, no. 11.

—— (1994). 'Die Kosaken. Traditionalismus und nationale Erneuerung in der Ukraine', *BIOst*, no. 23.

Dietrich Geyer (1986). 'Modern Imperialism? The Tsarist and Soviet

Examples', pp. 49–62 in Wolfgang J. Mommsen and Jürgen Osterhammel (eds) *Imperialism and After: Continuities and Discontinuities*. London: Geo. Allen & Unwin.

Saulius Girnius (1992). 'Progress in Withdrawal of Troops from Lithuania?', *RFE/RL Research Report*, vol. 1, no. 34 (28 Aug.), pp. 29–33.

—— (1993a). 'Lithuania's Foreign Policy', *RFE/RL Research Report*, vol. 2, no. 35 (3 Sept.), pp. 23–33.

—— (1993b). 'Lithuanian Politics Seven Months after the Elections', *RFE/RL Research Report*, vol. 2, no. 27 (2 July), pp. 16–21.

—— (1994). 'Lithuania: Former Communists Fail to Solve Problems', *RFE/RL Research Report*, vol. 3, no. 1 (7 Jan.), pp. 99–102.

Joachim Glaubitz (1994). 'Japan und Russland. Stand und Perspektiven ihrer Beziehungen', *BIOst*, no. 7.

Misha Gle ny (1992). *The Fall of Yugoslavia: The Third Balkan War*. London: Penguin, new edn.

Paul Goble (1993). 'Russia and its Neighbours', *Foreign Policy*, no. 90 (Spring), pp. 79–88.

Kjell Goldmann (1988). *Change and Stability in Foreign Policy. The Problems and Possibilities of Détente*. London: Harvester Wheatsheaf.

Alvin W. Gouldner (1977). 'Stalinism: A Study of Internal Colonialism', *Telos* no. 34, (Winter), pp. 5–48.

James Gow (1991). 'Deconstructing Yugoslavia', *Survival*, vol. XXXIII, no. 4 (July – Aug.), pp. 291–311.

—— (1993). 'One Year of War in Bosnia and Herzegovina', *RFE/RL Research Report*, vol. 2, no. 23 (4 June), pp. 1–13.

Anton Grizold (1993). 'The Shaping of Slovenian National Security', *European Security*, vol. 2, no. 3 (Autumn), pp. 407–20.

A.J.R. Groom and Paul Taylor (1994). *Frameworks for International Co-operation*. London: Pinter.

Guardian Weekly.

Janne Haaland Matlary (1993). 'The Development of Environmental Policy-making in Hungary: The Role of the EC'. Paper to be presented at the ECPR Joint Session of Workshops, Leiden 2–8 Apr. 1993 (CICERO: University of Oslo).

Richard N. Haass (1990). *Conflicts Unending: The United States and Regional Disputes*. New Haven, CT and London: Yale University Press.

Jeffrey Hahn (1991). 'Continuity and Change in Russian Political Culture', *British Journal of Political Science*, vol. 21, pp. 393–421.

Uwe Halbach (1994). ' "Failing States" ? Nationale, staatliche und ökonomische Festigkeit der südlichen GUS-Länder' (Parts I and II), *BIOst,* no. 20 and 21.

Peter van Ham (1994). 'Ukraine, Russia and European Security: Implications for Western Security', *Chaillot Papers*, no. 13 (Feb.) (WEU Institute for Security Studies).

Thomas T. Hammond (ed.) (1975). *The Anatomy of Communist Takeovers.* New Haven, CT and London: Yale University Press.

Peter Hanak and Joseph Held (1992). 'Hungary on a Fixed Course: An Outline of Hungarian History', pp. 164–28, in Joseph Held (ed.) *Columbia History of Eastern Europe in the Twentieth Century.* New York: Columbia University Press.

Michael Handel (1981). *Weak States in the International System.* London: Frank Cass.

Kyril Haramiev-Drezov (1993). 'Bulgarian-Russian Relations on a New Footing', *RFE/RL Research Report*, vol. 2, no. 15 (9 Apr.), pp. 33–8.

Bohdan Harasymiw (1969). 'Nomenklatura: The Soviet Communist Party's Leadership Recruitment System'. *Canadian Journal of Political Science*, vol. 2, no. 4, pp. 494–512.

Peter Hauslohner (1981). 'Prefects as Senators: Soviet Regional Politicians Look to Foreign Policy', *World Politics*, vol. XXXIII, no. 2 (Jan.), pp. 197–233.

Vaclav Havel (1990). 'The Chance That Will Not Return', *US News & World Report* (26 Feb.).

Michael Hechter (1975). *Internal Colonialism: The Celtic Fringe in British National Development 1536–1966.* London: Routledge & Kegan Paul.

Gerald B. Helman and Steven R. Ratner (1992–93). 'Saving Failed States', *Foreign Policy*, no. 89 (Winter), pp. 3–20.

Charles F. Hermann, Charles W. Kegley Jr. and James N. Rosenau (eds) (1987). *New Directions in the Study of Foreign Policy.* London: Harper-Collins Academic.

John Herz (1950). 'Idealist Internationalism and the Security Dilemma', *World Politics*, vol. 2 (Jan.), pp. 157–80.

Christopher Hill (1977). 'Theories of Foreign Policy Making for the Developing Countries', pp. 1–17 in Christopher Clapham (ed.) *Foreign Policy Making in Developing States*, Farnborough, Hants: Saxon House.

Magdalene Hoff and Heinz Timmermann (1993). 'Kaliningrad: Russia's Future Gateway to Europe?', *RFE/RL Research Report*, vol. 2, no. 36 (10 Sept.), pp. 37–43.

David Holloway and Jane M.O. Sharp (eds) (1984). *The Warsaw Pact: Alliance in Transition?* London: Macmillan.

Franklyn Holzmann (1974). *Foreign Trade under Central Planning.* Cambridge, MA: Harvard University Press.

Geoffrey Hosking (1991). *The Awakening of the Soviet Union*, rev. edn. Cambridge, MA: Harvard University Press.

Jerry Hough (1989/90). 'Gorbachev's Politics', *Foreign Affairs*, vol. 68, no. 5, pp. 26–41.

—— (1982). *How the Soviet Union is Governed*. Cambridge, MA: Harvard University Press.

Hungarian Observer (a Budapest monthly).

Samuel B. Huntington (1968). *Political Order in Changing Societies*. New Haven, CT: Yale University Press.

—— (1993). 'The Clash of Civilizations?', *Foreign Affairs*, vol. 72, no. 3, pp. 22–49.

Independent.

Information (a Copenhagen daily).

Interfax.

International Herald Tribune.

International Institute of Strategic Studies (1993). *The Military Balance 1993–94*. London: Brassey's.

Dan Ionescu and Alfred A. Reisch (1993). 'Still No Breakthrough in Romanian-Hungarian Relations', *RFE/RL Research Report*, vol. 2, no. 42 (22 Oct.), pp. 26–32.

Ghita Ionescu (1965). *The Break-up of the Soviet Empire*. Harmondsworth: Penguin.

ITAR-TASS.

Izvestia.

Robert H. Jackson (1990). *Quasi-states: Sovereignty, International Relations and the Third World*. Cambridge University Press.

Japan's Northern Territories (1992). MFA, Japan.

Géza Jeszenszky (1994). *Statement at the Conference for a European Stability Pact*, Budapest: MFA, Republic of Hungary.

JiJi Press (Tokyo).

Pertti Joenniemi (1993). 'The Baltic Countries as Deviant Cases; Small States in Search of Foreign Policies', pp. 187–226 in Pertti Joenniemi and Peeter Vares (eds) *New Actors on the International Arena: The Foreign Policies of the Baltic Countries*. Tampere Peace Research Institute, Research Report no. 50.

Robert A. Jones (1990). *The Soviet Concept of 'Limited Sovereignty' from Lenin to Gorbachev: The Brezhnev Doctrine*. London: Macmillan.

Roy E. Jones (1979). *Principles of Foreign Policy: The Civil State in its World Setting*. Oxford: Martin Robertson.

Christer Jönsson (1984). *Superpower: Comparing American and Soviet Foreign Policy*. London: Pinter.

Natalja V. Juchneva (1993). 'Der Antisemitismus in Russland heute', *BIOst*, no. 6.

Kornelia Jurgaitiené (1993). 'Romantic Nationalism and the Challenge of Europeanization: [the] Case of Lithuania', pp. 32–8 in Pertti Joenniemi and Peeter Vares (eds) *New Actors on the International Arena: The Foreign Policies of the Baltic Countries*. Tampere Peace Research Institute, *Research Report* no. 50.

Ryszard Kapuscinski (1991). *The Soccer War*. London: Penguin.

Sergei A. Karaganov (1992). 'Problemy zashchity interesov rossiisko orientirovannogo naselenia v "blizhnem" zarubezhe', *Diplomaticheski Vestnik* (15 Nov.), pp. 43–5.

—— (1993). 'Russia and Other Independent Republics in Asia', pp. 21–30 in 'Asia's International Role in the Post-Cold War Era', *Adelphi Paper*, no. 276.

—— et al. (1993). *What Has Gone Wrong with Western Aid to Russia?* Research Report for the Bertelsman Stiftung. Institute of Europe, Russian Academy of Sciences, Moscow, mimeo. (Dec.).

Georgi Karasimeonov and Mette Skak (eds) (1994). *Bulgaria and Denmark and the New Europe*. Sofia: St Kliment Ohridski University Press.

Ole Karup Pedersen (1970). *Udenrigsminister P. Munchs opfattelse af Danmarks stilling i international politik*. Copenhagen: Københavns Universitets Institut for Samtidshistorie og Statskundskab, Skrifter 2 & G.E.C. Gads Forlag.

Michael Kaser (1965). *COMECON: Integration Problems of the Planned Economies*. London: Oxford University Press.

Edy Kaufman (1977). 'Latin America', pp. 131–64 in Christopher Clapham (ed) *Foreign Policy Making in Developing States: A Comparative Approach*. Farnborough, Hants: Saxon House.

Morten Kelstrup (1991). 'Danmarks deltagelse i det internationale samarbejde – fra pragmatisk funktionalisme til aktiv internationalisme, pp. 289–311 in Henning Gottlieb and Bertel Heurlin (eds) *Fred og konflikt: Håndbog i sikkerhed og nedrustning*. Copenhagen: SNU.

Paul Kennedy (1988). *The Rise and Fall of the Great Powers: Economic Change and Military Conflict from 1500 to 2000*. London: Unwin Hyman.

Riina Kionka (1992). 'Baltic States Develop a New Ostpolitik', *RFE/RL Research Report*, vol. 1, no. 8 (21 Feb.), pp. 21–25.

Alexei Kiva (1992). 'A Superpower which Ruined Itself', *International Affairs* (Moscow), no. 2, pp. 13–22.

Walter Kolarz (1952). *Russia and her Colonies*. London: Geo. Philip.

Pål Kolstø (1993). 'The New Russian Diaspora: Minority Protection in the Soviet Successor States', *Journal of Peace Research*, vol. 30, no. 2, pp. 197–217.

—— et al. (1993). 'The Dniestr Conflict: Between Irredentism and Separatism', *Europe-Asia Studies (formerly Soviet Studies)*, vol. 45, no. 3, pp. 973–1000.

'Konstitutsia Rossiiskoi Federatsii' (*Rossiiskaia Gazeta*, 10 Nov. 1993).

Bahgat Korany (1983). 'The Take-off of Third World Studies? The Case of Foreign Policy', *World Politics*, vol. XXXV, no. 3, pp. 465–87.

—— (1984). 'Foreign Policy in the Third World', *International Political Science Review*, vol. 5, no. 1, pp. 7–20.

Andrei Kortunov and Alexei Iziumov (1990). 'Shto ponimat pod gosudartsvnennymi interesami?', *Literaturnaia Gazeta* (11 July).

Lydia Kossikowa (1993). 'Die Handelsbeziehungen Russlands mit den ehemaligen Unionsrepubliken: Tendenzen und Problem', *BIOst*, no. 23.

Wojciech Kostecki (1994). 'Polish Foreign Policy 1989–93: Interpreting Value Priorities', Centre for Peace and Conflict Research, Copenhagen, *Working Papers* no. 9/94.

Grzegorz Kostrzewa-Zorbas (1992). 'Security for the East Europeans', *Problems of Communism*, vol. XLI (Jan.–Apr.), pp. 148–9.

N.A. Kovalski, T.V. Nosenko and P.T. Podlesnyi (1993). 'Rossia v Chernomorskom regione', *Doklady Instituta Evropy* no. 4, Moscow.

Andrei Kozyrev (1993). 'The New Russia and the Atlantic Alliance', *NATO Review* (Feb.), pp. 3–6.

Heinz Kramer (1993). 'The European Community's Response to the New Eastern Europe', *Journal of Common Market Studies*, vol. 31, no. 2 (June), pp. 213–44.

Mark Kramer (1989/90). 'Beyond the Brezhnev Doctrine: A New Era in Soviet-East European Relations?', *International Security*. vol. 14, no. 3, pp. 25–67.

Krasnaia Zvezda (Moscow).

Viktor Kravchenko (1946). *I Chose Freedom: The Personal and Political Life of a Soviet Official*. New York: Charles Scribner's Sons.

James A. Kuhlmann (ed) (1978). *The Foreign Policies of Eastern Europe: Domestic and International Determinants*. Leiden: A.W. Sijthoff.

Joseph C. Kun (1993). *Hungarian Foreign Policy: The Experience of a New Democracy*. Westport, CO: Praeger.

Vytautas Landsbergis (1992). 'NATO and the Baltic States', speech made by the President of Lithuania, Vytautas Landsbergis, to the North Atlantic Council on 23 September 1992.

Gail W. Lapidus, Victor Zaslavsky with Philip Goldman (1992). *From Union to Commonwealth: Nationalism and Separatism in the Soviet Republics*. Cambridge University Press.

Natalia Lebedeva (1993a). 'Rospusk Kominterna i transformatsia ego v Otdel Mezhdunarodnoi Informatsii TsK VKP (b)', Paper for the conference 'Archives and Research in Russia and Eastern Europe, Ærø, Denmark, mimeo (3–6 Dec.).

Natalya Lebedeva (1993b). 'The Comintern and Poland 1939–1943', *International Affairs* (Moscow) (Aug.), pp. 83–94.

Paul Lendvai (1988). *Hungary: The Art of Survival*. London: I.B. Tauris.

——— (1990). 'Eastern Europe I: Liberalism vs. Nationalism', *The World Today* (July), pp. 131–3.

Laszlo Lengyel (1990). 'Europe through Hungarian Eyes', *International Affairs* (London), vol. 66, no. 2, pp. 291–7.

Leninskaia politika mira i bezopasnosti narodov (1982). Moscow: Nauka.

John W.R. Lepingwell *et al.* (1994). 'Russia: A Troubled Future', *RFE/RL Research Report*, vol. 3, no. 24 (17 June), pp. 1–12.

George Liber (1991). '*Korenizatsiia*: Restructuring Soviet Nationality Policy in the 1920s', *Ethnic and Racial Studies*, vol. 14, no. 1 (Jan.), pp. 16–23.

Anatol Lieven (1993). *The Baltic Revolution: Estonia, Latvia, Lithuania and the Path to Independence.* New Haven, CT: Yale University Press.

Arend Lijphart (1977). *Democracy in Plural Societies: A Comparative Exploration.* Berkley, CA: University of California Press.

Seymour Martin Lipset (ed.) (1964). Revolution and Counterrevolution (esp. chapter 'The modernization of contemporary European Politics'). London: Heinemann.

Lithuanian Weekly (Vilnius).

John Lough (1993). 'Defining Russia's Relations with Neighbouring States', *RFE/RL Research Report*, vol. 2, no. 20 (14 May), pp. 53–60.

Bill Lomax (1994). 'Hungary: The Transition to Democratic Politics', Paper for the Conference 'Forward to the Past? Continuity and Change in Political Development in Austria, Hungary and the Czech and Slovak Republics', University of Aarhus (7–10 Oct.).

Geir Lundestad (1975). *The American Non-Policy Towards Eastern Europe 1943–1947: Universalism in an Area not of Essential Interest to the United States.* Oslo: Universitetsforlaget/New York: Humanities Press.

Allen Lynch (1994). 'After Empire: Russia and its Western Neighbours', *RFE/RL Research Report*, vol. 3, no. 12 (25 March), pp. 10–17.

Martin McCauley and Stephen Carter (eds) (1986). *Leadership and Succession in the Soviet Union, Eastern Europe and China.* London: Macmillan.

James P. McGregor (1992). 'Czechoslovakia: A New Style for the Ministry of Foreign Affairs', *RFE/RL Research Report*, vol. 1, no. 3 (17 Jan.), pp. 22–6.

James McKay (1982). 'An Exploratory Synthesis of Primordial and Mobilizationist Approaches to Ethnic Phenomena', *Ethnic and Racial Studies*, vol. 5, no. 4 (Oct.), pp. 395–420.

James E. Mace (1984). 'Famine and Nationalism in Soviet Ukraine', *Problems of Communism*, vol. XXXIII (May–June), pp. 37–50.

Ferenc Majoros (1993). 'Die Nachbarschaftsverträge der Bundesrepublik Deutschland mit Ungarn und der Tschechoslowakei', *BIOst*, no. 14.

Magyar Hirláp (a Budapest daily).

Igor Malashenko (1990). 'Russia: The Earth's Heartland', *International Affairs* (Moscow) (July), pp. 46–54.

Neil Malcolm (1994). 'The New Russian Foreign Policy', *The World Today* (Feb.), pp. 28–32.

Martin Malia (1990). 'To the Stalin Mausoleum', *Dædalus* (Winter), pp. 295–344 (written under the pseudonym 'Z').

———— (1992). 'From under the Rubble, What?', *Problems of Communism* (Jan.–Apr.), pp. 89–106.

———— (1994). 'Another Weimar? Nationalist Dangers in Post-communist Russia–and the Glimmerings of a Market Society', *Times Literary Supplement* (25 Feb.).

Paul Marer (1984). 'The Political Economy of Soviet Relations with Eastern Europe', in Sarah Meiklejohn Terry (ed.) *Soviet Policy in Eastern Europe*. New Haven, CT/London: Yale University Press, pp. 155–88.

Peter Martin (1991). 'The Gabcikovo-Nagymaros Dam Dilemma', *Report on Eastern Europe* (16 August), pp. 6–11.

T.G. Masaryk (1972). *The New Europe*. Lewisburg: Bucknell University Press.

Vladmir Matveev (1992). 'The New Russian Diplomacy: The First Months', *International Relations*, vol. XI, no. 2 (Aug.), pp. 77–94.

James Mayall (1992). 'National and International Security after the Cold War', *Survival* (Spring), pp. 19–35.

John M. Mearsheimer (1990). 'Back to the future: Instability in Europe after the Cold War', *International Security*, vol. 15, no. 1, pp. 5–56.

Maksim Meier (1994). 'Kuda povorachivaet gosudarstvennii korabl?', *Novoe Vremia*, no. 5.

Teodor Melescanu (1993). 'Security in Central Europe: A Positive Sum-game', *NATO Review* (Oct.), pp. 12–18.

Natalie Melnyczuk (1991). 'Ukraine Develops an Independent Foreign Policy: The First Year', *Report on the USSR (RFE/RL Research Institute)*, vol. 3, no. 45 (25 Oct.), pp. 21–5.

Alfred G. Meyer (1961). 'USSR Incorporated', *Slavic Review*, vol. 20, no. 3 (Oct.), pp. 369-76.

Gianni de Michelis (1990). 'Reaching out to the East', *Foreign Policy*, no. 79 (Summer), pp. 44–55.

Kathleen Mihailisko (1993). 'Belarus: Neutrality gives way to "Collective Security" ', *RFE/RL Research Report*, vol. 2, no. 17 (23 Apr.), pp. 24–31.

'Military Policy Doctrine of the Republic of Bulgaria within the Framework of the National Security Policy' (1992), pp. 4–8 in *Bulgarian Military Review*. Pilot issue.

John H. Miller (1977). 'Cadres Policy in Nationality Areas: Recruitment of CPSU First and Second Secretaries in Non-Russian Republics of the USSR', *Soviet Studies*, vol. 29 (Jan.), pp. 3–36.

Helen Milner (1992). 'International Theories of Cooperation among Nations: Strengths and Weaknesses (review article), *World Politics*, vol. 44 (Apr.), pp. 466–96.

Romuald J. Misiunas (1994). 'The Archives of the Lithuanian KGB', *BIOst*, no. 3.

———— and Rein Taagepera (1993). *The Baltic States: Years of Dependence 1940–1990*. London: Hurst.

Wolfgang J. Mommsen (1977). *Imperialismustheorien: Ein Überblick über die neueren Imperialismusinterpretationen*. Göttingen: Vandenhoeck & Ruprecht.

Wolfgang J. Mommsen and Jürgen Osterhammel (eds) (1986). *Imperialism and After: Continuities and Discontinuities*. London: Geo. Allen & Unwin.

Le Monde.

Hans J. Morgenthau (1951). *In Defense of the National Interest: A Critical Examination of American Foreign Policy*. New York: Alfred A. Knopf.

———— (1967). *Politics among Nations: The Struggle for Power and Peace*. 4th edn. New York: Knopf.

James F. Morrison (1978). 'The Foreign Policy of Poland', pp. 129–66 in James A. Kuhlmann (ed.) *The Foreign Policies of Eastern Europe: Domestic and International Determinants*. Leiden: A.W. Sijthoff.

John Morrison (1993). 'Pereyaslav and After: The Russian-Ukrainian Relationship', *International Affairs*, vol. 69, no. 4, pp. 677–703.

Edward L. Morse (1976). *Modernization and the Transformation of International Relations*. New York: Free Press.

Moscow News.

Alexander J. Motyl (1988). *Will the Non-Russians Rebel? State, Ethnicity, and Stability in the USSR*. Ithaca, NY: Cornell University Press.

————(1990). *Sovietology, Rationality, Nationality: Coming to Grips with Nationalism in the USSR*. New York: Columbia University Press.

————(ed.)(1992). *Thinking Theoretically about Soviet Nationalities: History and Comparison in the Study of the USSR*. New York: Columbia University Press.

Hans Mouritzen (1988). *Finlandization: Towards a General Theory of Adaptation*. Aldershot: Gower.

———— (1993). 'The Two Musterknaben and the Naughty Boy: Sweden, Finland and Denmark in the Process of European Integration'. *Cooperation and Conflict*, vol. 28, no. 4, pp. 373–402.

MTI (the Hungarian news agency).

NeGa (Nezavisimaia Gazeta, a Moscow daily).

Népszabadság (a Budapest daily).

Neue Zürcher Zeitung.

Renée de Nevers (1994). 'Russia's Strategic Renovation', *Adelphi Paper* no. 289 (July).

New Scientist.

Ole Nørgaard (1985). *Politik og reformer i Sovjetunionen*. Esbjerg: Sydjysk Universitetsforlag.

———— (1993). 'The Societal Basis of Security: The Case of the New Independent States of the Former Soviet Union'. Paper presented to the conference 'Building Security for the Future', Baltic Regional Research Centre, Vilnius (2–3 Sept.), 1993 (mimeo, 11 pp.)

Alec Nove (1982). *An Economic History of the U.S.S.R.* Harmondsworth: Penguin.

Joseph S. Nye (1971). *Peace in Parts: Integration and Conflict in Regional Organization.* Boston, MA: Little, Brown.

John O'Loughlin (1993). 'Precursor of Crisis: Political and Economic Relations of the Soviet Union, 1960–90', pp. 31–52 in idem and Herman van der Wusten (eds) *The New Political Geography of Eastern Europe*, London/New York: Belhaven Press.

Jan Obrman (1990). 'Foreign Policy: Sources, Concepts, and Problems', *Report on Eastern Europe* (14 Sept.), pp. 6–16.

—— (1992). 'Russia and Czechoslovakia Sign Friendship Treaty', *RFE/RL Research Report*, vol. 1, no. 19 (8 May), pp. 17–21.

William E. Odom (1992). 'Soviet Politics and After: Old and New Concepts'. *World Politics* , vol. 45, no. 1, pp. 66–98.

Karoly Okolicsanyi (1994). 'Macroeconomic Changes in Hungary, 1990–1994', *RFE/RL Research Report*, vol. 3, no. 24 (17 June), pp. 21–6.

Martha Brill Olcott (1991). 'The Soviet (Dis) Union', *Foreign Policy*, no. 82 (Spring), pp. 118–36.

—— (1992). 'Central Asia's Catapult to Independence', *Foreign Affairs*, vol. 71, no. 3, pp. 108–30.

Edith Oltay (1992). 'Minorities as Stumbling Block in Relations with Neighbours', *RFE/RL Research Report*, vol. 1, no. 19 (8 May), pp. 26–33.

OMRI Daily Digest (Prague: Open Media Research Institute).

Lucjian T. Orlowski (1993). 'Indirect Transfers in Trade among Former Soviet Union Republics: Sources, Patterns and Policy Responses in the Post-Soviet Period', *Europe-Asia Studies (formerly Soviet Studies)*, vol. 45, no. 6, pp. 1001–24.

Finn Ostergaard Jørgensen (1994). 'The Baltic States between East & West, unpubl. MA thesis. Aarhus: Institute of Political Science.

Oxford Companion to Politics of the World (1993). Oxford University Press.

Tibor Palankai (1991). *The European Community and Central European Integration: The Hungarian Case*, Institute for East-West Security Studies, Occasional Paper, no. 21, Boulder, CO: Westview.

Maria Papadakis and Harvey Starr (1987). 'Opportunity, Willingness and Small States: The Relationship between Environment and Foreign Policy', pp. 409–32 in Charles F. Hermann, Charles W. Kegley Jr. and James N. Rosenau (eds) *New Directions in the Study of Foreign Policy.* London: HarperCollins Academic.

Jiri Pehe (1992). 'Czechoslovakia's Political Balance Sheet, 1990 to 1992', *RFE/RL Research Report*, vol. 1, no. 25 (19 June), pp. 24–31.

Nikolaj Petersen (1977), 'Adaptation as a Framework for the Analysis of Foreign Policy Behaviour', *Cooperation and Conflict*, no. 4, pp. 221–50.

——— (1993). 'Abandonment vs. Entrapment: Denmark and Military Integration in Europe, 1948–1951' pp. 199–225 in Norbert Wiggershaus and Roland G. Foerster (eds) *The Western Security Community, 1948–1950: Common Problems and Conflicting National Interests during the Foundation Phase of the North Atlantic Alliance*. Oxford/Providence, RI: Berg.

PHARE Projects (1993). *PHARE Projects Approved in 1990, 1991, and 1992 by Beneficiary Country and by Broad Sectors*, DGI-L1/L2, JD/ar (Jan.). EC: Brussels.

Boris M. Pichugin (1994). 'K perspektivam torgovo-ekonomicheskikh otnoshenii Rossii s Evropoi', *Mirovaia Ekonomika i Mezhdunarodnye Otnoshenia*, no. 2, pp. 61–72.

Richard Pipes (1964). *The Formation of the Soviet Union: Communism and Nationalism 1917–1923*. Rev. edn. Cambridge, MA: Harvard University Press.

———(1991). 'The Soviet Union Adrift', *Foreign Affairs*, vol. 70, no. 1, pp. 70–87.

'The Politics of Intolerance' (1994). Special issue of *RFE/RL Research Report*, vol. 3, no. 16 (22 April).

Politiken (a Copenhagen daily).

Nikolai P. Popov (1994). 'Vneshniaia politika Rossii (analiz politikov i ekspertov)', *Mirovaia Ekonomika i Mezhdunarodnye Otnoshenia*, no. 3, pp. 52–9; no. 4, pp. 5–15.

Karl Popper (1966). *The Open Society and its Enemies*. vols 1 and 2. London: Routledge & Kegan Paul.

Bruce D. Porter (1992). 'A Country instead of a Cause: Russian Foreign Policy in the Post-Soviet Era', *Washington Quarterly*, vol. 15, no. 3 (Summer), pp. 41–56.

Barry R. Posen (1993). 'The Security Dilemma and Ethnic Conflict', *Survival*, vol. 35, no. 1, pp. 27–44.

Elgiz Pozdnyakov (1993). 'Russia is a Great Power', *International Affairs* (Moscow), no. 1, pp. 3–13.

Pravda.

Geoffrey Pridham, Eric Herring and George Standford (eds) (1994). *Building Democracy? The International Dimension of Democratisation in Eastern Europe*. Leicester University Press.

Adam Przeworski (1991). *Democracy and the Market: Political and Economic Reforms in Eastern Europe and Latin America*. Cambridge University Press.

Lucian W. Pye (1990). 'Political Science and the Crisis of Authoritarianism', *American Political Science Review*, vol. 84, no. 1 (March), pp. 3–19.

Gavriel D. Ra'anan. (1983). *International Policy Formation in USSR: Factional 'Debates' during the Zhdanovschina*. Hamden, CT: Archon Press.

Alexander Rahr (1991). 'Russia's "Young Turks" in Power', *Report on the USSR* (22 Nov.).

—— (1992). '"Atlanticists" versus 'Eurasians" in Russian Foreign Policy', *RFE/RL Research Report*, vol. 1, no. 22 (29 May), pp. 17–22.

—— (1993a). 'The First Year of Russian Independence', *RFE/RL Research Report*, vol. 2, no. 1 (1 Jan.), pp. 50–7.

—— (1993). 'Power Ministries' "Support Yeltsin"', *RFE/RL Research Report*, vol. 2, no. 40 (8 Oct.), pp. 8–11.

Teresa Rakowska-Harmstone (ed.) (1984). *Communism in Eastern Europe.* 2nd edn. Manchester University Press.

Georg von Rauch (1974). *The Baltic States: The Years of Independence: Estonia, Latvia, Lithuania, 1917–1940.* London: C. Hurst.

Alfred A. Reisch (1990): 'Primary Foreign Policy Objective to Rejoin Europe', *Report on Eastern Europe* (28 Dec.), pp. 15–20.

—— (1992). 'Hungarian Foreign Ministry Completes Reorganization', *RFE/RL Research Report*, vol. 1, no. 13 (27 Mar.), pp. 34–40.

—— (1993a). 'Hungarian-Russian Relations Enter a New Era', *RFE/RL Research Report*, vol. 2, no. 2 (8 Jan.), pp. 5–10.

—— (1993b). 'Central and Eastern Europe's Quest for NATO Membership', *RFE/RL Research Report*, vol. 2, no. 28 (9 July), pp. 33–47.

—— (1993c). 'Hungary's Foreign Policy towards the East', *RFE/RL Research Report*, vol. 2, no. 15 (9 Apr.), pp. 39–48.

—— (1993d). 'Hungary Pursues Integration with the West', *RFE/RL Research Report*, vol. 2, no. 13 (26 Mar.), pp. 32–8.

—— (1993e). 'The Central European Initiative: To Be or Not to Be?', *RFE/RL Research Report*, vol. 2, no. 34 (27 Aug.), pp. 30–7.

—— (1994a). 'Consensus on Hungary's Foreign Policy Frayed by Elections', *RFE/RL Research Report*, vol. 3, no. 20 (20 May), pp. 42–8.

—— (1994b). 'Central Europe's Disappointments and Hopes', *RFE/RL Research Report*, vol. 3, no. 12 (25 Mar.), pp. 18–37.

William M. Reisinger (1990). 'The International Regime of Soviet-East European Relations', *Slavic Review*, vol. 49, no. 4 (Winter), pp. 554–67.

David Remnick (1992). 'Dons of the Don', *New York Review of Books*, 16 July.

Report on Eastern Europe. Munich: Radio Free Europe/Radio Liberty (weekly).

Report on the USSR. Munich: Radio Free Europe/Radio Liberty (weekly).

Reuters.

Charles Reynolds (1981). *Modes of Imperialism.* New York: St Martin's Press.

RFE/RL News Briefs. Munich: Radio Free Europe/Radio Liberty (weekly).

RFE/RL Research Report. Munich: Radio Free Europe/Radio Liberty (weekly).

Nicholas V. Riasanovsky (1969). *A History of Russia*, 2nd edn. Berkeley, CA: University of California Press.

Philip G. Roeder (1991). 'Soviet Federalism and Ethnic Mobilization', *World Politics*, vol. 23, no. 2 (Jan.), pp. 196–233.

—— (1993). *Red Sunset: The Failure of Soviet Politics*. Princeton University Press.

Jim Rollo and Alasdair Smith (1993). 'The Political Economy of Eastern European Trade with the European Community: Why so Sensitive?', *European Economy*, no. 16.

James N. Rosenau (1966). 'Pre-theories and Theories of Foreign Policy' pp. 27–93 in Barry Farrel (ed.) *Approaches to Comparative and International Politics*. Evanston, IL: Northwestern University Press.

—— (1969). *Linkage Politics: Essays on the Convergence of National and International Systems*. New York: Free Press.

——(1970). *The Adaptation of National Soceities: A Theory of Political System Behaviour and Transformation*. New York: McCaleb-Seiler.

—— (1971). *The Scientific Study of Foreign Policy*. New York: Free Press.

—— (1981). *The Study of Political Adaptation*. London: Pinter.

—— (1990). *Turbulence in World Politics: A Theory of Change and Continuity*. New York: Harvester Wheatsheaf.

Alf Ross (1967). *Hvorfor demokrati?* Copenhagen: NNF Arnold Busck, 2nd edn.

Rossiiskaia Gazeta.

Robert L. Rothstein (1976). 'Foreign Policy and Development Policy: From Nonalignment to International Class War', *International Affairs*, vol. 52, no. 4, pp. 598–616.

Jacques Rupnik (1988). *The Other Europe*. London: Weidenfeld & Nicholson.

'Russia's Foreign Policy Concept' (1993). *International Affairs* (Moscow), no. 1, pp. 14–16.

Anna Sabbat-Swidlicka (1992). 'Poland Investigates Radical Farmers' Union', *RFE/RL Research Report*, vol. 1, no. 38 (25 Sept.), pp. 19–25.

Sergej Saizew (1992). 'Separatismus in Russland', *BIOst*, no. 41.

Richard Sakwa (1991). 'The Politics of Reintegration: The Common European Home and Beyond', *Paradigms*, vol. 5, no. 1/2, pp. 1-16.

Sh. P. Sanakoev and N.I. Kapchenko (1977). *O teorii vneshnei politiki sotsializma*. Moscow: Mezhdunarodnye Otnoshenia.

Konstantyn Sawczuk (1975). *The Ukraine in the United Nations Organization: A Study in Soviet Foreign Policy, 1944–1950*. Boulder: East European Quarterly distributed by Columbia University Press, New York and London (Eastern European Monographs no. IX).

Karin Schmid (1993). 'Untergang und Entstehung von Staaten in Mittel-

und Osteuropa. Neue Entwicklungen in Staats- und Völkerrecht', *BIOst*, no. 34.

George Schöpflin (1986). 'Hungary' pp. 99–113 in Martin McCauley and Stephen Carter (eds). *Leadership and Succession in the Soviet Union, Eastern Europe and China*. London: Macmillan.

—— (1991a). 'Post-communism: Constructing New Democracies in Central Europe', *International Affairs*, vol. 67 (Apr.), pp. 235–50.

—— (1991b). 'National Identity in the Soviet Union and East Central Europe', *Ethnic and Racial Studies*, vol. 14, no. 1 (Jan.), pp. 3–14.

—— (1992). 'From Communism to Democracy in Hungary' pp. 96–110 in András Bozóki *et al.* (eds). *Postcommunist Transition: Emerging Pluralism in Hungary*. London: Pinter/New York: St. Martin's Press.

Getrude Schroeder (1992). 'On the Economic Viability of the New Nation-States', *Journal of International Affairs*, vol. 45, no. 2, pp. 549–74.

Joseph A. Schumpeter (1950). *Capitalism, Socialism and Democracy*. 3rd edn. New York: Harper and Row/London: Geo. Allen and Unwin.

Solomon M. Schwarz (1952). 'Revising the History of Russian Colonialism', *Foreign Affairs*, vol. 30, no. 3 (Apr.), pp. 488–93.

Randall L. Schweller (1992). 'Domestic Structure and Preventive War – Are Democracies More Pacific?', *World Politics*, vol. 44, no. 2, pp. 235–69.

Gerald Segal *et al.* (1992). *Openness and Foreign Policy Reform in Communist States*. London: Routledge.

Segodnia (a Moscow daily).

Dieter Senghaas (1981). 'Socialism in Historical and Developmental Perspective', *Bulletin of Peace Proposals*, vol. 12, no. 3, pp. 287–301.

Susan Senior Nello (1991). *The New Europe: Changing Economic Relations between East and West*. Hemel Hempstead: Harvester Wheatsheaf.

Hugh Seton-Watson (1952). *The Decline of Imperial Russia 1855–1914*. London: Methuen.

—— (1960). *From Lenin to Khrushchev: The History of World Communism*. New York: Praeger.

—— (1967). *The Russian Empire 1801–1917*. Oxford: Clarendon Press.

Ann Sheehy (1991), 'USSR–The All-Union and RSFSR Referendum of March 17: Results', *Report on the USSR* (26 Mar.).

—— (1992). 'The CIS: A Progress Report', *RFE/RL Research Report*, vol. 1, no. 38 (25 Sept.), pp. 1–6.

Arkady N. Shevchenko (1985). *Breaking with Moscow*. New York: Knopf.

Gerhard Simon (1986). *Nationalismus und Nationalitätenpolitik in der Sowjetunion: Von der totalitären Diktatur zur nachstalinschen Gesellschaft*. Baden-Baden: Nomos.

—— (1994). 'Russland: Hegemon in Eurasien?', *BIOst*, no. 6.

Herbert A. Simon (1947). *Administrative Behaviour*. New York: Free Press.

Jeffrey Simon (1993). 'Does Eastern Europe Belong to NATO?', *Orbis*, vol. 37, no. 1 (Winter), pp. 21–35.

Mette Skak (1991a). 'Centraleuropas nye udenrigspolitik', *Politica*, vol. 23, no. 3, pp. 275–91.

———— (1991b). 'East Europe, the Soviet Union and Europeanization: A Challenge for the European Community'. Paper presented to the 1991 Annual Meeting of the American Political Science Association, Washington, DC (29 Aug.–1 Sept.) (mimeo.).

———— (1992a). 'The Changing Soviet-East European Relationship', pp. 31–48 in Roger E. Kanet, Deborah Nutter Miner and Tamara J. Resler (eds) *Soviet Foreign Policy in Transition*. Cambridge University Press.

———— (1992b). 'Post-communist Foreign Policies: Initial Observations', *Cooperation and Conflict*, vol. 27, no. 3, pp. 277–300.

———— (1993a). 'Post-Soviet Foreign Policy: The Emerging Relationship between Russia and Northeast Asia', *Journal of East Asian Affairs*, vol. VII (Winter/Spring), no. 1, pp. 137–85.

———— (1993b). 'Rusland og Europa', *Økonomi og Politik*, vol. 66, no. 4, pp. 13–21.

———— (1933c). 'The EC Policy of the Visegrad Countries' in Ole Nørgaard, Thomas Pedersen and Nikolaj Petersen (eds) *The European Community in World Politics*. London: Pinter, pp. 118–36.

Barbara Skinner (1994). 'Identity Formation in the Russian Cossack Revival', *Europe-Asia Studies* (formerly *Soviet Studies*), vol. 46, no. 6, pp. 1017–38.

Ben Slay (1993). 'The Postcommunist Economic Transition: Barriers and Progress', *RFE/RL Research Report*, vol. 2, no. 39 (1 Oct.), pp. 35–44.

Den slovakiske regerings programerklæring (1994). Vedtaget d. (13 Apr.) (in Danish).

Robert M. Slusser (1962). 'The Role of the Foreign Ministry', pp. 197–239 in Ivo J. Lederer (ed.), *Russian Foreign Policy: Essays in Historical Perpective*. New Haven, CT/London: Yale University Press.

Anthony D. Smith (1981). 'War and Ethnicity: The Role of Warfare in the Formation of Self-images and Cohesion of Ethnic Communities', *Ethnic and Racial Studies* vol. 14, no. 4, pp. 375–97.

———— (1992). 'Ethnic Identity and Territorial Nationalism in Comparative Perspective', pp. 45–65 in Alexander J. Motyl (ed.) (1992). *Thinking Theoretically about Soviet Nationalities: History and Comparison in the Study of the USSR*. New York: Columbia University Press.

Glenn H. Snyder (1984). 'The Security Dilemma in Alliance Politics', *World Politics*, vol. 36, no. 4 (July), pp. 461–95.

Jack Snyder (1990/1). 'Averting Anarchy in the New Europe', pp. 104–40 in Sean M. Lynn-Jones (ed.) *The Cold War and After: Prospects for Peace*. Cambridge, MA: MIT Press (reprinted from *International Security*, vol. 15, 1990-1).

—— (1991). *Myths of Empire. Domestic Politics and International Ambition.* Ithaca, NY: Cornell University Press.

Vladimir Socor (1992). 'Russia's Fourteenth Army and Insurgency in Eastern Moldova', *RFE/RL Research Report*, vol. 1, no. 36 (11 Sept.), pp. 41–8.

Roman Solchanyk (1992). 'Ukraine and Russia: The Politics of Indpendence', *RFE/RL Research Report*, vol. 1, no. 19 (8 May), pp. 13–16.

—— (1993). 'Ukraine: A Year of Transition', *RFE/RL Research Report*, vol. 2, no. 1 (Jan.), pp. 58–63.

Aleksandr I. Solzhenitsyn (1990). 'Kak nam obustroit Rossiiu?', *Literaturnaia Gazeta* (18 Sept.).

Joseph Stalin (1936). *Marxism and the National and Colonial Question.* London: Lawrence and Wishart.

S. Frederick Starr (1978). 'Tsarist Government: The Imperial Dimension', pp. 3–38 in Jeremy R. Azrael (ed.) *Soviet Nationality Policies and Practices.* New York: Praeger.

John J. Stephan (1974). *The Kuril Islands.* Oxford: Clarendon Press.

John G. Stoessinger (1969). *The Might of Nations: World Politics in Our Time.* 3rd edn. New York: Random House.

Summary of World Broadcasts. BBC.

Ronald Grigor Suny (1989). 'Nationalist and Ethnic Unrest in the Soviet Union', *World Policy Journal*, vol. VI, no. 3 (Summer), pp. 503–28.

Bogdan Szajkowski (1993a). *Encyclopedia of Conflicts, Disputes and Flashpoints in Eastern Europe, Russia and the Successor States.* Harlow: Longman.

—— (1993b). 'Will Russia Disintegrate into Bantustans?', *The World Today*, vol. 49, nos. 8–9, pp. 172–6.

Roman Szporluk (ed.) (1976). *The Influence of East Europe and the Soviet West on the USSR.* New York: Praeger.

—— (1986). 'The Ukraine and Russia', pp. 151–82 in Robert Conquest (ed.) *The Last Empire: Nationality and the Soviet Future.* Stanford, CA: Hoover Institution Press.

—— (1989). 'Dilemmas of Russian Nationalism', *Problems of Communism*, vol. XXXVIII (July–Aug.), pp. 15–35.

—— (1992). 'The National Question', pp. 84–112 in Timothy J. Colton and Robert Legvold (eds) *After the Soviet Union From Empire to Nations.* New York/London: W.W. Norton.

Michel Tatu (1981). 'Intervention in Eastern Europe', pp. 205–64 in Stephen S. Kaplan *et al.*, *Diplomacy of Power: Soviet Armed Forces as a Political Instrument.* Washington, DC: Brookings Institution.

TASR (the Slovak news agency).

TASS.

Elizabeth Teague (1994). 'The CIS: An Unpredictable Future', *RFE/RL Research Report*, vol. 3, no. 1 (7 Jan.), pp. 9–12.

John Tedstrom (1989). 'USSR Draft Program on Republican Economic Self-Management: An Analysis', *Report on the USSR* (21 Apr.), pp. 1–8.

'Terms of Reference for the Council of Baltic Sea States' (1992). Copenhagen: MFA, reprinted in *Dansk Udenrigspolitisk Årbog*. Copenhagen: DJØF.

Heinrich Tiller/Hans-Henning Schroeder (1993). 'Machtkrise und Militär: Die russischen Streitkräfte während des Machtkampfes zwischen Präsident und Parlament im Herbst 1993', *BIOst*, no. 46.

The Times.

Heinz Timmermann (1992). 'GUS und Ostmitteleuropa: Strategien der neuen Eliten zur Aussenpolitischen An- und Einbindung', *BIOst*, no. 42.

—— (1993). 'Die Europapolitik Russlands und die russisch-deutschen Beziehungen', *BIOst*, no. 36.

Mikk Titma and Nancy B. Tuma (1992). 'Migration in the Former Soviet Union', BIOst, no. 22.

Rudolf L. Tökes (1990). 'Hungary's New Political Elite: Adaptation and Change', *Problems of Communism*, vol. XXXIX (Nov.-Dec.), pp. 44–65.

—— (1991). 'From Visegrad to Kraków: Cooperation, Competition, and Coexistence in Central Europe', *Problems of Communism*, vol. XL (Nov.-Dec.), pp. 100–14.

Lev Nikolaevich Tolstoi (1963). *Sobranie Sochinenii*, vols 4-7 ('Vojna i mir'). Moscow: Khudozhestvennia Literatura.

Vera Tolz (1992). 'Ministry of Security Official Gives New Figures for Stalin's Victims', *RFE/RL Research Report*, vol. 1, no. 18 (1 May), pp. 8–10.

Alfred Tovias (1991). 'EC-Eastern Europe: A Case Study of Hungary', *Journal of Common Market Studies*, vol. 29., no. 3 (Mar.), pp. 291–315.

Jan Arveds Trapans (1991). 'Baltic Foreign Policy in 1990', *Report on the USSR* (11 Jan.), pp. 15–18.

'Treaty on Good Neighbourliness and Friendly Co-operation between the Slovak Republic and the Republic of Hungary' (1995).

Jan F. Triska and David D. Finley (1968). *Soviet Foreign Policy*. London: Macmillan.

Robert C. Tucker (ed.) (1977). *Stalinism: Essays in Historical Perspective*. New York: W.W. Norton.

Ferdinand Tönnies (1957). *Community and Society (Gemeinschaft und Gesellschaft)*. Transl./ed. C.P. Loomis. East Lansing: Michigan State University Press.

Adam B. Ulam (1962). 'Nationalism, Panslavism, Communism', pp. 39–67 in Ivo J. Lederer (ed.) *Russian Foreign Policy: Essays in Historical Perspective*. New Haven, CT/London: Yale University Press.

—— (1973). *Stalin: The Man and his Era*. New York: Viking Press.

—— (1974). *Expansion and Coexistence: The History of Soviet Foreign Policy, 1917–1973*. New York: Praeger.

Frank Umbach (1993). 'The "Yugoslavisation" of the former Soviet Union and Western Crisis Management', *BIOst*, no. 45.

—— (1994). 'Russia and the Problems of Ukraine's Cohesion: Results of a Fact-Finding Mission', *BIOst*, no. 13.

Igor Usachev (1993). 'The Diplomacy of the Russian Empire', *International Affairs* (Moscow) (Oct.), pp. 111–19.

Nikolai Uspenky and Sergei Komissarov (1993). 'New Stage in Cooperation in the Baltic Region', *International Affairs* (Moscow) (Feb.), pp. 83–8.

Milada Anna Vachudova (1993). 'The Visegrad Four: No Alternative to Cooperation?', *RFE/RL Research Report*, vol. 2, no. 34 (27 Aug.), pp. 38–47.

Jiri Valenta (1984). 'Soviet Decisionmaking on Czechoslovakia, 1968', pp. 165–84 in idem and William C. Potter (eds), *Soviet Decisionmaking for National Security*. London: Geo. Allen & Unwin.

V. Stanley Vardys (ed.) (1965). *Lithuania under the Soviets: Portrait of a Nation, 1940–65*. New York/Washington/London: Praeger.

—— (1983). 'Polish Echoes in the Baltic', *Problems of Communism*, vol. XXXII (July–Aug.), pp. 21–34.

Peeter Vares (1993). 'Dimensions and Orientations in the Foreign and Security Policies of the Baltic States', pp. 3–31 in Pertti Joenniemi and Peeter Vares (eds) *New Actors on the International Scene : The Foreign Policies of the Baltic Countries*. Tampere Peace Research Institute, Research Report, no. 50.

Raimo Väyrynen (1989). 'Constraints and Opportunities in the Foreign Policies of Small States', pp. 52–63 in Bertel Heurlin and Christian Thune (eds) *Danmark og det internationale system. Festskrift til Ole Karup Pedersen*. Copenhagen: Politiske Studier.

Richard de Villafranca (1993). 'Japan and the Northern Territories Dispute: Past, Present, Future', *Asian Survey*, vol. XXXIII, no. 6 (June), pp. 610–24.

'Vneshniaia Politika stran Varshavskogo Dogovora' (1986). *Pervaia Polovina 80-x godov*. Moscow: Nauka.

Gudrun Wacker (1994). 'Die VR China und die Nachfolgestaaten der Sowjetunion'. Parts II and III *BIOst*, no. 12 and 27.

Ole Wæver et al. (1993). *Identity, Migration and the New Security Agenda in Europe*. London: Pinter.

Celeste A. Wallander (1992). 'International Institutions and Modern Security Strategies', *Problems of Communism*, vol. XLI (Jan.–Apr.).

Stephen M. Walt (1992). 'Revolution and War', *World Politics*, no. 3 (Apr.), pp. 321–68.

Sidney and Beatrice Webb (1937). *Soviet Communism: A New Civilisation.* vols I–II, 2nd edn. London: Longmans Green.

Kenneth N. Waltz (1979). *Theory of International Relations.* Reading: Addison-Wesley.

Gerhard Wettig (ed.) (1993). 'Sicherheits- und Bedrohungsperzeptionen in Ost- und Mitteleuropa', *BIOst*, no. 43.

Jan B. de Weydenthal (1993). 'Russia Mends Fences with Poland, the Czech Republic, and Slovakia', *RFE/RL Research Report*, vol. 2, no. 36 (10 Sept.), pp. 33–36.

────── (1994). 'Cross-Border Cooperation in East Central Europe', *RFE/RL Research Report*, vol. 3, no. 2 (14 Jan.), pp. 32–5.

Nicholas J. Wheeler and Ken Booth (1992). 'The Security Dilemma', pp. 29–60 in John Baylis and N.J. Rengger (eds) *Dilemmas in World Politics: International Issues in a Changing World.* Oxford: Clarendon Press.

Erik Whitlock (1994). 'The CIS Economies: Divergent and Troubled Paths', *RFE/RL Research Report*, vol. 3, no. 1 (7 Jan.), pp. 13–17.

Charles Wolf Jr. (1987). 'The Costs and Benefits of the Soviet Empire', pp. 121–40 in Henry S. Rowen and Charles Wolf Jr. (eds) *The Future of the Soviet Empire.* London: Macmillan.

Arnold *Wolfers* (1962). *Discord and Collaboration. Essays on International Politics.* Baltimore, MD: Johns Hopkins Press.

Victor Yasmann (1993). 'Legislation on Screening and State Security in Russia', *RFE/RL Research Report*, vol. 2, no. 32 (13 Aug.), pp. 11–16.

Victor Yasmann (1994). 'Security Services Reorganized: All Power to the Russian President?', *RFE/RL Research Report*, vol. 3, no. 6 (11 Feb.), pp. 7–14.

Yearbook of International Communist Affairs. Stanford, CA: Hoover .

Oran R. Young (1986). 'International Regimes: Toward a New Theory of Institutions', *World Politics*, no. 1 (Oct.), pp. 104–22.

Andrei Zagorski (1994). 'Die Entwicklungstendenzen der GUS: Von der Differenzierung zur Konsolidierung?', *BIOst*, no. 24.

John Zametica (1992). 'The Yugoslav Conflict', *Adelphi Paper*, no. 270.

Die Zeit.

Vladimir V. Zhirinovski (1993). *Poslednyi brosok na jug.* Moscow: LDP.

Jan Zielonka (1992). 'Security in Central Europe', *Adelphi Paper*, no. 272.

Voytek Zubek (1993). 'New Poland's Old Dilemma: the Polish Minority in Lithuania', *Ethnic and Racial Studies*, vol. 16, no. 4 (Oct.), pp. 656–82.

Vladislav Zubok (1992). 'Tyranny of the Weak', *World Policy Journal*, vol. IX, no. 2 (Spring), pp. 191–217.

Die Zukunft des Gebiets Kaliningrad (Königsberg) (1993). Special publication resulting from an international study group. *BIOst* (July).

INDEX

315